SANCTIONING MODERNISM

ROGER FULLINGTON SERIES IN ARCHITECTURE

SANCTIONING MODERNISM

ARCHITECTURE AND THE MAKING OF POSTWAR IDENTITIES

EDITED BY Vladimir Kulić, Timothy Parker, and Monica Penick

FOREWORD BY Frederick Steiner

UNIVERSITY OF TEXAS PRESS   AUSTIN

Publication of this book was made possible in part by support from Roger Fullington and a challenge grant from the National Endowment for the Humanities.

Copyright © 2014 by the University of Texas Press
All rights reserved

First paperback edition, 2015

Requests for permission to reproduce material from this work should be sent to:
  Permissions
  University of Texas Press
  P.O. Box 7819
  Austin, TX 78713-7819
  http://utpress.utexas.edu/index.php/rp-form

♾ The paper used in this book meets the minimum requirements of ANSI/NISO Z39.48-1992 (R1997) (Permanence of Paper).

LIBRARY OF CONGRESS CATALOGING-IN-PUBLICATION DATA

Sanctioning modernism : architecture and the making of postwar identities / edited by Vladimir Kulić, Timothy Parker, and Monica Penick. — First edition.
    pages   cm. — (Roger Fullington series in architecture)
  Includes bibliographical references and index.
  ISBN 978-0-292-75725-7 (cloth : alk. paper)
  ISBN 978-1-4773-0759-5 (paperback)
  1. Modern movement (Architecture) 2. Architecture and society—History—20th century. I. Kulić, Vladimir, editor of compilation. II. Parker, Timothy, editor of compilation. III. Penick, Monica, editor of compilation. IV. Doordan, Dennis P., author. Writing history.
    NA682.M63S26 2014
    724'.6—dc23   2013038461

doi:10.7560/757257

CONTENTS

Foreword   vii
FREDERICK STEINER

Preface   ix
VLADIMIR KULIĆ, TIMOTHY PARKER, AND MONICA PENICK

Acknowledgments   xii

Introduction. Writing History:
Reflections on the Story of Midcentury Modern Architecture   1
DENNIS P. DOORDAN

PART I. MODERNISM AND THE STATE

Introduction   8
VLADIMIR KULIĆ

1. Bucharest: The City Transfigured   11
   JULIANA MAXIM

2. The Scope of Socialist Modernism:
   Architecture and State Representation in Postwar Yugoslavia   37
   VLADIMIR KULIĆ

3. Czechoslovakia's Model Housing Developments:
   Modern Architecture for the Socialist Future   66
   KIMBERLY ELMAN ZARECOR

4. Sanctioning Modernism and Tradition:
   Italian Architecture, the Vernacular, and the State   90
   MICHELANGELO SABATINO

PART II. MAKING RELIGION MODERN

Introduction — TIMOTHY PARKER — 109

5. Uncertainty and the Modern Church: Two Roman Catholic Cathedrals in Britain — ROBERT PROCTOR — 113

6. "Humanly sublime tensions": Luigi Moretti's Chiesa del Concilio (1965–1970) — TIMOTHY PARKER — 139

7. Modernism and the Concept of Reform: Liturgy and Liturgical Architecture — RICHARD KIECKHEFER — 168

PART III: MODERNISM AND DOMESTICITY

Introduction — MONICA PENICK — 182

8. "Technologically" Modern: The Prefabricated House and the Wartime Experience of Skidmore, Owings and Merrill — HYUN-TAE JUNG — 186

9. "Modern but not *too* modern": *House Beautiful* and the American Style — MONICA PENICK — 219

10. House and Haunted Garden — SANDY ISENSTADT — 244

Further Reading — 269

Contributors — 274

Index — 277

FOREWORD

Just when an idea or a movement seems to have run its course, or merely run out of steam, a new mind and set of eyes come along and make it fresh again. Such is the case with *Sanctioning Modernism*, where three young scholars have brought together a new perspective on the Modern Movement. This triad—Vladimir Kulić, Timothy Parker, and Monica Penick—has enlisted an interdisciplinary band of other emerging and more seasoned academics as allies in this effort.

In doing so, the young and seasoned scholars go far beyond what modernism looks like and deeply probe its political, religious, and domestic consequences. These scholars help illustrate the observation by Kurt Lewin (1890–1947) that "there is nothing so practical as a good theory" (from *Field Theory in Social Science: Selected Theoretical Papers* [New York: Harper and Brothers Publishers, 1951]). The theory of modernism had far-reaching implications for the built environment.

These implications span the globe, and as the pages that follow illustrate, range in scale from our homes to state institutions. While the architectural story flows throughout, the contributors show how built form is related to our political, worship, and home lives. In other words, they address topics at our very essence as human beings.

The trio of sparkplugs behind this book deserves special recognition. As graduate students, they envisioned a collaborative endeavor. When most doctoral students look within, Penick, Parker, and Kulić reached out to each other and beyond. As they were completing their doctoral studies (and now, as they have gone on to academic posts—Vladimir at Florida Atlantic University, Timothy at Norwich University, and Monica at the University of Wisconsin–Madison), these three took on a demanding editorial endeavor. In the end, they have produced a wide-ranging work, and they also have contributed focused chapters themselves.

In many ways, modernism began as a positive movement. There was a belief that humans could envision and create a better world. In several ways, we have. In others, we have fallen short, and making the world a better place remains a work in progress. This book also began as a positive movement by its editors and contributors. That effort has produced the fine book, with its fresh perspective on modernism, that you now hold in your hands.

Frederick Steiner
Dean, School of Architecture
The University of Texas at Austin

PREFACE

This book is the product of an eponymous symposium held at the School of Architecture at the University of Texas at Austin in 2007. The organizers of the symposium—now the editors of this volume—were, at the time, doctoral students in Architectural History. We were all engaged in separate research projects set in the post–World War II decades, yet our individual themes, at first glance, seemed geographically and culturally disconnected, with little in common other than a chronological coincidence. This disparate view of history struck us as both problematic and auspicious. We wanted, then, to launch a new kind of dialogue and a new line of critical inquiry; our goal was to find a compelling and productive link, a deeper thematic and methodological similarity that would tie our work together and enrich the larger story of postwar architecture. This search ultimately converged around the question of the "sanctioning" of architectural modernism, with its broad popularization, validation, and institutionalization after World War II.

Indeed, if the Cold War conditioned an "anxious" postwar modernism, as Sarah Williams Goldhagen and Réjean Legault have claimed in their valuable collection, the period was also one of an optimistic—if not triumphal—modernism that reigned victorious after decades of trials and tribulations. In the Introduction to this book, Dennis Doordan rightly highlights the construction of the United Nations Headquarters in Manhattan, based on a scheme by Le Corbusier, as the symbolic moment of conquest. But the significance of that triumph can only be understood in light of Le Corbusier's legendary loss twenty years before at the competition for the Palace of the League of Nations in Geneva. It was this defeat that sparked the creation of organized international alliances that bolstered the modernist cause; of these, the Congrès Internationaux d'Architecture Moderne (CIAM) is perhaps the most notable. In the context of our work here, CIAM became a vital force in the "sanctioning" and canonization of modernism. This story may read as a heroic myth, but the very presence of institutionalized ideological agency in the narrative undercuts the metaphysical basis of canonical histories that viewed modernism as the predestined, unavoidable outcome in architecture's historical development. It is precisely this kind of agency that interests us in this book.

To study modern architecture in the early twenty-first century is to confront a subject whose coherence is continually contested. We are reminded at every turn that what makes modern architecture modern are emphatically not the canonical constructs that dominated the early histories of the Modern Movement. The historiography of modern architecture is the story of an ever-growing, ever-expanding set of reconsiderations, revisions, and rehabilitations. The scholarship of recent decades has amounted to a sustained critique of the canon, focusing upon all that had been left out, all that had been falsely championed, and all that formal or functional analysis inadequately addressed. Such inquiry has also pointed up the necessity of interdisciplinary approaches and has helped formulate or appropriate the myriad methodologies that are now routine. The dogged pursuit of these issues has surely led to an improved and enriched understanding of modern architecture even as it has made grasping the unity of the field ever more difficult, if not impossible.

For our generation of architectural historians, however, this noncanonical orientation is less about the hard-won result of sustained critique as it is the point of entry into the field. When we came of age, the postmodernist critique of modernist orthodoxies was already on the wane and a second round of evaluation of modernist legacies was in order, albeit this time devoid of the combative and prophetic character of its original incarnation. For us, a critical (if not wholly suspect) awareness of the grand narratives is a given. The question for us is how can we understand, formulate, and properly historicize the variegated and politically charged modernisms that the canonical histories were not ready to accept? Moreover, how do we approach the role of the now circumscribed canonical interpretations that form part of modern architecture's own history? Against the backdrop of this critical starting point, then, we believe that a careful look at the various constructs, uses, and appropriations of modernism itself—in its various guises, including the canonical—is a necessary and promising task.

It is no accident that the decades following the Second World War are the focus for so many emerging scholars of architectural history. The period is one in which modernism rapidly became entrenched. Modern architecture spread around the globe alongside increased modernization, urbanization, and postwar reconstruction—and it eventually won widespread acceptance. And yet it is during these decades, as the limits of conventional conceptions of modernism became palpable and concrete, that modernism was subject to increasing criticism. This pressure was exerted both internally and externally, through official institutions and other venues of discourse. Postwar modernism is marked, therefore, by a plethora of research opportunities, and not merely for the ongoing project of critically reforming the historical understanding of modernism. The postwar period is also an ideal setting for grappling with modernism's own history as a matter of modern identity: what did it mean to be "modern"? As posed within the context of modern architecture and therefore centered upon the building as artifact, this question inevitably involves multiple disciplines and realms of human experience; the answers take shape in manifold moments of contestation, appropriation, negotiation, and compromise.

It is in this sense of approaching modern identity in and through architecture that we conceptualized the present collection of essays: as explorations of the ways in which distinct institutions, practices, ideologies, traditions, and discourses sanctioned—or were sanctioned by—modernism, however fluidly or variously construed. Three specific spheres in which such engagement figured prominently organize the collection according to the political, religious, and residential settings in which such engagement mainly occurred. These thematic spheres directly correspond to our individual scholarly interests and expertise, but they also, we believe, contribute to a useful—although clearly not comprehensive—broader framework for reassessing the role of modern architecture in the construction of modern identities after World War II.

A brief Introduction to each thematic section will provide provisional orientation. But as the reader follows the story of any individual chapter, she will encounter abundant overlapping areas. Within a given case study, the religious form may be tinged with political implications, the political objective rooted in domestic ideals, or concepts of domesticity directly shaped by political ideology. The larger aim of this gathering of focused yet interrelated scholarship, then, is to contribute to a fuller understanding of modern identity as it is formed in and through architecture. The common themes of the political, the domestic, and the religious, as well as the common time frame, yield a fruitful picture of not only the previously unstudied particulars that belie any canonical view but also the uses to which such interpretations were in fact put.

ACKNOWLEDGMENTS

Many people contributed to making this book possible. First of all, we owe thanks to the faculty and staff of the School of Architecture at the University of Texas at Austin. Dean Frederick Steiner and Anthony Alofsin generously supported the project from the very start and helped us obtain the funding for the "Sanctioning Modernism" symposium from which this book originated, as well as for the book itself. Richard Cleary, Christopher Long, Francesco Passanti, and Danilo Udovički contributed their insights prior to and during the symposium. UT Austin graduate student Laura McGuire and the staff of the Alexander Architectural Archive helped us organize the accompanying exhibition (funded in part by the UT Austin Events Co-Sponsorship Committee). At the University of Texas Press, Jim Burr was a patient and supportive editor. Two outside reviewers provided valuable insights and suggestions; we thank them for their careful attention. Julia Dane was a diligent and thorough undergraduate assistant (supported by funding from the University of Wisconsin–Madison) whose tireless work made the completion of the manuscript much less stressful than it would have been without her. Thank you, Julia! Finally, heartfelt thanks to our colleagues who contributed their essays and worked patiently through several revisions to make this book as good as possible.

We owe gratitude to everyone mentioned. Much of the credit for this book is theirs; the errors are our own.

SANCTIONING MODERNISM

INTRODUCTION

WRITING HISTORY
REFLECTIONS ON THE STORY OF MIDCENTURY MODERN ARCHITECTURE

DENNIS P. DOORDAN

In a park-like setting along New York City's East River the United Nations stands proudly as an enduring symbol of... what? Today the UN buildings are assailed by some as the sinister architectural symbol of a new world order that threatens to strip nations of sovereign control over their own affairs. For others, the pristine geometry and midcentury palette of materials and artworks serve as a poignant reminder of the naïve hopes and disappointing achievements that trail in the wake of the promise of a new peaceful world order rising phoenix-like from the ashes of World War II. Six decades ago, the aluminum and glass curtain wall of the Secretariat Building and the daring design of the General Assembly Building heralded a new direction in postwar design and declared the triumph of modernism in architecture. Or did it? No one doubted the significance of the United Nations design. Writing in the pages of *Architectural Record*, Henry Stern Churchill called it "probably the most important architectural work of the century."[1]

But "important" did not necessarily mean good, and critics were quick to take issue with various aspects of the planning and design of the United Nations. After describing the novel features of the building, Churchill finally concluded that it still lacked something essential: emotional resonance. He concluded:

> The planning of the UN group is a triumph of clarity and ingenuity.... It is a triumph of technical skill, of structural ability, of mechanical engineering.... It is, in other words, a very fine example of American architectural skill. It is not, however, much more than that; and perhaps it could not be.... The failure is not the fault of the architects, but of the time in which no emotional symbols are possible because there is no deep belief, no emotional content in our lives.[2]

Even ardent champions of the kind of clarity, ingenuity, and technological sophistication to be found in the UN design expressed concerns about the way building activity was developing in the 1950s. A sense of unease, for example, comes through in some of Walter Gropius's writings and speeches of that era:

> After the revolution in our own ranks, which has brought clarification, we seem to be set for a new creative effort. So it might be appropriate to investigate how far our professional framework fits the condition of our times.... Let's see if the gigantic shift in the means of production has been sufficiently recognized by us. ... The architect is in a very real danger of losing his grip in competition with the engineer, the scientist and the builders.[3]

Henry Stern Churchill and Walter Gropius were hardly lonely figures trying to hold back the march of progress. They are representative of the professional culture to which they belonged, a culture wrestling with the uneasy feeling that too many of its triumphs bore signs of failure as well as success and too many of their critical assessments betrayed doubts as well as certainty.

The mid–twentieth century marked the emergence of modernist theory and architecture as the dominant force in design practice and education. Alternative design ideologies—traditional building, eclecticism, craft-based work—survived but occupied peripheral or minority positions within architectural culture.[4] This was an international architectural culture dominated by a concern for the following:

- The rationalization and the modernization of design thinking and architectural education
- The institutionalization of modernist planning principles (ultimately derived from the work of influential architects like Le Corbusier and organizations like the Congrès Internationaux d'Architecture Moderne
- The industrialization of architectural production (to whatever degree the local economic and technological infrastructure could support)
- The celebration of distinctively modern conceptions of creativity (which privileges novelty and invention over the refinement and extension of traditional formal vocabularies)

But as the remarks by Churchill and Gropius cited above suggest, to speak of an international culture of modernism does not require that we accept the idea that this culture was monolithic or uniform. As readers of this collection will note, at times the modernization campaigns that drove urban planning and social housing efforts were promoted as vital steps toward fostering egalitarianism in modern mass society. But the West held no monopoly on claims regarding the political significance of modern architecture. Juliana Maxim describes how plans for the redevelopment of the Floreasca quarter of Bucharest in the late 1950s and 1960s were interpreted as the vivid demonstration of modern design's ability to serve as the emblem of socialism's commitment to the sweeping transformation of Romania. The temptation to dismiss the official rhetoric surrounding these modernist-inspired planning efforts as the cynical manipulation of artistic ideals to promote different—and contending—political ideologies must be resisted. The end of World War II brought new opportunities for architects to participate in both the social and physical rebuilding of war-torn cities, but it did not bring a new consensus on fundamental questions concerning the relationship between political and architectural ideologies, the optimal way to integrate technology and design, or the organization of the professional practice. What it meant to be modern remained an open-ended question of tremendous concern to various constituencies and one that, inevitably, generated multiple answers.

It is against this background of promise and frustration that the articles collected in this anthology should be read. This collection grew out of a 2007 symposium, "Sanctioning Modernism," organized by the School of Architecture at the University of Texas at Austin. Two goals shaped the effort: presenting new scholarship on a series of specific architects and projects that belong to the mid-twentieth century, and exploring the implications of this new research for the writing of history. In the press release promoting the symposium, the organizers noted that the history of modernism in architecture has now been told many times, but the result, they lamented, consisted of "reductive partisan histories" and "an impoverished canonical view of modernism." In contrast, the material in this collection significantly enriches our understanding of mid-twentieth-century developments in modern architecture. The authors make a collective claim that this material constitutes an important chapter in the history of modernism. Beyond the light these chapters shed on specific design campaigns, this anthology prompts us to reconsider some of the common assumptions that have shaped popular accounts of modern architecture. The traditional grand narrative associated with modernism describes how a version of the International Style triumphs in the United States and Western Europe. This narrative then juxtaposes a triumphant modernism in the West to a regressive Socialist Realism imposed heavy-handedly on the socialist bloc of Eastern Europe and the Soviet Union. In place of this familiar scenario, the contributors to this anthology describe a more complex, nuanced picture of greater diversity within modernist architectural culture. In this effort they are aligned with those architectural historians who call into question the very possibility of writing a canonical history of modern architecture.

Canonical histories of architecture identify sets of paradigmatic examples that distill collective judgments of quality. As such, canonical history represents a definitive summation not just of what constitutes the best work of a period but also the correct way to perceive the design strategies and cultural values embodied in that work. Canonical histories thus constitute an intellectual "point of arrival": study these architects, buildings, and events and you will know the subject. Ideally, the values that shaped the formation of the canon go on to inform future historical scholarship, while fidelity to the paradigms presented is one important criterion employed by architects and critics to validate new designs. As the symposium's organizers recognized, the canonical account of architectural modernism had been under assault for more than three decades from multiple critical perspectives. Historians began to investigate the status of women within the architectural profession, recover their contribution, and decipher the encoding of gender roles and identities within the built environment. Critics of Eurocentrism called for a more nuanced appreciation of the relationship between centers and peripheries of industrial production and cultural consumption, while scholars of colonial and postcolonial experiences explored the role of architecture in the formation and maintenance of ethnic, racial, and national identities. The rise of structuralist and poststructuralist discourses opened up the discussion of the production of design theory and its role in shaping architectural practice. More recently, the revival of interest in classical and traditional architecture and the emergence of environmentally oriented critiques have pointed to vast lacunae in the historical assessment. For their part, the contributors to this anthology focused their investigations on the mid-twentieth century, a period, as they argue persuasively, that is full of opportunities for discovery.

The critique of canon production as the goal of history, though useful and, indeed, necessary, leaves open an important question. If the purpose of compiling a history of modern architecture is not just the validation of a single design orientation (i.e., modernism) through the certification of a canon, then to what end is the endeavor? How else can the historian's task be conceptualized? The answer to this question begins with recognizing that beyond satisfying immediate needs for shelter and service, every building is an argument concerning how the world might be. "Modern but not *too* modern," the title of Monica Penick's essay, neatly captures this. Her essay explores the role of critics like *House Beautiful*'s Elizabeth Gordon in setting the terms of the debate. Indeed, the contributions by Hyun-Tae Jung and Sandy Isenstadt vividly demonstrate just how malleable and contested the image of the American home was in mid–twentieth-century America.

At any given moment in time, different conceptions coexist of how the world might be. The respective merits of these conceptions are continually debated by architects, their clients and patrons, critics, design educators, and the general public. Rather than anointing some supposed "winners" in an epochal struggle to control the future, architectural history can serve as the thoughtful, probing record of the debate among various constituencies regarding how to conceptualize, fabricate, and evaluate the built environment. Such an approach to history is essentially pluralist in nature, treats diversity in architecture as a sign of vitality rather than confusion, and offers readers an intelligible portrait of complexity in place of a simplistic rendering of the past.[5]

So what debates were recovered for us in this collection? The answer begins with the title of this anthology, *Sanctioning Modernism*. The symposium organizers employed the term "sanctioning" in its positive meaning as authoritative approval (rather than the more negative use of the term to identify coercive or punitive restrictions). Who indeed sanctioned modernism or, for that matter, withheld its sanction? The roles of the state and various political entities figure prominently in this collection. Several chapters explore developments in Czechoslovakia, Romania, and Yugoslavia and document a modernist design culture that crossed political barriers such as the Iron Curtain more readily than perhaps has been previously imagined. But the ability to sanction was not reserved exclusively to organs of the state (indeed it never has been in the modern era). Corporate entities through their patronage, academic institutions through their role in shaping the knowledge base for architecture and planning, industrial concerns through their ability (or, in some cases, inability) to shape the material basis for architectural production, and the professional and popular press that is so instrumental in shaping public perception and understanding and framing cultural debate must all be factored into the study of who sanctions modern architecture.

The inclusion of material treating developments in Eastern Europe warrants an observation about the politics of writing history. The presentation in English of fresh research on national experiences in the former Eastern bloc is a relatively recent development in the historiography of modern architecture and sheds some light on the political context within which the writing of history is embedded. I am thinking here not of the overt ideological censorship of scholarly writing but rather of the limitations on scholarly activity imposed by the Cold War division of Europe into two antagonistic blocs. When, for example, I began my doctoral research at Columbia University in the late 1970s, opportunities for American graduate students to travel and conduct archival research behind the Iron Curtain were so constrained that it simply was not viable to propose dissertation topics in certain areas. Was my generation of graduate students aware that there were missing chapters in the account of modern architecture? Certainly. Could we go to Bucharest or Prague or Moscow and gain ready access to state and municipal archives? At that time, certainly not. The writing of history does not occur in a vacuum, and each generation of historians must contend with what is possible and accessible as well as with what is needed and available.

There is one additional entry to the above list of sanctioning bodies to be acknowledged: religious institutions. Three of the chapters in this collection explore various efforts to reconcile the concerns of modernist architects with the traditions of the Roman Catholic Church. The sheer volume of church building going on in parts of Europe and America in the second half of the twentieth century is noteworthy. Demographic changes left the existing building stock of churches in the traditional urban centers increasingly isolated from the actual communities they were intended to serve. The *centro storico* of Italian cities like Rome and Milan, for example, are amply provided with church building, but the new neighborhoods that sprang up on the urban periphery created a corresponding demand for new facilities. Demographic change is one of the drivers of architectural production. Efforts to address this need in Italy and elsewhere brought modern architects into contact with a set of questions that went to the core of the debate over what it meant to be modern. Could the emerging rational secular culture of modernism and the enduring faith-based culture of institutional religion reach a fruitful accommodation? Was there a metaphysical dimension to modernism that could be articulated sufficiently to sustain a constructive dialogue with the intellectual traditions of established faith? Could, in the cases examined in this anthology, the Catholic Church and mainline Protestant denominations trust and learn from the modernists to conceptualize institutional reform in terms of innovation rather than as a purifying return to earlier practices?

As the work presented here demonstrates, the past is as complex as the present. We should not be surprised to learn that what "sanctioned" modern architecture, that is, what arguments served to validate design decisions, varied from context to context. Beyond compiling a simple chronicle of who built what when and where, historians seek understanding through reflecting upon what people found persuasive as they struggled, as each generation must, with fundamental questions of how we can shape the built environment to serve human purposes and satisfy human needs.

NOTES

1. Henry Stern Churchill, "United Nations Headquarters: A Description and Appraisal," *Architectural Record* 111, no. 7 (July 1952): 104.

2. Ibid., 121.

3. Walter Gropius, "The Architect within Our Industrial Society," in *The Scope of Total Architecture* (New York: Collier Books, 1962), 73.

4. It is worth noting here that the reemergence of these alternatives to the dominant modernist worldview in the late twentieth century forms part of the story of postmodernism.

5. I develop this argument for a concept of pluralist history in the Introduction to my *Twentieth Century Architecture* (New York: Harry Abrams, 2002), ix–xvi.

MODERNISM AND THE STATE

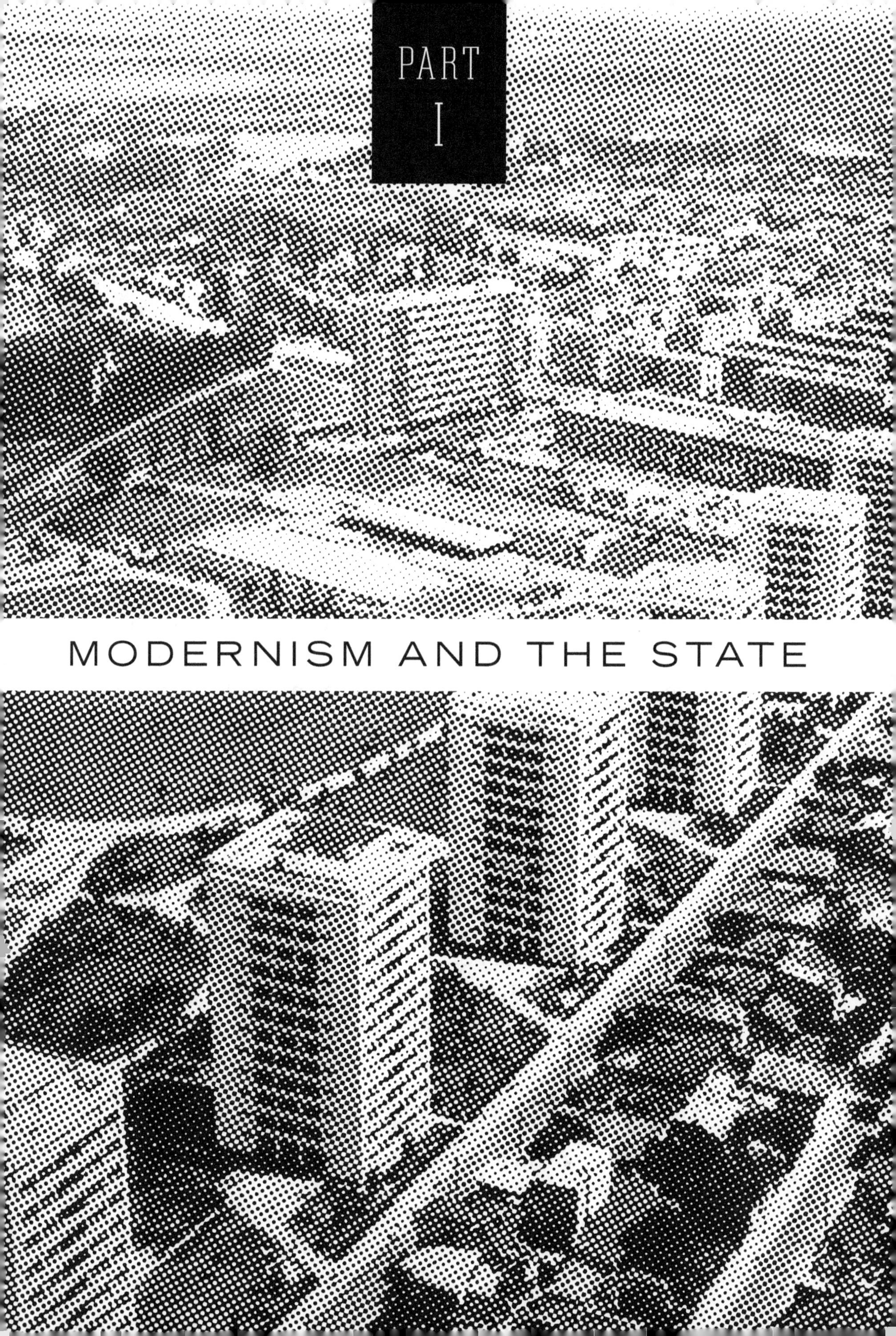

INTRODUCTION

VLADIMIR KULIĆ

During the two decades following World War II, various political entities across the world adopted modernist architecture in its different guises both for representational purposes and as an instrument of modernization. The period thus stood in contrast with the interwar years, when modernists struggled to attract official support, especially after the turbulent alliance between the avant-gardes and the varied central and local governments of the 1920s dissolved under the rising totalitarian forces. It was only in a few places such as Czechoslovakia and Turkey that architectural modernism before World War II was consistently accepted as the "official style" of political representation.[1]

By the late 1950s, however, states worldwide discovered that their own interests aligned with the logic of what historian James C. Scott called "high modernism": "a strong, one might even say muscle-bound, version of the self-confidence about scientific and technical progress."[2] The most poignant product of such an alignment, according to Scott, was the modern clean-slate city, laid out in accordance with the principles formulated by the gurus of modernism like Le Corbusier. Indeed, from Brasilia to Chandigarh and from New Belgrade to Albany, "high modernism" became the architecture of choice for state representation, as well as a device through which vastly different modernization projects were carried out. There was, however, nothing inherently natural about this alliance, as it was forged through a variety of specific dynamics and for a range of motivations, often dictated more by circumstances and pragmatic concerns than by the ideal principles.

Fragments of this complex history are already known: most notably, recent scholarship has uncovered how modernist architecture and design became enlisted in the "cultural Cold War," especially on the Western side of the confrontation.[3] The story, however, is far from complete even if one limits the perspective to the developed capitalist countries; when the view expands to the so-called second- and third-world countries, the dynamics appear to be almost completely unknown.[4] Of course, modernism was by no means a monolithic phenomenon either, and it acquired a particularly rich repertoire of forms after World War II, making the story of its mobilization for political purposes even more complicated.

The chapters that follow in this section focus on the politically complex region of east-central and southern Europe, which comprised countries from both sides of the Iron Curtain, including one, Yugoslavia, which straddled that divide. These countries shared many historical commonalities yet occupied very different positions on the geopolitical map of the Cold War, making them particularly suited for comparison. At the same time, the case studies explored here also highlight the fact that architectural modernism had many facets that cannot be reduced to a single monolithic description. Instead, the modernist paradigm comprised a great variety of expressions, motivations, and connotations, thus defying the stereotype of a universally applicable and politically neutral "International Style." If Italian architects sought to maintain a vital link with vernacular traditions as a way to elude rationalism's prewar association with the Fascist state, in Romania architects severed any connections with the past in order to signify the establishment of a new society. If in Czechoslovakia the state aspired to efficient standardization and typification of architecture, in Yugoslavia it embraced diverse modes of representation to buttress its internal and external legitimacy. The following four essays explore these diverse meanings of architecture as a way to problematize the complex relationships between modernism and the state after World War II.

NOTES

1. On Turkey, see Sibel Bozdoğan, *Modernism and Nation Building: Turkish Architectural Culture in the Early Republic* (Seattle: University of Washington Press, 2001). On Czechoslovakia, see Rostislav Švácha, *The Architecture of New Prague, 1895–1945*, trans. Alexandra Büchler (Cambridge, MA: MIT Press, 1995).

2. See James C. Scott, *Seeing Like a State: How Certain Schemes to Improve the Human Condition Have Failed* (New Haven, CT, and London: Yale University Press, 1999), 4.

3. See, among other titles, Jane C. Loeffler, *The Architecture of Diplomacy: Building America's Embassies*, 2nd ed. (New York: Princeton Architectural Press, 2010); and Annabel Jane Wharton, *Building the Cold War: Hilton International Hotels and Modern Architecture* (Chicago: University of Chicago Press, 2001).

4. For a pioneering effort on the mutual dynamic in the use of design in the ideological battle between the Soviet and American blocs, see Greg Castillo, *Cold War on the Home Front: The Soft Power of Midcentury Design* (Minneapolis: University of Minnesota Press, 2010). For efforts to expand the perspective to the developing world, see Lawrence J. Vale, *Architecture, Power, and National Identity*, 2nd ed. (London: Routledge, 2008); and Sandy Isenstadt and Kishwar Rizvi, eds., *Modernism and the Middle East: Architecture and Politics in the Twentieth Century* (Seattle: University of Washington Press, 2008).

1 BUCHAREST
THE CITY TRANSFIGURED

JULIANA MAXIM

BETWEEN DECAY AND RECONSTRUCTION: THE FLOREASCA NEIGHBORHOOD

On an April morning . . . a group of young architects and workers strolled through the [Floreasca district] around Rachmaninoff Street, which had once been deserted. They passed through three large plazas, through wide interior courts, which opened towards perspectives similar to Renaissance architectural visions. Teams of men and women were planting trees and flowers. They stopped in front of the colonnade of a large theater in neoclassical style. They walked along storefronts. In a library window was an art book titled *Projects for a Socialist City*. . . . They came to the lake, and on its shores, raised miraculously between air and water, was the Palace of Culture that the sun, shining on the hundreds of windows, seemed to cover in diamonds.[1]

I walk along lines of housing blocks, through the courtyards filled with flowers. . . . In the distance other blocks are being built. There are plans for 80 of them. . . . Already 15 are inhabited. A small town.

I enter block number 7, by chance.

Fancy that! You need only turn a valve to heat the radiator. You light a match and the gas stove warms up. You light another match, down in the laundry room, and the water heater starts boiling. You turn a faucet, and warm water fills the ceramic tub. You turn another one and hot water reaches the dishwasher in the kitchen. You press a button, and garbage disappears, down to the incinerator.

Thus live now the workers leading production lines, along with their families. Or even the functionaries. Or the intellectuals.[2]

Floreasca—where a real town stands by the park which replaced the abject pit of yore.[3]

FIGURE 1.1. R. Macry and M. Dumitru, Floreasca Towers, Bucharest, 1963. Illustrated in Grigore Ionescu, *Arhitectura '44–'69. Arhitectura în România în perioada anilor 1944–1969* (1969), 137.

The capital of the Romanian socialist state was described in the postwar decades as a place of beauty, order, and healthy comforts. The literature of the time abounded with edifying stories about a Bucharest where ordinary people, after long struggles, built contented, wholesome lives. Although highly ideological, these accounts testify nonetheless to the hold that the idea of a modern, clean, and efficient city had on the popular imagination, and to the central role architecture was granted in imagining and defining a socialist reality. The Floreasca district described in the opening quotes was one such place that accrued significant power in the symbolic landscape of postwar Bucharest and helped to shape the discourse about the socialist city in terms of awe-inspiring order, collective well-being, and radical transformation (figure 1.1).

By contrast, since the fall of the Iron Curtain, the West's encounter with the socialist built environment has been characterized by a sense of horror:

> Soviet-style apartment blocks are abundant. . . . They are gray and gloomy, the structural equivalent of a cloudy, motionless sky. We visited one [Bucharest] community where families were living in such apartments. No water. No electricity. Garbage spread out thickly across the courtyards, its stench hovering on the breeze. . . . No one on earth, not a single one of God's children anywhere, should ever have to live in arrangements anywhere close to what I found in this urban slum of Bucharest.[4]

> Solutions are sought for fixing, improving, recycling, adapting, and humanizing these drab, gray, uninspiring bedroom communities.[5]

In recent years, Romanian public opinion has come to regard Bucharest's numerous mass housing projects as a powerful metaphor for the disintegration of the system itself. Thus in a recent wave of Romanian movies that received broad international attention, it is the spaces themselves—bleak, ill-lit, deteriorated, Kafkaesque—that function as the primary visual signifiers of socialism. In films like Cristi Puiu's *The Death of Mr. Lazarescu* of 2005, Corneliu Porumboiu's *12:08 East of Bucharest* of 2006, and Cristian Mungiu's *4 Months, 3 Weeks, and 2 Days* of 2007, to name just a few, the camera uses the ravaged textures and endless concrete surfaces that encased life under socialism as chief expressive devices for gloom.

For the historian, however, the dismay the socialist city now conventionally triggers is but a poignant iteration of the outrage and repulsion that the newly installed Communist regime had expressed toward the laissez-faire capitalist city it inherited in 1948. As Bucharest's socialist housing projects become, in the imagination of the twenty-first century, the stand-in for urban misery and political failure, it is necessary to tell how the socialist urban project arose in the 1950s from an equally forceful criticism of the poverty, filth, overcrowding, and social and material injustice in the capitalist city. The long view on a development such as Floreasca shows how cycles of perceived decay and reconstruction overlap with cycles of political change, complicating the current condemnation of socialist mass housing: the Communist political and architectural project now seen as having brought misery and oppression to its inhabitants originated in an earnest effort to eliminate precisely those same conditions. Despite the West's revulsion at the monotonous landscape of the socialist housing districts, socialist city planning shared most of the modernist ideals, models, metaphors, and attitudes toward tradition. In its rise and fall, the story of the socialist city is also, in many ways, the story of modernism itself.

In the case of Bucharest, the socialist regime that came to power immediately after World War II inherited a dramatically increased urban population and a severe housing shortage that had led, in the 1930s and 1940s, to an explosion of unregulated shack-towns around the historical center. The architectural solutions and the accompanying rhetoric that have come to define the socialist city were in large part responses to the acute economic disparities reflected in the ring of slums surrounding its prosperous core. In particular, the juxtaposition between the extremes of opulence and misery offered a formidable condemnation of the defunct capitalist order:

> To the city's visitors, the center would appear with large boulevards bordered with elegant villas and tall buildings, while the periphery lacked all infrastructure.... This characteristic of the built environment in Bucharest perfectly represents the regime of exploitation. Between center and periphery, the bourgeoisie had erected insurmountable barriers.[6]

In the articulate critique of Bucharest's "anarchic development" and in the systematic solutions for its blighted peripheries—which came only in part as directives from Moscow—one finds, recycled and amplified, key principles of modernist planning. The city that the political and professional Communist elites erected on the wastelands of capitalism became, without any acknowledgment, one of the important laboratories for the application of modernist ideas regarding the city. As a result, the aging socialist districts currently dismissed as slums cannot be seen simply as proof of a political system's failure, but need to be examined in the larger historical context of the Modern Movement.

The socialist development of Floreasca between 1956 and 1963 on the northern edge of Bucharest illustrates with particular poignancy how the negative view of the preexisting city, understood as unjust and class-based, found a natural ally in rationalist urban planning. Before the advent of the socialist regime in 1948, Floreasca had been one the most infamous shantytowns of Bucharest, and G. Călinescu's resplendent architectural vision quoted at the beginning of this essay began amidst mud and weeds:

> Rachmaninoff Street was, at the extremity that opened on the [Floreasca] lake, a simple country road that ran between an earthen shore and a row of tall chestnut trees, next to which stood the fences of houses built on perpendicular streets as well as the walls of a former race horses' stable. Often, piles of hay and litter filled the air with a hybrid smell of freshly cut grass and acrid putrefaction. The streets that ran toward the lake carried boyars' names.... The earthen shore across the row of chestnut trees was, in summertime, covered in weeds grazed by the cattle of the surrounding inhabitants. On top of a hill stood the desolate red ruin of an abandoned house. Both the dirt road and the land next to the shore belonged to a subdivision that had been abandoned because of the [World War II] events.... Further down, the street was paved and had sewers, but was almost without any houses, as were the other streets of the subdivision.... Weeds came out irrepressibly through the pavement cracks, as if they wished to clean the earth's surface of its crust of stone.... An old rooster led its hens throughout this neighborhood that had been abandoned before being born. Some goats and their kids grazed

in the summer, and often a herd of muddy sheep led by a shepherd took over this wild place.[7]

This description of presocialist Floreasca, together with the quote at the beginning of this essay, frame one of the most popular Romanian novels of the 1960s, Călinescu's *Black Chest*. The book relies on Floreasca's wondrous transformation from slum to workers' promised land to guide a vivid narrative of aristocracy's demise and the rise of a generation of young, idealist, diligent workers. While Călinescu gently derides old Floreasca (and, by extension, much of old Bucharest) for its decrepit, rural air unsuited for a capital, other writings of the 1950s and 1960s openly denounce it as filthy and degraded—similarly presenting its degradation as evidence of the shortcomings of a previous political order. Despite being relatively close to the city center, presocialist Floreasca had no water or sewer lines, and its unpaved streets were lined with humid, dark, and poorly ventilated lodgings, often situated below street level. Year-round residents were workers, small artisans, or low-level functionaries who, unable to afford a room of their own, lived in dorm-like rooms where ten to fifteen people slept. Floreasca was bordered to the north by an infamous garbage dump (the "Floreasca pit") that attracted a population of ragpickers and, in wintertime, gypsies, the Romanian ethnic minority often stereotyped as lawless and wild (figure 1.2).[8]

Thus built on the site of a slum, socialist Floreasca not only provided affordable modern housing to a new group of residents but also staged a quasi-alchemical transmutation of garbage into a garden, and of a primitive village into a modern

FIGURE 1.2. The caption reads: "Bucharest, gypsy shacks next to landfill north of Bucharest." Postcard, 1930s. Collection of the Library of the Romanian Academy.

FIGURE 1.3. "The Floreasca district, before August 23 [1944] and today." Illustrated in *Arhitectura R.P.R.* 7, no. 5 (September-October 1959): 11.

city. As I will try to show, the modernism of the newly planned communities such as Floreasca was intended not only to solve with speed and efficiency the need for housing but also to counteract the irrational, uneven development characteristic of the old capital city under the fickle laws of the market. Images and texts of the time always contrast the newfound sense of order and prosperity with the preceding dejection and neglect. Photos of Floreasca, for instance, were carefully cropped to include hints of the old city, which is meant to appear in all its poverty, inefficiency, and obsolescence, while written sources preface descriptions of socialist architecture with accounts of the city's lamentable past (figure 1.3). Indeed, the conflict between the old order and the new one, and the victory of the second over the first, was one of the principal regulating metaphors of the Communist political sphere, and as such needed to be reflected again and again in aspects of everyday reality. The development of Floreasca between 1956 and 1963 illustrates how this ideological economy of struggle and transformation was progressively articulated in specific (and specifically modernist) architectural and urban terms—many of which came to define the socialist conception of the city.

Eventually, parts of Floreasca would also come to illustrate the reverse transformation, and today the cycle of decay, reconstruction, and decay is complete. Poorly maintained since the demise of the socialist state, the white towers have begun to peel and rust. The original smooth facades are now poked through with antennas and air conditioners, the orderly rhythm of loggias permanently disrupted by the accretion of screens, curtains, and canopies. The lawns are scrawny and soiled with garbage. Nature itself seemed to have taken its revenge, drowning the geometrical clarity of the towers with overgrown masses of greenery. Like in Călinescu's presocialist Floreasca, weeds push through the broken pavement.⁹

The example of Floreasca shows the extent to which the socialist city is framed through comparisons that foreground striking differences and ruptures rather than continuities. In the 1960s a place such as Floreasca represented the unquestionable triumph of socialist centralized intervention over laissez-faire dereliction; a generation later, in the 1990s, socialist mass housing was now used to demonstrate the flagrant shortcomings of Soviet-style state control over architecture. The contrasting tropes of renewal and decay, order and disorder, utopia and dystopic failure, and collectivity and anonymity repeatedly pit the urban ambitions of the socialist state against Western capitalist urban forms. I wish to show instead that the socialist city also belongs firmly within industrial capitalist urban models and their corresponding ideology of progress and rational dominion over the environment. Despite the rhetoric of antagonism, many links tie the postwar socialist city to earlier discussions of the modern urban experience that occupied Western European architects and political powers in the first half of the twentieth century. Floreasca, in all its embodiments—before, during, and after socialism—offers the opportunity to reflect on approaches to the city that had been attempted much before and far beyond socialism's rise to power in Romania.

SOCIALIST URBANISM:
MASTER PLANS AND LEGISLATION

Bucharest's transformation into a socialist city in the 1950s and 1960s resulted from the regime's uncompromising recourse to centralized planning, which, in the case of the capital, materialized in a series of master plans for its development. Seen as total and rational, the master plan and the pieces of legislation that accompanied it emerged in a climate of fierce condemnation for spontaneous, unregimented growth, which had produced most of the city's existing residential fabric. The plan also reflected a desire to eradicate old settlements that at times superseded even the more pressing need for housing.

In search of systems for cheap and rapid housing construction, and needing to clean up and reshape the city, the socialist architects abandoned the problem of giving form to single elements and instead embraced the city as the real unit of production. Methods of design and construction were rigorously standardized, leading to a sweeping transformation of the entire architectural discipline.¹⁰ These measures rapidly replaced a type of urban growth based on the small, individual, and endlessly variable dwellings that characterized most of old Bucharest with large-scale architectural projects commissioned by the state and based on standard types and series, technological efficiency, and economy.

The newly installed socialist regime in Romania made its first attempt at regulating city form with Resolution 2448 of November 1952, issued by the

Party's Central Committee and titled "Concerning the general plan for the socialist reconstruction of the city of Bucharest."[11] The resolution's scope was all-encompassing and established a structure of commissions and committees through which all architectural activity, from construction details to urban form, was to become state-funded and controlled. A State Committee for Architecture and Constructions (CSAC) was formed to vet and control all architectural and urban projects, with the goal to "ensure the application of a unitary line of principles throughout the field of architecture, and the systematization and construction of cities and constructions of all nature."[12] The resolution also regulated both the scope and organization of architects' work: architectural collectives were to first produce a master plan to be approved at the state level and then work within its bounds to redevelop the capital. (The Central Committee approved the master plan for Bucharest in 1958 and passed numerous subsequent revisions.) The system of vast architectural projects funded by the state and carried out by numerous state design agencies overseen by the State Committee for Architecture and Constructions brought to an end all private commissions and private architectural practice.

More significantly, the 1952 Resolution opened with a heavy-handed rhetorical outburst against the capitalist city:

> Towns and settlements throughout our country's territory have inherited a heavy burden from the bourgeois exploitative regime. Anarchically developed, according to the narrow-minded interests of the bourgeoisie and the landowners, our country's cities offered a striking contrast between the rich districts of the ruling classes and the poor ones, in which the workers lived in misery, in crumbling houses, without water, sewer, or light.[13]

By contrast, the resolution envisioned the socialist capital as a unified territory that was to be scientifically and systematically planned to respond to the needs of the workers and to remedy spatial inequalities. The resolution required that the size of the city be controlled and its perimeter fixed once and for all, which meant that all new development would be achieved through the densification of the existing urban territory. The resolution, along with countless other documents of the time, also insisted on achieving a certain architectural unity within the city to correct its existing contrasts. (One of the earliest applications of that principle was to establish a uniform building height along all of the boulevards crossing the city, unlike the more common model of the city as a pyramid in which buildings grow taller toward the center.) The resolution also called for erasing the contrast between center and periphery not only visually but also in terms of quality of construction, infrastructure, and services. For that purpose, daycare centers, schools, medical facilities, stores, markets, post offices, and other collective programs needed to be distributed "rationally" and equally throughout the city. The regulation, along with the master plan that subsequently emerged from it, also divided the city for the first time into single-function zones, such as the one that situated heavy industry on the city's outskirts. Similarly, extensive attention was given to creating and planning green spaces, resulting in a complex system of parks, from small neighborhood squares to a botanical garden, connected in a continuous green zone that served the "recreation needs of the workers."

Finally, the resolution contained specific indications about the large-scale planning and construction of housing. To that effect, it introduced the notion of complex, multifunctional residential ensembles generically named *cvartal*. These small territorial units rapidly became the planning device of choice in developing the socialist city and, as Floreasca well illustrates, the object of intense experimentation, adaptation, and evolution over the next two decades. At the time of the 1952 Resolution, the *cvartal* was defined as ranging between five and ten hectares in size, with spaces allowed for gardens and small parks. The density and height of the residential buildings were also specified—though in practice these guidelines were applied with significant variation.

Although never acknowledged as such, the 1952 Resolution was for all practical purposes the first official endorsement of certain modernist principles in an architectural historical line that previously had been colored by antimodernist sentiment. The resolution was indeed radically rewriting a previous master plan for Bucharest, which in 1935 had timidly tried to address disastrous housing conditions by legislating city limits, although that plan had remained largely unimplemented. The 1935 Master Plan had designated the traditional single-family, two-story house, with a common parting wall on one side and a garden at the back, as the most appropriate residential building type for the urban population. In the same stroke, the 1935 plan had declared the apartment building as unfit for Romanian workers, who were deemed still essentially rural in their mentality and habits. The text also warned that apartment living swayed its tenants toward Communism, while ownership of individual lots created a bond between the citizen and the land that counteracted Communist tendencies and was therefore preferable.[14] The important differences regarding the typology of the workers' housing between the 1935 Master Plan and the 1952 Resolution are key in understanding the socialist architectural agenda: while the first insisted on the single-family house with its individual plot of land and the swaying importance of private property, the second advocated groups of industrially produced residential blocks and collective spaces. In both cases, however, housing was seen as having the power to transform the mind-set of its inhabitants and therefore the structure of society as a whole.

After the 1952 Resolution, the Floreasca district underwent several stages of construction that illustrate the successive answers architects provided during the 1950s to the call for a "scientific and systematic planning of the city." By 1956, eighty-five apartment buildings had already been built (see figure 1.3). This first stage of development represented one of the new regime's first major projects in the capital and provided one of the earliest and most publicized applications of the *cvartal*. It also demonstrated the socialist state's forceful rewriting of prewar legacies. The project occupied a preexisting street grid initially destined to contain individual villas (as described by Călinescu) but canceled the original division of land by moving individual residential lots into larger land holdings that could accommodate an environment of apartment buildings and collective open spaces.

THE *CVARTAL* AND MODERNIST PLANNING

The *cvartal* was the principal channel through which principles of the modern movement were progressively activated on a large scale in Romania, even during a period conventionally considered to have been entirely dominated by the Socialist Realist doctrine exported by Moscow. Indeed, the *cvartal* of the 1950s joined together concerns for monumentality and classical composition with radically rationalist design solutions.

Writing about Floreasca in 1969, architectural historian G. Ionescu described it as "a little town able to accommodate 11,000 residents; it contains 5 large groups in which most of the housing blocks are placed linearly along the streets of the existing subdivision. Most of these blocks are built from IPB standardized units, have a uniform height of 3 floors plus ground floor, and occupy 30% of the ground surface, resulting in a net density of 450 inhabitants per hectare."[15] The early Floreasca was indeed a small world of neat, similar residential blocks on four levels, rigidly aligned along a street grid. The project successfully transformed what had been destined to become single-family houses into a dense collective dwelling environment boasting exceptional comforts for the time, such as modern kitchens, running hot water, new schools, and a cinema. The planning of the district and the design of the housing blocks were devised on strict scientific principles (such as, for instance, the IPB [Institut Proiect București] standardized construction modules, or the tightly quantified ratios and densities), but the economy of its construction and design coexisted with a monumental impulse. The composition of the district seems caught between the solution of a homogeneous grid, extendable according to need, and a composition built around an emphatic, Renaissance-like center, in this case marked by the cinema (figure 1.4).

The buildings are simple rectangular prisms, but their upper edges end in projecting cornices that read like an apology for the lack of a more prominent roof. Windows and doors are framed in relief, also in resistance to the unrelenting flatness of the walls; a concrete molding wraps around each building in order to suggest a plinth, and the treatment of the buildings' surface imitates the joints of stonework (figure 1.5). All these elements signified, albeit in a simplified form, that the classical vocabulary of building parts and urban spaces commonly associated with Socialist Realism existed, at least in the early 1950s, in awkward but nonetheless close conjunction with the modernist language of simplicity and economy and the abstract logic of standardization.

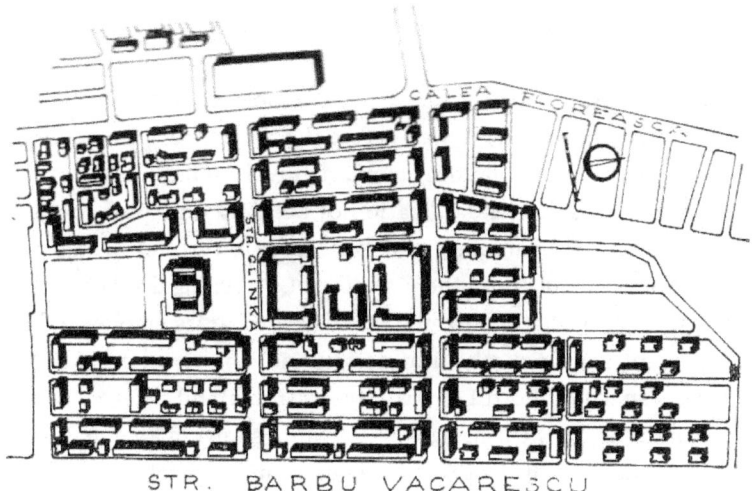

FIGURE 1.4. Corneliu Rădulescu and Associates. Early phase of the Floreasca district, planned according to the *cvartal* notion. Illustrated in Grigore Ionescu, *Arhitectura '44–'69. Arhitectura în România în perioada anilor 1944–1969*, 68.

FIGURE 1.5. Early mass housing in Floreasca, 1956–1958. Illustrated in Grigore Ionescu, *Arhitectura '44–'69. Arhitectura în România în perioada anilor 1944–1969*, 69.

One could argue that the seemingly unresolved architectural identity of Floreasca can be attributed to the reorientation forced upon the architectural profession by Khrushchev's rise to power in the Soviet Union in 1954 and his open condemnation of Stalinist aesthetic culture. But a look at other *cvartals* designed in Romania between 1948 and 1955, well before the Khrushchev-mandated stylistic austerity, shows that their planning similarly involved both significant attention to the typification and standardization of building units and the industrialization of construction techniques, and extensive concern for ornamentation. For instance, an article explaining the planning of a housing district in the town of Bacău in 1952 discussed at length the standardized units employed, boasting a rate of 80 percent standardization of design and construction (the standard units—*tronson*—specified both constructive systems and interior plans, and carried names such as "ISPROR nr 228-1953") while showing an equal fervor for the design and production of the capitals, volutes, and vegetal motifs in ceramic moldings that were to be applied on the facades.[16]

The ambiguity that was built into the *cvartal* of the 1950s, and the overlap between what appear to be contradictory positions about architectural expression and city form, stem from the *cvartal*'s complicated origin in the Soviet Union. The history of the *cvartal* is well beyond the scope of this essay, but its arrival on the Bucharest postwar planning scene is a good example of how architectural ideas formulated in the 1920s and early 1930s came to accommodate variable political and cultural contexts in the postwar. Indeed, the notion of *cvartal* that migrated to Romania in the early 1950s dated back to the 1930s. Exported by Moscow after World War II as the chief recipe for the socialist housing district, the *cvartal* was the result of early relations between the Soviet Union and the modernist avant-gardes. The theoretical and formal basis of the *cvartal* had been conceived at a time of close collaboration between European and Soviet architects between 1930 and 1934.

During the first Five-Year Plan (1928–1932) that marked the Soviet Union's grand turn toward industrialization, the government had systematically sought out and invited foreign architects and engineers to assist with the planning and building of new industrial centers and new socialist towns. The list of architects who spent several years in the Soviet Union, working alongside Soviet architects in newly formed central planning institutes, gives a sense of the extent to which the ideas of the early CIAM (Congrès Internationaux d'Architecture Moderne) generation, such as standardization and equitable distribution of space and low-cost mass housing, became intertwined with Soviet practices. Working in the Soviet Union in the 1930s were the Dutch J. B. van Loghem, the French André Lurçat, and the Czech Jaromír Krejcar, as well as two German teams, one under the direction of Hannes Meyer and composed of six young architects from the Bauhaus in Dessau, and one under the direction of Ernst May and composed of about twenty engineers and architects from Frankfurt (among them Walter Schwagenscheidt, Werner Hebebrand, Margarete Schütte-Lihotzky, the Dutch

Mart Stam, the Hungarian Fred Forbàt, and the Swiss Hans Schmidt). Many of these architects had been active participants in the early CIAM meetings at La Sarraz and Frankfurt, where the problem of "collective and methodical land policy," mass housing, and the conception of residential districts that integrated social and cultural institutions into a functional whole had first become matters of systematic research and debate.[17] Although the spare and functional character of the districts and towns (such as Magnitogorsk) conceived by these planning brigades was strongly criticized during the monumentalist backlash of the late 1930s and 1940s, the Stalinist decades nonetheless retained the *cvartal* as the basic planning unit, and with it much of the earlier planning principles: the need to decentralize and increase density at the periphery, the need to standardize construction, and the *cvartal*'s multifunctional aspect, with nurseries, shops, schools, and playgrounds arranged at walking distances from all housing.[18] Thus the *cvartal* migrated to Romania in the early 1950s invested with a double legacy: on the one hand, the ideological and technical positions of the German-speaking avant-garde; on the other, the compositional attitudes of Stalinism.

The Soviet and postwar socialist regimes shared with this early CIAM generation not only concrete solutions for the organization of the city, but philosophical ones as well, such as the condemnation of individual ownership of urban land. Indeed, the CIAM members of the late 1920s and 1930s (and later, as shown, for instance, in Josep Luís Sert's writings of the 1940s) had denounced private property as the main obstacle to urban reconfiguration:[19] "The chaotic division of land, resulting from sales, speculations, inheritances, must be abolished by a collective and methodical land policy," read the CIAM's initial declaration of 1928.[20] The transformation of small, privately owned parcels into state-owned large landholdings destined for high-rise and high-density housing, and, equally important, an approach to housing at the scale of the neighborhood are but two principles of socialist planning that correspond closely with those of the early CIAM.

The important professional contributions of foreign architects to Soviet planning in the 1920s and 1930s meant that Romania's socialist urbanism of the 1950s and 1960s, under Moscow's direct influence, was in fact establishing important lines of continuity with interwar European modernist thought. It was under Moscow's impulse that the architectural profession in postwar Romania eventually embraced wholesale the rational urbanism of the avant-garde of the first half of the century, renouncing its own historical skepticism toward collective forms of habitation. Indeed, in Romania, the official architectural culture of the authoritarian socialist regime proved much closer to the interwar European modernist avant-garde than to its own presocialist past, which, as seen in the 1935 Master Plan, had feared modernist planning as a possible instrument of Communism.

Although praised for its capacity to achieve density, the early *cvartals* such as Floreasca in the 1950s were quickly criticized for the rigidity of their layout, the monotony of their buildings and of their geometrical grid, the failure to address the problem of parking, and ultimately for the failure to fully and rapidly adopt

FIGURE 1.6. Floreasca towers, as seen from the lake. Postcard, before 1968. Collection of the author.

standardized and industrialized construction methods.²¹ By consequence, the design principles that had guided the development of Floreasca in the late 1950s were significantly revised. By 1963, six new residential towers signaled the beginning of a second wave of research and experimentation with housing that was to transform Bucharest profoundly throughout that decade (figure 1.6).

BUILDINGS IN A GARDEN: FROM *CVARTAL* TO *MICRORAION*

> [The architect] dreamed of a miners' town; . . . he saw it like a play of white cubes stretching on a vast and green meadow. Everything would have been very idyllic, and life in green and white, with all the benefits of civilization, would have been, needless to say, a happy one.²²

In the early 1960s, changes in the planning of housing districts clarify some of the seemingly unresolved aspects of the *cvartal*. The transformation occurs on the level of the architectural language—all remnants of neoclassical ornamentation and monumentality, now condemned by Moscow, vanish—but also, and more importantly, in the layout of the urban units, which in their new configuration and size come to be designated in Romania as *microraion*. In the Soviet Union, where both *cvartal* and *microraion* originated, the difference between them throughout the 1930s and 1940s is by no means clear and the two seem to have coexisted rather than succeeded each other. Their differentiation is further complicated by the fact that both terms have been translated in English as superblock (or sometimes as neighborhood unit).[23] In Romania, however, *cvartal* is a term that belongs clearly to the planning practices of the late 1940s and 1950s and which disappears in favor of *microraion* in the 1960s. This change in denomination illuminates an important shift in the planning of the residential district.

I suggest that the turn from the *cvartal* to the *microraion* is not, as an immediate reading would have it, an abandonment, in the wake of Khrushchev's speech, of Socialist Realism in favor of a return to a modernist line; instead, it signals Romania's socialist architectural culture's realignment from one modernist line to another, in a shift that could be usefully compared to the one that distinguished the hard rationalism of the early CIAM to the functionalist and more visually self-conscious proposals of a later CIAM. Bucharest's urban projects of the 1960s, including the six Floreasca towers of 1963, show new concerns that correspond closely to a text such as the Charter of Athens and therefore to CIAM's work of the late 1930s and 1940s—although, again, no acknowledgment of such ties is to be found in the socialist literature of the time.[24] Equally important, the shift from *cvartal* to *microraion* was propelled also by the need, frequently expressed in the contemporary literature, to build a new city in striking contradistinction to the old one. To that end, the *cvartal* was still too closely bound to the structures of the old city to satisfy the search for a fully expressed new urban condition.

In the early 1960s, the planning of the *microraion* increasingly emphasizes the autonomy of the residential buildings from the street, arranging them instead according to criteria (such as sun exposure, views, and quality of experience inside the *microraion*) that no longer take the surrounding city into account. Instead of the *cvartal*'s assimilation into an existing street pattern or urban block, it is the provision of green areas in all residential districts that becomes the central issue, as important, perhaps, as technological innovation and the rational disposition of buildings. The idea of large green open spaces, either as greenbelts around the city or as the setting for widely spaced apartment blocks, appears in all writing about the socialist city and seems to have been used to respond to criticisms about the overly controlled and monotonous built environment fostered by the monumental geometry of the *cvartal*. More importantly, it is the green areas' potential to function as the new collective spaces of the new districts, and to replace the civic centers of the old city with new, alternative ones, that seems to have determined the socialist regime's adherence to the charter's stance on green spaces. In the new socialist *microraion*, and very much in agreement with the charter's text, housing was removed from a traditional relationship with the street and turned inward, toward interior gardens and parks. As in the charter, collective life was increasingly conceived in relation to recreation. People and cars followed separate paths, and residential buildings often were not reachable by car but were accessed only by pedestrian alleys winding through green

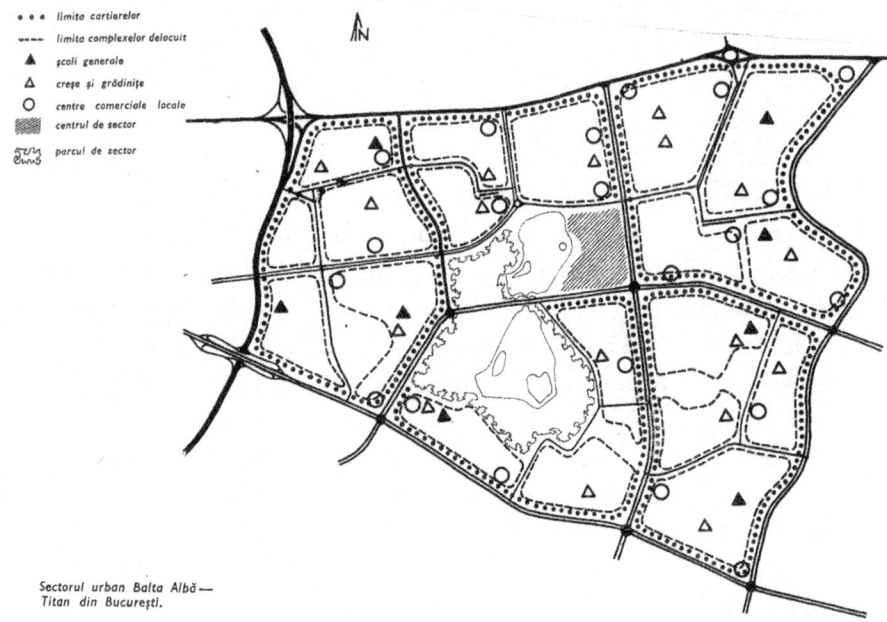

FIGURE 1.7. Plan of the Balta Albă housing district, with its subdivision in *microraions* (dotted lines). The district is centered on a lake and a large park. The legend indicates each *microraion*'s functional autonomy within the larger district, with day-care centers, schools, and commercial facilities. Illustrated in C. Lăzărescu, *Urbanismul în România*, 47.

---

spaces (figure 1.7). Much hinged, indeed, on the collective nature of such spaces. In Bucharest even the most modest single-family houses had been traditionally organized around a courtyard and a small garden plot, a relationship to the land that Romanian presocialist urban imagination had considered essential to the well-being of the urban lower and middle classes. The socialist model of the highrise in the middle of a park tried to restore some of that primordial access to nature, but it also made private claims over open space impossible. And while the apartment units inside mass housing developments were often privately owned and did not directly challenge the model of a family-centered private sphere, it fell upon the use of green spaces to effectively overturn the paradigm of ownership and instill a collective mind-set.

The *microraion* differed in important ways from the *cvartal* of the 1950s. Though similar in size (both could contain between 1,500 and 3,000 inhabitants), the *cvartals* were not conceived to function autonomously. The 1952 Resolution had stipulated only the rational distribution of basic services throughout the city, without linking these services necessarily to the *cvartals*. In practice, the barshaped residential blocks of *cvartals* of the 1950s, orderly and unidirectionally disposed along streets or around a clear, monumental center, were to function in continuation with the city. In contrast, the *microraion* was expected to produce

FIGURE 1.8. Floreasca towers. On the left (north) are the park and, further, the lake. The site previously housed a garbage pit. In the lower right corner (south) is the interwar neighborhood of single-family houses. In the upper-right corner is the first stage of socialist Floreasca from the late 1950s. Illustrated in *Arhitectura* 15, no. 4 (1967): 7.

new cities within the city: "The [*microraion*] can be defined as a clearly delimited part of a residential area, which accommodates a tightly knit and relatively autonomous collectivity."[25] The *microraion* rejected the grid and generated a street pattern that followed its own internal logic. Finally, the *microraion* completely unhinged the housing from the urban street, a phenomenon that urban theorists like Philippe Panerai and Jean Castex, for instance, called the "death of the urban block" and that, not incidentally, they traced back to Ernst May's plans for Frankfurt in the late 1920s.[26]

The six apartment towers built in 1963 on the edge of the former garbage pit are the last episode in Floreasca's socialist reconstruction (figure 1.8). The project, while on a much smaller scale than the *cvartal* that preceded it in 1956 or the *microraions* that were to follow in other parts of Bucharest, nonetheless clearly illustrates the search to overcome the historical characteristics of residential Bucharest, which would ultimately define the *microraion*. Indeed, the Floreasca towers are still caught in the attempt to mediate the encounter between socialist and presocialist visions of the city, before the *microraion* cast this encounter in the mode of a complete and unresolvable antinomy. Because the towers were built in relative proximity to the surrounding neighborhood, they plainly exposed the conflicts, physical and symbolic, that the socialist urban idea had triggered within the existing city.

For instance, whereas the later, fully developed *microraions* offered self-enclosed, functionally autonomous residential environments with their own internal circulation logic, the Floreasca towers still run along an existing street. But unlike the buildings of the 1956 development, the towers also turn their backs to the street, anticipating the principle of green space as the symbolic and physical center of the housing districts. Despite having four almost identical faces, subtle differences express the fact that the towers have been oriented away from the old city that borders them to the south and toward the new park (and former garbage pit) that opens on their northern edge. The facade containing the most windows opens onto the vista of the park and the lake, while the facade with the fewest windows turns toward the street. The entrance to each tower is also removed from the narrow street that borders the complex to the south and is located on the western side, accessible only to pedestrians, pointing to the separation between foot and car traffic that would characterize the *microraion*.

REPRESENTING THE CITY

The socialist state invested unprecedented financial resources in building the socialist city; in return, it enlisted workers' housing in a vast propaganda campaign meant to demonstrate the transformation of life under the new political order. The state, concerned with substantiating the claim that a qualitative leap had occurred from capitalism into socialism, came to rely heavily on architecture as key evidence of this transformation.[27] New neighborhoods such as Floreasca thus had a presence that extended well beyond their physical territory, becoming representational spaces that were showcased relentlessly in photographs and in writing. The Floreasca towers in particular were the object of numerous photographs that circulated in books, magazines, and thousands of postcards. I would argue that the photographs had a dual function. First, they actively countered the memory of the shantytown and garbage pit that many residents of Bucharest still might have associated with the name of Floreasca. To that end, the images established a visual register in stark contrast to the traits of the shantytown: while the informal settlement had followed neither zoning nor plan, photographs emphasized the precise alignment of the towers and the seriality of the construction.

FIGURE 1.9. Aerial view of Bucharest. In the foreground is the building that then housed the Council of Ministers. The six Floreasca towers are in the distance. The image puts in direct relationship the center of Communist political power and the new housing districts. Postcard, 1960s. Collection of the author.

Because descriptions of the *mahala* insisted on the "lowly" nature of its buildings, the vertical organization of socialist housing in general, and the height of the towers in particular, became not just an efficient way of using land but instead a visual symbol of strength and moral rectitude.[28]

The second function of the photographs was to give the Floreasca towers the status of recognizable landmarks (figure 1.9). The choice of angles and viewpoints emphasized their height, and large panoramas showed their silhouette rising above the city in the same way that steeples would have signaled, in other times, the civic heart of a settlement. These views, always taken from the center outward, imply a conception of the city in which the new peripheral neighborhoods have acquired a symbolic predominance equal to that formerly given to the historic core.

NEW, OLD, MODERN:
RATIONALISM VERSUS STYLISTIC MODERNISM

> An extraordinarily striking contrast existed between the old Floreasca pit, with its shanties, and, less than 30 meters away, a luxurious neighborhood where bourgeois owners and the upper classes lived lives of leisure.[29]

In the context of socialism's effort to distinguish itself from life under capitalism, the Floreasca towers were used to demonstrate how state-planned affordable mass housing could not only regenerate a slum but also counter the other extreme of capitalism's inequity: the inefficient, arbitrary, even frivolous formal variations of bourgeois architectural taste, exemplified by the small villas that bordered the towers to the south. The towers' rigorous alignment functioned, on the territorial level, as the seam between the class divisions of the capitalist city: extreme poverty in the form of the former garbage dump and shantytown on the north side, and wealth in the form of the upper-middle-class villas that still line the grid of streets to the south. The towers were meant to prove that socialism could transcend such class divides through architectural means and overcome, more specifically, the shortcomings of the bourgeois house. Instead of private, unique residences, highly individualized according to the specific personality and economic status of the owner, the towers provided efficient, mass-produced, unsentimental and status-free units. Here again, the photographs are explicit: while the towers rise boldly amidst vast open spaces, the bourgeois neighborhood in the background seems cramped and low; the streets of the latter are submerged in greenery that signals its old age—read obsolescence—while the towers appear unburdened by any accretion. More importantly, the towers are identical and abstract while the 1930s neighborhood is an eclectic agglomeration of scales, styles, forms, and materials (figure 1.10).

In their uncompromising repetition and standardization (the construction of Floreasca towers was touted as having used the most advanced technology of sliding casts for reinforced concrete), the towers were to be read as arguments for a kind of architecture that replaced the arbitrary demands of the individual patron and the unbound invention of the architect with spatial and constructive solutions that were instead reached rationally and for the collective good. Instead of the endless trends and variations that had led to Bucharest's urban "chaos," the standardization of architectural form contained the promise of a new political

FIGURE 1.10. 1930s street adjacent to the Floreasca towers (visible at the back). The two houses in the foreground illustrate the eclecticism of Romanian interwar architecture. On the right, the large brick house harbors neo-Byzantine motifs, while the small house to its left illustrates the "cubist" style defined by simplified geometric volumes and decoration. Photo by author, 2005.

and cultural unity, and of a legible expression of socialist power at the scale of the city. In the words of one commentator,

> We are no longer designing luxury villas, tenement housing or other sorts of buildings meant for speculative purposes that benefit an exploitative minority. . . . Architectural work today is no longer the personal problem of a creator, but a collective work supported by the state.[30]

Mass housing projects such as Floreasca spelled also a more general rebuttal of the particular form modernism had assumed in presocialist Romania. It is not incidental that the neighborhood adjacent to the towers contained some of the most representative examples of interwar experiments with modern forms, which in the eclectic architectural scene of 1930s Bucharest had been limited to posh private residences and had amounted mostly to exercises of architectural authorship and formal playfulness. The Floreasca project countered such surroundings with a restrained and repetitive formal solution that elided expression of status and revealed instead the logic of centralized planning, technology, and mass production. This rupture in the history of Romanian architecture not only reflects the shift from a capitalist to a socialist society but also activates two fundamentally different understandings of modernism: on the one hand, architecture as the subjective creation of unique works of art that aimed to achieve symbolic and aesthetic meaning; on the other hand, architecture as the large-scale production of replicable forms conceived for the requirements of society as a whole, which claimed to have eradicated all recourse to the affective and the symbolic.[31]

The development of Floreasca illustrates how, under socialism, prefabrication and standardization led to a general shift in scale from the design of single objects to that of large neighborhoods formed through the repetition of one building type, or from the singular to the collective. Far from being seen as monotonous, series of identical housing blocks were often the object of photographs that celebrated the clock-like regularity of their organization. Like products of the assembly line, they were presented not as individual objects, but as identical and interchangeable parts inside a larger order.

Despite having a strongly cultivated visual presence, the towers were not acknowledged as aesthetic objects. This was made quite clear in the only article about the towers that appeared in the magazine *Arhitectura* in 1963. Written in a matter-of-fact manner, the article concentrated on extensive technical facts and solutions to objective demands:

> We reached the following conclusions: [in this project] we have reduced the execution time by 30% compared to other current building systems; we have reduced the use of wood by 35%; . . . we have significantly increased the degree of industrialization, shown by a 25% increase of productivity of labor; . . . we have reduced the cost of construction by 3%.[32]

But it would be a mistake to accept—as the architects ask us to do—the argument that design was determined uniquely by pragmatic concerns for speed and economy. Even at its most pragmatic, the socialist regime's attitude toward architecture was in fact powerfully ideological, supported through many important rhetorical acts; while socialist architecture no longer produced meaning through conventional uses of composition, ornamentation, or rich materials, it still harbored the conviction that built form had the power to express and shape social and political ideals, and still aimed at finding ways to signify and effect progressive social development. An architecture conceived on an urban scale convincingly embodied a collectivist ideal, while standardization and technological process constituted a complementary attack on individualism and subjectivity (both the architect's and the inhabitant's), these aspects being made visible in the way in which the housing blocks are fully submitted, from their constructive process to their situation in space, to the inexorable logic of the series. The ideological underpinnings of architecture as a collective act also extended beyond the realm of political doctrine to reach into the heart of the definition of a work of art. By defining the design process as the organization of production, with its connotations of economy, speed, and repeatability, and with the neighborhood as its module, socialist architecture aimed to undermine what it saw as the bourgeois values of authenticity and uniqueness.

The architecture produced by the authoritarian Communist regimes of the postwar has rarely been discussed as a valuable episode in the history of the Modern Movement. And yet, a development such as Floreasca shows over and over how the effort to build a radically new socialist city forged direct ties with positions familiarly associated with the Modern Movement of the 1920s and, in adapting and amplifying them, revealed much of their tenor. By reconceptualizing architecture into a set of procedures and by making the satisfaction of collective needs its primary mission, socialist architects put in practice ideals such as the destruction of the creator's "aura" and the transformation of the creator into the producer, which had been formulated a generation earlier. In the periodical *Arhitectura*, the main architectural publication of the time, one finds explicit calls to de-subjectify the design process by replacing it with increasingly precise models of organization:

> We need to go from building piece by piece to the serial execution of constructions. . . . In this period during which new forms of construction appear, we need to verify our attitude towards architecture, and to reorganize in an entirely new way the problem of design . . . we need to liquidate the rift between execution and design. . . . Houses are not built to be looked at! . . . Therein lies the essential difference between socialist and bourgeois architecture: while the latter bears the mark of endlessly variable tastes of individual patrons, in our architecture, everything must be established with precision, through objective calculations. When the principles of such calculations will be established, there will be no place left for individual, arbitrary taste, for forever-changing fashions, for ephemeral distractions.[33]

> [Our years] mark the departure from design methods that were based on an archaic and narrow understanding of the relationship between form and content, both in architecture and in urbanism.[34]

For the historian, the recovery of the radical modernist language that lies at the core of postwar socialist architecture matters in reassessing not only the architectural legacy of Communism, but also the conventional narratives about what constituted the dominant architectural ideas in the postwar decades. At a time when, in the West, the Modern Movement was undergoing extensive revisions, shedding its radical political and scientific tone in favor of technically determined but nonetheless preeminent stylistic pursuits, socialist architecture was structured in reverse, fulfilling the aspirations of the early Modern Movement such as standardization and efficient production methods. Most accounts of the Modern Movement describe its development after the 1930s as the decline of the aspiration toward a fully rationalized city and the triumph of a largely apolitical aestheticism. The history of postwar socialist architecture reverses that verdict.

NOTES

1. G. Călinescu, *Scrinul Negru* (The Black Chest of Drawers) (Bucharest: Editura de Stat pentru Literatură și Artă, 1960), 854.

2. Ioachim Botez, *Prin București, odinioară și azi* (Through Bucharest, Past and Present) (Bucharest: Editura Tineretului, 1956), 74–75.

3. Constantin C. Giurescu, *History of Bucharest,* abbreviated translation (Bucharest: Publishing House for Sports and Tourism, n.d.), 110. Originally published as Constantin Giurescu, *Istoria Bucureștilor din cele mai vechi timpuri pînă în zilele noastre* (Bucharest: Editura pentru literatură, 1966).

4. Habitat for Humanity® International website, May 9–10, 2006, entry (website visited on May 30, 2006).

5. Peter Lizon, "East Central Europe: The Unhappy Heritage of Communist Mass Housing," *JAE* 50, no. 2 (November 1996): 104.

6. Alexandru Cebuc, "Aspecte din viața unor mahalale bucureștene din perioada 1900–1944" (Aspects of Life in Some Bucharest *Mahalale* in the Years 1900-1944) in *Materiale de Istorie și Muzeografie* 1 (1964): 101.

7. Călinescu, *The Black Chest*, 5.

8. Stoica, Luana-Irina, "La banlieue bucharestoise de l'entre-deux-guerres. Mahalaua—topos et réalité sociale." *New Europe College Annual Proceedings 1997–98*, 385. "The so-called 'rooms for rent' were mere shacks made out of wood planks and whitewashed on the inside. Living in conditions that did not satisfy even the most basic sanitary needs, overcrowded in unhealthy ways, thousands of people were falling ill." P. Daiche and A. Bene, "Aspecte ale dezvoltării edilitar-urbanistice ale capitalei între cele două războaie mondiale," in *Materiale de istorie ale orașului București*, vol 1 (1964): 131.

9. This was the condition of parts of Floreasca in the early 2000s. The rush to land and real estate speculation of the last ten years in Bucharest has accelerated the cycle of impoverishment and gentrification, and Floreasca is once more being developed and densified.

10. During 1960–1965, 300,000 apartments were erected with state funds in Bucharest. The projections were an acceleration of the rhythm to 80,000 to 100,000 apartments a year, in the hope of fully meeting the need for housing in the capital by 1975. Grigore Ionescu, *Arhitectura '44–'69. Arhitectura în România în perioada anilor 1944–1969* (Bucharest: Editura Academiei Republicii Socialiste România, 1969), 107.

11. Comitetul Central al Partidului Muncitoresc Român, *Hotărîre cu privire la planul general de reconstrucție socialistă al orașului București*. Resolution 2448 (Bucharest: Editura pentru literatură politică, November 1952). The Central Committee was the main administrative body of Romania's ruling Communist Party, which in 1954 was still called the Workers' Party of Romania. It subsequently changed its name to the Socialist Party of Romania.

12. Ibid.

13. Ibid.

14. Duiliu Marcu, G. M. Cantacuzino, R. Bolomey, I. Davidescu, T. Rădulescu, *Planul*

Director de Sistematizare. Rezumat al memoriului colectiv (Systematization Master Plan. Synopsis of the Collaborative Report) (Bucharest: Institutul Urbanistic al României, 1935).

15. Ionescu, *Arhitectura '44–'69*.

16. M. Silianu and Clement Stănescu, "Cvartal de locuințe într-un oraș nou din regiunea Bacău," *Arhitectura* 4 (1955): 23–28.

17. Hans Schmidt, "Architettura sovietica e paesi occidentali," in *Socialismo, città, architettura: URSS 1917–1937. Il contributo degli architetti europei* (Rome: Officina Edizioni, 1971), 266–267. It is interesting that the 1936 turn toward Socialist Realism in the architecture and urban planning of the Soviet Union was primarily a rebuttal of the May team's projects. The criticism concerned the schematic and uniform design of residential districts and new towns as well as the entire notion of the "functional city." For instance, when the workers encountered the early housing built by Mart Stam at Magnitogorsk, they unfavorably compared the spare modernist housing without balconies to tsarist ornate architecture, a terrible political verdict. Ibid., 271.

18. Maurice Frank Parkins, *City Planning in Soviet Russia* (Chicago: University of Chicago Press, 1953), 52.

19. Although Sert is uneasy about the abolition of private property, he concedes that land should be held in common: "The Neighborhood Unit requires a land unit. . . . Property owners may retain all their rights to the land, but the subdividing lines (the actual lot limits) within each new land unit would be removed as hindrances to the project planned." Josep Luís Sert, *Can Our Cities Survive? An ABC of Urban Problems, Their Analysis, Their Solutions* (Cambridge, MA: Harvard University Press, 1947), 74.

20. CIAM's La Sarraz Declaration (1928). In *Programs and Manifestoes on 20th-Century Architecture*, trans. Michael Bullock (Cambridge, MA: MIT Press, 1971).

21. See discussion of the inadequacies of the *cvartal* in Cezar Lăzărescu et al., *Urbanismul în România* (Bucharest: Editura Tehnică, 1977), 46.

22. Călinescu, *The Black Chest*, 661.

23. See, for instance, Parkins, who writes in 1953.

24. The work and writings of Helena and Szymon Syrkus in the late 1940s and 1950s remind us that, in socialist Poland at least, the charter was at once well known and criticized: "The demands of the Athens Charter have been completely satisfied in my country since 1945. . . . We of CIAM must revise our attitude. The Bauhaus is as far behind us as Scamozzi. It is time to pass from the Athens Charter to reality." Helena Syrkus, "Art Belongs to the People," in Sigfried Giedion, *Architecture, You and Me: The Diary of a Development* (Cambridge, MA: Harvard University Press, 1958), 86–88.

25. Lăzărescu et al., *Urbanismul în România*, 63.

26. P. Panerai, J. Castex, et al., *Formes urbaines, de l'îlot à la barre* (Marseilles: Parenthèses, 1997).

27. On the problem of the "qualitative leap" from capitalism to socialism, see Benjamin Robinson, "Socialism's Other Modernity: Quality, Quantity, and the Measure of the Human," *Modernism/modernity* 10, no. 4 (2003): 705–728.

28. "In these *mahala* crawls a larval world, with its horizon reduced to the limit. Swallowed day after day by the factory that squeezes out of them not only their strength but also their vital impulses, men grind all their inner possibilities, become dazed, renounce everything that is meaningful, uplifting, sublime." Getta Săvescu, "Tipuri bucureștene oglindite în literatura din deceniile 3 și 4 ale veacului XX" (Bucharest Types as Depicted in the Literature of the Third and Fourth Decades of the 20th Century), *Materiale de istorie ale orașului București* 6 (1968): 341.

29. Cebuc, "Aspects," 101.

30. "Marea sărbătoare" (The Great Celebration), *Arhitectura RPR* 7, no. 4 (July–August 1959): 5–6.

31. See Alan Colquhoun, "Symbolic and Literal Aspects of Technology," in *Essays in Architectural Criticism: Modern Architecture and Historical Change* (Cambridge, MA: MIT Press, 1981), 26–30. See also Colquhoun, *Modern Architecture* (Oxford: Oxford University Press, 2002), 169. Adolf Behne, for instance, described such a failed relationship within the Modern Movement as the split between Romantics and Rationalists: "two clear types can be distinguished: at their extremes are the rationalist and the romantic. In the context of architecture we have identified the consistent functionalist as representing one of these types, the romantic. His opposite is the consistent rationalist." Behne, *The Modern Functional Building*, trans. Michael Robinson (Santa Monica, CA: Getty Research Institute for the History of Art and the Humanities, 1996), 129–130.

32. V. Agent, "Blocuri-punct cu 12 niveluri în parcul Floreasca," *Arhitectura* 11, no. 3 (1963): 21.

33. V. Maslaev, "Despre problemele care îi frămîntă în prezent pe arhitecți" (Issues of Concern for Today's Architects), *Arhitectura* 6, nos. 1–2 (1958), 42–43.

34. Ionescu, *Arhitectura '44–'69*, 59.

2 THE SCOPE OF SOCIALIST MODERNISM
ARCHITECTURE AND STATE REPRESENTATION IN POSTWAR YUGOSLAVIA

VLADIMIR KULIĆ

Apart from the fact that they were both prominent architects in socialist Yugoslavia, at first sight, Vjenceslav Richter (1917–2002) and Bogdan Bogdanović (1922–2010) do not seem to have much in common. The former was an avant-gardist known for light, cool, geometricized structures that explored the limits of modernist tropes of abstraction, technology, and space. The latter created exuberant, allusive, symbolically charged monuments, often rustically hand-carved out of stone, which evoked a distant history rather than projecting the visions of a brave future. Even at a second look, there is not much that connects them, as they emerged out of two distinct artistic lineages from two distinct parts of former Yugoslavia: Richter was a prodigious—albeit more radical—product of the functionalist school of Zagreb, whereas Bogdanović was decisively influenced by the group of Belgrade Surrealists. It is only when we examine the origins and details of their careers that profound similarities emerge: common links to the pre–World War II left-wing culture, political engagement, almost compulsive production, oppositional stances to the architectural mainstream of the period, blurring of the boundaries between architecture and other disciplines, prolific writing, and, finally, their idiosyncratic yet powerful roles in creating some of the most symbolic representations of the Yugoslav socialist project.

In light of the conventional perception of post–World War II architecture, it is this last point that exposes both Bogdanović and Richter as rather odd representatives of the socialist world. Entrenched views reduce almost half a century of the production of built environments in Eastern Europe to two main stereotypes: the pompous monumentality of Socialist Realism (which is at least relatively well-researched because it provokes a certain dark fascination) and the endless monotony of repetitive panel buildings (which until recently have been deemed so bad that they do not deserve a closer study even as a cautionary tale).[1] Even these two stereotypes figure only among the relatively well informed, as most surveys of twentieth-century architecture pay no attention to postwar Eastern Europe.

This omission is particularly glaring in comparison with the several decades of efforts, sparked by postcolonial theory, at expanding the canon of modernism to include at least some token representatives of the so-called third world. In contrast, the "second world"—the "distinct, if ultimately truncated limb of modernity's tree," as Nancy Condee has cogently described it—has been consistently ignored; at first for rivaling the first-world conception of modernity, and then as a loser in the global "battle for hearts and minds."[2] Architecture is at a particular disadvantage here: first-world art history and art markets have at least acknowledged the so-called dissident art of socialist states, even if this politically motivated acknowledgment reduced the complexities of historical agency to a clear-cut opposition between the "official" and "dissident" art.[3] But there can hardly be such a thing as dissident architecture when all levers of patronage seem to belong to the state; therefore, all socialist architecture is understood as official and, by extension, not worth exploring, except maybe as a direct manifestation of politics. It is no wonder, then, that built environments of socialist Eastern Europe appear as an ultimate "non-architecture," devoid of any inherent aesthetic values, discourses, and significant practitioners worth knowing—precisely the key components traditionally used in the construction of architectural history.

Bogdanović and Richter defy such a framework. They both clearly eschewed the dissident status by creating some of the most effective architectural representations of the Yugoslav state, and yet they undoubtedly satisfied architectural history's conventional criteria of significance by formulating distinct original theoretical and practical positions, which attracted much attention in Yugoslavia and, occasionally, even abroad. In this chapter I will focus on their respective careers to problematize the stereotypes of socialist architecture and especially the term "socialist modernism," which has recently gained currency in fields ranging from music to visual arts. Commendable for expanding the perspective on postwar modernism, this term, with its need for special qualification, still seems to imply that socialism was not a natural condition for the development of modernism. Richter and Bogdanović complicate such views, since their careers demonstrate that a socialist system could provide fertile ground for the development of a wide variety of modern(ist) ideas. And while Yugoslavia was in some ways a special case, since it pursued its "own path to socialism" independent of Soviet tutelage, it was still a socialist state with all the essential features of such a system. In the lack of a reliable mapping of postwar architectural modernism in Eastern Europe, I will here use Yugoslavia as a representative to renaturalize the allegedly inherent antagonism between postwar socialism and the aesthetic innovations in architecture. Ultimately, however, my argument may be applicable to other parts of post-Stalinist Eastern Europe too: it can be argued that the scope of architectural discourses and practices that sprang from various left-wing traditions and existed under socialism is so broad that the designation "socialist modernism" can be used only in the most cursory way, as it reveals very little about the actual content of its designee.

MODERNISM(S) IN SOCIALIST YUGOSLAVIA

Socialist Yugoslavia sanctioned modernism. Such a blanket claim is especially easy to make in the context of architecture, in which modernism simultaneously had the connotation of an instrument of social modernization, a mode of cultural production, and a means of ideological representation. Thanks to its unexpected break from the Soviet bloc in 1948, Yugoslavia was only briefly touched by the political imposition of Socialist Realism; from that moment on, the country defined itself through its distinction from the Soviet-dominated East.[4] In the critical formative decade of the 1950s, the Yugoslav Communist leadership formulated a new political and economic system of socialist self-management, based on an allegedly more authentic interpretation of Marxism, and gradually released its iron grip over cultural production. After some initial disputes, high modernism in visual arts soon acquired broad acceptance, replacing Socialist Realism's demands for explicit ideological representation. Predominantly concerned with the means of expression rather than any social mission, this seemingly ideologically neutral art mirrored the appropriation of high modernism in the West as a weapon of the cultural Cold War.[5] Even its subsequent theoretical elaboration as "Socialist Aestheticism" had its parallels with Clement Greenberg's formalism, stressing art's liberation from the narrative burden of Socialist Realism and its autonomous logic. The difference, of course, was that in Yugoslavia such autonomy was appropriated to represent not a liberal democracy, but a self-managing socialism.[6]

Building on a strong tradition of prewar modernism, architecture after 1948 never really had to make any transition, since architectural Socialist Realism had never been clearly defined, let alone fully imposed.[7] By the end of the 1950s, modernist planning had redefined most of Yugoslavia's major cities. Floating white boxes and curtain-walled towers of new administration, office, and civic buildings thoroughly transformed their downtowns. And although it may have violated the personal tastes of some of the top party officials, especially the country's undisputed leader, Josip Broz Tito, the International Style amounted to a virtual new "official style" of the socialist state. Just like modernist art, the architecture of the International Style appeared to be politically too beneficial to provoke any serious official resistance: providing the immediately obvious signs of distinction from the Soviet bloc, it served for a while as an effective symbolic source of Yugoslavia's external legitimation.[8] Moreover, its short-lived domination, which lasted approximately until the mid-1960s, was perhaps the only period in which most of Yugoslav architectural production subscribed to at least some level of stylistic unity, an exceedingly rare moment in a country marked by a remarkable level of ethnic, religious, and cultural heterogeneity (figure 2.1).

Indeed, by the turn of the 1950s, some of the most important practitioners were already working on the margins of the new mainstream. Rather than appropriating international idioms wholesale, these architects hybridized the global

FIGURE 2.1. Kazimir Ostrogović, City Hall, Zagreb, 1955–1956. Photo © Wolfgang Thaler.

and the local to give shape to some of the basic concepts of the Yugoslav socialist project. The reception of Le Corbusier was indicative in this respect. Formerly proclaimed a bête noire by Socialist Realist critics, Le Corbusier quickly reestablished his primacy after 1950 as the most influential international modernist, not least because many of his prewar apprentices and collaborators were Yugoslavs who now held prominent positions as practitioners and educators in their home country. A retrospective of Le Corbusier's work, which toured the country in early 1953, was followed by an enthusiastic wave of distinctly Corbusian buildings in most major cities. By this time, however, architects like Edvard Ravnikar in Ljubljana and Juraj Neidhardt in Sarajevo—both collaborators at the *rue de Sèvre* studio in the 1930s—were already well past merely replicating the idiom of their *maître*. Neidhardt and his Slovenian colleague Dušan Grabrijan developed a regionalist reinterpretation of Le Corbusier, whose work, in their opinion, displayed many parallels with the vernacular architecture created in Bosnia under the Ottomans; hence they argued that an indigenous Bosnian modernism could be naturally developed from the local vernacular architecture. Their magnum opus, a monumental, five-hundred-page book titled *Architecture of Bosnia and the Way to Modernity*, presented Grabrijan's painstaking ethnographic research as a basis for Neidhardt's Corbusian projects, in an effort to reconcile local culture with the demands of the global civilization. Significantly, the book boasted a rare acknowledgment from Le Corbusier himself, who wrote a laudatory preface.[9] At the same time, Ravnikar worked on a different synthesis, combining his experiences in Le Corbusier's studio with the lessons of the Wagnerschule, which

FIGURE 2.2. Edvard Ravnikar, Memorial Complex in Kampor, Island of Rab, Croatia, 1953. Photo © Wolfgang Thaler.

he assimilated through his other famous mentor, Jože Plečnik. Ravnikar's 1953 Memorial Complex in Kampor at the Island of Rab (Croatia) marked a unique moment in this synthesis: a rigorous, geometricized landscape organized along a broken asymmetrical promenade architecturale, it employed abstracted classical elements hand-carved out of large monoliths to create a timeless atmosphere, simultaneously archaic and modern (figure 2.2).[10]

In both instances, the inspired aesthetic syntheses had decidedly political aspects. Neidhardt's efforts to create a modern architectural identity of Bosnia only became politically acceptable (although not exactly fully embraced) thanks to the federalist reorganization of the country, which was one of the basic tenets of the socialist revolution, in direct opposition to the unitary interwar monarchy.[11] In this context, it is also important to mention that both Neidhardt and Ravnikar subsequently became national "patriarchs" of modern architecture in two of Yugoslavia's constituent republics, Neidhardt in Bosnia-Herzegovina and Ravnikar in Slovenia, thus further reinforcing the logic of socialist federalism. Each designed the most visible architectural symbols of statehood in his own republic and exerted an enormous influence on generations of local students, virtually creating a recognizable national "school." Ravnikar also significantly contributed to another symbolic cornerstone of socialism by designing several exquisite war memorials, including the aforementioned complex at the Island of Rab. Since the official narratives of the genesis of socialist Yugoslavia consistently conflated the liberation war with the revolution, every war memorial at the same time served as a monument to socialism, too. In this respect, Ravnikar was one of several innovators who facilitated the important transition away from Socialist Realism by exploring new modes of architectural commemoration that did not rely on the stereotypical pathos of monumental figurative sculpture.

The range of modernist poetics in the architecture of socialist Yugoslavia was therefore quite broad almost from the very start; Ravnikar and Neidhardt were only two among a number of architects around the country who explored the varied aesthetic possibilities of the period. Ultimately, however, it was Vjenceslav Richter and Bogdan Bogdanović who expanded that range to its aesthetic and discursive extremes, while also devising the most explicit architectural symbols of the socialist state. Both men were extremely prolific and both constantly defied disciplinary borders; as architects, each carved his own professional niche, specializing in a single building type that constituted his experimental playground. Richter's domain was exhibition design, especially pavilions at various international shows; among the dozen or so that he designed, several rank as Yugoslavia's most poignant architectural representations abroad, all the more successful for attracting lavish praise and thus adding to the national prestige. Bogdanović, on the other hand, specialized in war memorials, creating some of the most iconic structures in this genre. Scattered all over the country, his works uniquely transcended the federation's internal ethnic borders and were effectively stamped upon the collective memory of the generations that grew up under socialism. As far as the visual properties of their products are concerned, these two architects could not have been more different, but they shared the ease with which they crossed the divisions between architecture and art and, more importantly, they shared common intellectual and artistic origins. In order to understand those origins, however, it is necessary to return to the interwar period and the activities of the left-wing intelligentsia in the Kingdom of Yugoslavia.

AESTHETICS AND POLITICS BEFORE SOCIALISM

Bogdanović and Richter owed their formation to two distinct but closely allied intellectual and artistic circles centered in Belgrade and Zagreb. Despite their divergent aesthetic programs, these circles were brought together by their left-wing inclinations and by the common antagonism to the ruling Karađorđević dynasty. Lacking consensus about the basic principles of internal organization, the Yugoslav monarchy was fraught with ethnic and class strife, further aggravated by the regime's persistent repression, which culminated in King Alexander's infamous 1929 dictatorship. The repression struck particularly hard at the local Communist Party, which was outlawed as early as 1921. But even though the party could publicly operate only through cover organizations and cultural outlets, it still attracted some of the most progressive intellectuals and artists of the period among its sympathizers.[12] Their devotion to the Communist cause, however, was put to a test in the early 1930s after Socialist Realism was imposed as the official aesthetic doctrine in the USSR. Like in many other countries, the reverberations of the Soviet events split Yugoslav left-wing intellectuals into two fiercely opposed camps, one siding with the "party line" of politically tendentious art, the other resisting it, arguing that artistic freedoms were compatible with revolutionary aspirations. Dubbed by historians the "conflict on the literary left," this split predominantly focused on literature, even though some prominent visual artists and architects took sides in it too.[13]

The camp opposed to Socialist Realism was by no means aesthetically monolithic, and it encompassed a range of positions. In Zagreb, its central figure was the well-known writer Miroslav Krleža, a Communist sympathizer and an outspoken defender of artistic freedoms. Although himself not exactly a radical modernist, the erudite Krleža understood modern art and architecture well and actively supported the group Zemlja (Earth), the most important socially engaged artistic group in Croatia. The group predominantly consisted of visual artists of divergent aesthetic directions, but it also included a number of modernist architects, such as the leading Croatian functionalist Drago Ibler.[14] Krleža's Serbian counterpart was Marko Ristić, a poet and the leader of the prolific group of Belgrade Surrealists, one of the early local strongholds of the international movement, developed in close contact with the Surrealist *Centrale* in Paris.[15] The group consisted of writers, poets, and visual artists, especially photographers, but no architects. Despite their divergent aesthetic persuasions, Krleža and Ristić were longtime friends and allies; at the eve of the war, they collaborated on the literary journal *Pečat* (Stamp), which marked the height of their confrontation with the "official line" of the Communist Party. Significantly, among its editors the journal also had two prominent Croatian functionalist architects: the already mentioned Ibler and his colleague Drago Galić.

Bogdanović and Richter were both intellectually formed in the heavily politicized atmosphere of the late 1930s, defined in the complicated triangle between the oppressive politics of the monarchy, the rising Fascist threat, and the divided left. Richter commenced his studies of architecture under such conditions in 1937 in Zagreb, at the time when that city was a hotbed of functionalism thanks to a large number of architects educated abroad, especially in German-speaking lands. Although most of these architects depended on typical bourgeois commissions, it was generally assumed that functionalism was associated with progressive politics and many prominent figures, like Ibler, were indeed involved in left-wing associations. Richter himself was politically active as a student and by 1939 he joined the Association of the Communist Youth of Yugoslavia, an illegal organization under the auspices of the Communist Party. He was well aware of the aesthetic controversies on the left; although not yet interested in how they concerned visual arts, as an architect he was firmly aligned with modernists.[16] Bogdan Bogdanović, on the other hand, became associated with leftist intellectual circles through his father, Milan, a Belgrade literary critic and a vocal opponent of the monarchy. Young Bogdan grew up virtually surrounded by prominent intellectuals (he met Krleža at the age of six), and early on became indoctrinated by Surrealism directly through Marko Ristić, who became his uncontested role model. Through family connections, Bogdanović also met some of Yugoslavia's most prominent modernist architects, which prompted him to begin fantasizing about creating a Surrealist architecture.[17] He became a student of architecture at the University of Belgrade in the fall of 1940, only six months before the German attack on Yugoslavia.

At the outbreak of the war, both Richter and Bogdanović had to interrupt their studies. Already known for his left-wing activities, Richter immediately joined the Communist-organized resistance and operated an illegal printing shop outside of Zagreb before being discovered by the police, wounded in an altercation, arrested, and interned in a camp in Vienna.[18] Five years younger, Bogdanović spent most of the war in desolate occupied Belgrade, but in the end somewhat reluctantly joined the Association of the Communist Youth and, in 1944, the already sizable Partisan units. During his one short year as a warrior, however, he quickly made up for the earlier inactivity: he joined the party, advanced to the rank of a deputy political commissar of his battalion, and, like Richter, got badly wounded in combat.[19] For each man, the active participation in the resistance ensured an unshakable political reputation after the war, since the Communist Party of Yugoslavia took complete control of the country even before the fights ended. Such reputation, no doubt, was bound to translate into a favorable status in the new society: both Richter and Bogdanović assumed teaching positions at the university as soon as they graduated, and they both acquired desirable commissions early on. But neither of them followed a typical path of an architect in a rapidly modernizing socialist state, which offered a chance to design whole cities and hundreds of dwellings in a few strokes. Instead, they chose to pursue their own unique artistic visions and to challenge the mainstream, ultimately reaching individual success, but never generating a new mainstream. That they both could rely on a political reputation in the process was probably only necessary.

CAREER SNAPSHOT 1: VJENCESLAV RICHTER AND AN AVANT-GARDE ARCHITECTURE FOR AN AVANT-GARDE SOCIALISM

Vjenceslav Richter started his professional career while still a student at the University of Zagreb in the late 1940s with the small but important commissions for various exhibition pavilions in Yugoslavia and abroad. For these commissions, he often collaborated with his colleagues, artists Ivan Picelj and Aleksandar Srnec, thus crossing the boundaries between architecture and art from the very beginning of his career. At a time when the regime strove to impose Socialist Realism as the exclusive paradigm of socialist creativity, these projects were striking not only for eschewing the traditionalist overtones and pathos typical of the Soviet doctrine, but also for incorporating explicit references to the interwar avant-garde. These included the Constructivist reduction of the design language to floating linear and planar elements held by exposed metal frames and trusses, to biomorphic shapes reminiscent of Surrealism and Hans Arp. Some shows even contained elements that seemed like direct quotes from Frederick Kiesler: concave walls, undulating ribbons, or strange, organic-looking columns. Indeed, Richter repeatedly acknowledged the avant-garde, especially Constructivism and the Bauhaus, as major influences on his work.[20] The origins of this interest were diverse and multifold. The memories of the interwar avant-garde were still very much alive in Zagreb, which had been well connected to the international context before the war.[21] Richter's professor and mentor, Zdenko Strižić, likely played an important influence in this respect: a prominent prewar modernist educated in Dresden with Hans Poelzig, he had famously won the competition for the Kharkiv Opera House in 1930, one of the last high-profile international competitions organized in the Soviet Union before the shift to Socialist Realism.[22] But what certainly helped Richter expand his horizons was also the fact that his work on exhibition pavilions allowed him to travel to the West long before it was possible for ordinary Yugoslavs, and thus to acquire firsthand information on the latest foreign architecture and design.[23] For example, during a trip to Chicago in 1950, while working on a Yugoslav pavilion there, he made a point of paying multiple visits to László Moholy-Nagy's Institute of Design at the Illinois Institute of Technology, a successor to the "New Bauhaus" that Moholy-Nagy had founded upon his arrival in the United States in 1937.[24]

The design for the 1950 exhibition *Highway* (in collaboration with Picelj, Srnec, and architect Zvonimir Radić) was exemplary both as a high-profile commission and as a striking example of modern design. The show celebrated one of the socialist state's top projects, the construction of the first modern highway in the country. Named the "Highway of Brotherhood and Unity," the road connected Yugoslavia's two largest cities, Belgrade and Zagreb, which both hosted the exhibition. Mounted on panels of various sizes, the displayed images floated freely in space, supported by exposed light structures. The walls behind were painted with primary colors in geometrical patterns, filled in with ideological symbols and the abstracted representations of signifiers of progress: radio transmitters, cranes, machines, etc. Intense dynamism permeated the design. This was the kind of three-dimensional montage—bringing together Communist ideology, passionate optimism and faith in progress, and avant-garde design language—that had not been seen since the demise of Russian Constructivism in the early 1930s, a message that, arguably, resonated powerfully with the contemporaneous political events. Namely, it was precisely in 1950 that Yugoslavia's Communist leadership began a series of thorough political and economic reforms, moving away from the Stalinist dogma and reinventing socialism based on a new interpretation of "authentic" Marxism-Leninism. The result was the invention of "workers' self-management," a system aimed at a gradual "withering away of the state" and its replacement with participatory democracy both at the workplace and in civic life. If the Communist Party of Yugoslavia was about to change its name to the

League of Communists to evoke Marx's original Communist League of 1848 and thus claim the legacy of authentic Communism, Richter's evocations of Constructivism similarly claimed the legacy of the original art of the October Revolution. This realignment of artistic and political avant-gardes was no coincidence for Richter, who saw his artistic activities as part of his political commitment and considered socialism as a precondition for a "general transformation of our image of the world."[25]

Despite its political potential, this message was not received without opposition from conservative forces and its acceptance required concerted activist efforts, which would color much of Richter's career. Such efforts were most significantly formalized through EXAT 51 (Eksperimentalni atelier—Experimental Studio), Yugoslavia's first successful independent group of artists after World War II.[26] Richter was the group's cofounder and chief ideologue. He wrote its *Manifesto*, arguing for a synthesis of visual arts in the creation of totally designed environments based on abstraction and continuous experimentation, thus explicitly building on the traditions of the progressive movements from the interwar period.[27] And while the *Manifesto* was somewhat defensive in its language, EXAT's members would soon extend an open challenge to the still entrenched conservatism through both their theoretical advocacy and their practical activities. Throughout the 1950s, Richter was at the forefront of such activist efforts, organizing public debates and engaging in polemics with the cultural establishment.[28] At the same time, his theoretical calls for a synthesis of visual arts were materialized in his pioneering work in the field of interior and product design. From 1950 to 1954 he was the chair of the Department of Architecture and Design at the short-lived Academy of Applied Arts in Zagreb, while he also continued to practice exhibition, interior, stage-set, and product design, consistently bringing together the various modes of visual arts into a unified expression. After the academy was dissolved, Richter formally joined an existing architectural office but in effect worked almost independently, while continuing to receive high-profile commissions.

Richter's greatest contribution to the architectural representation of Yugoslav socialism—and one of the pinnacles of his efforts to achieve a synthetically designed environment—was the highly praised national pavilion at the 1958 Universal and International Exposition in Brussels (figure 2.3).[29] The architect's winning design at a rather uninspired national competition in 1956 proposed a spectacular structure suspended from a central cable-stayed mast, its support reduced to one single point, which allowed a completely open ground floor. The jury praised the proposal's spatial and functional qualities, but from the very start expressed concerns about the viability of the suspension structure. This proved to be a major point of contention during the development of the project. Richter insisted on keeping the mast—going so far as to privately hire a structural engineer to prove his point—but the experts summoned by the organizing committee judged differently.[30] The architect's insistence on the suspension concept may be ascribed to his indebtedness to Constructivism, whose proponents had a penchant for such structures, famously exemplified in Ivan Leonidov's project for the Lenin Library in Moscow (1927) and Hannes Meyer's *Petersschule* in Basel (1926). The removal of the mast, therefore, also meant the removal of some of the project's avant-garde connotations, even though in its finished form the pavilion was still a small masterpiece and a full realization of Richter's ideas about the synthesis of visual arts.

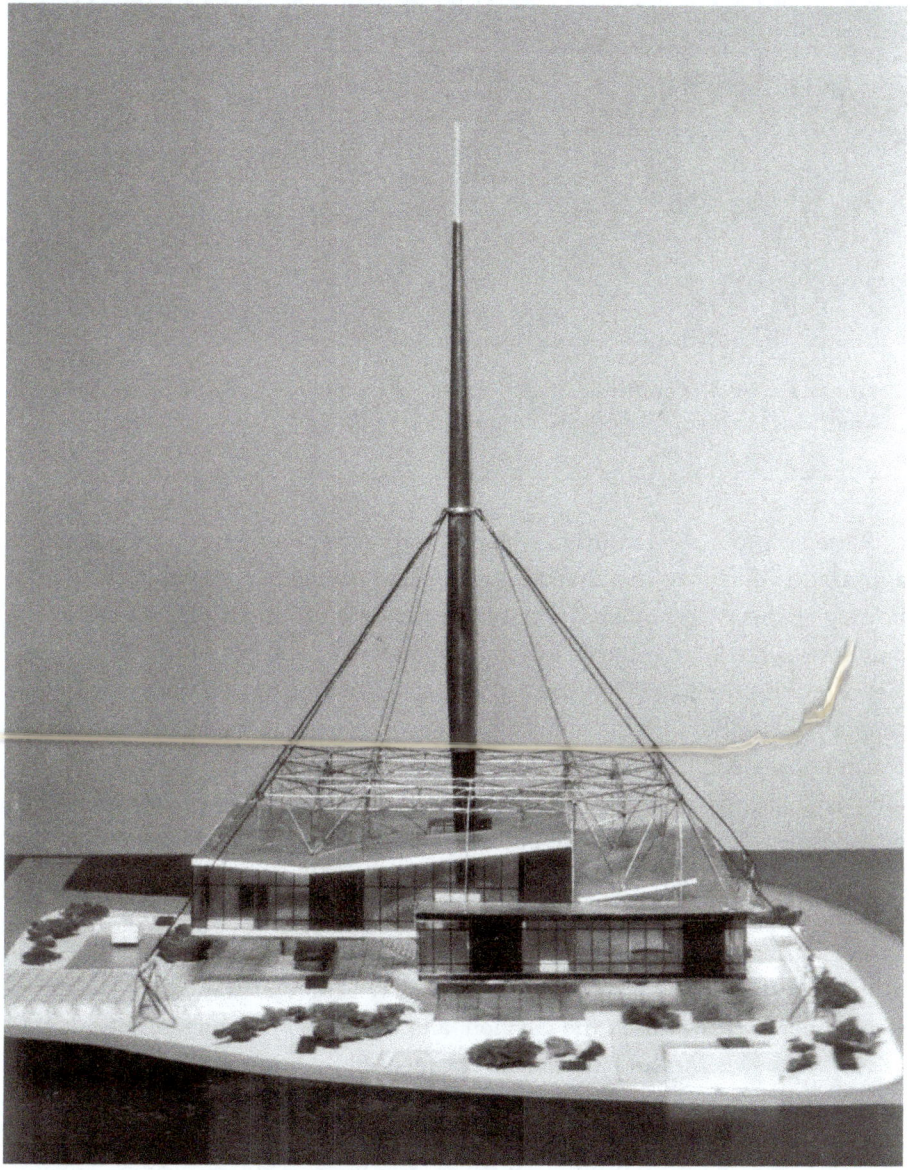

FIGURE 2.3. Vjenceslav Richter's winning competition entry for the Pavilion of Yugoslavia at EXPO '58 in Brussels, 1956. Archive of Yugoslavia, Belgrade.

FIGURE 2.4. Vjenceslav Richter, Pavilion of Yugoslavia at EXPO '58, Brussels, 1956–1958. Front view. Archive of Yugoslavia, Belgrade.

Raised on thin steel columns, the pavilion's weightless interlocking volumes appeared to float above a marble-paved plaza, creating a dynamic cascade of flowing spaces with no barriers between the exterior and interior. Part of the building's success lay in the fact that, compared to the overcrowded commercialism of much of the EXPO, it seemed like an embodiment of good taste. Rather than a fair pavilion, it resembled an elegant, sparsely furnished art gallery, in which every exhibit yielded to a dominating Mondrianesque aesthetic of three-dimensional grids, a "symphony in black and white" interspersed with occasional splashes of color.[31] Indeed, the building itself was the most successful part of Yugoslav participation at EXPO.[32] *Architectural Review* ranked it among the "six outstanding pavilions" at EXPO,[33] and the Belgian press described it as a "palace in steel, glass, wood, and marble whose elegance lies in its restraint."[34] Gurus of modernism such as Alfred Barr Jr. and Jean Cassou of the Paris Museum of Contemporary Art praised the pavilion, and students of architecture flocked to see it.[35] Many visitors and journalists commented that, in the visual noise of the EXPO, Richter's pavilion offered a welcome point of calm and repose.[36] One journalist particularly highlighted the building's photographic appeal, noting how it attracted amateur photographers always in search of good shots (figure 2.4).[37]

The overwhelmingly positive reception of the pavilion was in itself a political message and an important source of external legitimation for the Yugoslav socialist project. Framed by the already existing views of Yugoslav modern art as a symptom of the country's break from the Soviet orbit, the design was interpreted in decidedly political terms.[38] For example, transparency, the open ground floor, and the absence of any doors were understood as analogous to Yugoslavia's openness to foreigners, in sharp contrast to the countries behind the Iron Curtain (figure 2.5). Similarly, modesty and restraint indicated a focus on human values instead of megalomaniac representation, as was the case with the pavilions of the great powers.[39] A parallel with Ludwig Mies van der Rohe's 1929 Pavilion of Germany in Barcelona comes to mind here, one of the iconic buildings of interwar modernism and itself a modernist *Gesamtkunstwerk*. In either case, it was the building's open, free-flowing space, more than anything exhibited inside it, that couched powerful political messages: of a modern, peaceful, and democratic Weimar Germany instead of the conservative war-mongering Wilhelmine

FIGURE 2.5. Vjenceslav Richter, Pavilion of Yugoslavia at EXPO '58, Brussels, 1956–1958. Interior view. Archive of Yugoslavia, Belgrade.

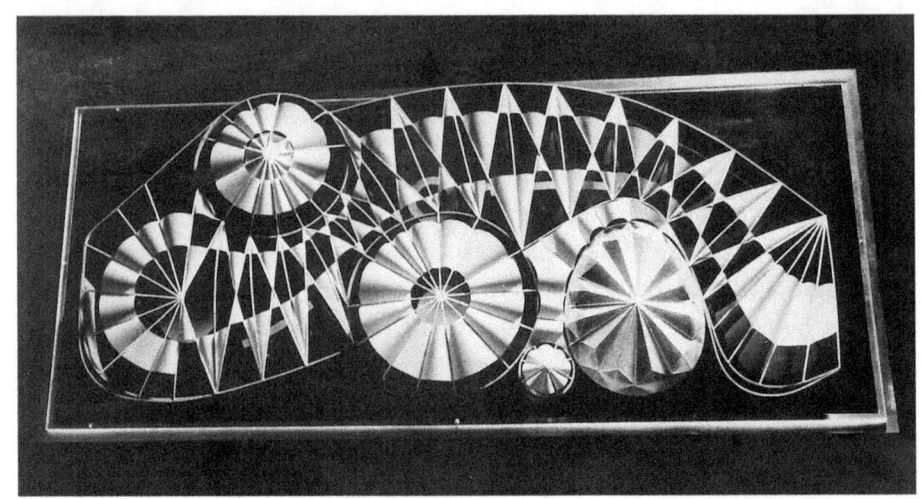

FIGURE 2.6. Vjenceslav Richter, Pavilion of Yugoslavia at the International Labor Exhibition, Turin, 1961. Model. Archive of Yugoslavia, Belgrade.

Empire, and of a reformed, open, and modern Yugoslav socialism liberated from Stalinist oppression.[40] In this context, one wonders if Richter's use of cruciform columns—similar to those in Barcelona—represented a pure coincidence, a conscious appropriation, or even a deliberate homage.

Subsequently, Richter realized only two more pavilions representing Yugoslavia, both in Italy and both much smaller than the one in Brussels. One was designed for the 1961 International Labor Exhibition and staged inside Pier-Luigi Nervi's Palace of Labor in Turin (figure 2.6). Based on a geometry of circular segments, it was a formally and technologically imaginative project, with hinged zigzagging roofs that could fold flat like an accordion for easy transport. Appropriate to the context of an exhibition of labor, here workers' self-management itself was the subject of the presentation, and Richter created another formally and spatially rich environment to showcase the virtues of the system. A centerpiece of the pavilion was a three-dimensional model of self-management that allowed visitors to explore the organization of the political system; combining rotating concentric rings in Plexiglas, the model was not unlike one of Rodčenko's or Moholy-Nagy's famous mobile installations.

Even more imaginative was the pavilion for the XIII Triennale in Milan in 1964 (figure 2.7). Although still exploring the possibilities of geometrical abstraction, it showcased Richter's increasing obsession with repetitive modules, also recognizable in a large series of his "systemic sculptures." The theme of the Triennale was spare time, and Richter was given virtually free reign by the show's commissar, his former EXAT colleague, architect Bernardo Bernardi. The two of them again chose to highlight self-management as the central theme, exploring how it "reflected in the sphere of spare time" through the activities of the various houses

FIGURE 2.7. Vjenceslav Richter, Pavilion of Yugoslavia at the XIII Triennale in Milan, 1964. Interior view. Archive of Yugoslavia, Belgrade.

of culture, workers' and people's universities, people's technical associations, and sports organizations.⁴¹ The design itself was a highly aestheticized spatial and formal exercise, which created a complete environment out of uniform thin wooden laths arranged in a three-dimensional orthogonal grid. Like an artificial forest, the freely arranged elements defined the space only in the fuzziest sense of the word; even the exhibited photographs were cut into thin strips, coalescing and dissolving as one walked around. As Maroje Mrduljaš argued, "the planar differentiation of space disappears here, giving way to a lattice-structure. . . . An 'isotopic' environment thus emerges that uncouples the visual permeability and the permeability of movement and inhabitation. The pavilion can be freely occupied or colonized with the exhibits . . . allowing the large photos with the scenes of leisure to float freely in space."⁴²

Richter's exercise in nonhierarchical spatial and visual organization clearly resonated with the pavilion's theme of leisure, but I would argue that it also revealed his idiosyncratic interpretation of self-management as an ultimate expression of human freedom. Yet again, the design stressed the subtle connection between its own avant-garde aesthetics and the avant-garde status of the Yugoslav system, ultimately winning the Golden Medal of the Triennale, a remarkable feat in light of the fact that Yugoslavia was the only socialist country in the show and that its presentation contained explicitly political overtones.⁴³ Although small, Richter's Triennale pavilion was aesthetically perhaps the most radical design with which Yugoslavia ever presented itself abroad; that something like it would ever be constructed for an official presentation was as much a testimony to Richter's unique artistic vision and his considerable political reputation as to his contribution to the sphere of artistic liberties in the previous fifteen years.

But what should have been the pinnacle of Richter's efforts at representing Yugoslav socialism ultimately remained unbuilt. The Museum of the Revolution of the Nations and National Minorities of Yugoslavia was intended to be one of the centerpieces of New Belgrade, the country's new socialist capital. Richter won the competition for the building in 1961, but the construction did not begin until 1978 at a less prominent—although still highly symbolic—position halfway between the buildings of the Federal Government and the seat of the League of Communists. With the declining power of the Yugoslav federation, however, it never advanced beyond the basement. If built, the museum would have been, in some important aspects, a much larger, more monumental, and somewhat more rigid reinterpretation of the Brussels pavilion, featuring interlocking exhibition spaces raised above a transparent ground level. Instead of the central suspension mast, this time the design featured dramatic sweeping skylights, another symbolic gesture evoking a sense of revolutionary triumph and optimism. The building's abandoned foundations, however, remain as a strangely appropriate symbol of the failed project of socialist Yugoslavia, tucked away and forgotten under the overgrown greenery.

Richter's architectural career similarly reached a dead end after this project, and for the rest of his life he would only design several low-profile structures. Instead, his interests increasingly shifted toward pure and applied art, as well as theory. His 1964 book *Sinturbanizam* (synthetic urbanism) was perhaps the most far-reaching utopian vision ever imagined by Yugoslav architects, proposing as it did a total compression of urban fabric into giant highly technological "ziggurats" as a way to reduce the waste of time in traffic and other unproductive activities in the fractured modern city.⁴⁴ Richter also continued expanding the boundaries of modern art through his participation in the circles that succeeded EXAT 51 and were active in the 1960s around New Tendencies, a Zagreb-based international movement that explored the systemic, scientific, and cybernetic potentials of art.⁴⁵ Boosted by the international exposure provided by his successes in Brussels, Italy, and elsewhere, Richter subsequently had a remarkable career as a sculptor whose "systemic sculptures" found their way to some of the world's most prestigious collections, including the New York Museum of Modern Art and the Tate Gallery in London.

CAREER SNAPSHOT 2: BOGDAN BOGDANOVIĆ AND THE STRATEGIES OF SOCIALIST COMMEMORATION

At the time when Richter began his advocacy for a synthesis of visual arts based on geometrical abstraction, Bogdan Bogdanović was still uncertain of his true calling as an architect. Repulsed by the extremely limited material conditions of the period, which reduced architecture to little more than purely utilitarian construction, he found a temporary refuge in urban planning and, following his graduation from the University of Belgrade's Technical Faculty in 1951, he began teaching at the Department of Urbanism. Soon after that, however, an opportunity arose that would determine his future career. Invited to participate in a limited competition for a monument to the local Jewish victims of the war, Bogdanović began studying the metaphysics of Judaism and for the first time discovered a method that allowed him to articulate his long-standing fascination with Surrealist art.[46] Metaphysics, mythology, and symbolism—all inherently related to commemoration—opened a window onto the collective subconscious and further, through Freudian psychology, to Surrealism, allowing the movement's methods to achieve a rare instance of architectural articulation.[47] His success at the competition and the subsequent positive reception of the monument indicated a direction that would allow Bogdanović to practice architecture as an artistic pursuit and to incorporate his flair for intellectual games, rather than to follow the path of instrumental rationality that he perceived as the order of the day. And despite the fact that he would not receive another commission for a memorial in almost a decade, his path was already essentially decided with this early work.

A small structure tucked away at the bottom of Belgrade's Sephardic Cemetery, the Monument to the Jewish Victims of Fascism consists of a processional dromos that leads through a "gate" formed by two wing-shaped walls toward a wrought-iron menorah behind (figure 2.8). The meaning is rather simple here, although unusual for a period when Socialist Realism still heavily influenced commemoration: a passage between the living and the dead, a transition from the material world to eternity, highlighted through a series of misaligned forced perspectives shaped by the main architectural elements. The rounded forms of the two walls perhaps evoke the biblical tablets of stone that Moses received on Mount Sinai.[48] What is remarkable, however, is the execution, which announced in a rudimentary way much of Bogdanović's future design methodology: evocative but never completely explicit forms; a complex relationship with history and memory; and a reliance on traditional materials and craftsmanship. The last is particularly striking, since Bogdanović used rubble from buildings destroyed during the war to construct parts of the memorial, with various friezes, capitals, and ornamental slabs clearly recognizable among its rustic stone blocks. This symbolic collage of disparate fragments certainly owed to the architect's interests in Surrealism; but a sensibility for textures and materials, as well as the overall

FIGURE 2.8. Bogdan Bogdanović, Monument to the Jewish Victims of Fascism in Belgrade, 1952. Photo by author.

references to classical antiquity, also revealed the lessons learned from the Slovene architect Jože Plečnik, whose work Bogdanović had discovered during the war.[49] As incongruent as it may seem at first sight, this amalgam was not without an underlying affinity, since Plečnik consistently subverted the rules of classicism throughout his career, instilling a sense of imaginative playfulness even into his most solemn designs, which appealed to Bogdanović's already formed Surrealist sensibilities.

Between his work on the Jewish monument and the end of the 1950s, Bogdanović worked mainly on urban plans for several small cities in Montenegro, but he also used this time to initiate a parallel career as a writer and theorist, countering even more explicitly the emerging dominance of modernism. Published first as a series of short articles in the daily Borba and several other Belgrade periodicals, and then as a book titled *Small Urbanism* (Mali urbanizam, 1958), Bogdanović's vision of the city stood in sharp contrast to the heroic modernization project that was in full swing across the country.[50] Even a cursory glance at the list of topics reveals a divorce from the rational, large-scale gestures of contemporaneous architecture and planning: "About a Fountain," "A Beautiful Old-Fashioned Courtyard," "The Living Image of the Street," "Roofs and Chimneys," "Picturesque Architecture," "A Great Master of the Small Urbanism" (devoted to Plečnik), etc. Instead, essays were paeans to the small scale, the picturesque, the quirky, and the irrational; they advocated preservation instead of destruction, asserted the importance of symbolism in urban life, and demonstrated a keen sense for the "texture of the street."

But *Small Urbanism* was not merely a collection of nostalgic elegies to a time gone by; it was aimed at improving the present situation and, perhaps even more importantly, at educating on how to love the city in its contradictory totality. The author that emerged in them was an observant *flaneur* who did not simply appreciate tradition, but also celebrated the various manifestations of modernity: the mysterious and phantasmagoric ways in which modern artificial illumination transforms the streets at night; the humor of new urban rituals, like processions of soccer fans; or the poetic dissonances between the old and the new. What Bogdanović opposed was not rationality itself—and certainly not modernization—but the *aesthetic* of rationalism, the functionalist turn toward the unimaginative and the regimented that modern architecture and urban planning had taken in a war-damaged country going through modernization at break-neck speed. He was not a conservative unable to understand the new, but a disenchanted insider who recognized the limitations of modernism all too well. After all, he had been personally acquainted with the country's pioneers of modernism from an early age, and it was perhaps this fact that provided him with confidence to raise his voice against the emerging dogma.

On the one hand, Bogdanović's criticism of mainstream modernism paralleled Team X's efforts at acknowledging the significance of human contacts and social life in the city; and despite his claims that he was never interested in the activities of CIAM (Congrès Internationaux d'Architecture Moderne), he praised some of the Team X projects (although never mentioning the architects).[51] On the other hand, Bogdanović was far more explicit than any of the Team X members in his advocacy for a harmonious continuity with history and nature, and his taste for symbolism and figural representation contradicted Team X's persistent abstraction. It is very tempting to see this position as an anticipation of postmodernism, especially in combination with some of his subsequent built projects, in which he used history as a repository of forms to be freely appropriated and transformed at will, disregarding the standard linguistic rules.[52] (This was also a lesson learned from Plečnik; it is no wonder that postmodernist architects like Michael Graves "discovered" Plečnik in the 1980s as an alleged precursor to postmodernism.) Perhaps the most obvious example in this respect was one of Bogdanović's very few "real" (or, at least, inhabitable) buildings, a remodeling of the nineteenth-century villa of Serbia's Queen Natalija near the city of Smederevo into a luxury residence for the guests of the Serbian republican government, done at the occasion of the first Summit of Non-Aligned Nations in 1961. A stylized neo-Palladian structure complete with simplified pediments, entablatures, and garlands, the redesigned villa was replete with self-consciously ironic gestures: classical elements used out of their normal context and made out of industrial components (such as iron pipes playing the role of comically thin Ionic columns), flattened ornaments that look as if cut out of cardboard, etc. The only reason not to consider this villa a real precursor of postmodernism—and it indeed preceded the house that Robert Venturi built for his mother in Pennsylvania by one year—was the fact that Bogdanović never developed further in this exact direction, his memorials relying on far freer and more imaginative reworking of historical motifs than postmodernism as we know it ever did.

Among the generations of architecture students educated in Belgrade, Bogdanović's second book, *The Futile Trowel: The Doctrine and Practice of the Brotherhood of Golden (Black) Numbers* (1963) attracted a cult-like following for its author. It was not exactly a manifesto of postmodern architecture, but it was in itself a postmodern text that deliberately blurred the lines between historical fact and fiction.[53] Defying a clear designation in genre, the book begins as a somewhat personal interpretation of the architecture of famous figures of classicism and their indebtedness to the Pythagorean glorification of numbers. The seemingly conventional text, however, soon devolves into a phantasmagoric meeting that brings together historical personalities that were in reality separated by decades, even centuries: Donato Bramante, Andrea Palladio, Luca Pacioli, Francesco Borromini, Guarino Guarini, Giambattista Piranesi, Claude-Nicolas Ledoux, Antoni Gaudí. Alleged members of a brotherhood initiated into the secrets of the "Great Number," their personalities transmute into each other's through history in their never-ending quest of "inner architecture." By the end of the book, the author himself joins their fictional gathering, together with several unidentified characters from his own time, and ends up an initiate himself. The haughty topic might have resulted in an unbearably pretentious text had Bogdanović's style been any less humorous. His distinguished characters thus often resort to less than dignified words and actions: they bang each other on the head with trowels, the hallowed symbol of their trade; they speak in street jargon; they use comical or insulting nicknames for each other, and so on.

It is almost uncanny to what degree *The Futile Trowel* anticipated the topics and methods of literary postmodernism that would emerge a decade or two later. The very title, with its hint to one of the symbols of freemasonry, indicates a fascination with esoteric knowledge and secret societies that would be a staple of writers like Umberto Eco. There is also a deliberate attempt to (mis)represent the material as based on historical facts: in a quasi-scholarly afterword, Bogdanović provides the alleged keys for reading the book, but they only further blur the line between the real sources and his fictional characters. Bogdanović's erudition is apparent and he uses it with playful ease to confound the reader page after page; but erudition conceals a deeper message that lies within the method itself: that for a patient student, history can be a repository of ideas and forms to be freely reinterpreted and rewritten. This kind of relativism is closely affiliated with subsequent postmodernist methods, although the ultimately oneiric quality of Bogdanović's text, reliant on the subconscious, the irrational, and the absurd, again reveals his great indebtedness to Surrealism. It was no coincidence that a second edition of *The Futile Trowel* was reissued in 1984, at a time that was finetuned to this kind of sensibility.

If in the period between *Small Urbanism* and *The Futile Trowel* Bogdanović did experience some kind of "initiation," it was probably much broader and deeper than the fascination with Pythagoreanism and classicism. During the "dry years" of the 1950s, when he had little chance to build what he considered his true calling, he further developed his interest in symbolic meaning sparked at the beginning of the decade. This interest was in line with the Surrealist fascination with psychology and the unconscious, but it also expanded into the study of anthropology and the writers such as Lucien Lévy-Bruhl, Claude Lévi-Strauss, Lewis Mumford, and others. As his subsequent books reveal—most of them musings on the history and meanings of cities and urban life—his eclectic interests developed into an erudite, although not exactly rigorous, knowledge of ancient mythologies, religion, ethnology, philosophy, etc.[54] But it was the memorials, which from the turn of the 1960s he began building with increasing regularity, that revealed his erudition most clearly. Operating from an extremely *longue-durée* perspective, Bogdanović combined disparate historical references with an almost frivolous ease, realizing that in memorials the associative and subconscious meanings tend to survive far longer than any precise, historically specific interpretations. Most of his memorials are, consequently, extremely open-ended and multivalent collages of forms and motifs, never explicit and at moments virtually self-referential. Bogdanović's writings and interviews reveal that he never intended to ascribe any precisely fixed meanings to his projects: not only did he delight in discovering the various popular interpretations of his own work, but he himself also offer varied and occasionally even contradictory interpretations.

What unites the almost twenty highly diverse memorials that Bogdanović designed in the two decades from the early 1960s until the early 1980s is that they all consistently blurred the lines between landscape, sculpture, and architecture; they reinterpreted the notions of materiality and craft, straddling the divides between the traditional and modern; and they embodied a sense of playfulness and improvisation that almost defies their solemn purpose. The so-called Slobodište ("Freedom-ground") near the central Serbian city of Kruševac (1960–1965) is as good an example of these qualities as any other. Designed to commemorate the local civilians killed as German hostages, it is a sprawling landscape consisting of several large, connected "craters" that envelope the visitor, creating their own world of sweeping grassy slopes isolated from their mundane suburban surroundings. Transforming the landscape with extensive earthwork was one of the staples of Bogdanović's projects, hinting at ancient burial mounds, the most primeval commemorative form. But in Kruševac this transformation was particularly massive, since the design was influenced by local circumstances that allowed Bogdanović to make an agreement with the management of the local bulldozer factory to test each newly manufactured machine by contributing to the excavations on the site.[55] The visitor moves through the landscape following a barely visible stone paving, irregular and overgrown with grass. One of the craters was shaped like an amphitheater, and it continues to be used for public performances to this day. The only objects one encounters are a strange circular stone gate that marks the transition between two neighboring spaces (its name, "Sun Gate," suggests a reference to Chinese gardens), and the twelve winged "souls" scattered over the slopes of the final crater, as if trying to fly out of it toward the sky (figure 2.9).

Each unique in details and roughly hand-carved in sandstone by local stonecutters, these sculptures embody Bogdanović's design method both in terms of his improvisational approach and of the open-ended meanings of the final product. The architect frequently worked directly with teams of local craftsmen without any definite drawings (much like one of his idols, Antoni Gaudí), and in the case of Kruševac, he roughly drew the shape of each winged sculpture directly on the block of sandstone, giving specific instructions about the desired technique to each individual craftsman. When the sculptures were ready, he spent a day with a group of local schoolchildren, who helped him specify the precise position of each piece by playing the role of walking sculptures and moving around the crater according to his instructions until the desired configuration was achieved. Thus, despite the fact that the construction took several years, the exact shape of the memorial was uncertain until the very end, and was determined literally through a children's play, as if to emphasize the architect's proclaimed intention of celebrating life rather than glorifying death. The specific interpretation of the memorial, however, remains open. According to one, the "winged souls" represented an explicit Orphic symbol, referring to a specifically Balkan branch in the tradition of classical antiquity.[56] According to another, however, they originated from the Minoan "horns of consecration," thus evoking a rather different body of myths.[57] Indeed, for an educated visitor, the stone "souls" attempting to fly out of the crater of "Hades" might evoke the very general contours of Orphic myths, which were generally related to the questions of life, death, and afterlife; the wings also seem to resemble lyres, the symbol of Orpheus's art. Bogdanović took great pleasure when such motifs, after having acquired a layer of patina, confounded the uninformed foreign archaeologists and anthropologists, who recognized the references but could not locate the objects in time; he saw their confusion as a proof that his work transcended cultures and epochs.[58] But such expert knowledge was never crucial in interpreting the memorials and it served only as a pretext for their evocative forms, open to individual interpretation, much like a dream that has a value only in relation to each specific dreamer.

That Bogdanović succeeded in bringing such an unconventional approach to reality was a remarkable feat considering that virtually all of his monuments commemorated the victims of the war and directly contributed to the official narrative on the genesis of the socialist state. And while some of his projects were small in scale and of significance only to the local communities, others, like the memorial complex at the site of the Jasenovac concentration camp in

FIGURE 2.9. Bogdan Bogdanović, the "Sun Gate" (top) and the "winged souls" (bottom) at the Slobodište Necropolis, Kruševac, Serbia, 1960–1965. Photos © Wolfgang Thaler.

FIGURE 2.10. Bogdan Bogdanović, Jasenovac Memorial Complex, Jasenovac, Croatia, 1959–1966. Photo © Wolfgang Thaler.

Croatia, ranked among the most high-profile commemorative endeavors in postwar Yugoslavia (figure 2.10). The conventional interpretation is that allowing this lack of any ideological signifiers was a calculated decision by the regime used to prove the existence of intellectual and artistic freedoms in the country, and thus to bolster its international reputation. But while Bogdanović's work did contribute in a certain measure to the regime's external legitimation, this could have been only its subsidiary role, since other buildings fulfilled that purpose far more efficiently (for example, Richter's exhibition pavilions). Moreover, the lack of explicit ideological representation was by no means unique to his monuments; it was a rule rather than an exception in postwar Yugoslavia. The chief audience for the commemoration of the war was domestic. By creating spaces and forms that sparked imagination and encouraged individual interpretations, Bogdanović's memorials created a personal connection to their audience, thus tying the individual and the collective together far more effectively than by employing explicit ideological signs. Their open-endedness and mythical allusions were essentially aligned with the overall tendency of the Yugoslav socialist state to mythologize the war, yet their lack of historical specificity helped downplay the fact that the war was fought not only against foreign occupation but also between Yugoslavia's own ethnicities, as well as on ideological grounds. Bogdanović himself often interpreted his memorials as symbols of hope and the triumph of life over death, contributing to the political project of ethnic reconciliation conducted under the banner of "brotherhood and unity."[59] His memorials thus aimed at the simultaneity of remembering and forgetting that is necessary, as Benedict Anderson has famously argued, for the forging of nations.[60] That some of them continue to enjoy popularity even after the atrocious war in which socialist Yugoslavia disappeared—and some indeed do—testifies to the surprising success of this strategy.

CONCLUSION

The obvious conclusion to draw from the comparison of Vjenceslav Richter and Bogdan Bogdanović is that architectural representations of postwar state socialism cannot be reduced to the stereotypes that have emerged at certain historical moments: the pompous gingerbread of Socialist Realism or the utilitarian drabness of the post-Stalinist period. The two architects stretched the aesthetic boundaries of socialist representation so broadly as to render such reductionist perspectives meaningless. Their work also defies another stereotype that is currently in the making: that of the otherworldly Brutalist fantasies built across Eastern Europe in the 1970s and 1980s, which allegedly came out of nowhere as the last gasps of a dying socialism.[61] The oeuvres of Richter and Bogdanović were not only visually different from such examples but also had deep theoretical and discursive roots, resulting as they did from years of patient explorations rather than momentary flights of imagination.

On a subtler note, however, Bogdanović and Richter also reveal that the socialist world was not insular from the broader international currents of modernism. Both architects were immersed in the postwar discourses on architecture and culture, maintaining close relationships with colleagues abroad, in the West as well as in the East. The aesthetic contrast between the two of them paralleled in important ways the dilemma between "techno-utopia" and "Architecture" that Felicity Scott identified as the defining fault line of the 1960s and 1970s in the West, pitching the disciplinary dissolution into technological utopianism against the retreat into the time-tested disciplinarity of Architecture with a capital A, which ultimately ended in postmodernism.[62] But if Richter's architectural visions indeed converged with the techno-utopias and Bogdanović's with postmodernism, they both were nevertheless original achievements produced under very particular social and cultural conditions. Rather than having to choose whether to conform to or resist the culture of late capitalism, as their colleagues in the West did, Bogdanović and Richter worked in and for a real revolutionary society that, despite all its inherent shortcomings, at least promised to resolve the many contradictions of modernity. Richter thus never resorted to ironic or negative criticism, as did some of the Western techno-utopias, and Bogdanović's populism never flirted with commercialism, as did much of postmodernism. Instead, they found a way to intervene in social reality and give architectural shape to the hope of achieving a more just society. They succeeded at keeping the connection between the aesthetic and social revolutions alive, thus realizing some of the dreams of their avant-garde predecessors. That these dreams materialized in such divergent ways only testifies to the diversity of what we consider avant-garde.

NOTES

1. Several recent studies have finally started exploring the topic of prefabricated socialist housing, for example, Kimberly Elman Zarecor's *Manufacturing a Socialist Modernity: Housing in Czechoslovakia, 1945–1960* (Pittsburgh: University of Pittsburgh Press, 2011), or Mark B. Smith's *Property of Communists: The Urban Housing Program from Stalin to Khrushchev* (DeKalb: Northern Illinois University Press, 2010).

2. See Nancy Condee, "From Emigration to E-migration: Contemporaneity and the Former Second World," in *Antinomies of Art and Culture: Modernity, Postmodernity, Contemporaneity*, eds. Terry Smith, Okwui Enwezor, and Nancy Condee (Durham and London: Duke University Press, 2008), 235–236.

3. As an example, see Aleš Erjavec, ed., *Postmodernism and the Postsocialist Condition: Politicized Art under Late Socialism* (Berkeley, Los Angeles, and London: University of California Press, 2003).

4. For a discussion of Yugoslavia's symbolic others, see Dejan Jović, "Communist Yugoslavia and its 'Others,'" in *Ideologies and National Identities: The Case of Twentieth-Century Southeastern Europe*, ed. John Lampe and Mark Mazower (Budapest and New York: CEU Press, 2004), 277–302.

5. The literature on the cultural Cold War is vast; on architecture and design, see Greg Castillo, *Cold War on the Home Front: The Soft Power of Midcentury Design* (Minneapolis: University of Minnesota Press, 2010).

6. The term Socialist Aestheticism was coined in 1963 by the literary critic and theorist Sveta Lukić in *Savremena jugoslovenska literatura (1945–65)* (Belgrade: Prosveta, 1968). Socialist Aestheticism was imported into art theory by Belgrade art critics Miodrag B. Protić and Lazar Trifunović in the early 1980s to retroactively explain the art of the late 1950s and 1960s. Although they both appropriated Lukić's basic definition as an autonomous art that focuses on its own expressive possibilities, they ascribed it opposing values, each grinding his own critical ax. For Protić, the term positively connoted the liberation from Socialist Realism and its representational demands; see Miodrag B. Protić, *Jugoslovensko slikarstvo šeste decenije-nove pojave*, exhibition catalogue (Belgrade: Muzej savremene umetnosti, 1980), 14. Conversely, Trifunović emphasized the other side of Lukić's definition: an "art for art's own sake" divorced from social reality and the ills of modern life; see Lazar Trifunović, *Enformel u Beogradu*, exhibition catalogue (Belgrade: Umetnički paviljon Cvijeta Zuzorić, 1982); reprinted in Trifunović, *Studije, ogledi, kritike* (Belgrade: Muzej savremene umetnosti, 1990), 124.

7. For more, see my dissertation, "Land of the In-Between: Modern Architecture and the State in Socialist Yugoslavia, 1945–65" (PhD diss., University of Texas at Austin), 44–73.

8. On the appropriation of high modernism in socialist Yugoslavia and its role in the country's external legitimation, see Vladimir Kulić, Maroje Mrduljaš, and Wolfgang Thaler, *Modernism In-Between: The Mediatory Architectures of Socialist Yugoslavia* (Berlin: Jovis, 2012), 36–40.

9. See Dušan Grabrijan and Juraj Neidhardt, *Arhitektura Bosne i put u suvremeno* (*Architecture of Bosnia and the Way to Modernity*) (Ljubljana: Državna založba Slovenije, 1957). For a summary, see Kulić, Mrduljaš, and Thaler, *Modernism In-Between*, 87–89.

10. See William J. R. Curtis, Tomaž Krušec, and Aleš Vodopivec, *Arhitekt Edvard Ravnikar, spominski kompleks na otoku Rabu, 1953* (*Architect Edvard Ravnikar, Memorial Complex on the Island of Rab, 1953*), exhibition catalogue (Ljubljana: Dessa, 2004); also William J. R. Curtis, "Abstraction and Representation: The Memorial Complex at Kampor, on the Island of Rab (1952–53) by Edvard Ravnikar," in *Edvard Ravnikar: Architect and Teacher*, eds. Aleš Vodopivec and Rok Žnidaršič (Vienna: SpringerWienNewYork, 2010), 33–50.

11. For example, Neidhardt and Grabrijan had already developed their basic argument before the war, but it only became politically acceptable as a statement of Bosnian identity with the establishment of the federal state under socialism, which allowed the creation of the federal republic of Bosnia and Herzegovina.

12. Part of the reason why the Communist Party was so attractive to progressive intellectuals, especially outside of Serbia, was that it consistently opposed not only the pronounced social injustices in the monarchy but also the unitary concept of the state under hegemony of a Serbian dynasty. Class struggle was thus tightly bound to ethnic politics, the persistent cause of political strife throughout the short life of the kingdom.

13. On the "conflict on the literary left," among other sources, see Stanko Lasić, *Sukob na književnoj ljevici 1928–1952* (Zagreb: Liber, 1970).

14. Miroslav Krleža, "O slučaju arhitekta Iblera," in *Književna republika* (Zagreb) 2 (1921–22): 170–173.

15. Facing a similar choice as their French brethren, most Belgrade Surrealists sided with André Breton and remained faithful to the movement, thus confronting the Communist Party. None of them chose Louis Aragon's way of espousing Socialist Realism. Even Konstantin-Koča Popović, a talented Surrealist poet who became a legendary resistance general during the war and a high official in postwar Yugoslavia, did not embrace Socialist Realism; he instead abandoned poetry altogether.

16. Richter's interview for Radio Belgrade with Miloš Jeftić, January 27, 1990, unpublished transcript, National Library of Serbia.

17. These included Drago Ibler from Zagreb, as well as the Prague-educated Serb Nikola Dobrović, who at the time practiced in Dubrovnik, but after the war became the Head Architect of the City of Belgrade.

18. For Richter's political engagement, see Jeftić, interview with Vjenceslav Richter.

19. Author's interview with Bogdanović, May 2005.

20. See Marijan Susovski, ed., *Richter* (Zagreb: Muzej suvremene umjetnosti, 2003), 15–17. See also Jeftić, interview with Vjenceslav Richter, 20.

21. Croatian architects were particularly well informed of the latest avant-garde achievements, since many of them studied with famous modernists in Austria and Germany, and the Yugoslav branch of CIAM was based in Zagreb under the leadership of Drago Ibler.

22. Susovski, *Richter*, 15.

23. These included the fairs in Stockholm (1949), Vienna (1949), Hannover (1950), Paris (1950), Chicago (1950), etc.

24. Susovski, *Richter*, 17.

25. In Richter's view, artists were supposed to be leaders in the construction of socialism rather than to merely follow, or retreat from, the realities of social life. Such a position continued the socially minded concerns of the interwar avant-garde, radically denying the separation of visual media and arguing for continuity in the design of human environments, from the smallest scale of individual objects to the largest scale of the city. This position is perhaps best exemplified by his 1964 book on "synthurbanism" (synthetic urbanism), which explicitly stated the connection between socialism and continuity in the design of human environments, from the smallest scale of individual objects to the largest scale of the city; see Vjenceslav Richter, *Sinturbanizam* (Zagreb: Mladost, 1964).

26. On EXAT, see Ješa Denegri and Želimir Koščević, *EXAT 51: 1951–1956* (Zagreb: Galerija Nova, 1979).

27. For an English translation of the *Manifesto*, see "Exat 51: Manifesto," in *Impossible Histories: Historical Avant-Gardes, Neo-Avant-Gardes, and Post-Avant-Gardes in Yugoslavia, 1918–1991*, eds. Miško Šuvaković and Dubravka Đurić (Cambridge, MA: MIT Press, 2003), 539.

28. For example, Richter responded to Socialist Realist critic Grgo Gamulin, who criticized modernism's "captive forms," with a text entitled "Captive Theories." See Vjenceslav Richter, "Zarobljene teorije," *Krugovi* 1 (1952): 84–91.

29. For a detailed discussion of the construction and reception of the Pavilion of Yugoslavia at EXPO '58, see my article "An Avant-Garde Architecture for an Avant-Garde Socialism: Yugoslavia at EXPO '58," in *Journal of Contemporary History* 46, no. 1 (January 2012): 161–184.

30. Richter hired engineers Draganić and Špringer to estimate the suspended construction, and they claimed to be able to calculate and build it within the required time, with only a marginal rise in expenses. See Richter's letter to the Commissariat, August 11, 1956, Archive of Yugoslavia, Belgrade (Arhiv Jugoslavije, hereafter AJ), Fond 56, Fascikla 1.

31. "Symphony in black and white" was a description published in the Belgian Communist daily *Drapeau Rouge*; quoted in "Izveštaj TANJUG-u," May 10, 1958, AJ, Fond 56, Fascikla 24.

32. Reports of officials and hosts of the pavilion are virtually unanimous in such estimates; see AJ, Fond 56, Fascikla 6.

33. See "Six Outstanding Pavilions: Jugoslavia," in *Architectural Review* 124, no. 739 (August 1958): 116–118.

34. "Première manifestation au pavillon yougoslave," *Le Peuple* (Brussels), February 4, 1958.

35. See the reports of the pavilion hosts: "Izveštaji domaćina paviljona," AJ, Fond 56, Fascikla 6.

36. See "Knjiga utisaka," AJ, Fond 56, Fascikla 26.

37. An article in the Belgian paper *Le Peuple* described the pavilion as "A Miracle of Elegance and Good Taste"; partial translation of the original text in "Izveštaj TANJUG-u," May 10, 1958, AJ, Fond 56, Fascikla 26.

38. About foreign views of Yugoslav architecture, see my essay "'East? West? Or Both?' Foreign interpretations of Architecture in Socialist Yugoslavia," *Journal of Architecture* 14, no. 1 (2009): 87–105.

39. These were all comments of foreign visitors; see "Izveštaji domaćina paviljona."

40. For this interpretation of the Barcelona pavilion, see Wolf Tegethof, "From Obscurity to Maturity: Mies van der Rohe's Breakthrough to Modernism," in *Mies van der Rohe: Critical Essays*, ed. Franz Schulze (New York: Museum of Modern Art, 1989), 29–94.

41. See Bernardo Bernardi, "Jugoslavija na XIII Trijenalu," in *Arhitektura* (Zagreb) 19, no. 90 (1965): 41–43.

42. See Maroje Mrduljaš, "Otvorene arikulacije institucija i 'bitna praksa,' Istraživačka arhitektura u Hrvatskoj u periodu 1953-1974. unutar konteksta internacionalne interne kritike modernizma," (master's thesis, University of Zagreb, 2011), 52.

43. Also participating were Italy, France, the United States, Mexico, Belgium, Finland, Brazil, West Germany, Austria, Great Britain, Holland, Switzerland, and Canada; "Jugoslavija na XIII Trijenalu."

44. See Richter, *Sinturbanizam*. For a short summary of the argument, see Kulić, Mrduljaš, and Thaler, *Modernism In-Between*, 220–221.

45. See Margit Rosen, ed., *A Little Known Story about a Movement, a Magazine, and the*

Computer's Arrival in Art: New Tendencies and Bit International, 1961–1973 (Karlsruhe: ZKM; Cambridge, MA: MIT Press, 2011).

46. Bogdanović described the events that led to his design for the Jewish Memorial in his autobiography *Ukleti neimar* (Split, Croatia: Feral Tribune, 2001), 93–95.

47. Bogdanović acknowledged the influence of the French ethnologist Lucien Lévy-Bruhl, who, in turn, greatly influenced Carl Gustav Jung's concept of the "collective subconscious"; author's interview with Bogdanović, May 2005.

48. I thank David Raizman for this suggestion.

49. Author's interview with Bogdanović, May 2005.

50. See Bogdan Bogdanović, *Mali urbanizam* (Sarajevo: Narodna prosvjeta, 1958).

51. On CIAM, Bogdanović in an interview with the author, May 2005; on Van den Broek and Bakema's Lijnban in Rotterdam, see "Dve razmere," in *Mali urbanizam*, 134–138.

52. Belgrade architectural historian Ljiljana Blagojević described Bogdanović as "one of the first postmoderns"; see Ljiljana Blagojević, "Postmodernism in Belgrade Architecture: Between Cultural Modernity and Societal Modernization," in *Spatium* (Belgrade) 14, no. 25 (September 2011): 23–29.

53. Bogdan Bogdanović, *Zaludna mistrija: doktrina i praktika bratstva zlatnih (crnih) brojeva* (Belgrade: Nolit, 1963).

54. For an exhaustive overview of Bogdanović's literary oeuvre, see Vladimir Vuković, *Bogdan Bogdanović: Das literarische Werk* (Vienna: Anton Pustet Verlag, 2009).

55. Bogdanović in an interview with the author, May 2005.

56. Ibid.

57. See Architekturzentrum Wien, *Bogdan Bogdanović. Memoria und Utopie in Tito-Jugoslawien* (Vienna: Architekturzentrum Wien and Wieser, 2009), 74.

58. Bogdanović in an interview with the author, May 2005.

59. Ibid.

60. See Benedict Anderson, *Imagined Communities: Reflections on the Origin and Spread of Nationalism* (London, Verso, 1983).

61. This stereotype has been recently disseminated mostly through the various photographic monographs; see, among many others, Frédéric Chaubin's *CCCP: Cosmic Communist Constructions Photographed* (Cologne: Taschen, 2011), or Roman Bezjak's *Socialist Modernism* (Ostfildern, Germany: Hatje Cantz, 2011).

62. See Felicity Scott, *Architecture or Techno-Utopia: Politics after Modernism* (Cambridge, MA: MIT Press, 2010).

3 CZECHOSLOVAKIA'S MODEL HOUSING DEVELOPMENTS
MODERN ARCHITECTURE FOR THE SOCIALIST FUTURE

KIMBERLY ELMAN ZARECOR

In the aftermath of World War II, Czechoslovakia began a process of national transformation and reconstruction that ultimately led to more than forty years of Communist Party rule. During the war and immediate postwar years, its multiethnic population became more homogeneous with the decimation of the Jewish population, the loss of Subcarpathian Ruthenia to the Soviet Union, and the expulsion of three million people of German descent. Internal and regional migration was also common as the government encouraged Slavs to resettle in the "borderlands" (Sudetenland) where properties and businesses confiscated from Jews and Germans were distributed to new settlers. One year after the May 1945 liberation of Prague, democratic elections were held and a new coalition government formed with strong representation from the Communist Party, which received almost 38 percent of the total vote, due in part to its prominent participation in the borderlands resettlement efforts.

In the summer of 1946, the coalition government announced the "Two-Year Plan," intended to return the country to 1937 economic conditions by the end of 1948. Provisions included restoring industrial capacity and infrastructure, improving transportation systems, and constructing at least 125,000 new housing units. One of the most ambitious housing initiatives of the Two-Year Plan was the Model Housing Development Program (Vzorné sídliště) at the Communist-led Ministry of Labor and Social Affairs. With start-up funds from the United Nations Relief and Rehabilitation Administration (UNRRA), the ministry set out to "build two or three housing developments, which would be tested and worked through in practical terms as examples for further building projects around the country."[1] Three Czech cities were chosen as pilot sites: Most, a city in the borderlands near the East German border; Kladno, a mining city about twenty miles northwest of Prague where the Communist Party of Czechoslovakia was founded; and Ostrava, a mining and steel-producing city in northeast Moravia.

Through a discussion of the three Model Housing Development sites, this chapter explores the transformation of postwar architectural practice in the context of rebuilding and resettlement efforts in Czechoslovakia.[2] These sites provide a complex record of the changing understandings of modernism in the early socialist period in Czechoslovakia. At the start, the neighborhoods were an attempt to return to interwar aesthetics, with buildings designed by individual architects featuring unadorned facades, flat roofs, metal details, and horizontal industrial windows. Some resembled Czech social housing projects of the 1930s and others looked like the contemporary Scandinavian projects copiously illustrated in the main architecture journal, *Architektura ČSR* (Czechoslovak Architecture), which resumed publication in the summer of 1946.[3] Prominent interwar modern architects participated in the program, including Josef Havlíček, who would represent Czechoslovakia in the United Nations design competition in 1947; Václav Hilský, who was known for his work on 1930s social housing complexes; and Jiří Štursa, a follower of avant-garde theorist Karel Teige. Their ambition was to find an architectural and spatial vocabulary to express the optimistic hopes of a new society, one that was shaped by a left-wing social agenda and the Communist Party itself.

Construction should have been finished by the end of the Two-Year Plan, but the work was delayed by material shortages, a lack of urgency, and the multitude of changes surrounding the February 1948 Communist Party takeover. In late 1948 the incomplete projects were handed over to Stavoprojekt, the newly established state-run system of architecture and engineering offices that replaced all private firms. The following year the individually designed buildings that had been part of the initial projects were abandoned and construction continued using larger standardized and repeated blocks chosen from a catalogue produced by Stavoprojekt. The final phase of major construction at the sites occurred during the period of Socialist Realism in the early 1950s when these standardized blocks were decorated with neoclassical and vernacular details according to principles adopted from Soviet architecture.

As a case study of early postwar architecture in Eastern Europe, the Model Housing Development Program provides new insight into the shift from interwar to postwar concepts of modernity and the role of the state in shaping these understandings. In the specific case of Czechoslovakia, where the avant-garde survived until the end of the 1930s, most architectural historians have portrayed the start of World War II as the end of modernism.[4] In a characteristic statement, Stephan Templ describes the postwar period as a "half century of darkness."[5] Yet buildings designed between 1945 and the Communist takeover in 1948, many with clear connections to the 1930s, defy such definitive pronouncements. Recognizing the continuities, Templ himself refers to them as the "feeble afterglow" of the avant-garde.[6] Jan Sedlák describes them as "the last traces of functionalism."[7] This chapter argues that, rather than an endpoint, this short period between the war and the Communist takeover was a critical bridge between the individually focused architectural practice of the interwar years and the model of collective work put forward within a socialist framework after 1945.

As this transformation occurred, the stylistic vocabulary of the avant-garde coexisted for several years with the new organizational strategies and working methods brought about by state involvement in architecture. With the creation of Stavoprojekt and its centralized institutional structure for professional practice, concepts such as standardization and typification were given priority over architects' individual desires for creativity. Functional and quantitative measures began to take precedence over aesthetics. A new framework for architectural production emerged, one that emphasized industrial and material requirements over formal characteristics, thereby ending the era of architecture as an individual artistic pursuit. With the advent of Socialist Realism in 1950, the question of aesthetics returned again for a short time, but new methods of industrial production and collective work had already become the basis for socialist architectural practice.

CZECHOSLOVAKIA AFTER WORLD WAR II

The architectural developments of the late 1940s in Czechoslovakia must be situated within a specific and unique context. Despite the tendency to describe all of the Eastern Bloc as a homogeneous region, the countries had distinct histories and wartime experiences, leaving each of them with varied problems, strengths, and political configurations in 1945. With its history of democratic rule in the interwar years and a relative lack of physical and economic damage during the occupation,[8] Czechoslovakia was poised to recover more quickly from the war than its devastated neighbors like Poland and Germany. At the same time, the experience of the 1938 Munich Pact, when France and Great Britain ceded part of Czechoslovakia to Germany without the Czechoslovak government's consent, set a tone of mistrust between Prague and its Western allies. This changed the course of postwar politics in the country by making the Soviet Union the more appealing economic and political ally.

This was evident in the April 1945 Košice Program, drafted in Moscow during the closing days of the war under Soviet supervision. Conceptually wide-ranging and ambitious, the document laid out a new framework for postwar governance and determined much about the experiences of the country's inhabitants after 1945. Economically, the immediate goals were the nationalization of large industries and the redistribution of confiscated German, Jewish, and Hungarian property to Czechs and Slovaks.[9] All right-wing political parties were banned for collaborating with the Nazis during the war.[10] The six remaining center and center-left parties, including the Communists and the Social Democrats, ruled as a coalition called the National Front. The Košice Program also called for popularly elected national committees to be formed at the local, district, and regional levels to manage public affairs. This form of governance was described as a "people's democracy."[11]

Despite the prominent role of the Communist Party in the coalition, the rhetoric of the National Front did not include outright Marxist language. Historian Bradley Abrams notes that at this time the Communists did not demand "the wholesale transplantation of Soviet culture onto Czech and Slovak consciousness."[12] Instead, Communist intellectuals formulated an argument that emphasized "patriotism, national traditions, [and] the progressive quality of the national character" as the foundations of the party's legitimacy.[13] These efforts were rewarded in May 1946 when the Communist Party received 40 percent of the popular vote in the Czech lands and 30 percent in Slovakia; combined this was almost 38 percent of the total.[14]

The National Front government ruled from May 1945 until February 1948. In this time it oversaw the start of economic recovery, massive population expulsions and transfers, and the creation of a homogeneous nation-state that needed to establish its own identity.[15] There were many challenges. Food was in short supply across the country, with rations as low as 1,300 calories a day in May 1945, which increased to 1,800 calories by the end of the year but still remained low through the 1940s.[16] The far east of the country, Subcarpathian Ruthenia, was ceded to the Soviet Union at the end of the war, resulting in the loss of 850,000 inhabitants. The Jewish population was also decimated through emigration and extermination in concentration camps. Only 44,000 of the 356,000 people who identified their religion as Jewish in the 1930 census remained in the country by 1945. Many of those who stayed then left in 1948 or with another wave of emigration in 1968. By 1980, only 9,000 Jews lived in Czechoslovakia.[17] But the largest population loss was due to the expulsion of citizens determined to be of German descent. In 1945 and 1946, three million citizens were forcefully expelled from the country as a form of war retribution and for what was justified at the time as a national security measure.[18] As a result, Czechoslovakia's population shrank dramatically from 15,900,000 in May 1945 to only 12,003,000 in December 1946.[19] These losses contributed to the extreme labor shortages that plagued the country for decades.[20]

The social and cultural consequences of the war proved to be the most destructive.[21] In 1939, 70 percent of the population of Bohemia, Moravia, and Silesia was Czech; by 1950, this number had grown to 94 percent.[22] As historian Nancy Wingfield has shown, the loss of the country's long-established German community created the need to construct a "new collective memory" for the country, one that "used socially organized forgetting—exclusion, suppression, and repression—on the one hand, and socially organized remembering—the deliberate invention, emphasis, and popularization of elements of consciousness—on the other . . . to legitimate the new 'purer' postwar Czechoslovak nation-state."[23] Beyond the outright anti-German propaganda common in political rhetoric, aspects of "forgetting" included changing building, street, and city names from German to Czech, removing monuments related to historic German figures, and forbidding the use of the term "Sudeten" after May 1945.[24] The construction of this new collective memory focused largely on using a shared Slavic past to unify Czechs and Slovaks, whose modern histories and wartime experiences had been different.[25] Within architecture, this was achieved, on one hand, by emphasizing the shared vernacular heritage of the region and, on the other, by highlighting the modernizing and progressive character of Czech and Slovak architecture in the interwar period.[26]

The population was also in motion at the time as large numbers of Czechs and Slovaks moved from the interior of the country to the borderlands where they were promised properties including confiscated businesses and homes. Between 1945 and 1950, one out of every four Czechs left their homes to try to build a new life there.[27] One of the most serious obstacles to these resettlement efforts was a lack of housing. Although there were as many as 640,000 apartments and homes in the region in the government's possession by 1946, some belonged to Czechs returning to the area, some were primitive even by interwar standards, and others had suffered war damage and needed reconstruction.[28] Historian Zdeněk Radvanovský describes "a catastrophic lack of housing" that was a "burning problem for practically all new settlers in the borderlands."[29]

There were also localized population shifts occurring within the borderlands and other industrial regions around cities such as Zlín and Ostrava. New factories needed housing for their workers. The existing housing stock around the country was problematic, not only because of the number of units or their condition, but because units were needed in places where there had not been housing previously. Although the transfers of Germans ended in 1947 and the population stabilized, the housing shortages in the borderlands continued into the 1950s.[30] The Ostrava region suffered similar problems as its coal-mining and steel industries expanded rapidly in the late 1940s and early 1950s. Given these challenges, architects quickly recognized the crucial role the profession could play in the further development of the socialist economy and society. At Stavoprojekt, emphasis was quickly placed on strategies for providing housing as quickly and efficiently as possible.

THE POSTWAR AGENDA

Providing new housing units was a necessity for rebuilding the economy, but it also had symbolic value for the regime. Architects were soon involved in debates about what socialist housing might be in Czechoslovakia. Just as the earliest postwar Communist Party rhetoric emphasized patriotism, national traditions, and the nation's progressive character, Czech and Slovak architects looked to the local interwar avant-garde as the most appropriate source of formal inspiration. This was made easier by the continued presence of prominent interwar architects who survived the war, many of whom stayed in Czechoslovakia and emerged as leaders in the postwar professional community.[31] In this sense, what occurred in 1945 was the regrouping of the avant-garde rather than the adoption of avant-garde forms by another generation of architects, a context specific to Czechoslovakia because of its experiences immediately before the war.

The most radical change in the rhetoric involved how to provide the urgently needed housing. Czechoslovakia's political and intellectual climate had moved to the left by 1945 as a response to Fascism and the events in Munich. This gave the leftist faction within the architectural community new authority to promote its long-standing agenda, which included building mass housing, changing the country's class structure, and exposing the nature of capitalist excess and exploitation.[32] Demands for the nationalization of the building industry, which had seemed naive in the 1930s, were now met with support from the profession and the government as part of a larger nationalization program instituted in the fall of 1945.[33] The leadership of the newly formed Block of Progressive Architectural Associations (Blok architektonických pokrokových spolků) argued for the consolidation of professional and material resources—collective work executed to regulated standards—as well as a clearly articulated agenda for architectural practice that established the architect as a critical and indispensable voice in the debates. State support was crucial to these goals, and one of the earliest demands was the creation of government institutes to investigate aspects of the building industry such as housing strategies, prefabrication, the economics of construction, building standards, and the relationship of people to the natural environment.[34]

At the same time, the state itself was formulating an approach to housing design, one grounded in a belief that architecture was fundamentally a social and economic endeavor and not a creative or formal act. Potential investors in state-sponsored housing projects, namely ministries, national committees (local political councils), and nationalized enterprises, had vowed to provide as much new housing to their constituencies as possible, especially in the borderlands and developing industrial regions. Simple, inexpensive units were essential to that goal. Given the scale of the housing problem, the shortage of building materials, and the lack of available skilled labor, government officials agreed with architects that new design and construction strategies had to be found.

The government's official involvement in planning for new housing construction had started as early as October 1945 when ministries began to survey employees about their housing conditions only to find significant shortages.[35] To address this problem, a housing advisory board was established in January 1946 with five committees to look at the financial, housing, land, organizational, and technical aspects of the crisis.[36] Members included politicians, institutional administrators, and representatives of various ministries. The technical committee, charged with setting standards for apartment units and building practices, soon split into two subcommittees.[37] One was for "building construction and materials" and was led by architect Karel Pilát, who would later administrate the Model Housing Development Program. The other considered "sociological and statistical research" and was led by architect Jiří Štursa, who had been a proponent of Karel Teige's concept of "scientific functionalism" in the 1930s. The separation and the lack of focus on formal issues indicated something of the new context in which architects had to operate.

The government issued a decree on July 16, 1946, declaring that 125,000 new apartment units would be built during the Two-Year Plan. The new Ministry of Technology was given the task of deciding how best to fulfill this target. Of the total number requested, 70,000 units were to be rehabilitated after suffering damage in the war; 30,000 would be completely rebuilt as part of the reconstruction efforts; and 25,000 new units would be provided specifically for industry and building cooperatives. One-third of the units would be in single-family houses and the rest in apartment buildings.[38] For the next six months, Štursa's subcommittee for sociological and statistical research worked on apartment and single-family house designs that would come to be known as "Two-Year Plan Apartments." The standardized plans were prepared just in time for the implementation of the Two-Year Plan on January 1, 1947.[39] In this first iteration, the 65-square-meter (700-square-foot) furnished "family units" for four to six people had two bedrooms with a living room, water closet, bathroom, pantry, and a small kitchen; these could be built as apartments, row houses, or single-family houses.[40] Furnished "bachelor" apartments were limited to twenty-five square meters (270 square feet) and contained a single large living space, water closet, bathroom, and small kitchen.[41]

Architect Karel Storch, who visited Stockholm, Helsinki, and Copenhagen as part of an official 1946 delegation, described very similar apartments in *Architektura ČSR* when he wrote about an "international consensus in the housing standard."[42] He argued that after years disconnected from this international building culture, Czechs and Slovaks needed to bring their housing standard closer to that of the more advanced Northern Europeans. He was critical of the German concept of the "minimum dwelling," popularized in the 1930s through CIAM (Congrès Internationaux d'Architecture Moderne). These units were reduced to the absolute minimum of space and functional requirements for sleeping and bathing, even eliminating the kitchen in favor of collective dining in some examples. Rather than the "vacuous economic liberalism" of the minimum dwelling concept, Storch believed instead that "the symbol of housing culture" was "the demarcation of function in each room, in every room—not only those in which the functional uses are given by their fixtures or other building systems."[43] The result was what he termed the "differentiated apartment" with a large living room; small, ventilated kitchen; a pantry, a separate water closet and bathroom; and segregated sleeping rooms for parents and children. These specifications matched those of the Two-Year Plan units and would influence the design of the first standardized units after 1948.

THE MODEL HOUSING DEVELOPMENTS

Announced the same month as the 125,000-unit target, the Model Housing Development Program was the most ambitious and important housing project of the Two-Year Plan.⁴⁴ Kladno, Most, and Ostrava were logical first sites given the housing needs in the borderlands and industrial regions. The Ministry of Labor and Social Affairs administered the program and appointed local building associations to oversee the work in each city. Association members included representatives from the ministry, local industrial concerns such as mines, chemical plants, and steel mills, and local and regional national committees. The individual associations were responsible for developing the program, writing budgets, and choosing architects to design the master plan and standardized building types with the intention that they could be replicated at other sites. The financial support provided to the projects by local interest groups meant that a specified number of the housing units would be reserved for their employees. In the case of the Ostrava development, for example, Vítkovíce Ironworks was entitled to 20 percent; the Ostrava-Karviná Regional Coal Mines and the Ostrava Chemical Enterprise each had 15 percent; and the regional, state, and local national committees claimed the remaining 50 percent.⁴⁵ In Kladno and Most, the local mining collectives were the primary beneficiaries.⁴⁶

The association in each city hired four or five architects to work on the master plan and individual buildings for their development. In Kladno, the design group included Josef Havlíček and Václav Hilský, both of whom had been respected avant-garde architects in Prague before the war.⁴⁷ Jiří Štursa, who led the subcommittee that proposed the Two-Year Plan Apartments, worked on the teams in Most and Ostrava.⁴⁸ The building sites, chosen for their proximity to local industries and the potential to connect to existing city infrastructure including transportation networks, consisted of land already in the possession of the state, supplemented by the purchase of individual tracts.⁴⁹ The Ostrava site was the largest, with a plan to build a housing development for 7,500 residents in 1,800 units (figure 3.1).⁵⁰ Kladno and Most were planned for 5,000 people in 1,200 units (figure 3.2).⁵¹

Architect and project administrator Karel Pilát from the Ministry of Labor and Social Affairs wrote that the work was inspired by three important precedents: Ebenezer Howard's Garden City from 1898; Tony Garnier's Industrial City from 1917; and Le Corbusier's City for Three Million Inhabitants of 1922.⁵² Like these precedents, each of the project proposals included housing, schools, shopping areas, community centers, health clinics, parks and open green spaces, garages, and mass transportation to local industries and urban centers. In Ostrava there was also a hotel, dormitory, and youth center in the main square. Housing was provided in a mix of single-family homes, row houses, and two- to five-story apartment buildings with a few taller buildings, such as eight-story housing blocks built in parallel rows in Ostrava and eleven-story towers in Kladno.⁵³

In Most and Ostrava, Jiří Štursa produced diagrams of the master plans, what he called "analyses of the gravitational circles" of the site. These illustrated the hierarchical relationships between the different programs and their distances

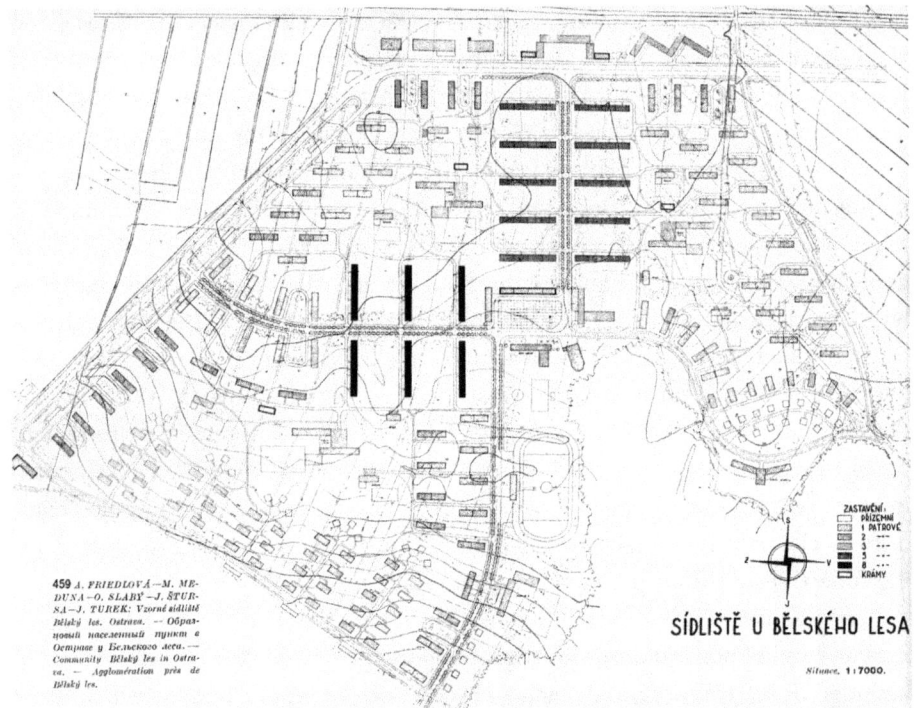

(ABOVE) FIGURE 3.1. Anna Friedlová, Vladimír Meduna, Otto Slabý, Jiří Štursa, and Jaroslav Turek, Model Housing Development, Ostrava. Plan. *Architektura ČSR*, 1947.

(OPPOSITE PAGE, TOP) FIGURE 3.2. Josef Havlíček, Václav Hilský, Miroslav Koněrza, and Emil Kovařik, Model Housing Development, Kladno. *Architektura ČSR*, 1947.

(OPPOSITE PAGE, BOTTOM) FIGURE 3.3. Jiří Štursa, Model Housing Development, Most. Diagrams showing "analyses of the gravitational circles." *Architektura ČSR*, 1947.

---

from the housing clusters (figure 3.3). These diagrams were descendants of charts and diagrams utilized by Štursa and his collaborators in the 1930s under the rubric of scientific functionalism.[54] For example, each sector in Most had two locations for services such as tailors, butchers, and hairstylists and one grocery store; at the center of the development was a department store. The schools followed the same pattern, with at least three schools in each sector: one day-care center, one elementary school, and one middle school; a single high school was located in the center.[55] Ostrava followed a similar distribution pattern, although the planned settlement pattern was denser. Because of this, there were fewer day-care centers and elementary schools in the plan, although one assumes that each one would have been larger to accommodate a similar overall number of students.[56] There was also a conscious effort to make the apartments equidistant from other amenities. For example, residents would have to walk no more than ten minutes from their apartment to a tram stop.[57]

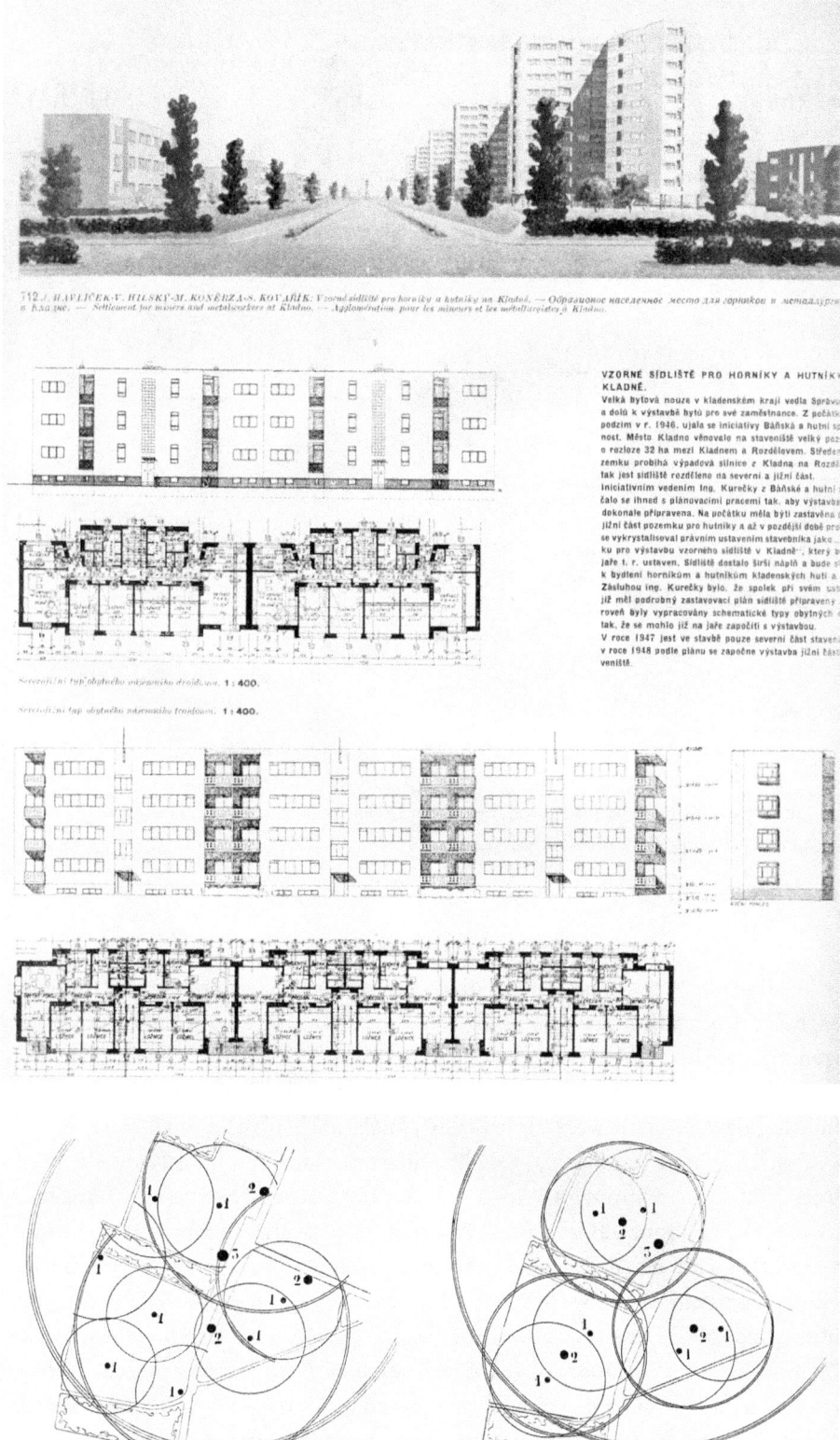

CZECHOSLOVAKIA'S MODEL HOUSING DEVELOPMENTS

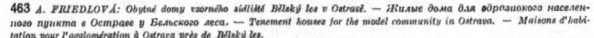
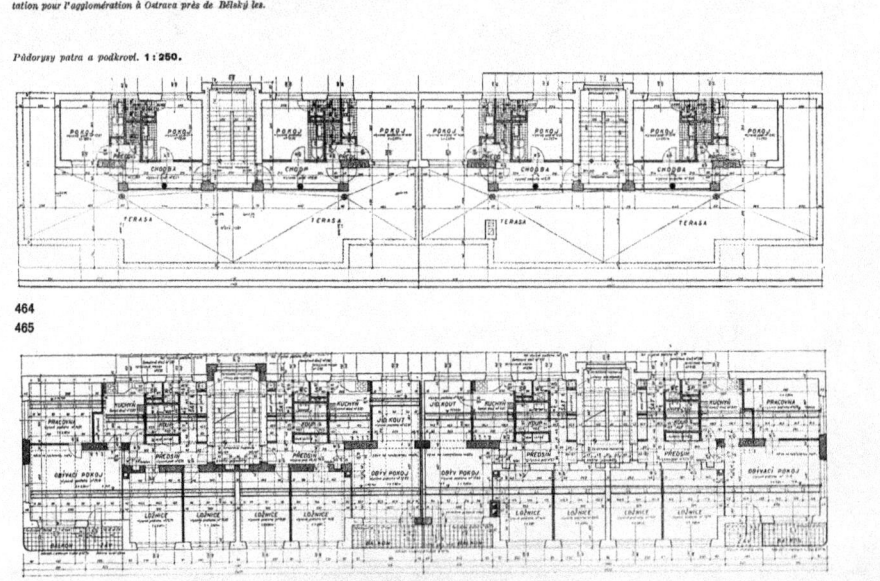

FIGURE 3.4. Anna Friedlová, Model Housing Development, Ostrava. Design for apartment buildings. *Architektura ČSR*, 1947.

In addition to the master plans prepared by the four- and five-member teams, each architect submitted plans for individual buildings to a limited competition, the results of which were decided by the association.[58] With their flat roofs and horizontal facade compositions, the apartment buildings proposed for each housing development were stylistically consistent with the modernist tendencies of the period (figures 3.4, 3.5). The apartments were typically two-bedroom units that followed Štursa's Two-Year Plan proposals and Storch's Scandinavian-inspired ideas about differentiated apartments, although in most cases the units were larger, with eat-in kitchens or separate dining rooms. Some one-room bachelor apartments were also proposed; in Ostrava they were located on the penthouse floor of the five- and eight-story buildings, although they were not built in the final projects. The most distinctive development was Kladno with a combination of modest three-story blocks punctuated by Y-shaped apartment towers on *pilotis* designed by Josef Havlíček, who was about to leave for New York to represent Czechoslovakia on the United Nations design team.[59]

FIGURE 3.5. Anna Friedlová, Model Housing Development, Ostrava. Apartment building after renovation. Photo by author, 2006.

THE PROJECTS AFTER 1948

Despite these auspicious beginnings, the Model Housing Development Program did not proceed as planned. Material and labor shortages, general disorganization, and a lack of urgency meant that little was accomplished at these sites in 1947 and 1948. Twenty of the three-story, fifteen-unit apartment blocks designed by Josef Havlíček and Václav Hilský were started in Kladno in 1947, but according to Havlíček, construction "stagnated" until after the Communist takeover in February 1948.[60] In Ostrava, only fifteen of the seventy buildings planned for the first phase were started by 1948. Jiří Štursa's proposal for parallel rows of eight-story blocks lining the main north-south boulevard was abandoned.[61] Instead, in September 1947 the association chose Anna Friedlová and Jaroslav Turek, local architects and members of the master plan committee, to build eleven and four apartment blocks, respectively.[62] Friedlová's four-story blocks included 112 two-room apartments in seven buildings and 116 one-room bachelor apartments in four buildings. At almost ninety square meters (970 square feet), her two-room units were similar to but larger than Štursa's Two-Year Plan units, with either a separate dining room or workspace and more storage.[63] Turek's four buildings were smaller, only three stories, and less elegant with large open balconies on the entrance side and smaller balconies at the rear (figure 3.6). No community

FIGURE 3.6. Jaroslav Turek, Model Housing Development, Ostrava. Apartment building. Photo by author, 2006.

buildings, schools, or commercial businesses were started during this time. Residents of the few completed units were left without the promised services until another construction phase in the mid-1950s.

Stavoprojekt took over management of the still incomplete Model Housing Developments when it was established in September 1948. As an organization, its mandate included transitioning architectural practice from its artistic and creative origins to a model that saw design as a form of industrial production. In a speech at the first nationwide meeting of regional administrators, Stavoprojekt director Jiří Voženílek stated that "achievement" in the building industry "depends first and foremost on how quickly it succeeds in reorganizing the scattered debris of handicraft businesses into enterprises governed by planning and the method of industrial production."[64] Deputy director Otakar Nový added that "in order to transition the building industry from handicraft to production, we must transform our building sites into factories."[65]

Within this new framework, the individually designed buildings that were initially proposed for the Model Housing Developments posed a problem. The fundamental mandate of the three associations—to build modest, comfortable housing units for workers in key industries—did not change, but the planned units did not meet the new Stavoprojekt guidelines for standardized housing construction; instead, they were grouped under the label of "atypical." Compounding the problem were budget overruns. When the program failed to deliver the promised units by the end of 1948, the construction budgets had to be increased. It was difficult to acquire building materials not already forecast in the first Five-Year Plan, which went into effect on January 1, 1949.

The situation created a conflict between the local associations and the new central administration. Frustration was evident in discussions at association gatherings in each city. At a committee meeting of the Association for the Construction of the Model Housing Development in Kladno on December 22, 1949, tempers flared as representatives from the Czechoslovak Building Works (the umbrella organization for enterprises in the building industry including contractors and the Stavoprojekt network), local companies, and the ministries argued over whom to blame for the failure to produce more units. It came out during the meeting that the Czechoslovak Building Works had published newspaper articles claiming that 110 percent of the plan for the housing settlement had been fulfilled, even though the association knew that the correct number was 53 percent—126 units as of December 22.[66] There were complaints that costs would have been lower if local craftsman had been employed to do the work. The discussion eventually returned to the question of the housing units. One local engineer commented that the demands for fulfilling the plan would increase in 1950 and "in Ostrava, they should have built 6,000 homes by 1950—how should they do this if at this point they can't even finish 300?"[67]

Similar concerns were voiced at the meeting of the association in Ostrava, where the political pressure to deliver units was even more intense. Common complaints cited a lack of building materials and a shortage of labor.[68] Once Stavoprojekt had taken over the project, the association sent repeated requests to the Czechoslovak Building Works for assistance; however, the work remained behind schedule and over budget.[69] By 1950, the level of dissatisfaction with the poor management hit a fever pitch. Three years into the project, many housing blocks in Ostrava lacked basic necessities like central heating, proper attic insulation, or lighting. According to one resident:

> The electrical work is very negligent. It is not only that many already occupied apartments don't have enough fixtures, it's that the occupants cannot get light in all of the shared spaces, mainly there are no fixtures in any of the stairways or basement. Practically the whole housing development, with the exception of the apartments, is completely unlit in the evening and at night.[70]

Under these less-than-ideal conditions, the Model Housing Developments were a constant reminder of the failure of the Two-Year Plan and the challenge to make improvements as quickly as possible in order to keep up with the planning targets.

To remedy the situation, the leadership of Stavoprojekt actively pursued standardization and typification for all building types. In residential construction, a limited number of apartment blocks, which would become known as the T-series, were designed and approved for use in all projects by 1950 (figure 3.7). Starting in

FIGURE 3.7. Model Housing Development, Ostrava. Standardized apartment building, 1950. Photo by author, 2004.

1951, technical manuals for each building sector were published by Stavoprojekt research institutes to codify and convey these designs to the regional offices.[71] The T-series units were similar in size and layout to the Two-Year Plan Apartments, but stylistically they were less modern without the avant-garde details of the buildings designed between 1945 and 1949. The buildings had plain facades, punched windows, and pitched roofs, which gave the overall impression of being inspired by vernacular examples. Although as hypermodern as factory-produced objects, the T-series blocks signaled a change in emphasis within the design culture. An international interwar aesthetic was replaced with a local and self-consciously national conception of what socialist modernism might look like. This was an early sign of the influence that Soviet Socialist Realism and its historicist preferences would have in Czechoslovakia over the next five years.

SOCIALIST REALISM

The stylistic shift from interwar modernism to a local variant of Socialist Realism did not occur immediately after the Communist takeover in 1948. Through the end of the 1940s, the architectural leadership at Stavoprojekt remained committed to modernist forms and the profession was protected from the encroachment of Soviet Socialist Realism through strong connections to the political elite. By early 1950, however, the Soviets were putting pressure on the regime to conform more closely to its expectations. Strict adherence to the "Soviet model" of cultural production soon became a political necessity and new leadership was appointed at Stavoprojekt to implement the changes within the local offices.

Socialist Realism as a concept remains difficult to define. Recent scholarship describes the Soviet variant of the style across all forms of cultural production as having multiple formal, material, and linguistic expressions that share common traits such as the belief in the absolute power of the Communist Party and its basis in Marxism-Leninism, an unfailing optimism about the future, and a preference for decorative and historicist aesthetics.[72] In Czechoslovakia, the political rhetoric of a "national road to socialism" and the country's need to define its own postwar identity after the loss of its German and Jewish populations led to an emphasis on vernacular forms. Following the Soviet slogan "national in form, socialist in content," architects who embraced the style looked not only to the architecture of Czech and Slovak villages but also to the Bohemian Renaissance in the sixteenth century, when Prague was an imperial capital. This provided a broad palette to work from, and at the same time, the small scale of many of the exemplars predicted that Czechoslovak Socialist Realist buildings would be much smaller and more humane than in the Soviet Union where the monumentality of eighteenth-century St. Petersburg was an important model.

Planning for the next phase of the unfinished Model Housing Developments had to be adjusted to this new context. Although some new construction of T-series apartment blocks had occurred on the sites since 1948, the developments were still far from finished. In the Ostrava case, Jiří Kroha, a modernist turned Socialist Realist who was the favorite architect of Communist Party leader and president Klement Gottwald, was asked in the summer of 1952 to design the next phase of the Ostrava Model Housing Development. The neighborhood, which had been named Ostrava-Bělský Les in 1947, was renamed Ostrava-Stalingrad in 1950.[73] A longtime Marxist and professor at Brno University of Technology, Kroha was one of the first Czech architects to advocate for the widespread adoption of a local variation on Soviet Socialist Realism. He built a reputation as an exhibition designer for prominent state events such as the Slavic Agricultural Exhibition in 1948 and as a polemicist in *Architektura ČSR*, where he published numerous articles on the topic. The Communist government rewarded him with accolades and the opportunity to lead the only autonomous design office in the country, the Master Atelier of National Artist Jiří Kroha.[74]

In starting his work in Ostrava, Kroha had to contend with the existing master plan from 1947, the fifteen original three- and four-story apartment buildings that had been started before 1948, and clusters of T-series buildings that had been constructed on the site from 1950 to 1952. His design for phase two included a civic square and a new entrance on the northern end of the site leading to a row of larger, more decorative residential buildings that fronted the street between the entrance and the square. The buildings were, in fact, the next generation of standardized T-series blocks embellished with decorative flourishes to give the desired Socialist Realist effect (figure 3.8). The civic buildings, which had been called for in the original master plan, included a health clinic, a post office, a culture house, a children's nursery, schools, grocery stores, and a department store

FIGURE 3.8. Model Housing Development, Ostrava. Garden facade of a standardized apartment building by the office of Jiří Kroha, 1952. Photo by author, 2006.

FIGURE 3.9. Model Housing Development, Ostrava. Department store from 1952 by the office of Jiří Kroha, shown after 1956. Photograph Collection/Ostrava Municipal Archives.

FIGURE 3.10. Model Housing Development, Kladno. Towers under construction. *Bydlení v Československu*, 1958.

(figure 3.9).[75] Stylistically, the project was representative of Kroha's idiosyncratic take on Socialist Realism, inspired by Czech and Slovak vernacular motifs and nineteenth-century examples such as Fourier's Phalanstère. Some of his signature elements included arcades connecting the health clinic and post office to the main commercial street and a classically inspired decorative scheme with stucco relief work, statuary, and column-pilaster combinations. The most successful aspect of Kroha's intervention was the readability of the neighborhood's urban composition with the addition of the entrance and the square.

The developments in Most and Kladno followed similar trajectories.[76] Josef Havlíček, the lead designer at the Prague office of Stavoprojekt in the 1950s, continued to work on the Kladno master plan for many years. In 1956 he redesigned the tall buildings that had been planned along the development's main boulevard. The Y-shaped towers on *pilotis* transformed into small skyscrapers reminiscent of New York City with strong vertical forms, wide bases, and square setbacks (figure 3.10). Completed in 1959, the buildings were neither stylistically Socialist Realist nor modern, indicating ambivalence to the trends in architectural styles at the time.[77] In Most, later T-series buildings with Socialist Realist details were built to fill in much of the initial site by the mid-1950s. The city itself, in the heart of the brown-coal basin of the borderlands, became infamous in the 1970s when the government tore down the historic city center and relocated a Baroque church in order to mine underground coal deposits that were judged more valuable than the historic buildings themselves. On higher ground, adjacent to the already built Model Housing Development, a new concrete city emerged with large housing blocks and a massively scaled urban core, which bore no relationship to the original city. The new city remains one of the poorest and least desirable in the country, although the area around the original Model Housing Development remains relatively stable.[78]

CONCLUSION

Although the Model Housing Developments did not become models for future neighborhoods as initially intended, the continued attention paid to them through the 1950s indicated the symbolic importance of this program to the regime. As difficulties continued for the designers, investors, and residents, the project itself became a microcosm of the larger problems faced by the state as it transitioned from a complex and diversified capitalist economy to a planned economy. Failure to complete the projects was in this sense a failure of the new system. Changes to the formal character and construction methods of the Model Housing Developments from their earliest incarnation in 1946 to the designs of the mid-1950s clearly illustrated the transformations occurring within the design culture at Stavoprojekt. By 1949, architects were no longer artists designing single commissions for their clients. Instead the practice of architecture became a collective endeavor tied more to state ambitions for quick and inexpensive housing than to avant-garde principles of form and function.

When considered in hindsight, there are many things the state could have learned from the Model Housing Development Program that would have predicted some of the problems which architects and investors faced throughout the Communist period. During the Two-Year Plan, it was already apparent that labor and materials would have to be carefully considered and aggressively sought out. The need to coordinate multiple investors, contractors, and architects complicated bureaucratic and decision-making processes and held up the pace of construction. The loss of individual authorship, and therefore the changing nature of architectural practice, was also evident from the start. In the search to find a strategy that could be repeated around the country, standardized and typified buildings were much more attractive to investors than hiring individual architects to produce site-specific designs.

For these reasons, the architect's role fundamentally changed after 1950 as the nature of design moved away from creative work and toward factory production. Many architects of the interwar generation found this compromise hard to accept. By the early 1950s, younger and more ideologically driven practitioners had taken the lead in the debates about the future of socialist design. These young, ambitious, and politically minded architects were the same group who would quickly embrace Socialist Realism and then abandon it once again in the wake of the deaths of Stalin and Gottwald.

Despite the challenges that were already evident, the post-1948 government embraced repetitive planning on the neighborhood scale and encouraged projects that provided shared services to large numbers of residents in low-rise, high-density developments constructed with standardized apartment blocks. Many politicians and architects saw this as the best solution to the critical housing shortage, although they knew it could significantly reduce the design quality of individual units. This strategy remained part of Stavoprojekt's working methodology until 1989 and the end of Communist Party rule, but the execution of such projects was always difficult as labor and material shortages disrupted schedules, shoddy craftsmanship was rampant, and the building sector never delivered as many buildings as expected. The history of the Model Housing Developments and the changing understandings of socialist modernity offer insights into the architectural strategies of the regime and why, ultimately, the Czechoslovak state failed to provide the promised quality and quantity of housing.

NOTES

1. Karel Pilát, "Výstavba vzorných sídlišť a jejich poslání (The Construction of the Model Housing Developments and Their Mission)," *Architektura ČSR* 7, no. 6–7 (1948): 204.

2. This essay is adapted from material in my book; see Kimberly Elman Zarecor, *Manufacturing a Socialist Modernity: Housing in Czechoslovakia, 1945–1960* (Pittsburgh: University of Pittsburgh Press, 2011).

3. For more on the 1930s, see Rostislav Švácha, *The Architecture of New Prague, 1895–1945*, trans. Alexandra Büchler (Cambridge, MA: MIT Press, 1995); Rostislav Švácha, Sona Ryňdová, and Pavla Pokorná, eds., *Forma sleduje vědu/Form Follows Science* (Prague: Jaroslav Fragner Gallery, 2000).

4. See, for example, Kenneth Frampton, "A Modernity Worthy of the Name: Notes on the Czech Architectural Avant-Garde," in *El arte de la vanguardia en Checoslovaquia 1918–1938/The Art of the Avant-Garde in Czechoslovakia 1918–1938*, ed. Jaroslav Anděl (Valencia: Institut Valencia d'Art Modern, 1993), 231; Karel Teige, *The Minimum Dwelling*, trans. Eric Dluhosch (Cambridge, MA: MIT Press, 2002), xxiv–xxv.

5. Stephan Templ, *Baba: The Werkbund Housing Estate Prague* (Basel; Boston: Birkhäuser, 1999), 12.

6. Ibid.

7. Zdeněk Lukeš and Jan Sedlák, "Doznívání funkcionalismu (The Last Traces of Functionalism)," in *Česká architektura, 1945–1995 / Czech Architecture, 1945–1995*, ed. Karel Dušek (Prague: Obec architektů, 1995), 20–27.

8. Boris P. Pešek, *Gross National Product of Czechoslovakia in Monetary and Real Terms, 1946–58* (Chicago: University of Chicago Press, 1965), 2.

9. See Zdeněk Radvanovský, "The Social and Economic Consequences of Resettling Czechs into Northwestern Bohemia, 1945–47," in *Redrawing Nations: Ethnic Cleansing in*

East-Central Europe, 1944–1948, ed. Philipp Ther and Ana Siljak (Lanham, MD: Rowman and Littlefield, 2001), 243.

10. Melissa Feinberg, *Elusive Equality: Gender, Citizenship, and the Limits of Democracy in Czechoslovakia, 1918–1950* (Pittsburgh, PA: University of Pittsburgh Press, 2006), 193.

11. Radomír Luža, "Czechoslovakia between Democracy and Communism, 1945–1948," in *A History of the Czechoslovak Republic 1918–1948*, ed. Radomír Luža and Victor S. Mamatey (Princeton, NJ: Princeton University Press, 1973), 393; Feinberg, *Elusive Equality*, 193.

12. Bradley F. Abrams, *The Struggle For the Soul of the Nation: Czech Culture and the Rise of Communism* (Lanham, MD: Rowman and Littlefield, 2004), 94.

13. Ibid., 92.

14. Luža, "Czechoslovakia between Democracy and Communism," 404.

15. On aspects of memory and national identity in this period, see Nancy M. Wingfield, "The Politics of Memory: Constructing National Identity in the Czech Lands, 1945 to 1948," *East European Politics and Societies* 14, no. 3 (2000): 246–267.

16. Martin R. Myant, *Socialism and Democracy in Czechoslovakia, 1945–1948* (Cambridge and New York: Cambridge University Press, 1981), 56, 185–186.

17. Jaroslav Krejčí and Pavel Machonin, *Czechoslovakia, 1918–92: A Laboratory for Social Change* (New York: St. Martin's Press, 1996), 34–37. See also Benjamin Frommer, *National Cleansing: Retribution against Nazi Collaborators in Postwar Czechoslovakia* (Cambridge and New York: Cambridge University Press, 2005), 25–26.

18. Radvanovský, "Social and Economic Consequences of Resettling," 243.

19. John Shute, "Czechoslovakia's Territorial and Population Changes," *Economic Geography* 24, no. 1 (1948): 39.

20. See Myant, *Socialism and Democracy in Czechoslovakia*, 63–75; Martin R. Myant, *The Czechoslovak Economy, 1948–1988: The Battle for Economic Reform* (Cambridge and New York: Cambridge University Press, 1989), 137–142; John N. Stevens, *Czechoslovakia at the Crossroads: The Economic Dilemmas of Communism in Postwar Czechoslovakia* (Boulder, CO; New York: East European Monographs, Distributed by Columbia University Press, 1985), 214–220; Eagle Glassheim, "Ethnic Cleansing, Communism, and Environmental Devastation in Czechoslovakia's Borderlands, 1945–1989," *Journal of Modern History* 78 (March 2006): 68–73.

21. There is a growing body of scholarly work in English on the broad implications of the expulsions; see Glassheim, "Ethnic Cleansing"; Nancy Wingfield, "The Politics of Memory"; Ther and Siljak, *Redrawing Nations*; David Gerlach, "Working with the Enemy: Labor Politics in the Czech Borderlands, 1945–48," *Austrian History Yearbook* 38 (2007); Eagle Glassheim, "National Mythologies and Ethnic Cleansing: The Expulsion of the Czechoslovak Germans in 1945," *Central European History* 33, no. 4 (2000): 463–486.

22. Chad Carl Bryant, "Either German or Czech: Fixing Nationality in Bohemia and Moravia, 1939–1946," *Slavic Review* 61, no. 4 (2002): 683.

23. Wingfield, "The Politics of Memory," 246.

24. Ibid., 256–264.

25. Ibid., 249–251, 58.

26. The vernacular interest can be seen in the work of architects like Dušan Jurkovič; see Christopher Long, "'The Works of Our People': Dušan Jurkovič and the Slovak Art Revival," *Studies in the Decorative Arts* 12, no. 1 (Fall–Winter 2004–2005): 2–29.

27. Adrian von Arburg, "Tak či onak. Nucené přesídlení v komplexním pojetí poválečné sídelní politiky v českých zemích" (One Way or the Other: Czechoslovak Resettlement Policy and Its Effects in the Bohemian Lands after World War II), *Soudobé dějiny* 10, no. 3 (2003): 253.

28. Karel Janů, *Nájemné z bytů v pohraničí* (Rent from Apartments in the Borderlands) (Prague: Svoboda, 1946), 15.

29. Radvanovský, "Social and Economic Consequences of Resettling," 244.

30. Ibid., 253.

31. They included Bohuslav Fuchs, Jaroslav Fragner, Karel Janů, Josef Havlíček, Václav Hilský, Jiří Kroha, Oldřich Starý, Jiří Štursa, and Jiří Voženílek.

32. Two well-known books on these themes by members of the interwar avant-garde are Jiří Kroha, *Sociologické fragment bydlení* (The Sociological Housing Fragment) (Brno: 1932, c1973), and Teige, *The Minimum Dwelling*. Teige's book was originally published in Czech in 1932 as *Nejmenší byt*.

33. For an analysis of the economy from 1945 to 1948, see Jan M. Michal, "Postwar Economic Development," in *A History of the Czechoslovak Republic 1918–1948*, eds. Luža and Mamatey, 428–460.

34. "Memorandum Bloku architektonických pokrokových spolků," 2.

35. The letter was referred to in a response from the Postal Ministry; see Letter to Ministerstvo dopravy-veřejná správa technická (Ministry of Transportation-Public Technical Committee) from Ministerstvo pošt (Postal Ministry), November 14, 1945, Ministerstro techniky (Ministry of Technology) (henceforth MT), carton 267, National Archives (henceforth NA).

36. Meeting minutes for the five committees can be found in MT, cartons 267, 302, NA. On state employee housing, see Ministerstvo techniky, "Potřeba bytů pro státní zaměstnance" (The Need for Apartments for State Employees), October 25, 1947, MT, carton 267, NA.

37. "Záznam o II.plenární schůzi Poradního sboru pro bytovou výstavbu konané 7.května 1946" (Record of the 2nd Plenary Meeting of the Advisory Board for Housing Construction on May 7, 1946), May 7, 1946, pp. 5–7, MT, carton 302, NA.

38. "Zápis o poradě konané podle vládního usnesení o přípravních opatřeních k provádění budovatelského programu vlády" (Minutes of the Meeting on the Preparatory Arrangements to Implement the Government's Building Program), August 1, 1946, p. 1, MT, carton 303, NA.

39. Plans signed by Jiří Štursa on December 23, 1946, can be found in MT, carton 302, NA.

40. "Směrnice pro stavbu bytů v rámci bytové stavební obnovy a výstavby dvouletého plánu" (Directives for the Construction of Apartments in the Framework of Building Rehabilitation and Construction during the Two-Year Plan), December 31, 1946, MT, carton 302, NA.

41. Ibid.

42. Karel Storch, "Mezinárodní shoda v bytovém standardu" (The International Consensus in the Housing Standard), *Architektura ČSR* 6, no. 5 (1947): 140–141.

43. Ibid., 140.

44. Pilát, "Výstavba vzorných sídlišť a jejich poslání," 204. Extensive archival documentation survives about the Ostrava Model Housing Development. See fonds: MT, cartons 348–351, NA; Spolek pro výstavbu vzorného sídliště v Ostravě-Zábřeh (Association for the Building of the Model Housing Development in Ostrava-Zábřeh, henceforth Spolek), Archiv města Ostravy (Ostrava Municipal Archives, henceforth AMO), Ostrava, Czech Republic; Vládní komise pro výstavbu Ostravska (Government Commission for the Building of Ostrava), Zemský archiv v Opavě (Regional Archive in Opava), Opava, Czech Republic.

45. "Zápis o poradě konané dne 26.listopad 1946" (Minutes of the Meeting on November 26, 1946), November 26, 1946, Spolek, carton 1, AMO.

46. Pilát, "Výstavba vzorných sídlišť a jejich poslání," 205.

47. Ibid., 204–205. The Kladno team also included Miroslav Koněrza and Emil Kovařík;

Most—Karel Kuthan, Jiří Novotný and Ferdinand Fencl; Ostrava—Anna Friedlová, Vladimír Meduna, Otto Slabý, Jiří Štursa, and Jaroslav Turek.

48. Jiří Štursa, "Sociálně organisační předpoklady pro plánování vzorného sídliště v Ostravě a Mostě" (The Socially Organized Conditions for the Planning of a Model Housing Development in Ostrava and Most), *Architektura ČSR* 7, no. 6–7 (1948): 207–209.

49. For example, the records of the land purchase in Ostrava can be found in MT, carton 348, NA and the meeting minutes of the association in Spolek, cartons 1–20, AMO.

50. Pilát, "Výstavba vzorných sídlišť a jejich poslání," 205.

51. Jiří Štursa, "Vzorné sídliště v Mostě" (The Model Housing Development in Most), *Architektura ČSR* 7, no. 6–7 (1948): 210–213; Josef Havlíček, *Návrhy a stavby* (Projects and Buildings) (Prague: Státní nakladatelství technické literatury, 1964), 70–77. Havlíček would continue working on various projects at the Kladno site until 1959.

52. Pilát, "Výstavba vzorných sídlišť a jejich poslání," 201–202.

53. Havlíček, *Návrhy a stavby*, 70–77; Pilát, "Výstavba vzorných sídlišť a jejich poslání," 201–206; Štursa, "Sociálně organisační předpoklady pro plánování vzorného sídliště v Ostravě a Mostě," 207–209; Štursa, "Vzorné sí dliště v Mostě," 210–213.

54. For examples, see Karel Janů, *Socialistické budování (oč půjde ve stavebnictví a architektuře)* (The Building of Socialism [What's at Stake in Construction and Architecture]) (Prague: Ed. Grégr a syn, 1946).

55. Štursa, "Vzorné sídliště v Mostě," 210.

56. Pilát, "Výstavba vzorných sídlišť a jejich poslání," 203.

57. Ibid.

58. For discussions of the projects and their early construction phases, see MT, cartons 347–351, NA. For Ostrava, see Spolek, AMO.

59. Havlíček, *Návrhy a stavby*, 74. In plan, his original project for the United Nations competition (a three-winged conical tower) was very similar to the Kladno project; see ibid., 97.

60. Havlíček, *Návrhy a stavby*, 70.

61. See Martin Strakoš, "Nová Ostrava a její satelity—část 1" (New Ostrava and Its Satellites, Part 1), *Stavba*, no. 3 (2003): 58–63; Martin Strakoš, "Nová Ostrava a její satelity—část 2" (New Ostrava and Its Satellites, Part 2), *Stavba*, no. 4 (2003): 59–64.

62. "Zápis o schůzi spolku pro výstavbu vzorného sídliště v Ostravě, konané dne 30.září 1947" (Minutes of the Meeting of the Association for the Construction of the Model Housing Development in Ostrava, Sept. 30, 1947), September 30, 1947, MT, carton 348, NA.

63. Pilát, "Výstavba vzorných sídlišť a jejich poslání," 204.

64. "Zápis I.celostátní porady vedoucích všech oddělení Stavoprojektu" (Minutes of the First Nationwide Conference of the Heads of All Stavoprojekt Departments), p. 18, speech by Jiří Voženílek, MT, carton 431, NA.

65. Ibid., 25, speech by Otakar Nový.

66. "Zápis 13.schůze výboru Spolku pro výstavbu vzorného sídliště, konané dne 22.prosince 1949 v domě oddechu SO v Kladně" (Minutes of the 13th committee meeting of the Association for the Construction of the Model Housing Settlement, Dec. 22, 1949, at the SO Recreational Center in Kladno), p. 1, MT, carton 350, NA.

67. Ibid., 3.

68. See, for example, "Výstavba vzorného sídliště—informace o provádění nátěrů" (The construction of the model housing settlement—information on painting), May 19, 1948, carton 351, MT, NA.

69. See, for example, "Výstavba vzorného sídliště—provádění jeho výstavby" (The construction of the model housing settlements—executing the construction), August 31, 1949, carton 351, MT, NA.

70. "Zápis o schůzi představenstva Spolku pro výstavbu vzorného sídliště v Ostravě

konané dne 23.srpna 1950 v úřadovně předsedy KNV v Ostravě s.Arnošta Matýska" (Minutes of the Meeting of the Board of Directors of the Association for the Construction of the Model Housing Settlement in Ostrava, Aug. 23, 1950, in the Office of the President of the Regional National Committee in Ostrava, comrade Arnošt Matýsek), MT, carton 351, NA.

71. The only surviving copy of any of these guides in a library or archive is the twelve-volume 1952 guide for industrial buildings at the National Library in Prague. *Typisační sborník 1952* (Typification Guide 1952), 12 vols. (Prague: Průmyslové výdavatelství, 1951–1952).

72. See Evgeny Dobrenko and Eric Naiman, eds., *The Landscape of Stalinism: The Art and Ideology of Soviet Space* (Seattle: University of Washington Press, 2003).

73. See Strakoš, "Nová Ostrava a její satelity—část 1," 58–63; Strakoš, "Nová Ostrava a její satelity—část 2," 59–64.

74. For more on Kroha in the 1950s, see Kimberly Elman Zarecor, "Stavoprojekt and the Atelier of National Artist Jiří Kroha in the 1950s," in *Jiří Kroha (1893–1974)—Architect, Painter, Designer, Theorist: A 20th-Century Metamorphosis*, ed. Marcela Macharačková (Brno: Era; Muzeum města Brna, 2007), 328–365.

75. Jiří Kroha, "K základním otázkám první konference architektů v ČSR" (On the Fundamental Questions of the First Conference of Architects in Czechoslovakia), *Architektura ČSR* 11, no. 5–6 (1952): 139–150.

76. Updates on the model housing developments can be found in 1958 and 1959 articles on housing in Czechoslovakia; see Ferdinand Balcárek and Karel Storch, "Deset let typisaze v Československu" (Ten Years of Typification in Czechoslovakia), *Architektura ČSR* 17, no. 7 (1958): 293–308; Josef Havlíček, "Z dostavby sídliště Vítězného února v Kladně" (On the Completion of the Housing Development on Victory of February Street in Kladno), *Architektura ČSR* 18, no. 4 (1959): 210–214; Jiří Hrůza, "Sídliště na Mostecku" (The Housing Developments of the Most Region), *Architektura ČSR* 17, no. 2 (1958): 62–63.

77. Havlíček, *Návrhy a stavby*, 72.

78. For more on Most, see Eagle Glassheim, "Most, the Town that Moved: Coal, Communists, and the 'Gypsy Question' in Post-War Czechoslovakia," *Environment and History* 13, no. 4 (2007): 447–476.

4 SANCTIONING MODERNISM AND TRADITION
ITALIAN ARCHITECTURE, THE VERNACULAR, AND THE STATE

MICHELANGELO SABATINO

From the early 1920s to the late 1950s the dialectic of modernism and tradition, whether classical or vernacular, characterized the Italian state's architectural patronage.[1] This essay investigates post–World War II state-sponsored building initiatives, mainly housing, and the architectural debates accompanying their design and realization. It sets them against the backdrop of Italian architectural discourse on identity that surfaced during the Fascist period (1922–1943) and continued to weigh heavily on the decisions of architects and urban designers in postwar democratic Italy. The essay focuses on the role that appropriation of extant vernacular building traditions and the abandonment of classicism played in facilitating the emergence of a regionalist modernism sanctioned by the state during the postwar years. In critically examining the renewed interest in the vernacular (ordinary buildings and objects manufactured by and for the agrarian peasantry), first "discovered" by ethnographers and geographers during the 1910s and afterward in the 1920s by artists and architects, I argue that Italian postwar modernism emerged because the state's nationalist identity agenda based on classicism was sidelined in favor of an interest in regionally inflected vernacular traditions. What makes Italy's contribution to a broader international mid-twentieth-century discourse on architectural modernism during those years distinctive is that *sanctioning modernism* and *sanctioning tradition* overlapped strategically. During those years, the deployment of tradition in the service of a discourse on cultural, political, and social identity was critical to the ways the Italian state chose to represent its priorities at home and abroad.

In terms of high-profile state-sponsored architectural realizations during the postwar years, one need only recall the differences in approach that surfaced between Italy and other countries at the 1958 Brussels World's Fair, whose symbol became the surreal Atomium by André Waterkeyn.[2] At the first international exposition to be held after the end of the traumatic Second World War, Italy's facade-less "village," characterized by its stereotomic walls and traditional spatial

FIGURE 4.1. Ernesto Rogers et al., Italian Pavilion, Brussels, 1958. Rendering. BBPR Archive/Milan Polytechnic.

configuration typical of Mediterranean hill towns, contrasted with the ethereal tectonic qualities of Egon Eiermann's pavilion for Germany and the ornamental monumentality of Edward Durell Stone's U.S. Pavilion (figure 4.1). While Eiermann's modernist pavilion avoided any overt association with tradition, Italian architects associated with Studio Architetti BBPR and Ernesto N. Rogers (as well as Lodovico Barbiano di Belgiojoso and Enrico Peressutti), such as Adolfo De Carlo, Ignazio Gardella, Giuseppe Perugini, and Ludovico Quaroni, sought to recalibrate the ambivalent relationship between modernism and tradition that came to distinguish the Fascist regime's strategic embrace of classicism.[3] Recall, for example, the bombastic classicism that characterized much of the architecture and urban planning behind the Fascist regime's last sustained effort in self-promotion via world fairs—the E42 (Esposizione Universale Roma) in Rome that was canceled due to the onset of World War II.

Unlike most progressive architects who fled Nazi Germany only to return decades later or who never again set foot in their homeland, the majority of architects who had previously worked with the Fascist regime remained in Italy during the postwar years.[4] For many of these architects, a renewed interest in the

FIGURE 4.2. Adalberto Libera (with Adolfo Amitrano), Casa Malaparte, Capri, 1942. Photo by author.

vernacular tradition helped to distance themselves from classicism and its associations with Fascism. By challenging the historiography of twentieth-century Italian architecture, which breaks the subjects into periods generally coincident with wars, as misleading, I would like to demonstrate that such breaks assume a simplistic linear cause-and-effect relationship between politics and culture. Manfredo Tafuri was the first architectural historian in Italy to declare that "the essential continuity between Italian design of the prewar period and that of the years from 1945 to 1960 is an historical fact that has not yet been sufficiently recognized."[5] To be sure, the difficult negotiation between modernism and tradition in the service of Fascist cultural politics—whether Giuseppe Terragni's embrace of abstract classicism in his Casa del Fascio in Como (1936) or Adalberto Libera's vernacular-infused rationalist Casa Malaparte in Capri (1942)—meant that international recognition of Italy's "new" architecture under Fascism was late in coming from militant critics who viewed modernism as antithetical to tradition (figure 4.2). Not by coincidence, up until the 1960s and 1970s, when major historiographical revisions began, Futurism continued to be considered Italy's only contribution to the avant-garde precisely because of the antitraditional bias of its most celebrated proponents, Antonio Sant'Elia and Filippo Tommaso Marinetti. Citing the Italian Pavilion in Brussels and other realizations of the 1950s that engaged modernism and tradition, English architecture critic and historian

Reyner Banham accused Italian architects of "infantile regression" in the name of Neo-Liberty.⁶ Banham openly questioned why Ernesto N. Rogers, "the hero-figure of European architecture in the late Forties and early Fifties," appeared to be abandoning modernism for a tradition-infused "Neo-Liberty." Banham could simply not fathom why talented Italian postwar architects had abandoned the example set by Futurist trailblazer Sant'Elia.

An exception to this trend among non-Italian historians and critics to marginalize Italy's contribution to modern architecture on the basis of its dialogue with tradition is found in Sigfried Giedion's *A Decade of New Architecture* (1951). Giedion's book includes buildings realized under Fascism such as the Studio Architetti BBPR's sun-therapy colony in Legnano (1938) despite its implicit dialogue with classical tradition by way of the two-story portico and symmetrical bathing pavilion. Alfred Roth's publication *The New Architecture Presented in 20 Examples*, published nearly a decade earlier in 1940, also included the sun-therapy colony. Critical reappraisals of Italian architecture under Fascism during the late 1960s and 1970s coincided with the rise of Neo-Rationalism spearheaded by architects like Aldo Rossi (1931–1997) and Giorgio Grassi (1935–).

REGIONALIST MODERNISM FOR DEMOCRATIC ITALY

Italy's modernism developed out of late-nineteenth-century debates over what constituted national identity in the arts and architecture in a country composed of diverse regional vernaculars and a formidable classical tradition. This predicament of reinventing its modern Italian identity—first after unification in 1861, then following the Fascist coup of 1922—was questioned again after the end of World War II when the recent memory of excesses of Fascist nationalism led architects, artists, and intellectuals to carefully rethink the role of *Italianness*. A popular referendum in 1946 led to the establishment of a democratic republic, changing, at least on a parliamentary level, the political circumstances of architectural practice, which had been regimented by laws set up by the Fascist regime.⁷

During the postwar years the need for housing was imperative, due to not only the destruction of cities from bombardment but also the mass migration of rural labor from the southern and central regions of Italy, in which farmers abandoned their villages and towns to seek employment in the industrial cities of Milan, Genoa, and Turin. This led the new democratic government—financially supported by the American Marshall Plan—to support a series of modernist architectural and urban planning initiatives aimed at "rebuilding the house of man" in both physical and spiritual terms.⁸ The primary state-sponsored housing agency, INA-Casa, was founded in 1949 as part of the "Piano Fanfani." This program, named after the political leader Amintore Fanfani, who sought to implement the construction of 300,000 dwelling units, commissioned Italian architects to design housing for the working class. In Rome, the Tiburtino (1950–1954) by Ludovico Quaroni and Mario Ridolfi and the Tuscolano III (1950–1954) by Adalberto Libera

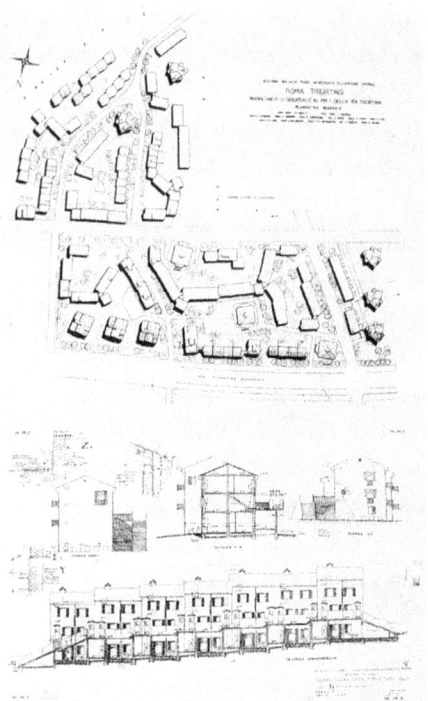

FIGURE 4.3. Mario Ridolfi, Tiburtino Row House, 1950–1954. Drawing (elevation, section, and plan). INA-Casa, Rome.

are among the most distinguished realizations of a program that tended to employ low-tech vernacular materials and construction processes for reasons that were mainly pragmatic and "cultural" (low-cost manual labor and easily available materials) (figure 4.3).

Another important initiative was La Martella (1951–1954), a postwar New Town at the outskirts of the southern Italian town of Matera, sponsored by the UNRRA-Casas (United Nations Relief and Rehabilitation Administration), a major building program that complemented the efforts of INA-Casa (figure 4.4).[9] Both of these housing initiatives received American financial support, and both of them "recycled building types that had been developed before the war and were still within Italian domestic architectural traditions."[10] In all of these postwar realizations supported by the state, architects and urban planners were mindful of the political risks surrounding large-scale initiatives such as the Fascist New Towns realized for the Pontine Marshes—including Littoria (1932, now Latina), Sabaudia (1934), Pontinia (1935), Aprilia (1937), and Pomezia (1939)—because these had required a strong central authority to execute. A reaction against this sort of top-down power dynamic and a new enthusiasm for neighborhoods emerged in large part dictated by fear of history repeating itself and as a result of the fragile economy of postwar Italy.[11]

In Rome, the multiphased realizations for Tiburtino and the Tuscolano III set the architectural standard for state-sponsored housing that sanctioned modernist design which appropriated the formal and material qualities of vernacular buildings, towns, and hamlets. Despite the reactionary political and social objectives of the antiurban policies of Benito Mussolini's Fascist regime, interest in vernacular building traditions associated with agrarian peoples still appealed strongly to Italian architects of the postwar period because their organic materials and human scale represented an antithesis to most of the classically inspired buildings clad in "noble" materials such as travertine endorsed by Mussolini's megalomaniacal regime.[12] Despite the strategic use of classicism to represent Fascist authority, the propaganda literature of Fascist New Towns, for example, abounds with images of stark neo-vernacular cottages. For postwar architects

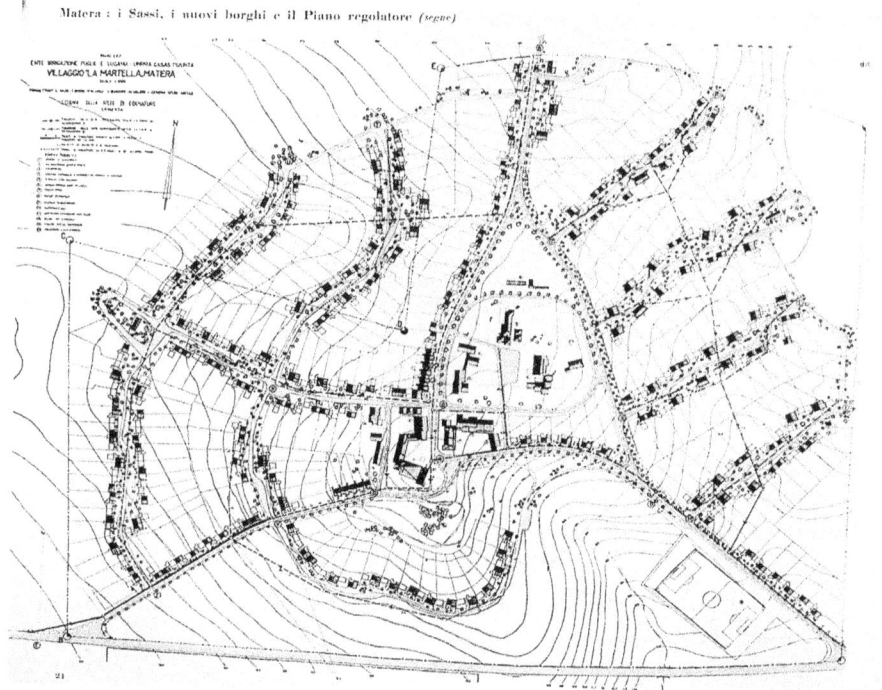

FIGURE 4.4. Ludovico Quaroni et al. (L. Agati, F. Gorio, P. M. Lugli, M. Valori), "La Martella," Matera, 1951–1954. Plan. *Urbanistica*, n. 15–16, 1955.

working on behalf of the democratic Italian State, reusing cues from regional vernacular traditions was less threatening than classicism because of the latter's overpowering association with overt nationalism and the collapsed Fascist regime. Significantly, the lead architects involved in these projects such as Mario Ridolfi and Ludovico Quaroni (Tiburtino) and Adalberto Libera (Tuscolano III, 1950–1954) had also designed a number of classically inspired and thoughtful buildings for the Fascist regime.

In the case of Tiburtino, for example, Ridolfi and Quaroni sought to reference the vernacular with a series of practical and cultural considerations. First, they selected and combined different housing types. By so doing, they sought to temper the potentially alienating qualities of uniformity by selecting a variety of low-density horizontal row houses alongside high-density vertical towers. By eschewing a homogeneous rationalist grid in favor of winding roads typical of villages or towns, these architects sought to respond to the changes in the topography of the site and in so doing temper the abstraction of utopian planning with site-specific place-making strategies. Postwar architects in Italy did not view appropriating cues from the extant vernacular tradition as turning their backs on modernism but simply as finding new modes of regionalist expression that avoided the relentless repetition of the international style which eventually surfaced in such contemporary U.S. public housing complexes as Hellmuth, Yamasaki and Leinweber's Pruitt Homes and Igoe Apartments in St. Louis, Missouri (1955). With their sociological emphasis on community and its architectural correlate, collective form, the INA-Casa (and UNRRA-Casas) complexes also offered an alternative to the aggressive urban palazzo type that invaded Italian cities during the Fascist era and increased during the postwar years thanks to a huge rise in privately funded, developer-driven initiatives in collusion with local authorities. Here the state-sponsored initiatives that simultaneously sanctioned modernism and tradition were oftentimes overshadowed by an enormous volume of poorly designed and conceived buildings which cropped up all over Italy but shared little of the sophistication of Tiburtino's and Tuscolano III's regionalist declinations.

Extant vernaculars inspired regionalist modernist projects in more varied ways so as to address the social realities and psychological needs of rural families being consolidated into the urban working class. While an enormous quantity of the rural peasantry left Italy altogether at the turn of the twentieth century, internal emigration from the countryside to the industrial cities of central and northern Italy in the 1950s characterized postwar economic and demographic cycles. The designs of the new postwar communities sought to re-create the spatial intimacy and social compactness of rural settlements, in which public and private spaces were often interlocked. Although the new housing estates built in Rome and elsewhere shared approaches with their counterparts in Milan, Genoa, and Turin—especially in terms of unit planning and construction standards—their architectural languages differed insomuch as they combined regional traditions with modernist idioms in distinctive ways. For example, earth-toned stuccos and brick ornaments were used by Ridolfi in his Tiburtino neighborhood row houses to echo the "minor architecture" of nearby hill towns (the so-called *Castelli romani*) of the Latium region, whereas the whitewashed stucco finish typical of southern Italian vernacular was used by Quaroni for the neo-vernacular dwelling units of his La Martella (figure 4.5).

Fascist ideology promoted a populism grounded in a top-down paternalistic relationship between the state and its citizens. Not surprisingly, even the relationship between modernism and tradition in state-sponsored architecture and urban planning initiatives during those years was often more prescriptive than a matter of choice. Classicism was the Fascist regime's preferred language for public buildings insofar as it conveyed an authority that was already claimed by emperors and popes, whereas the vernacular tradition (the typical "cottage" known as the *casa colonica*) was only deployed within the realm of domesticity in which the stakes of representing national identity were decidedly lower. In contrast, postwar architects were less interested in these hierarchies and more intent on producing architecture that seemed to open a dialogue with the social needs and cultural identities of the inhabitants of the new neighborhoods.

If consensus was achieved by way of heavy-handed propaganda and manipulation in the interwar Fascist years, its formation during the postwar years rested

FIGURE 4.5. Mario Ridolfi, Tiburtino Row House. Detail. Photo by author.

on grassroots strategies. Regional vernaculars were thus appropriated by postwar architects, many of whom had worked for the Fascist regime, to rethink modernism in terms of regionally specific identities. During these years Italian architects carefully studied and deployed lessons from Italy's rural heritage not only in the realm of public housing but also in such building types as ski lodges and weekend retreats for the Italian "leisure class," the wealthy northern urban elites who turned to nature on the weekend to escape the chaos of the city. Significant examples of these experiments in transforming extant Alpine vernacular forms and materials are the ski lodge at Lago Nero in Sauze d'Oulx (1946) and the Casa del Sole hotel in Cervinia (1955), both by the Turin architect Carlo Mollino, and Franco Albini's youth hostel Albergo Rifugio Pirovano, also in Cervinia (1952). Although these were not state-sponsored buildings, they indicate that Italians of different social classes were comfortable with embracing modernism and tradition even within the realm of leisure. Whether directed toward state- or privately funded initiatives, extant vernacular buildings helped bolster the search for a modernist Italian architecture tempered by regionalist identities.

Postwar developments within and outside of the domain of state-financed architecture were paralleled (if not spearheaded) by innovations in literature, film, and art. In the wake of an enduring romance during Fascism with the "myth of the Mediterranean" (with all of its classical iterations in art, architecture, and literature), Italy's intelligentsia turned their attention during the postwar years to the poetry of "reality" as seen through the experiences of the agrarian and working-class proletariat.[13] Left-wing Neorealist architects looked for guidance to Antonio Gramsci's posthumously published *Letteratura e vita nazionale* (1950) and, subsequently, Alberto Asor Rosa's *Scrittori e popolo: Saggio sulla letteratura populista in Italia* (1965). Such pioneering Neorealist films as Michelangelo Antonioni's *Gente del Po* (1943) focused on the day-to-day lives of ordinary people such as poor fishermen instead of celebrating the heroics of Italy's past glories. Luchino Visconti's film *La Terra Trema* (1948) was loosely based on the "verismo" of writer Giovanni Verga's 1881 novel *I Malavoglia* (The House by the Medlar Tree) and depicted the struggles of fishermen in a small Sicilian village. In the same vein as Visconti's films, Pier Paolo Pasolini and other directors explored the rugged vitality of the peasantry and working-class proletariat by employing non-professional actors, and in doing so they paralleled Italian architects' sustained interest in "anonymous," "unpedigreed" buildings.

Among architects, artists, and filmmakers, the "culture" of the marginalized peasantry, of the South in particular, occupied a central place. Carlo Levi's autobiographical book *Christ Stopped at Eboli—The Story of a Year* (first published in 1945 and translated into English in 1947), an account of the author's exile, imposed on him by the Fascist regime, to the "God forsaken" region of Lucania (currently known as Basilicata), reflects the continuum of interwar experiences and postwar reflections (figure 4.6).[14] Levi's account helped usher in the Neorealism movement in postwar Italian film, art, and architecture. The gripping, poetic tale of the year Levi spent among the southerners of the Basilicata region attracted the interest of intellectuals, artists, and architects in Italy and beyond. His fascination with the natural and built environment of Basilicata was reflected in the ethereal palette of whites and pinks in the paintings he produced during his time away from Turin: "It had been hard at first. Grassano, like all the villages hereabouts, is a streak of white at the summit of a bare hill, a sort of miniature imaginary Jerusalem in the solitude of the desert."[15] Like the

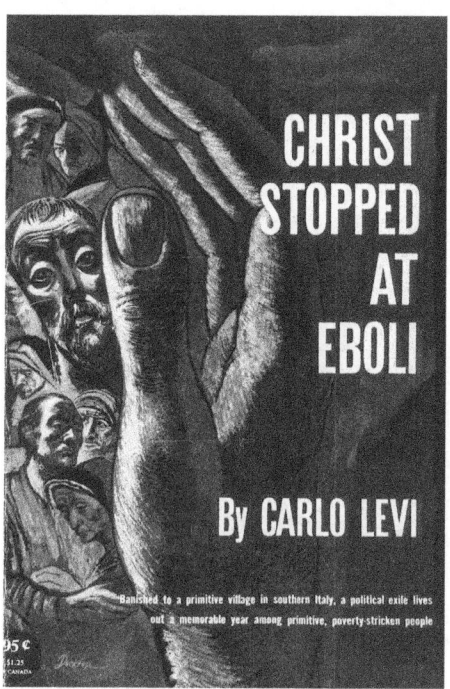

FIGURE 4.6. Carlo Levi, *Christ Stopped at Eboli* (1945). Book cover. New York: Farrar, Straus and Co., 1947.

accounts of the rural, disenfranchised peasantry of the Agro Romano by the artist and social reformer Duilio Cambellotti, Levi's work recalls the "heroic atmosphere" and otherness of "timeless" peasants living in remote hill towns.[16] During his exile, Levi observed the customs and mentality of an archaic agricultural society that had remained virtually unchanged by the rise of industrialization in other parts of the country.

Fascination for the dignified yet modest quotidian realities of the Italian peasantry extended beyond Italy's national borders. A case in point is the collaboration between American photographer Paul Strand and the Italian playwright Cesare Zavattini for their *Un Paese: Portrait of an Italian Village* (published in Italian in 1955 and translated into English in 1997). Zavattini's essay accompanied Strand's stark, psychologically penetrating black-and-white photographs of the rural environment of Luzarra and its inhabitants. Zavattini wrote, "Let's look together at Paul Strand's photographs, beneath which you can read the secret thoughts of my fellow-townsmen. The words are substantially theirs, and I think I rarely betray their spirit. And those people you see, those who speak, weren't chosen by us specifically because they had something to say."[17] Only a year after the publication of Strand's photographic essay, the writer Italo Calvino added to the growing postwar interest in the peasantry by publishing an important anthology of Italian folktales he gathered from existing works originally written (or recounted) in local dialects.[18]

These social and cultural struggles to come to terms with the needs of the "people" (i.e., the agrarian peasantry and working-class proletariat), as well as to distance themselves from the failures of the Fascist regime, informed the choice of terms in architectural discourse concerning the appropriation of the vernacular tradition in the early 1950s. The Milanese architect Giancarlo De Carlo employed the phrase *architettura spontanea* (spontaneous architecture) in the 1951 Milan Triennale exhibition he curated with Franco Albini and Giuseppe Samonà to describe extant vernacular buildings and environments featured in the exhibition (figure 4.7). De Carlo's term "spontaneous architecture" was the most widely circulated on account of the exhibition and echoed the content, if

FIGURE 4.7. Giancarlo De Carlo et al., *Mostra di architettura spontanea* (Spontaneous Architecture Exhibition), Milan Triennale, 1951. Photographer unknown.

FIGURE 4.8. Giuseppe Pagano and Werner Daniel, *Architettura rurale italiana* (Italian Rural Architecture), Milan Triennale, 1936. Exhibition. Photographer unknown.

not the exact terminology, employed by curators Giuseppe Pagano and Werner (Guarniero) Daniel in their Milan Triennale exhibition of 1936 and catalogue titled *Architettura rurale italiana: Funzionalità della casa rurale* (Rural Italian Architecture: Functionality of the Rural House) (figure 4.8). Pagano wrote thus about rural architecture of Italy:

> The repertory of rural architecture reveals an immense encyclopedia of abstract forms and creative expressions with obvious connections to the land, climate, economy, and technology. As such, an examination of rural architecture, conducted with these above mentioned criteria in mind, is useful and necessary to understand the causal relationships that the stylistic analysis of architecture has led us to forget. Rural architecture represents the first and immediate victory of man extracting sustenance from the land. Although it is a victory dictated by necessity, it is not devoid of artistic achievements.[19]

During the postwar years, the discourse of modernism in Italy was enhanced by numerous definitions of vernacular architecture. The architectural historian Egle Trincanato adopted the term "minor architecture" to describe the non-architect-designed buildings of Venice in her book *Venezia minore* (1948), which she wrote based on research conducted during the interwar years. The architect-historian Roberto Pane, in his essay "Architettura e letteratura" (Architecture and Literature) (1948), added even more currency to the concept of *architettura minore* (minor architecture) that had been used during the 1920s by such proponents of "contextualism" as Gustavo Giovannoni and Marcello Piacentini.[20]

While other concepts and terms such as "organic architecture" also relied on some basic principles of vernacular building practices with its relationships to site and the nature of materials, critic and historian Bruno Zevi denied its relationship to Neorealism.[21] Even though most architects throughout Italy who were actively involved in state-sponsored realizations shared a common desire to rethink the dialectic of modernism and tradition during those years, the debate was polarized between Rome and Milan. The positions were centered on Zevi's journal *Metron* and the Association for Organic Architecture (APAO) in Rome, Ernesto N. Rogers's journal *Casabella-Continuità*, and the Movimento Studi Architettura (MSA) in Milan.[22] Historians have acknowledged these different positions by contrasting the expressionist Neorealism of the Monument to the Fosse Ardeatine by Mario Fiorentino, Giuseppe Perugini et al. (1944–1947) with the pristine, Neo-Rationalism of Studio Architetti BBPR's Milan Monument to the Dead in the Concentration Camps in Germany (1946).[23] Despite these linguistic differences, Italian architects and intellectuals collectively agreed that the alienating qualities of international-style modernism could be tempered with a creative dialogue with tradition.

FROM CAVES TO COTTAGES:
A NEW VILLAGE FOR THE OUTSKIRTS OF MATERA

Completed in 1954, the village of La Martella outside the town of Matera in southern Italy's Basilicata was one of the most significant postwar realizations in which vernacular housing types like the *casa colonica* were reimagined as part of an autonomous community for peasants. The peasants had been inhabiting cave dwellings referred to as "sassi di Matera" (stones of Matera). Ludovico Quaroni led the team of architects, which included Michele Agati, Federico Gorio, Piero Maria Lugli, and Michele Valori. Commenting on the design, De Carlo lauded the "realism" of its conception and realization: "The urban planners who designed this village did not think about realizing an ideal utopian dream city. But rather, confronted with the problem of having to build an organism that could provide housing for a group of peasants originally living in the 'Sassi' of Matera, they began their work thinking about the real limits of this problem."[24] For De Carlo, La Martella demonstrated how extant models of rural architecture could be employed to promote agreeable living conditions for a low-income community. In the case of La Martella, housing coexisted with small artisanal *bottege* (workshops), a church, and other service-oriented buildings aimed at creating an autonomous and self-sufficient community (figure 4.9).

Quaroni's La Martella shared some similarities with the state-financed New Towns of the Roman littoral realized under Fascism during the mid-1930s. However, the political and economic conditions that made these projects possible during the interwar years changed radically after the fall of Fascism. Although the New Towns combined gridded and winding street patterns, most postwar housing estates steered clear of orthogonal layouts. Despite the naturalistic picturesque quality of the meandering streets, the serial designs of the duplex houses of La Martella suggest the fusion of the "spontaneous" preindustrial

FIGURE 4.9. Ludovico Quaroni and collaborators (Federico Gorio, Michele Valori, Piero Maria Lugli, Michele Agati), La Martella, Matera, 1954. Plan. IN-ARCH, Rome.

vernacular and machine-age serial production. Like the Fascist New Towns, which also adopted the whitewashed *casa colonica* (cottage) as a basic type for housing displaced peasant communities, La Martella offered living conditions that provided peasant families with highly improved hygienic conveniences, such as access to plumbing, while providing spaces for sustaining their sense of identification with the traditions of the region and with the rituals of agrarian life. The neo-vernacular designs of La Martella separated living space from agrarian workspaces unlike the *sassi*, where animals and their custodians often shared quarters.[25]

Despite the good intentions behind the planning and realization of La Martella, a number of its inhabitants complained about leaving the sassi. This reaction to the top-down paternalism, however benevolent, of the architectural professionals who were called to address the *questione meridionale* (the Southern Question) surfaced as the debate over modernism and tradition ensued. As the differences between the industrial North and the agrarian South became increasingly accentuated and, through television, better known after the mid-1950s, social tensions intensified. This paternalistic attitude, especially diffuse among "book-fed" intellectuals and professionals, had already been denounced by Antonio Gramsci and was repeated in the postwar years by philosopher-anthropologist Ernesto De Martino and a number of writers.[26] Despite the shared pursuit of rebuilding Italy's national image and self-esteem after the devastating outcome of Fascism, disparity between the rich of the industrial North and the poor of the agrarian South was even more troublesome during the mid-1950s when Italy's so-called economic miracle began.

TIBURTINO AND TUSCOLANO III:
NEW NEIGHBORHOODS FOR THE PROLETARIAT

If La Martella was one of the most celebrated postwar examples of architectural Neorealism in Italy's South, the Tiburtino designed by Ridolfi and Quaroni in collaboration with other architects was central Italy's most lasting contribution. The white surfaces and basic "cubist" volumes associated with interwar Rationalist design, which resurfaced in the neo-vernacular cottages of Quaroni's La Martella, were replaced in Ridolfi's row houses for the Tiburtino neighborhood by the tactile, organic textures of ornamental brick and the ochre-tone surfaces typical of *Castelli romani*. Despite the assertive presence of housing types reflecting modernist concepts of *Existenz minimum* such as the *casa torre* (apartment tower) and *casa in linea* (town or row house–type), the informal, welcoming atmosphere of the Tiburtino neighborhood is that of an Italian hill town conveyed through grade changes and winding streets. Although the overall quality of the different buildings of the neighborhood is noteworthy (with designs by architects such as Mario Fiorentino, Carlo Aymonino, and Federico Gorio), Ridolfi's *case a schiera con ballatoio* (row houses with balconies) are the most evocative because

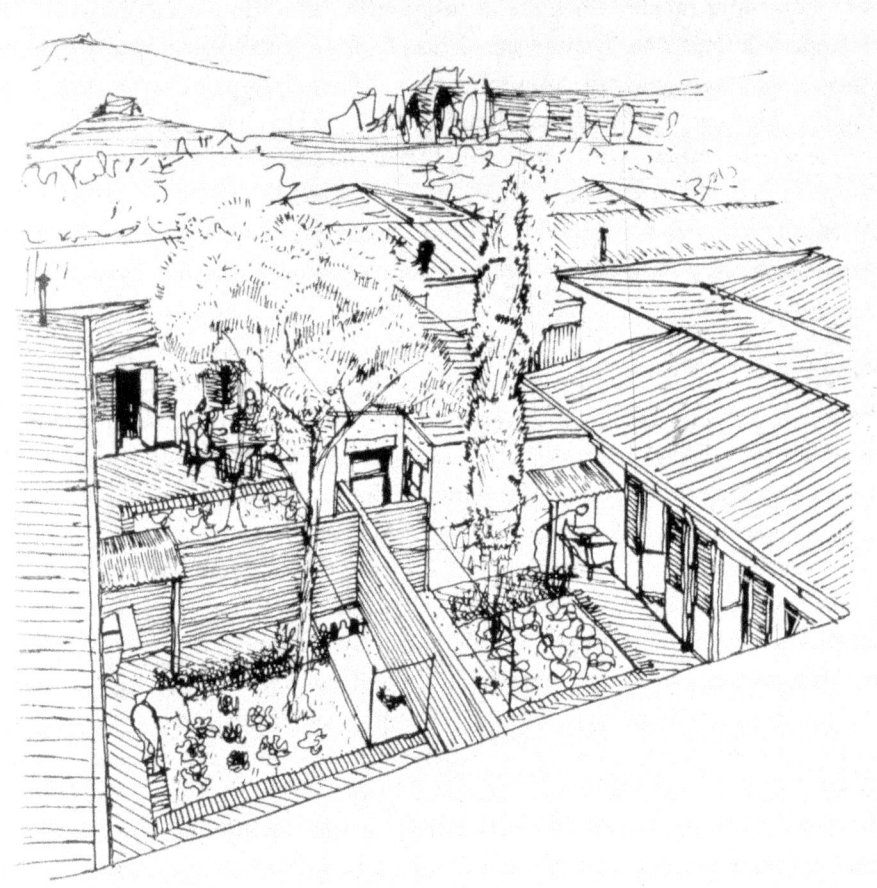

FIGURE 4.10. Adalberto Libera, Tuscolano, Rome, 1950–1954. View of courtyard houses. *Casabella-Continuità* 207, 1955.

he exploited the changing topography of the site to create a terraced effect and a continuous above-street-level promenade. With this project, Ridolfi became the first of the postwar architects to introduce ornamental brick screens that echoed the "gelosie" typically found in the agrarian buildings the inhabitants abandoned when moving to the city.[27]

Adalberto Libera's housing for the Tuscolano III neighborhood of Rome, also built under the auspices of INA-Casa, employs the classical and vernacular courtyard type as the primary model for one-story housing (figure 4.10). In this state-sponsored housing initiative, Libera too grappled with how to reconcile modernism and tradition. Zevi grasped the innovative qualities of the complex, referring to it as a *grattacielo straiato* (reclining skyscraper) or as a "horizontal Unité d'Habitation."[28] Like Tiburtino, Tuscolano III was a self-contained community in which inhabitants were offered basic services along with their domestic units. Although the simple, introverted quality of the facade-less Tuscolano III units shared little with Libera's iconic Casa Malaparte completed under Fascism in 1942, they are linked by a common commitment to reinterpreting the Italian (and Mediterranean) vernacular tradition. In adopting the common *domus* type for collective housing, Libera demonstrated that the vernacular was a fertile source that continued to inform Italian architecture under Fascism as well as Democracy.

As the "other" of classicism, the vernacular tradition was associated with the peasantry and its built environments and was appropriated by architects during the postwar years. While classicism was a source of contention after the end of the Fascist regime, the appropriation of extant vernacular buildings associated with the rural peasantry tended to bring architects of different political persuasions together to fulfill the needs of working-class communities. The vernacular traditions of the "subaltern" class—to use the vivid adjective coined by Gramsci—displaced the towering classical monuments of modern-day caesars and popes in the discourse of mid-twentieth-century Italian architecture and urbanism. Architects in Italy engaged by the state tempered modernism with regional traditions to achieve forms of architectural expression that could respond to the psychological and practical needs of the new working class. To dismiss this enterprise as antimodern, as some militant critics such as Reyner Banham have done (a case in point is his reaction to Italy's pavilion for the Brussels World's Fair of 1958), is to ignore its significant and recurring discursive role. The vernacular has functioned as the dialectical other of classicism, distancing itself from association with militarism, oppression, and violence. Only by resisting a reading that sees the appropriation of the vernacular as a conservative phenomenon can one begin to appreciate its dialectical role in the Italian state's desire to synthesize modernism and tradition during the postwar years.

NOTES

1. For an in-depth analysis of this topic, see my recent books: *Pride in Modesty: Modernist Architecture and the Vernacular Tradition in Italy* (Toronto and Buffalo: University of Toronto Press, 2010) and, with Jean-François Lejeune, *Modern Architecture and the Mediterranean: Vernacular Dialogues and Contested Identities* (London: Routledge, 2010). I wish to thank the organizers of *Sanctioning Modernism—A Symposium on Post-WWII Architecture*, Vladimir Kulić, Monica Penick, and Timothy Parker, for inviting me to share my research with colleagues and students. A special thank-you goes to my session chair Vladimir for his assistance throughout the entire process.

2. For an overview of the exposition, see Rita Devos and Mil de Kooning, eds., *L'architecture moderne à l'Expo 58* (Brussels: Fonds Mercator et Dexia Banque, 2006); in particular see Geert Bekaert, "Un volto sincero—Le Pavillon Italien," 131–143.

3. Ernesto Rogers, "The Future Was Not to Be Seen at Brussels," *Architects Year Book 9* (1960): 132–139.

4. Stephanie Barron and Sabine Eckmann, *Exiles + Emigrés—The Flight of European Artists from Hitler* (New York: Harry N. Abrams, 1997), in particular see 210–252.

5. Manfredo Tafuri, "Design and Technological Utopia," in *Italy: The New Domestic Landscape; Achievements and Problems of Italian Design*, ed. Emilio Ambasz (New York and Florence: Museum of Modern Art and Centro Di, 1972), 388–404.

6. Reyner Banham, "Neoliberty—The Italian Retreat from Modern Architecture," *Architectural Review* 125.747 (April 1959): 231–235.

7. For a history of postwar Italy, see Paul Ginsborg, *A History of Contemporary Italy: Society and Politics, 1943–1988* (London and New York: Penguin Books, 1990); Martin Clark, *Modern Italy, 1871 to the Present* (New York: Pearson Longman, 2008).

8. See Dennis Doordan, "Rebuilding the House of Man," in *The Italian Metamorphosis, 1943–1968*, ed. Germano Celant (New York: H. N. Abrams, 1994), 586–595.

9. See Marida Talamona, "Dieci anni di politica dell'Unrra Casas: dalle case ai senzatetto ai borghi rurali nel Mezzogiorno d'Italia (1945–1955). Il ruolo di Adriano Olivetti," in *Costruire la città dell'uomo – Adriano Olivetti e l'urbanistica*, ed. Carlo Olmo (Milan: Edizioni di Comunità, 2001), 173–204.

10. Paolo Scrivano, "Signs of Americanization in Italian Domestic Life: Italy's Postwar Conversion to Consumerism," *Journal of Contemporary History* 40, no. 2 (April 2005): 317–340.

11. Paolo Nicoloso, "Genealogie del piano Fanfani 1939–1950," in *La grande ricostruzione. Il piano Ina-Casa e l'Italia degli anni 50*, ed. Paola Di Biagi (Rome: Donzelli, 2001), 33–62. See also Sergio Pace, "Una solidarietà agevolata: il Piano INA-Casa, 1948–49," *Rassegna* 54 (June 1993): 20–27.

12. For an overview of classicism in Italian interwar architecture, see Giorgio Ciucci, "Italian Architecture during the Fascist Period—Classicism between Neoclassicism and Rationalism: The Many Souls of the Classical," *Harvard Architectural Review* 5 (1987): 76–87. See also Spiro Kostof, *The Third Rome, 1870–1950: Traffic and Glory* (Berkeley: University Art Museum, 1973), and Antonio Cederna, *Mussolini urbanista. Lo sventramento di Roma negli Anni del Consenso* (Rome and Bari: Laterza, 1979).

13. On Neorealism and architecture, see Bruno Reichlin, "Figures of Neorealism in Italian Architecture (Part 1)," *Grey Room* 5 (Fall 2001): 78–101, and "Figures of Neorealism in Italian Architecture (Part 2)," *Grey Room* 6 (Winter 2002): 110–133; and Maristella Casciato, "Neo-Realism in Italian Architecture," in *Anxious Modernisms: Experimentation in Postwar Architectural Culture*, ed. Sarah Williams Goldhagen and Rejean Legault (Cambridge, MA, and Montreal: MIT Press and CCA, 2000), 25–53. See also Vittorio Magnago Lampugnani, "The Myth of Reality: Notes on Neorealism in Italy 1946–56," in *Architecture and Arts 1900/2004: A Century of Creative Projects in Building, Design, Cinema, Painting, Sculpture*, ed. Germano Celant (Milan: Skira, 2004), 75–79.

14. Carlo Levi, *Cristo si è fermato a Eboli* (Turin: Einaudi, 1945), translated as *Christ Stopped at Eboli* (New York: Farrar, Straus and Co., 1947), republished by Farrar, Straus and Giroux in 2006. A film adaptation directed by Francesco Rosi appeared in 1980.

15. Ibid., 15. On Levi as a painter during his period of exile, see Pia Vivarelli, ed., *Carlo Levi e la Lucania. Dipinti del confino 1935–1936* (Rome: De Luca, 1990).

16. Duilio Cambellotti, "La campagna romana ante bonifica," in *Duilio Cambellotti—Teatro—Storia—Arte*, ed. Mario Quesada (Palermo: Edizioni Novecento, 1982), 211–219.

17. Published in Italian as Cesare Zavattini, *Un paese* (Turin: Einaudi, 1955); translated as *Un Paese: Portrait of an Italian Village*, trans. Marguerite Shore (New York: Aperture, 1997).

18. Italo Calvino, *Fiabe italiane. Raccolte dalla tradizione popolare durante gli ultimi cento anni e trascritte in lingua dai vari dialetti* (Turin: Einaudi, 1956); translated as *Italian Folktales Selected and Retold by Italo Calvino* (New York: Harcourt, 1980).

19. Giuseppe Pagano, "Documenti di architettura rurale," *Casabella* 8, no. 95 (November 1935): 18–25. See my translation of Pagano's text in "Pride in Modesty: Giuseppe Pagano's "Architettura rurale," "Documenting Rural Architecture by Giuseppe Pagano," *Journal of Architectural Education* 63, no. 2 (March 2010): 92–98.

20. Republished in Roberto Pane, *Architettura e arti figurative* (Venice: Neri Pozza Editore, 1948), 63–73.

21. "L'architettura organica secondo Bruno Zevi e la 'riscoperta' di Wright in Italia," in Fabrizio Brunetti, *L'architettura in Italia negli anni della ricostruzione* (Florence: Alinea Editrice, 1986): 125–142.

22. On the history of *Metron*, see Maristella Casciato, "Gli esordi della rivista 'Metron': Eventi e Protagonisti," *Rassegna di architettura e urbanistica* 117 (September–December 2005): 45–55. For a translation of the founding constitution of APAO, see Joan Ockman and Edward Eigen, eds., *Architecture Culture, 1943–1968—A Documentary Anthology* (New York: Rizzoli, 1993), 68–69.

23. See Amedeo Belluzzi and Claudia Conforti, *Architettura italiana, 1944–1994* (Bari and Rome: Laterza, 1994); Fabrizio Brunetti, *L'architettura in Italia negli anni della ricostruzione* (Florence: Alinea Editrice, 1986); and Manfredo Tafuri, *History of Italian Architecture, 1944–1985* (Cambridge, MA and London: MIT Press, 1989).

24. Giancarlo De Carlo, "A proposito di La Martella," *Casabella-Continuità* 200 (February–March 1954): v–viii.

25. See Amerigo Restucci, *Matera. I sassi* (Turin: Einaudi, 1991).

26. See Ernesto De Martino, *Sud e magia* (Milan: Feltrinelli, 1959; repr. 2000); Claudio Barbati, Gianfranco Mingozzi, and Annabella Rossi, eds., *Profondo sud. Viaggio nei luoghi di Ernesto De Martino a vent'anni da Sud e magia* (Milan: Feltrinelli, 1978); Ernesto De Martino, *The Land of Remorse: A Study of Southern Italian Tarantism* (London: Free Association, 2005; originally published in Italian as *La terra del remorse* [Milan: Saggiatore, 1961]).

27. For an overview of Ridolfi's work, see Federico Bellini, *Mario Ridolfi* (Bari and Rome: Laterza, 1993).

28. Bruno Zevi, "The Italian Rationalists," in *The Rationalists: Theory and Design in the Modern Movement*, ed. Dennis Sharp (London: Architectural Press, 1978), 118–129, and in Andrea Oppenheimer Dean, *Bruno Zevi on Modern Architecture* (New York: Rizzoli, 1983), 107–113.

PART II

MAKING RELIGION MODERN

INTRODUCTION

TIMOTHY PARKER

The essays in this section address a phenomenon that, from certain points of view regarding modern identity, remains virtually invisible. A long-standing trope of modernity is that it emerges insofar as religion, superstition, and their premodern cognates diminish. Thus, for instance, the modern world is roughly equated with not only the sociopolitical results of industrialization but also the philosophical implications of the scientific revolution and Enlightenment rationality, eventually yielding a disenchanted world, however incomplete its achievement may remain. Such a view is clearly reductive and simplistic, as the spate of "post-secularization" literature during recent decades in religious studies and elsewhere demonstrates.[1]

Nevertheless, a central (even if not defining) condition of modernity is surely an increasing critique of religion, and it has taken many forms. One strong thread of this development in the West was the eighteenth-century remaking of religion according to the use by liberal Protestants of anthropological and sociological perspectives upon human history, such that the distinction between religion and superstition was used to relegate the communal, ritual, and typically Catholic forms of religious practice to the premodern or colonial world. By the mid-twentieth century, the comparative, historical, and phenomenological methods that had come to dominate the academic study of religion emphasized the idea of mystical experience that is understandable in terms of symbol and myth, yet exists essentially beyond specific religious institutions, texts, and moral codes and is therefore open to appropriation in forming a general theory of religion.[2] Whether such a general theory of religion would in fact refer to something real, whether religion was sui generis or was instead an ideological construct inherited from the developments sketched above, remains a subject of some controversy.[3] But along the way, multiple critiques of religion developed, from Nietzsche's broad proclamation of the death of God,[4] to other nineteenth-century proponents of a "hermeneutics of suspicion,"[5] to more focused efforts at "demythologization,"[6] to the functional demise of the institutional metanarrative of Western Christendom due to its progressive disestablishment, to the mere waning of religious authority amidst splintering denominational claims.

Such critiques surely exercised their influence on the emerging fields of art and architectural history. And against the backdrop of religious subjects having traditionally dominated these fields, it should be no surprise that religious art and architecture would tend to fall out of the picture during the twentieth century. But they by no means ceased to be produced. It is all the more relevant, then, to address such work expressly in the context of the formation, contestation, and experience of modern identity.

The essays that follow in this section concern the complicated interrelationship between religious and architectural engagement with modernity in Western Christianity following World War II. Of central importance in this context was the Second Vatican Council (1962–1965), the major event by which the Roman Catholic Church sought to open itself to the modern world. When considered against matters of patronage, reception, interpretation, and the specifics of time and place, however, the various and conflicting roles such events could play are made evident.

The same is true with regard to the sanctioning of modernism. In the case of two new cathedrals in Britain, it appeared amidst manifest ambiguity and uncertainty, yet with surprising results. In the case of Luigi Moretti, it served as the foil against which religious institutional change would be architecturally interpreted and celebrated. And throughout the twentieth century, attempts to articulate and advocate for modern architecture were interwoven with efforts to reform and update liturgical practice. Through distinct but complementary methods and analyses, these essays demonstrate not only the complexity of a relatively unstudied part of architectural history but also the value of bringing into dialogue the multiple discourses and histories involved in the phenomenon of modern religious architecture.

NOTES

1. It is also a particularly Eurocentric view, which appears increasingly anomalous when considered from a global perspective. See Peter L. Berger, ed., *The Desecularization of the World: Resurgent Religion and World Politics* (Grand Rapids, MI: W. B. Eerdmans Publishing Co., 1999).

2. For a fuller explanation of the debates surrounding "religion," see E. E. Evans-Pritchard, *Theories of Primitive Religion* (Oxford: Oxford University Press, 1965) and Steven M. Wasserstrom, *Religion after Religion: Gershom Scholem, Mircea Eliade, and Henry Corbin at Eranos* (Princeton, NJ: Princeton University Press, 1999).

3. See especially Timothy Fitzgerald, *The Ideology of Religious Studies* (New York: Oxford University Press, 2000).

4. The theme appears more than once in Nietzsche's work. See, for example, "The Madman," in *The Gay Science*, ed. and trans. Walter Kaufmann (New York: Vintage, 1974 [1882, 1887]), 181–182.

5. The phrase comes from Paul Ricoeur and refers particularly to Nietzsche, Freud, and Marx. See Paul Ricoeur, *Freud and Philosophy: An Essay on Interpretation*, trans. Denis Savage

(New Haven, CT: Yale University Press, 1970) and Merold Westphal, *Suspicion and Faith: The Religious Uses of Modern Atheism* (Grand Rapids, MI: Eerdmans, 1993).

6. The key text is Rudolf Bultmann, *The Mythological Element in the Message of the New Testament and the Problem of Its Re-interpretation, Part I: The Task of Demythologizing the New Testament Proclamation; Part II: Demythologizing in Outline* (London: SPCK, 1953 [1941]).

5 UNCERTAINTY AND THE MODERN CHURCH

TWO ROMAN CATHOLIC CATHEDRALS IN BRITAIN

ROBERT PROCTOR

The 1960s witnessed the most significant changes in the history of the Roman Catholic Church (and, arguably, in Christianity) since at least the Reformation and Counter-Reformation. A major liturgical reform was announced at the Second Vatican Council of 1962 to 1965 and was subsequently implemented throughout the Church. This reform marked an endorsement of previous calls for change from theologians, liturgy scholars, and ordinary priests around the world; known as the Liturgical Movement, it now has a well-documented historical narrative.[1] Yet in Britain these changes came suddenly to many clergy and faithful, since few had any significant awareness of the movement, unlike their counterparts in continental Europe.[2] Meanwhile, from outside the Church came the threat of secularization: Christianity had begun to lose its status and purpose in British society, and churchgoing was being abandoned in all denominations on an unprecedented scale. Attendance at non-Catholic churches declined continuously throughout the twentieth century, accelerating sharply during the 1960s, while Roman Catholic attendance peaked in 1960 only to be followed by a sudden and dramatic exodus of the faithful.[3] On matters of faith and, above all, of liturgical practice, where the greatest reforms took place and had the greatest impact on parish life, this period may be characterized as one of uncertainty and sometimes even of crisis.

While the Church was accepting modern ideas in its religious practice, it was also doing so in its art and architecture. Indeed, throughout the Western world, the three decades after the Second World War saw great freedom and experimentation in church design, willingly sponsored by church authorities, and Britain was no exception. When postwar restrictions on materials were gradually lifted in the mid-1950s, large numbers of modern churches sprang up in new housing estates, often built by architectural firms specializing in the type. From Gillespie, Kidd and Coia's youthful and avant-garde Brutalist work around Glasgow to Weightman and Bullen's modern monumental churches in Liverpool and Burles,

Newton and Partners' civic-minded New Empiricism, modern architecture for the Roman Catholic Church was prolific and varied. Other denominations' church architecture was similarly diverse.[4] At the same time, British church architecture could be resolutely traditional: architects such as H. S. Goodhart-Rendel and F. X. Velarde sustained eclectic and individual approaches based on historical models, and Italian Romanesque and Byzantine styles remained popular into the 1960s.[5] The diversity of church architecture in Britain therefore generally reflects the great range of architecture in a period where modernism had become increasingly varied and complex across two generations of architects, yet continued to coexist, often in hybrid forms, with more traditional principles. Uncertainty and change characterized the architecture of this period as well as its religion.

Such diversity and change in both fields made for a rich multiplicity of expressions at the points where they met. This chapter explores two strongly contrasting examples of these meetings, in two of the most significant Roman Catholic projects of the postwar period in Britain: Liverpool Metropolitan Cathedral and Clifton Cathedral in Bristol. The Metropolitan Cathedral of Christ the King in Liverpool was designed in 1960 and opened in 1967, and therefore spans the period of upheaval marked by the Second Vatican Council (figure 5.1). Its architect, Frederick Gibberd, brought a distinctive brand of modernist principles to his design, principles which were ideally placed to meet the specific conditions surrounding the project's conception. The Cathedral of Saints Peter and Paul in Bristol for the Diocese of Clifton came later, designed in 1965 and opened in 1973 (figure 5.2). Its project architect, Ronald Weeks of the Percy Thomas Partnership, was younger than Gibberd, and his ideas and process of design were very different, in a period when liturgical reforms were becoming more established, and in a diocese with different needs.

In each case, the diocesan clients found themselves in a situation of uncertainty and instability. Despite such a context, they attempted to fix their ideas about the Church into an architectural form by commissioning significant new buildings. The interactions between clients and architects in these two projects reveal that despite the surface expressions of confidence which such large-scale new buildings suggested, uncertainty remained a characteristic of the design process, with distinctive architectural results. At Liverpool and Clifton, two different approaches to architecture offered differing solutions to the crisis of purpose and meaning in the Church. An examination of these case studies can therefore suggest some of the ways in which modern architecture colonized, and was accepted into, the conceptual space opened up by such uncertainty and the particular forms it took to occupy that space.

GIBBERD'S MODERNISM

Frederick Gibberd belonged to the prewar generation of British modernist architects, having been involved in the Modern Architecture Research (MARS) Group

FIGURE 5.1. Frederick Gibberd, Liverpool Metropolitan Cathedral, Liverpool, 1960–1967. Photo by Elsam, Mann and Cooper, 1967. Architectural Press Archive/RIBA Library Photographs Collection.

FIGURE 5.2. Percy Thomas Partnership, Cathedral of Saints Peter and Paul, Clifton, Bristol, 1965–1973. Photo by author, 2008.

(the British wing of the Congrès Internationaux d'Architecture Moderne, or CIAM) and becoming an establishment figure after the war with public commissions, most notably as architect-planner for Harlow New Town in Essex. In his book on Liverpool Metropolitan Cathedral, he made his modernist intentions apparent. Function was seemingly paramount, for example, as he asserted that "there is [. . .] no distinction between the approach to the design of a cathedral or, say, a hospital."[6] The cathedral's novel structure in concrete and use of on-site prefabrication and a crane in construction were technically innovative and therefore represented an architecture concerned with modern progress in building methods. Significant British modern artists were chosen to contribute to the building, notably John Piper and Patrick Reyntiens for the stained glass, in a decisive break with traditions of figurative religious art. Gibberd's design also engaged with modern urban concerns: he referred to the concept of a "city crown," more familiar from the early twentieth century, to justify its tall circular form, and vehicular circulation was threaded underneath the church through its podium.[7]

Nevertheless, there was a strain of more conventional values that tempered, and sometimes contradicted, this modernist description of intention. The materials of the building were, by the standards established in the 1950s by the younger generation of architects and the New Brutalist discourse, "dishonest": there was sandstone facing to the brick side chapels; the doors were of fiberglass with a bronze coating; and mosaic tiles were used to clad the external concrete. This ambivalence in the use of materials was one aspect of the extensive criticisms of the building that appeared in the architectural press on its opening in 1967. Robert Maxwell, for example, derided the cathedral's "lack of formal precision and control" and deplored its concessions to "tastefulness."[8] Gibberd explained his choices of material pragmatically on grounds of economy and appearance: raw concrete, he said, would become stained and therefore less structurally legible in Liverpool's wet and polluted climate.

Gibberd's only statement of principle on the matter of materials was given in a footnote: "It is said to be more truthful to expose them [i.e., concrete surfaces], but on that count one should also expose the plumbing and leave rooms unplastered," he wrote.[9] Yet this was exactly what the New Brutalists proposed and ruthlessly carried out in built works such as Alison and Peter Smithson's Hunstanton Secondary School in Norfolk.[10] In the matter of materials, therefore, Gibberd took a more traditional stance than his younger contemporaries, preferring to subordinate structural materials to essentially decorative or symbolic treatment. Meanwhile, architects influenced by the New Brutalism used plain and exposed materials in church architecture to achieve an expression of purpose in other ways. Gillespie, Kidd and Coia's churches, for example, used timber, brick, and reinforced concrete to create a distinctively massive, monumental but economical architecture. At St Bride's Roman Catholic Church at East Kilbride, a tall brick box and tower on a hilltop reflected the Church's concern for permanence in a more austere form of modern architecture (figure 5.3).[11]

FIGURE 5.3. Gillespie, Kidd and Coia, St Bride's Roman Catholic Church, East Kilbride, Scotland, 1958–1964. Photo by G. Forrest Wilson. The Glasgow School of Art Archives and Collections.

It is not just the approach to materials, however, which distinguished Gibberd's brand of modernism. Perhaps more fundamentally, he insisted throughout his book on the necessity for the architect to direct the collaborative work through his imaginative genius: "The ultimate determinant lies within the personality of the designer, the architect. It is his task to produce a unified work of art which communicates his feeling about the nature of the building."[12] It was in the nature of the cathedral type, he argued, to exceed its functional requirements, demanding a supplementary symbolic and artistic program: "Architecture is an art, imagination or feeling enters into the making of it and, of all buildings, a cathedral is expected to be the most imaginative in conception. [...] The spires of Lichfield [a medieval cathedral] are quite useless structures, they serve no practical purpose: they are symbols of man's belief in a spiritual life."[13] This argument justified his use of the circular form and pinnacled tower as a symbolic reference to the crown of thorns that stands metonymically for the cathedral's dedication to Christ the King.

Disparaging comments on this aspect of his design appeared, sometimes thinly veiled, in the publications overseen by the New Churches Research Group (NCRG) and its influential founder, Peter Hammond, and in Birmingham University's

Centre for Worship and Religious Architecture. In his introduction to a collection of papers given at NCRG conferences, Hammond complained that "Churches are built to 'express' this and to 'symbolize' that. We have churches which look like hands folded in prayer; churches which symbolize aspiration or the anchor of the industrial pilgrim's life; churches which express the kingship of Christ; churches shaped like fishes, flames, and passion-flowers. There are still very few churches which show signs of anything comparable to the radical functional analysis that informs the best secular architecture of our time."[14] Several papers in the series that followed made similar allusions to Liverpool. Charles Davis, a Roman Catholic theologian, saw expression as largely irrelevant to church design: "To make one's first aim in building a church the expression, in stone, brick or concrete, of some religious theme, such as the kingship of Christ, is to make church architecture trivial because of social irrelevance."[15] Liverpool Metropolitan Cathedral seems to have been a frequent object of critical discussion in such gatherings of clergymen and church architects informed by the Liturgical Movement. The discourse on church architecture, especially in its formulation by Hammond, tended to discuss the liturgical brief as a functional program and to consider the church primarily, and narrowly, as a functional building.

Gibberd claimed in his book that such liturgical function was at the heart of his design, nodding to the Liturgical Movement in a pithy sentence: "The circular form is a natural grouping in which the people have a sense of physical proximity both to the activities in the sanctuary and to each other, which latter emphasizes the communal aspects of worship."[16] Earlier, however, he had frankly admitted to a shortage of knowledge about the functions of a church: "I know very little indeed about the design of modern ecclesiastical building. [. . .] I have only the slightest knowledge of the new Liturgical Movement: if, for example, someone says that a bishop's throne must be behind the high altar, or that the font may be associated with the sanctuary, then I cannot question these statements."[17] Instead, he emphasized the aesthetic basis of his design, including the influence of Renaissance centralized churches. Critics in Britain were already generally rejecting circular church plans with central altars as being functionally and symbolically inappropriate for the liturgy. Although it was agreed that centralized plans could enable greater participation of the laity in worship, Hammond and other critics showed that the liturgy demanded a hierarchical organization and spatial form to express the unequal relationship between the priest or minister and the congregation. Other liturgical aspects of Liverpool were also criticized: its level floor was said to hinder participation of the congregation in worship, and the closed axial choir was thought to obstruct a direct relationship and ritual movement between the high altar and Blessed Sacrament chapel (figure 5.4).[18]

Gibberd's approach to the design of Liverpool Metropolitan Cathedral was therefore seen by some as functionally deficient, and as giving too great a role to aesthetic and symbolic motives in its design. Gibberd, meanwhile, clearly asserted that these were important, even claiming to have produced an initial

FIGURE 5.4. Frederick Gibberd, Liverpool Metropolitan Cathedral, Liverpool, 1960–1967. Interior viewed from side gallery showing entrance to the left, high altar in the center, and Blessed Sacrament chapel to the far right. Photo by author, 2012. Stained glass by John Piper and © Patrick Reyntiens. All rights reserved, DACS 2013.

design of inspired genius during a few hours of frenzied drawing while locked in his study.[19] This design method and, most crucially, its success at Liverpool arose through the circumstances of the cathedral's commissioning and the role of its client.

COMPETITION FOR LIVERPOOL:
CONCEPTIONS AND MISCONCEPTIONS

The architect's conviction in the genius of his design would have been confirmed by his success in the international competition for Liverpool Metropolitan Cathedral announced in 1959 and judged the following year. In winning this competition, Gibberd's design defeated nearly three hundred others, including entries from well-established architects such as Denys Lasdun (architect of the National Theatre in London) and Clive Entwistle, and Roman Catholic architects with previous knowledge of church design such as Gerard Goalen and C. H. R. Bailey of Kuala Lumpur, whose entry received second place. Gibberd's plan, though liturgically questionable, was bold and diagrammatic, and its success in the competition affirmed that his design method of formal artistic inspiration was appropriate and natural (figure 5.5). Such inspiration could seem almost divine, as it did to Bailey, who in a letter to the archbishop attributed his second prize to his prayers to Our Lady of Perpetual Succour.[20]

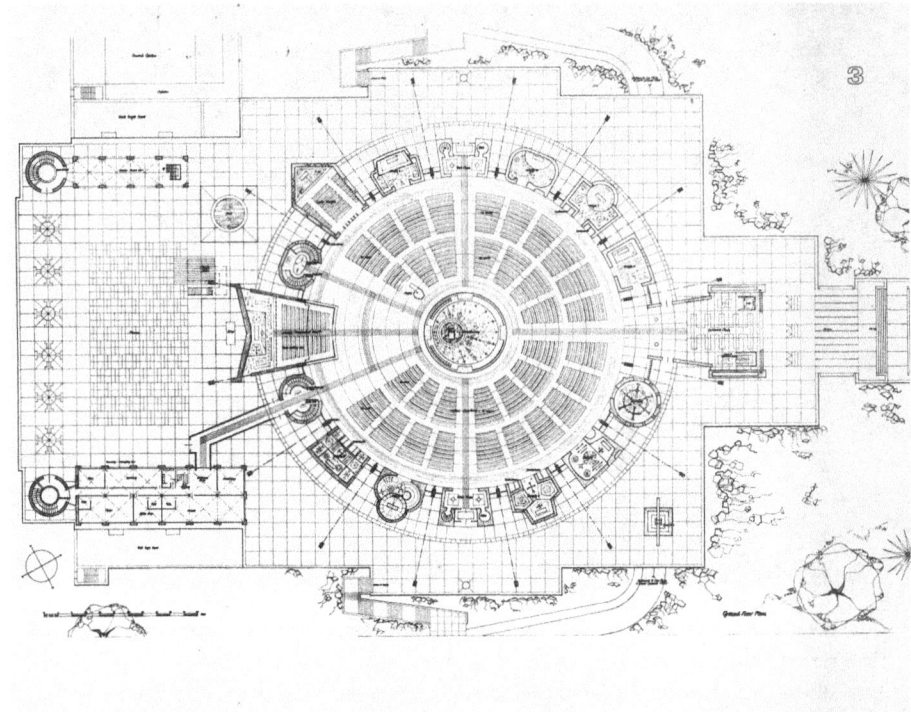

FIGURE 5.5. Frederick Gibberd, Liverpool Metropolitan Cathedral, Liverpool, 1960–1967. Plan drawing by Frederick Gibberd from competition entry, 1960. RIBA Library Photographs Collection/courtesy of the Gibberd Garden Trust.

The client's use of a competition to produce the building motivated this formal artistic method, since there could be no dialogue between architect and client until a plan had been selected. The competition's published *Conditions and Instructions* confirmed the value that would be attached to aesthetics, as the second publication containing answers to competitors' mainly technical questions was prefaced by a letter from the archbishop explaining that liturgical niceties were not in fact important: "for your consolation you should know that the Assessors will look first for a splendid conception," he wrote.[21]

This competition was influenced by that for Coventry Cathedral in 1950, which also produced a much-criticized building by another prominent architect of Gibberd's generation, Sir Basil Spence. The connection between the two competitions is clear from Liverpool's modeling of the published rules on Coventry's and, perhaps most decisively, from the appointment of Spence to the panel of three assessors.[22] The non-architect assessor representing the client at Liverpool was the archbishop himself, John C. Heenan. The volume of Heenan's autobiography concerned with his time at Liverpool tells the story of the selection procedure, but surprisingly fails to make any comment on the criteria for judgment and gives no mention of the range or nature of the projects submitted. Heenan had been assured by Spence that the selection would not be difficult to make, and that good plans would emerge of their own accord. Heenan described how the assessors moved quickly and independently among the plans with little discussion, soon finding that they had short-listed only a few schemes between them.[23] It seems that liturgical considerations came a distant second to architectural aesthetics.

If the competition lent itself to a particular kind of design—the "splendid conception"—this was thanks to the client's initial failure to understand or agree upon the nature of the cathedral. The competition brief itself was vague, with little in the way of specific guidance about liturgical form and nothing to say about what the client thought the social purpose of the building was to be. Such conceptual problems as whether the cathedral was to be considered a monumental symbolic institution, a site for large ceremonial gatherings or pilgrimage, or a working parish church were left unstated. The competition could have been seen as an almost magical way both of producing a design and of reaching consensus on the cathedral's future where none yet existed. Heenan noted, "Not everyone was enthusiastic about the new design but all agreed that it was good to have put an end to speculation."[24] Uncertainty was thus at the heart of the process, the reason for this method of arriving at a design, favoring a particular kind of diagrammatic and graphically potent solution.

The use of a competition to produce such a necessarily bold design had a logical connection to the cathedral's circumstances. It was first intended to provide a radical and realistic alternative to the painfully slow continuation of the original Byzantine design by Sir Edwin Lutyens, with the competitors limited to a budget of a million pounds, a stringent figure for a building originally destined to accommodate a congregation of three thousand faithful. The swift completion of the cathedral would also have enabled the television celebrity Heenan to leave a personal legacy to the archdiocese during his brief sojourn in the city from 1957 to 1963 on his progress through the Roman Catholic hierarchy (his path led from bishop of Leeds upward to archbishop of Westminster and then cardinal). An iconic modern building could also represent a contemporary identity and a rallying point in the city and the region for the thriving Roman Catholic community, strongly working-class and predominantly Irish, in opposition to Giles Gilbert Scott's neighboring, and also incomplete, Gothic Anglican Cathedral. While Gibberd used architectural reasons to justify his design, these institutional motives ensured its success.

Gibberd's scheme was easily readable, approaching a Beaux-Arts classical *parti* in its simplicity, with a central altar (actually slightly off-center in the original design), a ring of side chapels, and a dramatically soaring elevation. It was a clear and logical, but nevertheless expressive, solution to the problem of the cathedral. Since all the competition entries were sent back to their architects, very few others are now known beyond those that were published. From those few that are available, it is possible to appreciate Gibberd's design all the more. Even

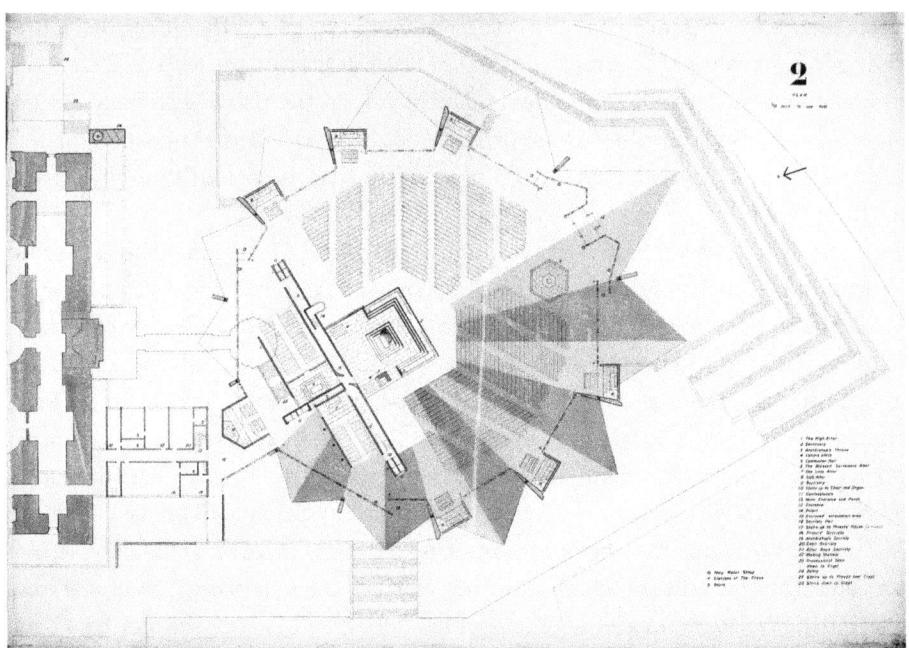

FIGURE 5.6. Unexecuted competition plan drawing for Liverpool Metropolitan Cathedral by Denys Lasdun, 1960. Denys Lasdun and Partners/RIBA Library Drawings and Archives Collections.

the short-listed schemes included many that were stylistically dated, naïve, and cumbersome. Others were very rough (such as a compact but incomplete modern Byzantine design by Oliver Hill) or simply dull (like the fussy eighteenth-century scheme by Norman Harrison).[25] More daring schemes than Gibberd's, including C. H. R. Bailey's and Clive Entwistle's, might have seemed dangerously unfeasible. One distinguished rival was Denys Lasdun, whose plan was based on a more strictly functional approach to liturgy, with an open sanctuary at one side of a circle surrounded by a horseshoe of seating. Behind its altar was a core of liturgical elements sandwiched between walls (including confessionals and projecting pulpit); unlike Gibberd's design, Lasdun's side chapels were carefully concealed from sight lines to the high altar (figure 5.6).[26] The low folded-slab roof of Lasdun's design did not possess the elevational impact which Gibberd's had achieved. Lasdun, though similar in age to Gibberd, demonstrated greater sympathy with the Liturgical Movement, and his design was in accordance with Hammond's rejection of monumentality and symbolism. Those qualities, disparaged by some, were precisely what Gibberd provided and what his client desired. The assessors' first comment was to praise the winning scheme's symbolic potency: "The design is full of imagination and powerfully expresses the Kingship of Christ."[27]

The simple clarity of Gibberd's design was achieved despite, rather than because of, the competition conditions. When the results of the competition were announced and the assessors' comments released to the architectural press, sharp criticisms were made of the insufficient criteria for judgment and apparently arbitrary justifications. A design by Arthur Bailey, for example, with an unusual arrangement of congregational seating flanking a central altar like transepts, was accorded third place, but criticized by the judges because its Lady chapel was given higher hierarchical and liturgical status than the Blessed Sacrament chapel, a problem which could have been solved simply by renaming them.[28] Meanwhile, one scheme was awarded a commendation even though it was described by the judges as seeming "to lack specifically religious quality" and having "failed as a cathedral building."[29] The assessors' decisions appeared to architects to be incomprehensible and confused, suggesting that the clients had no clear idea of what they desired of the building beyond a simplistic visual statement.

This is also confirmed by the competition's *Conditions and Instructions*, which were vague on the aspects of most importance to the physical planning of the building and at times contradictory. Some awareness of the Liturgical Movement seems evident, notably in the central premise of Archbishop Heenan's introductory letter that the high altar must be the focus of the building. Yet even this clear statement was not endorsed within the list of compulsory requirements, which were vague on such general concepts and specific only on details. The high altar had to be designed so that Mass could be said by a priest either facing the people or with his back to them (the latter noted as "the common practice," and so implicitly given preference). It was also specified that the sanctuary should be "clearly visible" to the congregation, and that "if desired, the seating may nearly encircle the High Altar and Sanctuary, to bring the people as near as possible," a statement which was, typically, immediately compromised by noting, "This is not a condition." More conservatively, however, competitors were given a list of processional routes that specified a "centre aisle," and a communion rail was required "separating the Sanctuary from the remainder of the church."[30]

The inadequacy of these rules became apparent when competing architects wrote to ask for clarification, and a further publication was compiled to answer their queries. Many competitors expressed frustration at the lack of any description of liturgical practice, which suggests their own lack of research. Typical, for example, was this question from architect R. G. P. Nunan's list of desired clarifications: "In the carriage of the Blessed Sacrament between the Chapel of the Blessed Sacrament Altar and the High Altar, is it desired that the Procession should walk out of the Main Sanctuary, and if so is there any preference as to which side: may it be in the Main Sanctuary, with public entrance from the Nave[?]," an inquiry which suggests either confusion over liturgical practice or a confused idea for a scheme.[31] Other architects' questions revealed their lack of understanding of Roman Catholic rituals and their meanings. Hidalgo Moya of Powell and Moya, for example, asked, "When Mass is offered at the High Altar, does transubstantiation occur at the High Altar or at the Chapel of the Blessed Sacrament? If the latter is the case, should that part of the service be visible and audible from the main body of the nave?"[32] Architects faced the difficult problem that any definition of liturgical action suggested a physical space, and that an architect's prior conception of a space might have obscured or obstructed a liturgical action. More practically, perhaps, competitors were worried that a template for the correct solution already existed in the clergy's minds.

The answers to most of these questions were vague or prohibitive. The route for the carriage of the Blessed Sacrament between the chapel and the high altar and the position of the archbishop's throne were "left to competitors." Other confusing points were left unresolved with a note about how few of the conditions were actually mandatory. The client's reticence was supposed to release competitors to exercise their imaginations without regard to the building's purpose. The archbishop's second prefatory letter explained his desire to elicit a wide field of potential solutions: "We are anxious that no architect should be excluded through neglect of some unimportant feature of the building. We have left you as free as possible to use your imagination. [. . .] You should not, therefore, worry unduly about the many details suggested in the 'should' clauses. We have been deliberately vague about the High Altar and sanctuary which, as I have already told you, should be the focal point of your design."[33] This response to the architects' questions reveals the uncertainty of the client (the archdiocese), whose representatives did not know or could not agree upon, and refused to formulate, their brief. It was this uncertainty that prompted the competition and led to Gibberd's robust design.

DESIGN INDECISIONS

Despite the visual certainty inherent in the chosen scheme, such uncertainties resurfaced during the building's construction whenever definite decisions had to be made and a liturgical form threatened to become fixed by the architecture. By the time work began, knowledge of the Liturgical Movement had become widespread in architectural discourse in Britain, thanks above all to Hammond's publications, especially his influential book *Liturgy and Architecture* of 1960.[34] Hammond and his colleagues proposed a method based on a dialogue between architect and client to establish a functional, liturgical brief. The church building was, he thought, primarily an instrument for the Eucharistic liturgy, in which the congregation was to take an active part. Gibberd's project architect, John (or Jack) B. Forrest, was evidently aware of these ideas and prepared lists of questions for the Cathedral Committee's Liturgical Sub-Committee as the detailed design of the sanctuary took shape. The answers, however, were frequently uninformative and prevaricating.

The question of a "throne" for the exposition of the Blessed Sacrament makes a good example. The practice of exposition was distinct from the Mass and involved placing the host in view of the congregation while prayers were said, both in private devotions and more communal services. This static, visual devotion to the Blessed Sacrament was not much admired by Liturgical Movement writers, who preferred to emphasize the primacy of the Eucharistic rite. Yet it was still regularly carried out in Britain at this time and required a means of displaying the host in a monstrance, usually placed on the altar or high up in a reredos. The reredos was also falling out of favor, viewed as an irrelevant and distracting decorative screen that would draw attention away from the focal point of the altar and the liturgical ceremony that surrounded it. The question of providing a means for displaying the Blessed Sacrament had been raised at the time the competition rules were written. Two contributors to the committee sent notes in favor. "Exposition of the Blessed Sacrament should be considered. Surely a throne is necessary," wrote one, while another gave it a specific location, "behind the High Altar."[35] It was eventually omitted from the competition conditions, but it emerged as a subject again when the high altar was being designed. To Forrest's question, "Will there be a temporary throne for Exposition of the Blessed Sacrament?" (a permanent one having presumably been ruled out as blocking the view of the Blessed Sacrament chapel), the initial answer penciled in for the committee's discussion was "probably yes," and the final answer was "It should not affect the design of [the] altar," and therefore did not need to be considered at all.[36]

Similarly, there was no conclusive answer to the question of placement of the canons' stalls and the archbishop's throne. After having inspected a mock-up of a proposed permanent arrangement, the committee requested a demountable and portable version instead.[37] Gibberd had expressed to the archbishop his desire to create a more dignified permanent throne than the wooden one finally designed, but, in another vacillation, Heenan insisted, "I am very much of the opinion that it would be best not to make any decision about the Archbishop's Throne and the Canons' Stalls until the Cathedral is actually functioning. [. . .] You could, if you wished, have a permanent throne provided it is movable."[38] Less than a year before the cathedral's opening a decision had yet to be made, and Gibberd expressed his anxiety and regret at not having found a solution.[39] The architectural effect of such advice was to produce a concept of the building as an expressive shell, within which liturgical functions could be organized and reorganized through flexibility of furnishings, a modern conception hitherto more common in other building types. Those elements that were most fixed—the railed-off baptistery near the entrance, for example, or the ring of side chapels—proved the value of this approach when they became obsolete by the time of the later phases of implementing the Vatican reforms in the late 1960s and early 1970s. Perhaps the only truly fixed point in the occupation of the building was the marble block of the high altar at its center, but even this element was originally conceived as dressed with a frontal cloth so that it could function as a frame for variable liturgical furnishings.

Much of the uncertainty surrounding the liturgical detailing of the cathedral arose from the abrogation of previous liturgical regulations that occurred during the Second Vatican Council. The Council's Constitution on the Sacred Liturgy of

December 1963 (just preceding the construction of Liverpool's liturgical furnishings and sanctuaries) did not contain any definite reforms, its only immediate effect being to suspend those parts of canon law that dealt with church design, leaving the Church in a state of apprehension.[40] To an architect or clergyman halfway through the design of a major church building, the likelihood of a radical change in Church practice might have seemed potentially disastrous. While some change was anticipated long before Vatican II, the announcement within the 1963 Constitution of the broad principle of "active participation" of the laity, without any detail as to how this was to be achieved, left the future open to speculation. To make a radical change in a church design following some European precedents might have seemed to some a dangerous presumption. To proceed with an old-fashioned design in the name of caution would have risked a futile expense.

The effects of this liturgical uncertainty can be seen at Liverpool. Archbishop Heenan's explanation for his ambivalence over the position of the celebrant at the high altar was that "Liturgical practice is developing continually in the Catholic Church,"[41] and the same problem crept into other aspects of the design. The side chapel and Blessed Sacrament chapel altars were all originally to be designed for the priest to stand with his back to the congregation. As late as 1964, the Liturgical Sub-Committee tried to prevent any permanent design work on the Blessed Sacrament chapel in case later alterations were required and suggested that "temporary steps, predella, altar etc." might be used for the cathedral's opening. This delay caused Gibberd some distress: "It is a very great pity indeed that we cannot have final instructions on the Blessed Sacrament Chapel as this is one of the places in the Cathedral where temporary works would be the most visually disastrous," he wrote to the committee chairman, Thomas McKenna.[42] He obviously convinced his client to make a decision, as the Liturgical Sub-Committee later reported that "His Grace [Heenan's successor, Archbishop George A. Beck] suggested, and the Committee approved, that the traditional design of altar for the Blessed Sacrament Chapel without facilities of Mass facing the people should be followed."[43] A year later the committee changed its mind, finally ruling out the possibility of Mass in the traditional position.[44] This decision was problematic because of the limited space in the chapel for the placement of the altar and the need to find a position for the tabernacle, limitations which would not permit the equivocation that proved to be so typical elsewhere in this building's design. In other words, when a decisive arrangement emerged, it was only as a pragmatic solution to a visual and spatial problem rather than a principled expression of liturgy or theology.

The state of anxiety over liturgical questions at this period cannot be blamed for all of the uncertainty that attended the cathedral's design and execution. Another reason that applied in some cases was a simple ignorance of how such decisions could be framed as a debate over meaning or principle. This is especially clear for the design of the high altar. Even the Liturgical Sub-Committee seems to have debated the form of this crucial liturgical element only on the basis of the

Church's rules, about which it exhibited confusion: "there seemed to be considerable difference of opinion on the question of the design of the Altar, but there was general agreement that it should consist basically of the mensa and support," recorded the minutes.[45] Whether or not the discussion involved any theological debate, the resolution was to "write to the Architect to inform him that: (a) the Altar should consist of one piece of solid stone table or mensa with a support or supports; (b) the support itself could take the form of a solid block of marble," a brief for the design which, again, failed to communicate any definite intention.[46]

What is notably absent from this conclusion is any mention of the symbolic meanings of the altar, particularly of the subtle play between communal meal and priestly sacrifice on which a design combining elements both of table and of altar could represent a commentary. The terms of such a debate were available to the committee at the time—indeed the conference in Liverpool in 1962 at which Gibberd himself had spoken included a paper by Catholic theologian Charles Davis on "The Christian Altar"—but there is no evidence that the cathedral used these terms to formulate a position for the architect.[47]

Such a lack of knowledge is confirmed by the committee's idea that the sidechapel altars should be of wood, so that "each altar could then be considered as an individual work of art."[48] This statement reveals a surprising ignorance of one of the major criticisms of Coventry Cathedral's high altar, namely that it had been designed as an element in an artistic installation rather than as a functioning liturgical object. If there was a liturgical motivation for this treatment of Liverpool's side altars, it would have been in the increasing redundancy of secondary altars. Concelebration, however, which eventually made side chapels largely irrelevant, only became common after the cathedral's completion, so it is perhaps more likely that Liverpool's side altars were influenced by Coventry's purely symbolic, nonliturgical "Hallowing Places."[49] Gibberd's solution for the high altar, the marble block, must therefore have had its motivation in his consideration of the altar's visual impact within the space and perhaps through the study of appropriate precedents such as Le Corbusier's altar at Ronchamp, and not in the application of a theological principle. Gibberd had few theological principles to work with: his client gave him stipulations about form without explaining the theoretical concepts from which those forms derived.

The clergy's failure to brief the architect with their own definite conceptions left a vacuum that Gibberd filled with his own aesthetic certainties. In the case of the artworks, the client's uncertainty allowed the architect a high degree of freedom. Gibberd and Heenan together visited the monks at Buckfast Abbey in Devon who had created figurative windows for Gerard Goalen's Church of Our Lady of Fatima at Harlow, the New Town for which Gibberd was planner. Gibberd disliked what he saw and rejected the monks' proposal that the cathedral lantern should display figures of Christ the King and the twelve apostles, which would have been barely distinguishable.[50] With more abstract precedents in mind, Gibberd instead persuaded the archbishop and the committee to commission John

FIGURE 5.7. Frederick Gibberd, Liverpool Metropolitan Cathedral, Liverpool, 1960–1967. View of Blessed Sacrament Chapel, including reredos painting and tabernacle design by Ceri Richards, 1966–1967, and stained glass by Ceri Richards and Patrick Reyntiens. Photo by Henk Snoek, ca. 1967. Architectural Press Archive/RIBA Library Photographs Collection. Artworks © Patrick Reyntiens and Ceri Richards. All rights reserved, DACS 2013.

Piper and Patrick Reyntiens after organizing a visit to see their work at Coventry Cathedral. Their trinity of sunbursts for Liverpool's lantern was visually more appropriate to the scale of the building and high position of the lantern.

Similarly, the abstract windows, reredos painting, and artistic tabernacle in the Blessed Sacrament chapel were commissioned from a fine artist, Ceri Richards, despite the concerns of the clergy.[51] Gibberd, with Reyntiens, persuaded them to accept Richards's work, convincing them of its artistic value. The Blessed Sacrament chapel's qualities as an artwork apparently predominated over its liturgical and devotional functions (figure 5.7). Gibberd's visual certainties resolved the clergy's doubts.

A LITURGICAL BRIEF: CLIFTON CATHEDRAL

In contrast to the cathedral in Liverpool, Clifton Cathedral in Bristol was the result of an entirely different architectural design process, however much the building may have in common superficially with Gibberd's cathedral.[52] Like Liverpool, it made use of modern construction techniques, here of in situ reinforced concrete and precast panels. It showed a concern with its urban environment through a raised podium to incorporate cars and secondary facilities, and a pointed tower form to mark its significance from a distance. Modern artists employed on the decorative scheme included William Mitchell for the Stations of the Cross in cement (Mitchell had carried out decorative sculpture at Liverpool for the doors and bell tower) and Henry Haig for an abstract scheme of stained glass using concrete tracery, as at Liverpool. When the Diocese of Clifton began to consider finding an architect in 1965, they approached the Royal Institute of British Architects about a competition and were sent the conditions for Liverpool as a model. But the bishop, Joseph E. Rudderham, "acting upon advice received from competent people," decided against a competition, a choice that would have a profound effect on the method of design.[53]

At Liverpool, the primary motivation for the abandonment of Adrian Gilbert Scott's reduced version of Lutyens's scheme and the abrupt shift to a new cathedral came from the personal vision of its new archbishop. At Clifton, the bishop was much less decisive about the need for the building. An individual offered to donate nearly all the money for a new cathedral on condition that it was only spent for that purpose. He had his own vision for the building as "a place of worship and a monument to Almighty God," as he later wrote to the bishop.[54] Nevertheless, he wished to remain anonymous and had only a small part in the conversations that took place over its design. Rudderham, meanwhile, did not immediately accept the money but consulted widely among his clergy, many of whom argued that it would be an inappropriate use of resources, citing world poverty and hunger, and even in one case the "spirit of poverty as expressed in the Vatican Council Documents," as more urgent moral imperatives.[55] It was with some reluctance that the bishop finally pursued the project, therefore, and only after the nineteenth-century pro-cathedral had been shown to be structurally deficient, with no funds available to repair it.

From the beginning, this spirit of tentative consultation was also present on the side of the architects. In accepting the commission, the architects of the Percy Thomas Partnership wrote, "We look forward to developing a close working relationship with you and your representatives so that we can examine in depth the function and requirements of a modern cathedral in the community today. We are sure that only such a close working relationship between Architect and Client can achieve the level of 'Architectural Seriousness' advanced by the New Liturgical Movement."[56] In this statement their knowledge of the architectural discourse in Britain concerning the Liturgical Movement is very clear. The term "Architectural Seriousness" refers to an essay of that title by architect and lecturer Lance Wright in Peter Hammond's edited collection of 1962, *Towards a Church Architecture*, in which the author urged modern architects to refrain from symbolism in addressing the functional problems of the church.[57] Hammond also argued that architect and client should collaborate in design. While at Liverpool the client's uncertainty over the cathedral was countered with a decisive visual image in the competition drawings, at Clifton the architects themselves adopted a posture of uncertainty as their starting point for design.

In late 1965, within a few months of accepting the commission, architect Ronald Weeks and others of the Percy Thomas Partnership produced a large design document entitled the "Liturgical Brief," perhaps referring to an essay of that name by Hammond.[58] This document dealt rigorously with every aspect of Clifton Cathedral's functions, liturgical and otherwise, using text and diagrams, the latter sometimes consisting of abstract indications of priority, directionality, and spatial relationships (like a bubble diagram) and at other times with more literal drawings of sections, plans, furnishings, and people (figure 5.8). On the right-hand side of each page was a blank column for "clerics' comments," gradually filled with notes in revised versions. Each element of the building was considered in relation to its uses and to its interconnections with every other element. There were diagrams showing processional routes through the building for different ceremonies and the locations of celebrants and servers at various points in time, right down to considerations of the way in which people queued for confession and the purposes of artworks, such as the Stations of the Cross, which "must create a physical movement around [the] church." "Active participation" of the congregation was given consideration through a range of possible seating plans drawn for discussion with the clergy. The fan shape was noted by them as "very acceptable," provided the altar was positioned "such that [the] angle of command [was] satisfactory," and this option was finally chosen. The building committee included a leading exponent of the early Liturgical Movement in Britain, the Dominican Gregory Murray, and it is likely that he influenced many of the decisions.

The architects' treatment of the baptistery was exemplary and further dem-

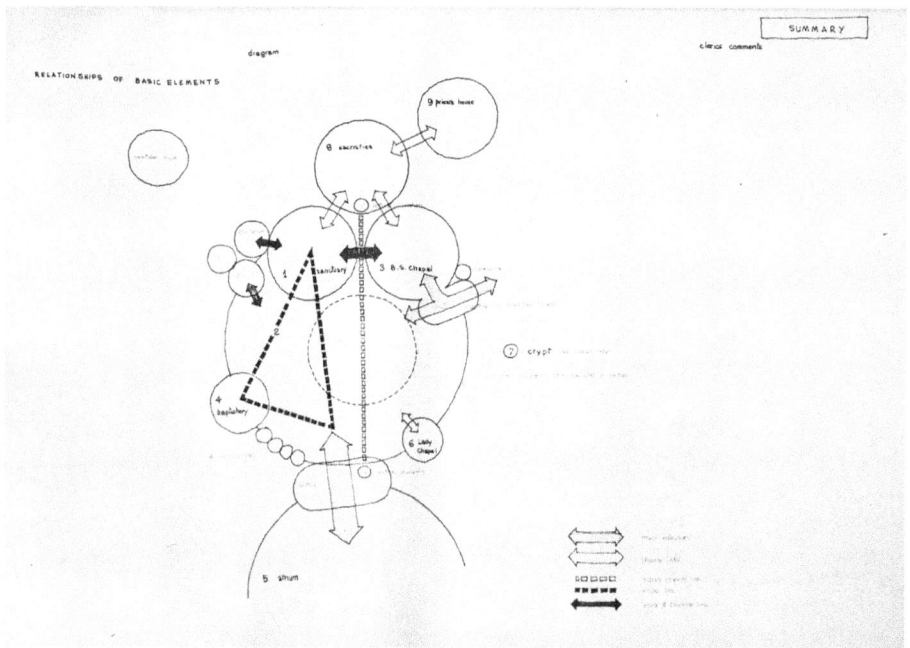

FIGURE 5.8. Architect Ronald Weeks of the Percy Thomas Partnership, Cathedral of Saints Peter and Paul, Clifton, Bristol, 1965–1973. Page from "Liturgical Brief" showing "Relationships of Basic Elements" for Clifton Cathedral, ca. 1966. Clifton Diocesan Archives, courtesy of the Trustees of the Roman Catholic Diocese of Clifton.

onstrates their approach (figure 5.9). A diagram showed a circular plan, with font and celebrant at its center surrounded by a U-shaped gathering of people ("normally 10–12 participants") as the ceremony usually occurred. A "symbolic diagram" was then drawn, showing a sloping descent of the catechumen into and through water (labeled "death"), accompanied by "the 'illumination' (white light)" above, and followed by "(life) resurrection" shown with an arrow ascending toward the altar. These proposals show that the architects were reading widely about both the liturgical and symbolic purposes of their subject, had conversed with their client in depth, and also had brought their own ideas to the discussion. Weeks wrote that the architecture then followed logically from their complex outline of functions: "It is this diagram which has finally been built on plan and moulded in three dimensions to create the internal environment."[59] The interior of Clifton Cathedral has a quality of openness rather like that of Liverpool, but this was intended to allow fluid movement between different areas, and the liturgical elements seem more definitely fixed and appropriate to their allotted places (figure 5.10). If, finally, there is a sense of certainty in this building, it is one of organization rather than of image.

The approaches of Gibberd and Weeks were therefore quite different. Gibberd took on the role of art-architect in response to a lack of direction from the client.

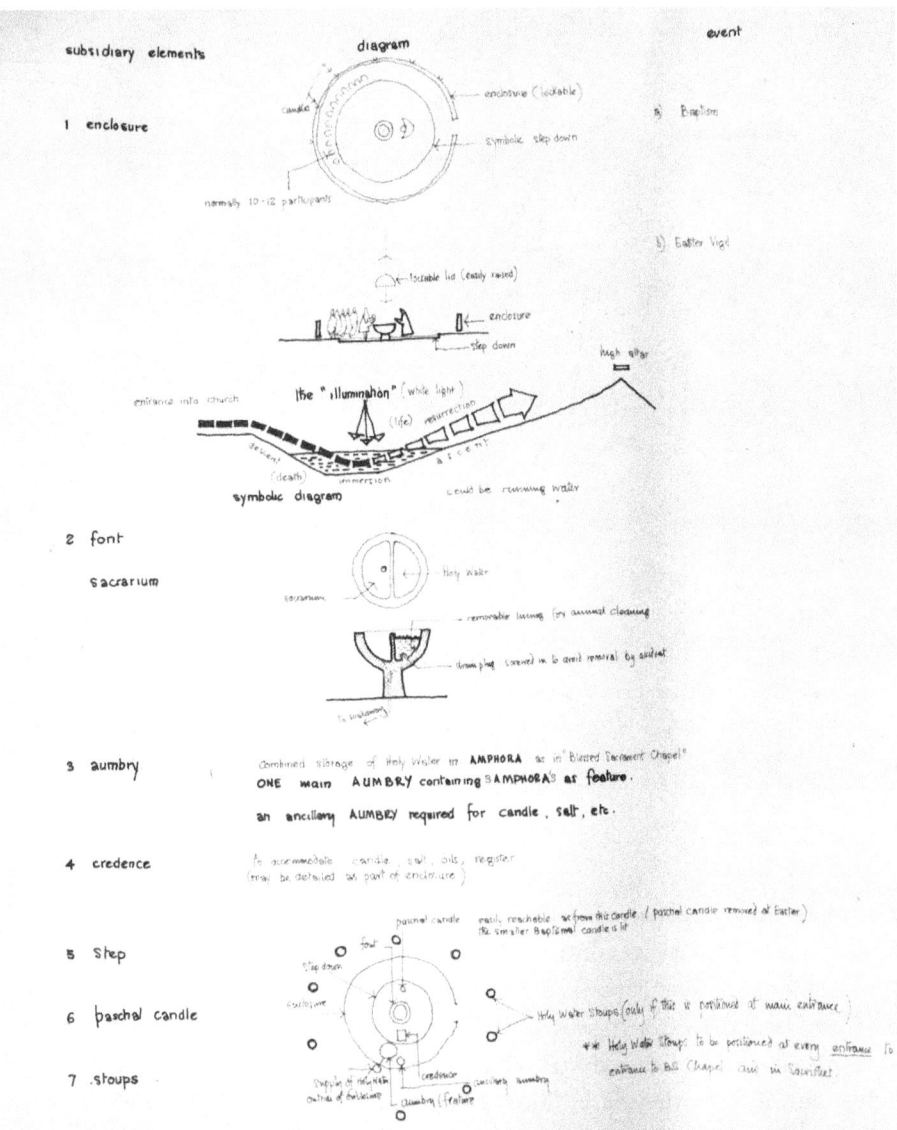

FIGURE 5.9. Ronald Weeks of the Percy Thomas Partnership, Clifton Cathedral. Baptistery sketches for Clifton Cathedral, ca. 1966. From Clifton Diocesan Archives, courtesy of the Trustees of the Roman Catholic Diocese of Clifton.

Weeks's role was more that of a coordinator of the client's requirements, weaving them into a hierarchical and meaningful whole. These stances reflect differing trends in modern architecture in this period. Weeks was more in tune with the collaborative sociological methods that had been adopted by architects of state schools in the immediate postwar period. These design methods had been developed before the war, especially at the Architectural Association architecture school in London.[60] One of the most notable later applications of a sociological

FIGURE 5.10. Percy Thomas Partnership, Clifton Cathedral, 1965–1973. Interior viewed from rear of the nave; note the baptistery in the distance to the left of the sanctuary. Photo by Brian Middlehurst, 1973.

method of design was by the firm of Robert Matthew, Johnson Marshall and Partners (RMJM) in their campus for the new University of York. For this project the architects drew complex diagrams of the buildings' uses in discussion with their client, planning the architecture of the scheme around the functional drawings that emerged and subsequently deriving its elevations primarily from planning and technical requirements, including the use of a prefabricated reinforced concrete system of construction.[61] Some features of the diagrams even appeared almost literally transcribed into physical form, such as the covered walkways that connected separate buildings. At Clifton, the architects did not eschew aesthetic expression, but, as examples, manipulated light for its symbolic meanings and raised a tower off-center over the sanctuary. Yet as at York, Clifton Cathedral's exterior consisted of a cladding of precast aggregate panels, suggesting an anti-monumentalism and a spirit of economy rather different from Liverpool's facing materials of stone, mosaic, and bronze.

The Roman Catholic diocese of Clifton differed greatly from that of Liverpool: without the latter's strong sectarian divisions and with a smaller and more middle-class population of faithful, it was perhaps not a place where a bold architectural statement seemed urgent or necessary. Moreover, neither its bishop nor its architects appeared to wish to use architecture as a way of leaving a mark for posterity, as did both Heenan and Gibberd. Designed and built later in time than Liverpool, Clifton Cathedral benefited from an increasing certainty over the reforms of the Second Vatican Council. By the time construction finally began in 1970, the New Order of Mass had been devised, distributed, and enforced. Nevertheless, the wide range of church experiments of the 1960s had not resulted in any widespread agreement over plan types, and so the architectural implications of the new liturgy remained ambiguous. In other ways, too, it was still a period of uncertainty, marked by an economic crisis that postponed construction and resulted in curtailments to the work and characterized by a wholesale abandonment of church attendance, which left Liverpool Metropolitan Cathedral almost empty on Sunday mornings and confidence in the Church's future wavering. The place and the atmosphere were different, and therefore so was the architecture.

CONCLUSION

If one were to follow the Liturgical Movement's priorities, as historians of church architecture often have done in the last few decades, the comparison between the Roman Catholic cathedrals in Liverpool and Clifton would be an easy one to make. Liverpool could be proved to be liturgically conservative and naïvely designed, while Clifton could be seen as a model of liturgically advanced and sophisticated planning. Gibberd and his clients could be viewed as not having taken seriously enough the liturgical, functional requirements of the building, and for not having undertaken a serious dialogue between them to establish a liturgical brief. Weeks and the Clifton clergy, meanwhile, would be praised for their intimate and knowledgeable collaboration. Yet such an interpretation would miss a vital point.

Perhaps even because of the problems encountered during its design, Liverpool Metropolitan Cathedral is visually stunning in a way that might not have been the case if a purely liturgical brief had been puritanically followed. The "splendid conception" of Gibberd's circular plan and conical section is powerful and daring, and arises precisely from his rejection of strict adherence to liturgical function and his Beaux-Arts method of producing a clear diagrammatic *parti*, in opposition to the material or functional priorities of younger designers. This method was a direct result of the competition process, with its nebulous rules and tendency to produce a striking image. The client's hesitancy and anxiety were repeatedly countered by the decisiveness of a visually minded modern architect, whose more old-fashioned conception of his role as imaginative artist lent a necessary authority to his voice for those he had to convince. Perhaps a more confident clergy would have produced a building that lacked the strength of identity and architectural confidence of Gibberd's design. Because of its clergy's neglect of strict liturgical function, Liverpool obtained a modern building that was appropriate to its time and location.

The certainties and uncertainties at Liverpool and Clifton almost seem to be reversed in each. At Liverpool, the interior is cluttered with indecisive liturgical furnishings, but these can easily be ignored as the scale and form of the space, the central altar and *baldachino*, and colors of light predominate. At Clifton, the various elements of the interior are coherently placed and legible, while the exterior is unassuming. Behind those differences of appearance are different architectural modes of working and different kinds of modernism. Both buildings show how modern architecture could gain access to a fundamentally conservative institution through a historical moment of transition and uncertainty. They show how modern architects' various orthodoxies and moralities could represent convincing solutions to the crises of meaning and authority that typified the condition of modernity for the Church, as they did for much of society and its other institutions. Uncertainty is therefore embodied in the architecture in many ways: in the possibility for aesthetic experimentation; in the juxtaposition of the temporary and expedient with the striking and daring; in the occasional fortuitous accidents produced by revelatory agreements and disagreements between the people involved in design. Liverpool Metropolitan Cathedral raises the distinct possibility that a primarily visual certainty could act for both architect and client to fill the modern void where other forms of conviction were absent. It might further suggest that such a condition prevailed elsewhere in modern architecture.

ACKNOWLEDGMENTS

I would like to thank Timothy Parker and his colleagues at the University of Texas at Austin for their invitation to participate in the symposium and book. The costs of image licenses for this essay were defrayed by a Dorothy Stroud publication grant from the Society of Architectural Historians of Great Britain, to whom I am very grateful. I would also like to thank Meg Whittle of the Liverpool Archdiocesan Archives, Father J. A. Harding of the Clifton Diocesan Archives, Ronald Weeks, Judi Loach, Ambrose Gillick, and Barnabas Calder.

NOTES

1. See, for example, John Fenwick and Bryan Spinks, *Worship in Transition: The Twentieth Century Liturgical Movement* (Edinburgh: T. & T. Clark, 1995).

2. J. D. Crichton, "The Liturgical Movement from 1940 to Vatican II," in *English Catholic Worship: Liturgical Renewal in England Since 1900*, ed. J. D. Crichton, H. E. Winstone, and J. R. Ainslie (London: Geoffrey Chapman, 1979), 60–78.

3. This is well described by Callum G. Brown, *Religion and Society in Twentieth-Century Britain* (Harlow: Pearson, 2006).

4. A useful summary is given by Elain Harwood, "Liturgy and Architecture: The Development of the Centralised Eucharistic Space," in *Twentieth Century Architecture* 3 (1998): 50–74; on Frances Pollen, see Alan Powers, *Frances Pollen: Architect, 1926–1987* (Oxford:

Robert Dugdale, 1999); on Gillespie, Kidd and Coia, see Robert Proctor, "Churches for a Changing Liturgy: Gillespie, Kidd and Coia and the Second Vatican Council," in *Architectural History* 48 (2005): 291–322.

5. On Goodhart-Rendel, see Alan Powers, ed., *H. S. Goodhart-Rendel, 1887–1959* (London: Architectural Association, 1987); on Gilbert Scott, see Gavin Stamp, "'A Catholic Church in Which Everything Is Genuine and Good': The Roman Catholic Parish Churches of Sir Giles Gilbert Scott," in *Ecclesiology Today* 38 (May 2007): 63–80.

6. Frederick Gibberd, *Metropolitan Cathedral of Christ the King, Liverpool* (London: Architectural Press, 1968), 17.

7. Ibid., 48–56, 138, 68–74, 35–38, 42–43; on the "city crown," or *stadtkröne*, see Volker Welter, *Biopolis: Patrick Geddes and the City of Life* (Cambridge, MA: MIT Press, 2001).

8. Robert Maxwell, "Liverpool Round-House," in *Architectural Design* 36, no. 6 (June 1967): 256.

9. Gibberd, *Metropolitan Cathedral*, 56, footnote.

10. See especially Reyner Banham, *The New Brutalism: Ethic or Aesthetic?* (London: Architectural Press, 1966).

11. Proctor, "Churches for a Changing Liturgy," 302.

12. Gibberd, *Metropolitan Cathedral*, 18.

13. Ibid., 12, 16.

14. Peter Hammond, "A Radical Approach to Church Architecture," in *Towards a Church Architecture*, ed. Peter Hammond (London: Architectural Press, 1962), 15–37 (quote on p. 23).

15. Charles Davis, "Church Architecture and the Liturgy," in Hammond, *Towards a Church Architecture*, 107–127 (quote on p. 108).

16. Gibberd, *Metropolitan Cathedral*, 22.

17. Frederick Gibberd, "The Liverpool Metropolitan Cathedral," in William Lockett, ed., *The Modern Architectural Setting of the Liturgy* (London: SPCK, 1964), 55–69 (quote on p. 55).

18. William White, "The Altar and the Liturgy," in *RIBA Journal* 74, no. 7 (July 1967): 281–285.

19. In discussion with the archbishop, see John C. Heenan, *A Crown of Thorns: An Autobiography, 1951–1963* (London: Hodder and Stoughton, 1974), 301.

20. C. H. R. Bailey to Archbishop John C. Heenan, August 28, 1960, Liverpool Roman Catholic Archdiocesan Archives, Cathedral Collection (henceforth LAA/CC), S2/VIII/A/10.

21. "Comment on the Liverpool Catholic Cathedral Competition," in *Architectural Design* (October 1960): 425–426 (quote on p. 425); typescript letter from Archbishop John C. Heenan for preface to answers to competitors' questions, LAA/CC, S2/VIII/A/17.

22. The Coventry conditions are present in the archive among the documents preparatory to the competition: *Coventry Cathedral Architectural Competition. Conditions and Instructions to Competing Architects*, October 1950, LAA/CC, S2/VIII/A/2. The Liverpool conditions were published as *Architectural Competition for the Metropolitan Cathedral of Christ the King, Liverpool: Conditions and Instructions to Competing Architects* (Liverpool: [n. pub.], 1959). See also Heenan, *Crown of Thorns*, 294. Further evidence includes meeting minutes, "New Cathedral Competition," June 4, 1959, LAA/CC, S2/VIII/A/1; and letter from T. E. Hall to Canon A. Maguire (Secretary of the Cathedral Executive Committee), May 11, 1959, LAA/CC, S2/VIII/A/3 (indicating the hasty drafting of the conditions by assessor David Stokes).

23. Heenan, *Crown of Thorns*, 299–301.

24. Ibid., 303.

25. Oliver Hill's scheme: DR 126/3(1–6), Royal Institute of British Architects (RIBA) Drawings Collection, London; Norman Harrison's scheme: PA 584/3(1–5), in ibid.

26. Lasdun scheme: PA 2100/5(1–8), RIBA Drawings Collection, London; see also

"Competition: Metropolitan Cathedral of Christ the King, Liverpool," in *The Architects' Journal*, September 1, 1960, 313–333 (quote on p. 333).

27. Ibid., 313.

28. "Competition: Metropolitan Cathedral of Christ the King, Liverpool," in *The Architects' Journal*, September 1, 1960, 313–333 (quote on p. 325).

29. Assessors' Report, reproduced with illustrations of winning and commended schemes, in *The Architect and Building News*, August 31, 1960, 267–280 (quote on p. 277).

30. *Conditions and Instructions*, 3, 15, 19, 17.

31. R. G. P. Nunan to Monsignor Turner (Competition Secretary), November 27, 1959, LAA/CC, S2/VIII/A/12.

32. Hidalgo Moya (Powell and Moya) to [Mgr Turner] (Competition Secretary), December 14, 1959, LAA/CC, S2/VIII/A/13.

33. Draft letter from Archbishop John C. Heenan for preface to answers to competitors' questions, undated, LAA/CC, S2/VII/A/17.

34. Peter Hammond, *Liturgy and Architecture* (London: Barrie and Rockliff, 1960).

35. "Schedule for New Cathedral. Canon O'Sullivan's Observations" and anonymous note, "New Cathedral. Schedule of Accommodation," LAA/CC, S2/VIII/A/4.

36. Anonymous undated "Notes for Meeting on 30th October 1963 with Monsignor McKenna re: Sanctuaries," and "Recommendations of Liturgical Sub-Committee for Final Answers to Questions Submitted by Mr. Forrest to Monsignor McKenna, 30th October 1963," LAA/CC, S2/XI/A/4.

37. Cathedral Executive Committee, meeting minutes, December 9, 1966, LAA/CC, S2/XI/A/7.

38. Archbishop John C. Heenan to Frederick Gibberd, March 2, 1961, LAA/CC, S2/IX/A/29.

39. Gibberd to Monsignor T. G. McKenna, [n.d., August 1966], LAA/CC, S2/X/A/108.

40. The principal documents were the "Constitution on the Sacred Liturgy," trans. Joseph Rogers, in Austin Flannery, ed., *Liturgy: Renewal and Adaptation*, 7th rev. ed. (Dublin: Scepter Books, 1968), 2*-29*; and Congregation of Rites, "Inter Oecumenici: On Implementing the Constitution on Liturgy," trans. Austin Flannery, in ibid., 37*-59*; see also Fenwick and Spinks, Worship in Transition, 67–69; R. Kevin Seasoltz, *New Liturgy, New Laws* (Collegeville, MN: Liturgical Press, 1980), 134; Proctor, "Churches for a Changing Liturgy," 294–296.

41. Draft preface to answers to competitors' questions, LAA/CC, S2/VII/A/17.

42. Gibberd to McKenna, February 5, 1964, LAA/CC, S2/X/A/37.

43. Cathedral Executive Committee, Liturgical Sub-Committee, meeting minutes, April 21, 1964, LAA/CC, S2/XI/A/5.

44. Cathedral Executive Committee, meeting minutes, July 9, 1965, LAA/CC, S2/XI/A/6.

45. Cathedral Executive Committee, meeting minutes, October 8, 1964, LAA/CC, S2/XI/A/5.

46. Ibid.

47. Charles Davis, "The Christian Altar," in Lockett, *Modern Architectural Setting of the Liturgy*, 13–31.

48. Cathedral Executive Committee, meeting minutes, May 13, 1965, LAA/CC, S2/XI/A/6.

49. On Coventry Cathedral, see Louise Campbell, *Coventry Cathedral: Art and Architecture in Post-War Britain* (Oxford: Clarendon Press, 1996).

50. Cathedral Executive Committee, meeting minutes, October 12, 1961, LAA/CC, S2/XI/A/2.

51. Archbishop George A. Beck to Gibberd, June 29, 1965, LAA/CC, S2/X/A/75; Gibberd to McKenna, [n. d., August 1966], LAA/CC, S2/X/A/108.

52. Published sources on Clifton Cathedral include Ronald Weeks and Kate Wharton, "Architectural Heritage Year 2075," in *Architect*, May 1975, 24–25; Peter Ansdell Evans, "Clifton's Catholic Cathedral," in *The Architects' Journal*, July 11, 1973, 70–72; and Kate Wharton, "Genesis of a Cathedral," in *The Architect and Building News*, January 1 and 15, 1969, 22–29.

53. Bishop Joseph E. Rudderham to Anthony Rossi, July 23, 1965, Clifton Roman Catholic Diocesan Archives, Cathedral Box (henceforth CDA/CB), miscellaneous correspondence folder.

54. [Name withheld at Cathedral's request] to Rudderham, February 18, 1970, CDA/CB, miscellaneous correspondence.

55. Various correspondence, quotation from Report of Deanery Meeting at St Mary's, Bath, December 14, 1969, in ibid.

56. Frederick S. Jennett (Sir Percy Thomas and Son [later named the Percy Thomas Partnership]) to Rudderham, July 19, 1965, in ibid.

57. Lance Wright, "Architectural Seriousness," in Hammond, *Towards a Church Architecture*, 220–244.

58. Peter Hammond, "A Liturgical Brief," in *The Architectural Review*, April 1958, 240–255. The document, "Liturgical Brief," referred to in what follows is stored separately in CDA/CB. For a more complete discussion of the design process at Clifton Cathedral, see Robert Proctor, "Modern Church Architect as Ritual Anthropologist: Architecture and Liturgy at Clifton Cathedral," *Architectural Research Quarterly* 15 (2011): 359–372.

59. Ronald Weeks, "The Design and Construction of the Cathedral Church of SS. Peter and Paul, Clifton," *Pax* (autumn/winter 1973): 60–69 (quote on 62).

60. See Andrew Saint, *Towards a Social Architecture: The Role of School-Building in Post-War England* (London: Yale University Press, 1987), e.g., 2–5.

61. Stefan Muthesius, *The Postwar University: Utopianist Campus and College* (New Haven: Yale University Press, 2000), 128–137; Saint, *Towards a Social Architecture*, 214–218.

6 "HUMANLY SUBLIME TENSIONS"
LUIGI MORETTI'S CHIESA DEL CONCILIO (1965–1970)

TIMOTHY PARKER

In 1967, Luigi Moretti (1907–1973)[1] published in *Fede e Arte* a pointed essay, "Where two or three are gathered in my name... (Matthew 18:20)," concerning the "great perplexity" facing architects of new churches in the wake of the sea change that was the Second Vatican Council (1962–1965).[2] Observing the "dangerous, or at least incautious, vehemence" with which otherwise sincere architects prematurely produced "a flood of purely formalistic designs," Moretti lamented the too-frequent consequence of "bare, denuded" churches.[3] The verbal terms of this judgment and disparaging visual characterization echo a description Moretti had given a work of his own, albeit with approval: the Commemorative Chapel (or Sacrario dei Martiri) at the Foro Mussolini, Rome (1940).[4] Built to honor martyrs of the Fascist revolution and the last of three religious projects Moretti designed for the Fascist regime, the Sacrario was "austere and naked" precisely because Moretti sought neither to rely upon inherited forms nor to forge a new symbolic language but rather to work out of the "spirit" of tradition such as it was in Rome.[5] He had become convinced that inherited symbols and forms no longer had adequate communicative capacity and marked instead a broad cultural crisis of Western liberal civilization having reached a dead end. As symbols became increasingly abstract and objective, the modern view of reality became overly simplified; thus, for Moretti, the crisis was especially one of waning spiritual reality.[6] As a strategy for response, he developed a studied indifference to the connotations of styles and forms, which kept him relatively disassociated from the prevailing architectural currents of Italian modernism. But after the war he lauded the Second Vatican Council as a promising effort to address this very crisis. Insofar as the Council offered a newly reformed perspective upon reality as framed by the relation between the human and the divine, a new architecture—most especially a new religious architecture—was then genuinely possible. While he remained averse to developing new form languages through explicit signs or

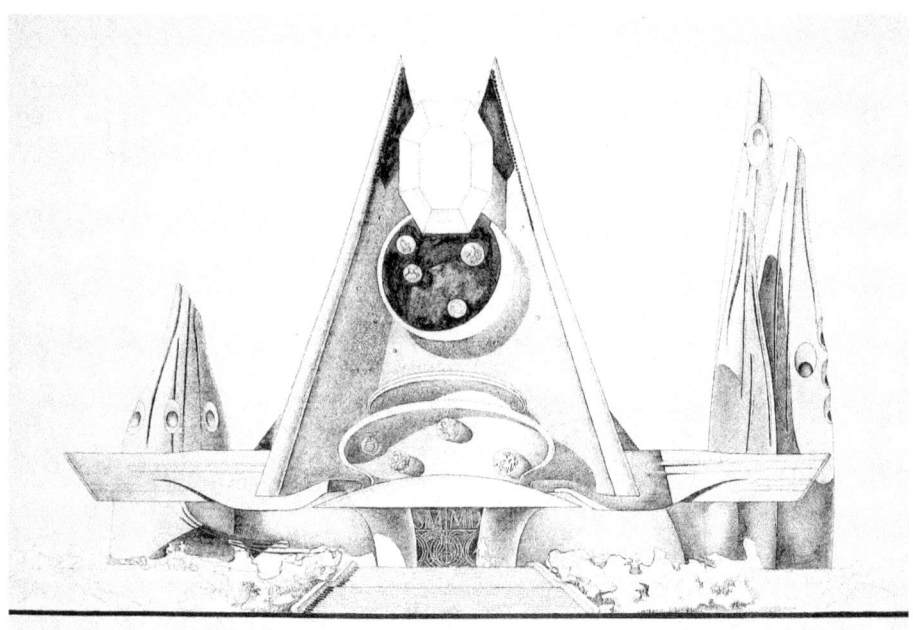

FIGURE 6.1. Luigi Moretti, Sancta Maria Mater Ecclesiae, 1965–1970. Front elevation. Central State Archive, Rome, Luigi W. Moretti Archive, Box 91, "Relazione."

symbols, he strove to avoid the emptiness of those early churches after the Council, which he judged to be a consequence of creating "form without content."[7]

The themes raised in the foregoing episode involve the constituent parts of the interpretive challenge raised by modern religious architecture, as situated within the theological, sociopolitical, and architectural context of postwar Italy and as explicitly explored in Moretti's Sancta Maria Mater Ecclesiae, the so-called Chiesa del Concilio, 1965–1970 (figure 6.1).[8] An unbuilt project for a new Roman Catholic parish church, the design Moretti sought would embody and celebrate the achievements of the Council and thereby tackle the crisis of meaningful form as it is encountered in the case of a modern parish church. Despite not being built, Moretti's project remains significant because of the effort he made to root his proposal in the theology of the first document promulgated by the Council, the *Sacrosanctum Concilium* (also known as the "Constitution on the Sacred Liturgy," December 4, 1963). Furthermore, to consider it in this light is also to consider a frequently sought or claimed but in fact fairly rare phenomenon: an architectural design whose primary identity and driving motivation is the expression of explicitly stated ideas.[9]

In the design, Moretti emphasized radical novelty even as he described and justified it through explicit reference to far-flung and heavily interpreted historical precedent. Questions of form and its relation to content are present but are addressed with such an emphasis on spatial and bodily experience, and their various theological underpinnings, that they often appear sidelined. In this regard, it is helpful to approach Moretti's work with not only a phenomenological orientation but also a conception of form that meaningfully serves such an orientation. This can be found by considering ornament, arguably the element of architecture most directly related to form and content, primarily in terms of function. Ornament is also directly related to modern identity in architecture, as the polemics surrounding ornament, from its purported banishment to efforts at inventing it anew, frame much of the ongoing challenge of understanding modernism.[10] A promising approach to ornament that emphasizes its function and is rich in implications regarding modernism is that developed by Oleg Grabar in *The Mediation of Ornament*, in which ornament is much less about the appearance of forms than the functions they perform, fundamentally various mediating functions.[11] This shifts the discussion, albeit tenuously, away from form per se, which will enable a better understanding of Moretti's work.

In this chapter I will consider the Chiesa del Concilio in terms of Moretti's stated theory, as articulated in the most pertinent of his writings and as evident in his broader practice. The juxtaposition of his design with his theory, driven as they both are by his reflections on the possibilities for modern religious architecture embodied in the Second Vatican Council, will also suggest a stance toward the interplay of modern identity and religious experience that is traditional and yet critical, consistently eschewing nostalgia.

Chief among the relevant writings is Moretti's unpublished brief for the design of Sancta Maria Mater Ecclesiae, which includes an interpretation of *Sacrosanctum Concilium*. Also directly pertinent to the project are the implications of earlier reflections on the Council ("Dove due o tre") and his analysis of the architectural, historical, and theological aspects of the communicative crisis mentioned above ("Spazi-luce nell'architettura religiosa").[12] But Moretti was working within multiple contexts, the most immediate of which is the design and construction of postwar churches in Italy. More broadly, the sociopolitical context of the period raised specific challenges concerning matters of modern identity, religious practice, and architectural culture. And more broadly still, the theoretical challenges of modern religious architecture are rooted in the historical emergence of the communicative crisis Moretti laments.

THE PROBLEM OF MODERN RELIGIOUS ARCHITECTURE

The very concept "modern religious architecture" tends in many ways toward contradiction. Whatever else it may suggest, religion appears to be about binding together (re-legio) with reference to a historical, even primordial, unity centered upon a creator or a transcendent realm.[13] Whether the object of such binding is stated mainly in terms of ontology or tradition (as in the narrative roots of myth), it surely involves a high view of history. Indeed, religious practices are hardly comprehensible apart from the traditions that have formed them. Yet the complicated set of phenomena and constructs that constitutes "the modern"—including the broad matrix of developments known as modernization as well as movements to embrace, express, or engage such developments under the banner of modernism—is regularly understood to signify a critique of, or distancing from, history and tradition, in the name of progress and the commitment ever to be new.[14] Even more to the point, however, the emergence of modernity is in many respects, if not consistently and universally, a secularizing phenomenon.[15]

To be sure, "modernity" and its cognates as here described are underdetermined: they disguise a wildly varying set of experiences and intentions, not all of which are set in opposition to history or tradition nor shift away from religious identity or practice. Nevertheless, both views—breaking from history and increasing secularization—gained sufficient traction to mark the historiography of modern architecture with a relative silence regarding religious buildings, especially when considered against their dominance across previous centuries. But by now modern religious architecture has been widely disseminated for more than fifty years and its first exemplars are at least a century old.

What sense is there, then, to the notion that a building is both modern and religious? In what manner are these descriptors reconciled, held in tension, or otherwise related? To consider the "religious identity" of a building is to take a typological approach to architecture, which in turn is to ask what is a church (or mosque, temple, etc.) and how do viable models develop and change over time? That answers to such questions display increasing difficulty in obtaining a broad purchase as modernity emerges is a central aspect of the crisis of meaningful form.

In his *The Bavarian Rococo Church: Between Faith and Aestheticism*, philosopher Karsten Harries traces this history and locates this communicative crisis of religious architecture in the Enlightenment's apotheosis of reason and the attendant aesthetic approach to art.[16] In this view, art must be pure and so cannot serve anything, including religion. Thus architecture is caught between two problematic positions: either it is useful but not beautiful, or it is beautiful but not fully architecture. But, what is a church? By any standard open to the matter of significant form, it must be a complete work of architecture, which is to say that it must be both beautiful and practical—yet precisely this is impossible in the aesthetic view of things.[17] Invoking significant form suggests that ornament is the central phenomenon, as in fact Harries concludes. Looking toward Moretti, however, if ornament is conceived solely by way of its intermediary function, following Oleg Grabar, then the problem of form may be opened up to new possibilities for modernity that do not presume a stock of commonly understood forms. But this requires a closer look at the question of how art is related to religion across the possibilities of figuration and abstraction.

Adolf Loos's critique of ornament is a central moment in the formation of modern identity in architecture, notwithstanding that it is still widely misconstrued.[18] Harries considers the nature of Loos's critique in some detail, highlighting two commonly overlooked aspects: the suggestion that ornament is related to religion and the notion that it evokes transcendence. Amidst his economic and cultural arguments against ornament that is no longer viable, Loos acknowledges the value to artisans of hours spent making ornament, calling them "holy hours." And for Harries, under the sway of the aesthetic approach such art would be self-justifying: "Art for art's sake is the ornament of modern life." Yet he glosses the creation of ornament by saying that "it attunes its creator to a larger order" and observes that ornament, despite the rhetoric, clearly has some hold on Loos that goes beyond mere nostalgia.[19] He even closes the book with an appeal concerning the Bavarian Rococo churches he has analyzed as displaying this death of ornament: if these churches still somehow exert some claim upon us, then surely the aesthetic approach must be unacceptable, however much any coherent community of meaningful form or notion of beauty as a sign of transcendent beauty may seem to be forever gone for us.[20]

As Harries observes, Immanuel Kant, the philosopher who most definitively articulates Enlightenment thought regarding art, identifies ornament as one of the few examples of fully autonomous, and therefore pure, artworks, thereby denying its architectural function of mediation. This is clearly one of the stops along the road to abstract art, for the Enlightenment's philosophical standard of pure autonomy requires that art serve no purpose; thus even figuration is impure insofar as it serves a representational purpose.[21] Indeed, the final sentence of Harries's Introduction sums it up: "The rococo church dies as the aesthetic sphere claims and gains autonomy. A once coherent value system splinters. One of the splinters is modern art."[22]

Particularly relevant here is the theory of the French philosopher Jacques Maritain, first fully articulated in *Art and Scholasticism* (1920). This was a clear reaction against the Kantian aesthetic approach that sought to move ahead by reaching back to Scholastic thought in a sort of retrieval. Far from relying on the received formulae of Scholasticism as it had trickled down from the nineteenth century, against which Catholic modernist theologians railed, Maritain went to the sources and retrieved them so that artistic form and its relation to religious content could be reconceived. For Maritain, art is an intellectual virtue and therefore is not tied to any specific concrete form. Rather, it is the internal form of the work of art that counts, such that the abstract is in fact the spiritual.

> What is required is not that the representation exactly conform to a given reality, but that through the material elements of the beauty of the work there truly pass, sovereign and whole, the radiance of a form ... and therefore of a truth. ... Here we have the formal element of imitation in art: the expression or manifestation, in a work suitably proportioned, of some secret principle of intelligibility which shines forth. It is upon this that the joy of imitation bears in art. It is also what gives art its value of universality.[23]

Maritain's is an antirepresentational theory of art that nonetheless claims a high view of art's value for religion in a modern world: it provides access to universal truth, it enjoys absolute artistic freedom, and it is simultaneously ever new yet deeply rooted in the central philosophical tradition of the Church.[24]

Maritain's philosophy of art was foundational for many modern artists, Catholic and non-Catholic alike, and Maritain himself played a crucial role in shaping the Council's reforms as they pertained to the arts. His approach was also coherent with the historical stance underlying *ressourcement*, the method of renewal employed by the advocates of the *nouvelle théologie* and most directly responsible for the reforms of the Second Vatican Council.[25] As a strategy it was both traditional and radical: *ressourcement* is usually translated with the phrase "back to the sources," suggesting an attitude of skepticism toward the present because of what it considers to have been lost in the ongoing development of tradition. That is, it posits a break in history to reach back and retrieve something that had become obscured but is in fact more authentic for being original, which in turn is brought forward to provide content for contemporary reform. Thus, it is traditional in its appeal to the past yet radical in its potential for disrupting current trajectories.

Such developments as these emerged, however, only against the sociopolitical backdrop of a Fascist "reactionary modernism" and a Vatican intransigence against modern culture and theological innovations, in contrast to which Italians then established their first democratic republic (1946) and the institutional Church embarked upon the remarkable rapprochement with modernity that was the Second Vatican Council.[26] In 1907 Pope Pius X had declared "modernism" to be "the synthesis of all heresies" (*Pascendi Dominici Gregis*), a position generally continued by subsequent popes and which led to the censure and suppression of modernist theologians during the 1950s under Pius XII. Such institutional intransigence and resistance to all that was modern was by then surely stirred up and complicated by the recent Fascist past, the end of which provided the immediate instigation for reappraising modernity and working toward resolving a long-developing identity crisis. The Church's embroilment in the quasi-religious practices of the Fascist regime (whose totalitarian capitalization of technology was just one sign of its implicit modernity, reactionary historicizing gestures notwithstanding), against the backdrop of the failure to adequately combat the Holocaust from the highest level, was a key aspect of this identity crisis.[27] Its nineteenth-century origins were most clearly seen in the dismantling of the Church's temporal powers resulting from the unification of the Italian state during the 1860s, amidst a paradoxical consolidation of institutional power in the papacy culminating in the declaration of papal infallibility during the First Vatican Council (1869–1870).[28] Thus in the years immediately following the end of the Second World War, it was hardly to be expected that the Church would soon signal a major reorientation toward the modern world, as was evident from the initial announcement of the Council on January 25, 1959, by Pope John XXIII.[29]

The social and political identity crisis that was at work here is so often seen in contrast to the Fascist years but is best understood against the longer interplay between the myth of Italy and the concrete history that eventually led to unification.[30] The postwar context for these issues was characterized by multiple, conflicting efforts, resulting in an overall indeterminateness.[31] Furthermore, due perhaps mainly to the recurrent failure to resolve matters of collective identity, in the postwar years there was a decline of interest in nationalism or patriotism of any kind.[32] The complexity of the debates only increased as the Fascist–anti-Fascist dualism gave way to that of Communist–anti-Communist, especially as the anti-Fascists were very different than the anti-Communists in identity and emphasis, and each had varieties and subspecies within.[33] More specifically, the Church that had always resisted and opposed the liberalism of democracy in favor of monarchy, and subsequently had befriended Fascism in part to better oppose Communism, aligned itself with this political liberalism after the war for the first time in history, marked especially by Pope Pius XII's 1944 Christmas Message.

A similar identity crisis emerged in the realm of architectural discourse during these years, marked by a distinct note of critique directed toward modernism's developing reception. An important intervention in this regard was by the art historian and professor Giulio Carlo Argan.[34] In the 1957 article "Architettura e ideologia" he sought to reclaim the moral and political edge to modernism, which had been present in the Bauhaus and other early modernist endeavors but had since become subordinated to if not completely eclipsed by an aesthetic ideology. Materially changing the world for the better through the careful application of modern technology was the real meaning of attention to function, not any look of functionalism. His chief diagnosis of the sociopolitical cause underlying the decline of modernism's ethical import was the failure to see the choice between technocracy and humanism as a false choice: technology and its employment could and must be an integral part of any viably modern humanism.[35]

Argan's article came in the midst of the renewed criticism of modernism from within, so to speak, that was oriented toward reforming it away from its perceived inhumane and alienating aspects (as well as its merely aesthetic aspects). The formation in 1957 of the "Team 10" group within the Congrès Internationaux d'Architecture Moderne (CIAM) is a key international example of this development.[36] More locally, the Italian debate over so-called Neo-Liberty architecture, such as BBPR's Torre Velasca in Milan (1954), concerned the question of whether such formal experiments constituted a betrayal of modernism toward an antihistorical (because not fully modern) romanticism. The same charge was leveled at Le Corbusier's pilgrimage chapel Notre Dame du Haut in Ronchamp, France, also completed in 1954, by Argan and others.

The decade of the 1960s was marked more by further change and rupture than by any development or resolution of these critiques. In fact, increasing controversy over reforming modernism amidst the broader political and cultural changes provoked altogether new approaches, perhaps best exemplified by the appearance, both in 1966, of the protest architecture of Superstudio and Archizoom, as well as of two publications regularly described as provoking the move into postmodernism: *Complexity and Contradiction in Architecture* by Robert Venturi (1925–), and *L'architettura della Città* by Aldo Rossi (1931–1997).[37] Thus the postwar period featured an identity crisis in architecture as well as in Catholicism, both having distinct expressions in Italy and Rome, which converge to make the challenge of modern religious architecture all the more palpable.[38] That the prospects for such endeavors were fraught with difficulty is suggested by the apropos remark by Catholic theologian Edward Schillebeeckx (1914–2009): "After two centuries of resistance, Catholics embraced the modern world just at the moment when the modern world began to distrust itself."[39]

Church architecture in postwar Italy reflects this period of multiple identity crises. As architect and historian Sandro Benedetti notes, there is hardly any possibility of summarizing the whole landscape: many churches were built, but all within an architectural culture that mostly ignored matters of religious architecture during these years, so that they remain broadly unknown.[40] Considering the centrality of religious import to such work, Benedetti holds up Saverio Muratori (1910–1973) and Luigi Moretti as emblematic of two fundamentally opposed ways of articulating the problem. Muratori, writing in 1956, identified the difficulty in terms of prevailing sociopolitical culture in postwar Italy: the freedom required of art was caught between the dominance of Crocean aesthetics and the subsequent spread of Marxist materialism. His idiosyncratic answer was to build explicit juxtapositions of old and new as instantiations of difficult mediation (e.g., his "baroque" church S. Maria dell'Assunzione, in the Tuscolana area in Rome, 1954).[41] Moretti's view centered on a communicative crisis of form and content; his solution to it, mediated by the events of the Council, is embodied in his Chiesa del Concilio.

More generally, the broader landscape of postwar Italian church architecture exhibits three main characteristics: 1) there was a new confidence when compared to the relative timidity of architects during the preceding decades; 2) new churches displayed an extreme formal simplification, especially in the presbytery; and 3) an interest in the dynamic spatial quality of the nave found expression longitudinally, vertically, and in striking uses of materials.[42] Despite the confidence and experimentation, the situation in Italy was far behind that in France, Germany, or Switzerland with respect to liturgical reform and innovation. Nevertheless, even in Italy there were signs for those attentive to them, as with Pius XII's suggestion of coming reform in his encyclical *Mediator dei* (November 20, 1947). The leading places for liturgical experimentation and reform within Italy were the dioceses of Milan, Turin, and Bologna. Milan led the way from the 1930s and 1940s with the earliest experiments, as in the work of Cesare Cattaneo (1912–1943) and Mario Radice (1898–1987), and later Enrico Castiglioni (1914–2000), though nothing in Milan was ever as organized as in Bologna.[43]

Benedetti takes the case of the Diocese of Bologna, under the leadership of

Cardinal Giacomo Lecaro (1891–1976), to encapsulate the movement from the experiments, greatly increased after 1955, to the virtual abandonment of religious import in the "crisis of the sacred" brought on by a turn to a new functionalism.[44] Indeed, through the journal *Chiesa e quartiere* and the founding of the Centro di Studio e Informazione per l'Architettura Sacra in the mid-1950s, the Diocese of Bologna sponsored conferences and spurred a vibrant movement focused upon modern church architecture and its surrounding urban challenges, including work by Le Corbusier and Alvar Aalto.[45] Common characteristics of the work included: efforts to integrate clergy and congregation; centralized plan organizations and interior focus; translation of traditional procession into a wrapping around the central area; and the idea of the church as refuge within the city.[46] By the late 1960s, Lecaro was calling for a completely neutral conception of the church, the better to address the functional problems in the midst of the contemporary city, with no appeal to any "sense of the sacred" or theological importance of the liturgy, let alone any attempt at communicative form.[47]

This movement roughly parallels a broader one that contrasts the new confidence and open, listening attitude of the Church to the world embodied by the Second Vatican Council, with the increasing confusion by the late 1960s over conflicting interpretations of the Council's reforms.[48] Benedetti suggests the work of Giovanni Michelucci (1891–1990) as emblematic of such a development, evolving as it did from the 1950s through the 1970s into more expressionist forms, which appeared more as icons of the turbulent times than as embodiments of any specific liturgical or theological value (and at times worked against such values).[49] Moretti's work aimed instead at direct liturgical and theological principles, rooted as it was in the specific reforms of the Council.

LUIGI MORETTI: BACKGROUND AND DEVELOPMENT

Luigi Moretti was Roman through and through. Born in Rome in 1907, he lived on the same street, via Napoleone III, for most of his life. Raised by his mother, he kept a small studio in the building of his youth—even much later in life after he was married in 1968. He attended a prestigious secondary school, Collegio San Giuseppe, Istituto de Merode, and then the Regio Scuola di Architettura from 1925 to 1930. Moretti graduated with the highest honors and won the Valadier Prize for the best thesis. His earliest work was centered on the study and restoration of monuments, on which he built a solid reputation.

The year after graduating, he assisted Gustavo Giovannoni in history and restoration courses and continued to pursue work in the studio he had opened while still a student. He had several collaborators, including painters, and their work ranged widely, including advertising, interior design, and exhibition planning. That same year he also worked on the Trajan markets with Corrado Ricci, through whom he met Renato Ricci, then undersecretary of Educazione Nazionale, who appears in turn to have introduced Moretti to Felicia Abruzzese, an important contact within elite Fascist society.⁵⁰ An increased profile came to him in short order: in 1933, at just twenty-seven years of age, he was named director of the technical office of the Opera Nazionale del Balilla, the organization behind the Fascist youth movement. This role brought involvement, even when not direct commissioning, in major projects for the government. But commissions were plentiful in any event: Moretti designed almost fifty projects or buildings for the regime. Furthermore, if many architects took on such work, he was surely prominent among them by virtue of working on projects of special interest to Mussolini, thereby ensuring not only attention from him but also greater coverage by the press.⁵¹

Perhaps the most important, public, and monumental of these projects was the Foro Mussolini (now Foro Italico), for which he assumed from Enrico Del Debbio (1891–1973) the responsibility to coordinate the various projects contained therein.⁵² Moretti also designed several of the individual elements: the Casa delle Armi (1933–1936), the Piazza dell'Impero (1937), the Palestra del Duce (1936), and the Sacrario dei Martiri (1940–1941).⁵³ He also oversaw the design of local headquarters for the organization throughout Italy and designed several headquarters himself. As his career progressed, Moretti developed something of a following, for which he rented a villa in Tivoli where he and his entourage would retreat and join friends, clients, and others for occasional festivities and creative collaboration. While it is unclear who was typically included in this group, Moretti was surely becoming well known within the Fascist party and its extended community, and he had among his clients many party officials.⁵⁴

Professionally, Moretti retained a distinctive individual voice. He was not tied to any of the major movements and was outspoken in his criticism of the major modernist school, the Rationalists, declaring in an interview that it was "born on paper, where it will live and die infallibly."⁵⁵ Indeed, his touchstones were found throughout history and included artists and architects from ancient Greece and Rome to Michelangelo to Baroque Rome. As a collector of eighteenth-century paintings and classical busts as well as contemporary art, he opened and operated a gallery in the 1950s. His involvement with Fascism is difficult to assess fully, but Cecilia Rostagni suggests that his work was guided as much by the myth of Romanità as anything more overtly political, especially as the idea of Rome was hardly a myth to Moretti. He never sought an architectural language for Fascism as much as he simply strove to form for Rome an appropriately "new face" of a "new people" through architectural order and clarity, but above all by transcending the past without contradicting or opposing it. Rome was already sacred to Moretti and therefore beyond political ideas. The political content of his work seems mainly focused upon gathering together the new Fascist monuments with the already present historical ones, to progress only in the spirit of continuous change that always operates out of a living tradition.⁵⁶

Despite conflicting reports from biographers, it seems Moretti largely disappeared from public life from 1942 to 1945. He supported the Repubblica Sociale

Italiana, Hitler's puppet state led by Mussolini in Salò, and after the war's end he was arrested and imprisoned for several months in Milan for trying to found a new political party. In prison he met Count Adolfo Fossataro, with whom he would gradually reenter Roman society by way of a joint venture, Cofimprese, pursuing housing and other rebuilding efforts, first in Milan and then in Rome.[57] Nonetheless, amid the postwar controversies the Italian press largely ignored him until the mid-1950s, though even in this period his work was covered in a few foreign publications.[58]

Back in Rome, Cofimprese was dissolved in 1956, but Moretti continued work in the speculative rebuilding of the city, becoming chief architect for the large real-estate company Società Generale Immobiliare. Despite being very much on the outside of the political currents of postwar Roman society, Moretti nonetheless gained support through a combination of factors, including success in the newly capitalist suburban development, major commissions such as commercial headquarters in significant sites, and family ties that came with his marriage in 1968 to Maria Teresa Albani, an heiress of one of the most prominent Roman families. He also enjoyed a remarkable level of professional success, winning a series of prominent regional, national, and international awards from 1957 to 1964, including being named a member of the Accademia di San Luca and an honorary member of the American Institute of Architects.[59] Following his reintegration into Roman society and resumption of professional advancement, Moretti worked on urban and international projects through the late 1960s.

There was an important theoretical aspect to Moretti's work as well, especially in the postwar period. In what was undoubtedly in part a self-promotional effort, he produced a short-lived journal, publishing seven issues over three years. *Spazio* (1950–1953) was characterized by provocative graphic design and research driven by a deeply synthetic approach to the subject matter, such as historic architecture studied with an eye to the most theoretical aspects of contemporary discourse, with inventive and at times unusual methods. For instance, in the article "Strutture e sequenze di spazi," he pursued a study of the spatial qualities of architecture by modeling in positive, three-dimensional form the interior spaces of well-known buildings as a way to understand the phenomenological aspect of spatial experience through the inversion of material and immaterial form.[60] He often studied patterns or forms through close-up photographs of the elements involved and careful, detailed proportional and geometric analysis alongside.[61] Indeed, this combination of careful attention to form in all its particularity and far-reaching consideration of spatial experience in all its subtlety both marks his architecture as distinctive and makes it all the more difficult to categorize in any traditional fashion. It also naturally brings into question any presumed correspondence between form and content, especially as this pertains to the formal aspects of ornament understood as mediation. Moretti used clay models in the design process from 1933 and seems to have been preoccupied with what he took to be the Baroque notion of monolithic, modeled conceptions of architecture.[62]

In the late 1950s he worked to advance what he called "parametric architecture," a study of architectural and mathematical relationships, first through the Istituto Nazionale per la Ricerca Matematica e Operativa per l'Urbanismo (IRMOU) beginning in 1957 and then, with Michel Tapié, through the International Center for Aesthetic Research in 1959. This work was presented at the Milan Triennale in 1960, to extensive media coverage. The 1950s also marked an increased interest and involvement in activities concerning religious architecture.[63] Moretti began to form a professional relationship with Giovanni Fallani in 1956, then director of the Pontifical Commission for Sacred Art in Italy; in 1961 he participated in the 9th Week of Sacred Art (where he presented the talk that would become the essay "Space-Light in Religious Architecture"); in 1963 he joined a public debate in Turin on Italian sacred architecture; and he was nominated to the jury for new churches in Rome in 1967, governed by the Pontifical Office for the Preservation of the Faith and the Provision of New Churches in Rome, wherein he represented architects from Rome and Lazio.[64]

In some respects, these efforts were all wrapped up in the project for Sancta Maria Mater Ecclesiae, and, indeed, Marco Mulazzani sees it as a culmination of Moretti's experiments in plastic unitary form, especially as the full integration of form, light, and structure into a single "unified absolute."[65]

The concrete occasion of the project for the church Sancta Maria Mater Ecclesiae was a public workers' housing development (1960–1965) planned for the area immediately to the southwest of the E42/EUR (Esposizione Universale Roma), called "Decima." The EUR had originally been planned as the site of the 1942 World's Fair Exposition (E42) and a showcase of Fascist culture, all of which were eclipsed by the war and marked the area with ambivalence for the postwar population. The church was designed to fit into and cap one edge of the new complex, for which Moretti was the architect in charge of urban planning. He was also the architect, along with Vittorio Cafiero, Adalberto Libera, and Ignazio Guidi, for the housing itself, comprising a series of sinuous blocks, four- or five-story buildings set upon *pilotis*.[66] The housing was built, but Moretti's church never was. A church for the parish was later built about a mile to the southwest, designed by Giorgio Pacini in 1985–1987.[67]

However, the idea of a new parish church dedicated to Mary as Mother of the Church originated at the Second Vatican Council itself. As one of a few surprise announcements at an allocution on November 18, 1965, during the final session of the Council, Pope Paul VI declared he would build a church dedicated to Mary, Mother of the Church. On December 8 of the same year, the final day and official close of the Council, the pope blessed a cornerstone for the new church.[68] Significantly, Moretti refers specifically to the closing days of the Council in his reflections on the great challenge facing architects who would design new churches, calling out Paul VI's closing address (December 7, 1965) as a "stupendous speech" that clarified the spirit with which one should proceed.[69] Furthermore, the following day, immediately after blessing the cornerstone of the church-to-be, the pope introduced several speeches that were closing addresses from the Council as a whole to various particular audiences, including one "To Artists" as "the guardians of beauty in the world." This was likely written by Jacques Maritain, whose aesthetic vision of modernism, critical of modernity without becoming nostalgic, would find an uncanny similarity in Moretti's ideas as they are given to explain the design for the Chiesa del Concilio.

Overall, the Decima housing development was organized around two cross axes, with the church planned for the southwest end of one, its opposite end heading toward the Tiber. According to Moretti's description of the project as presented to the housing authority, the entire complex was conceived as a house, so as to maximize opportunities for bumping into other human beings, making physical interaction practically inevitable. This was to be achieved through the formal interplay among the undulating facades and the resultant intervening pedestrian spaces, streets, and intersections.[70] That is, Moretti conceived the urban planning as primarily a matter of spatial creation, whose form factors would then be directed to enhancing the lived experience therein.

SACROSANCTUM CONCILIUM

The Second Vatican Council was an unexpected and remarkable event. Less than six decades had passed since Pius X had declared "modernism" to be "the synthesis of all heresies" (1907), and the reactionary mode had continued through the 1950s with Pius XII and his censure and suppression of modernist theologians. After Pius died (on October 9, 1958) and John XXIII was elected his successor, no one expected any major changes, but on January 25, 1959, the new pope announced the Council. As it happened, many of the theologians that had been silenced by Pius XII played an important role in the preparation for the Council. Furthermore, the charter of the Council itself stands out rather forcefully when compared to all previous such events in terms of its sheer proportion, its nature and focus, its openness to the laity and the broader world, the style of its discourse, its specific decisions, and its guiding principle of *aggiornamento*.[71]

Concerning church architecture, the first document promulgated at the Council, the Constitution on the Sacred Liturgy, or *Sacrosanctum Concilium*, has often been seen as having mandated an adoption of the *domus ecclesiae* model (church as house for the assembly of worshipers) over against a previously dominant *domus dei* model (church as house of God).[72] But the change it effected was more indirect, if still substantial.

The document in fact said relatively little about architecture. The original schema for the Constitution did have specific suggestions attached but the Council discussion settled instead on broad guidelines rather than laws. There followed Instructions that went into more detail (September 1964), such as recommending the placement of the high altar away from the wall so that celebration with the presider facing the people would be made possible. Still, neither the placement nor the *versus populum* celebration were mandated. Yet the rise in Eucharistic practice as the standard rite in many places, along with the "banquet-character" of the rite and the cultural increase of "community-consciousness" during these years, together so changed common practice that by 1966 the Constitution was widely held to have mandated such changes when it did no such thing, and the subsequent Instruction merely enabled them.[73]

What, then, does the Constitution on the Sacred Liturgy say?[74] First, there is an introduction followed by seven parts, only the last of which concerns "sacred art and furnishings," which in turn includes architecture. Major themes of the Introduction pertain to the nature of the Church and have in common a union of potentially opposed or conflicting tendencies: the Church is human as well as divine, visible as well as invisibly equipped, active as well as contemplative, and present in the world as well as not truly at home here. The first section expressly concerns liturgical reform, and four principles or concepts stand out: "full active conscious participation" of the laity in the liturgy is encouraged; "noble simplicity"[75] is held up as a guiding aesthetic principle; liturgy is a communal, not an individual, activity; and the use of the vernacular language is allowed (though not mandated).

Subsequent sections concern the Eucharist, other sacraments, the Divine Office (accounts of saints and martyrs should accord with the facts of history), the liturgical year (it should suit the conditions of modern times), sacred music (chant and organ music is treasured, but the Church is open to other possibilities), and, finally, sacred art and furnishings. This last section features three observations, the most closely tied to the problem of architecture to be found in the entire document: no style is uniquely suited to church usage; the prevalent art of contemporary times should yet be given "free scope" as long as it is exercised with "due reverence and honor"; and sacred images used for veneration may be retained, but their use should be moderated to keep the practice properly ordered.

MORETTI ON *SACROSANCTUM CONCILIUM*

In the unpublished brief prepared to accompany the formal presentation of the design for Sancta Maria Mater Ecclesiae, Moretti pursued a rather inventive meditation on what he took to be the overarching meaning of *Sacrosanctum Concilium* for the purposes of modern church art and architecture.[76] He begins by reviewing some challenges bequeathed by history. Considering the development of architecture from 1750 onward, he insisted that while there had been great examples of architecture among "sacred buildings," there had not been "churches" of high expression.[77] Instead, there had reigned a "domination of form for form's sake," without content or meaning.[78] And with the Enlightenment transformation of neighborly love into mere social contract, whatever meaning may have lain dormant in the liturgy was then reduced further still, leaving only a functionalist answer to a liturgy that was felt to be ever more "habitual, tired, and worn out."[79] Moretti observed that it was significant that *Sacrosanctum Concilium* was the first document issued by the Council; it was a sign of the crisis. It was equally significant that the document avoided strict formulae or explicit directives to architects. Nevertheless, Moretti identified some guidelines as discernible therein.[80]

Here it is remarkable that Moretti did not proceed with the "noble simplicity" principle or with any other aspect of the document obviously related to art or architecture. Rather, he identifies three main categories of guidelines: objectivity, love, and prayer.[81] Objectivity refers to the document's insistence upon the intrinsic goodness of all of creation and the attendant focus upon quotidian reality, and runs counter to both positivists and idealists.[82] Love refers especially to love of the neighbor and is based on the human-God analogy. It implies two lessons for Moretti that have distinct relevance for the postwar Italian setting: he contends that Marxism arose only because Christian love declined, and that any community must be "materially visible" to be real or actual.[83] Finally, liturgical prayer is fundamentally communal and involves both thought and action. Nevertheless, there is room for the public-private distinction, as expressed through the distinction between (public) liturgy and (private) devotion.[84]

Moretti moves on from here with what he takes to be the implications regarding church architecture. Several themes emerge. First, new church architecture would inevitably be speculative. It is no mere extension of a continuing tradition, nor is it a recovery of a remote yet still viable one. Also, there should be no arbitrary form without meaning. Rather, the situation and challenge require forms with both new and ancient meanings. In whatever form, the assembly of persons is properly at the center of such a new church, and it should be filled with a diffuse and clear light.[85]

Building upon the idea of the assembly of persons at the center, Moretti considers that a community is the sum of its parts, and these constitute the various forms of individual as well as communal prayer. Accordingly, the new church architecture should provide concatenations of spaces for such.[86] Also following from this idea of assembly and prayer is the notion that the church should be a refuge from the external world, which Moretti suggests be achieved through the exclusion of "elements recalling visual construction."[87]

The aim here is no mere separation for separation's sake, but all is oriented toward the goal of exalting the gathered community. Architecturally, such a "temple" exalts only with "absolutely new forms," in an environment of "space-light," featuring "abstract forms in an atmosphere of humanly sublime tensions" that together bring about "an infinite and indissoluble inseparable unity."[88] Hardly suggestive of any one model, *domus dei*, *domus ecclesiae*, or otherwise, Moretti's conceptual interpretation of the guiding themes of objectivity, love, and prayer toward concrete expression in architectural form trades at every turn upon some strategy of mediation, perhaps best encapsulated on the whole by his phrase "humanly sublime tensions."[89]

SANCTA MARIA MATER ECCLESIAE

How, then, does Moretti envision such ideas taking physical and phenomenal form as an architectural celebration of the Council? First, as it remained an unbuilt project and emphasized the conceptual content over specifics of construction, Moretti presented the church in various media and with differing apparent aims at work. Furthermore, as one of his tenets was to avoid marks of recognizable constructive traditions, the ideal seems to have been a somewhat atectonic approach, which raises the question of whether Moretti's church is in any plausible way buildable (figure 6.1).

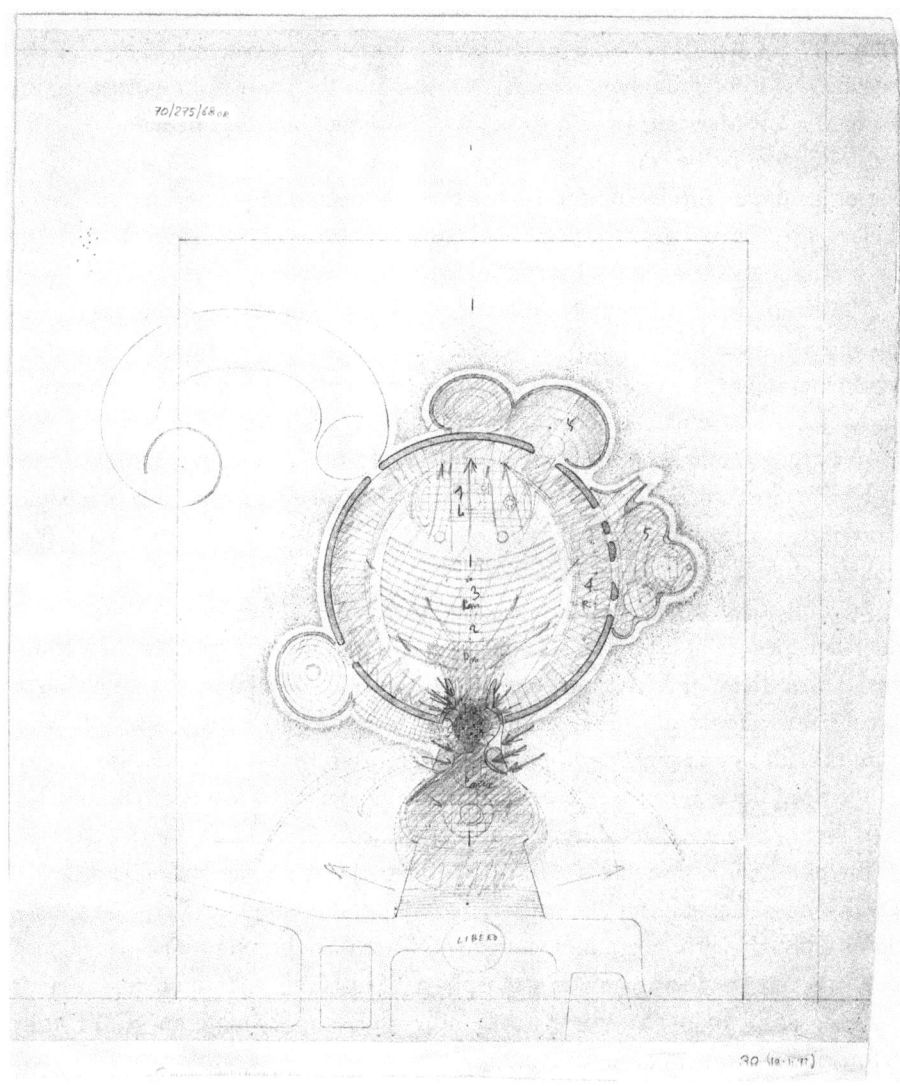

FIGURE 6.2. Luigi Moretti, Sancta Maria Mater Ecclesiae, 1965–1970. Design drawings. Central State Archive, Rome, Luigi W. Moretti Archive, 70/275/68OR.

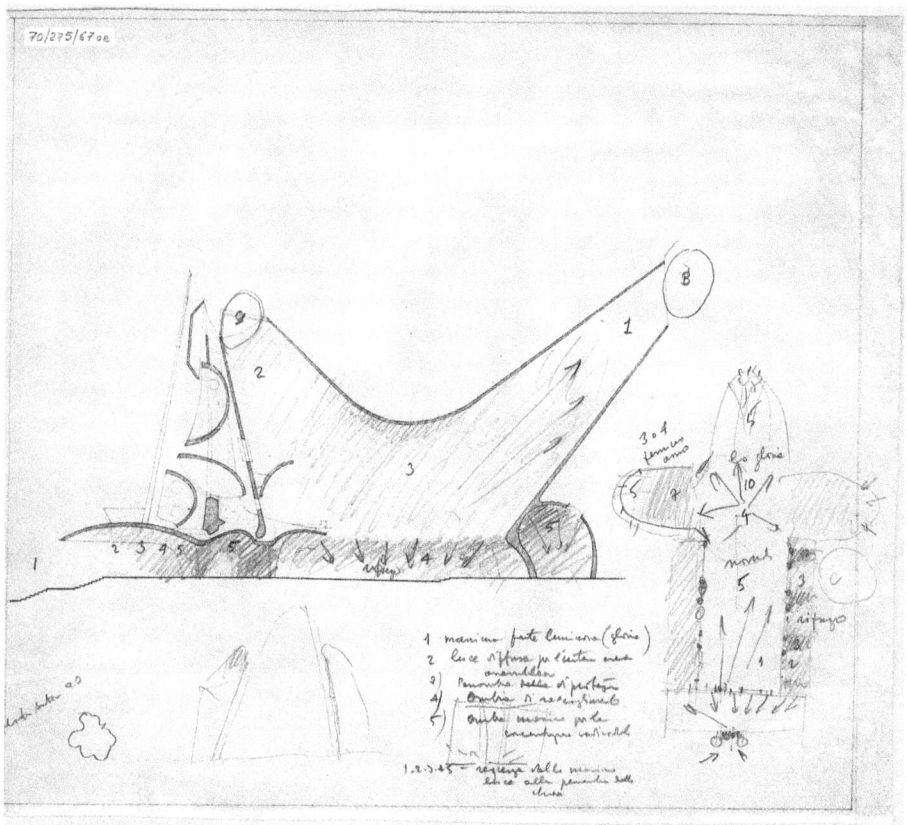

FIGURE 6.3. Luigi Moretti, Sancta Maria Mater Ecclesiae, 1965–1970. Design drawings. Central State Archive, Rome, Luigi W. Moretti Archive, 70/275/67OR.

Moretti's description of the church in his brief begins with the entry. Many drawings show the architect working out in great detail some way to understand and control the phenomenological experience of moving into and through the church (figures 6.2 and 6.3). One enters underneath a broad covering and then through a zone of constriction or spatial compression, moves through a momentary reprieve or breath and on through another, lesser place of compression, and then bursts out into the interior of the church. Beyond a mere attempt to orchestrate a dramatic entry, Moretti suggests a sort of analogue, mapping the procession onto a typical plan of a traditional Latin-cross church (figure 6.3). Here he lists the successive stages of a downright historically conditioned model, formally represented in abstract plan forms, but translates them into a new form that is structured by spatial experience and the notion of "space-light." In the final package of presentation material for the design, he distills these considerations into a set of conceptual diagrams that seek to explain how various levels and qualities of light help to define the concatenation of zones within the church as well as to coordinate with and reinforce the spatial compression-expansion scheme

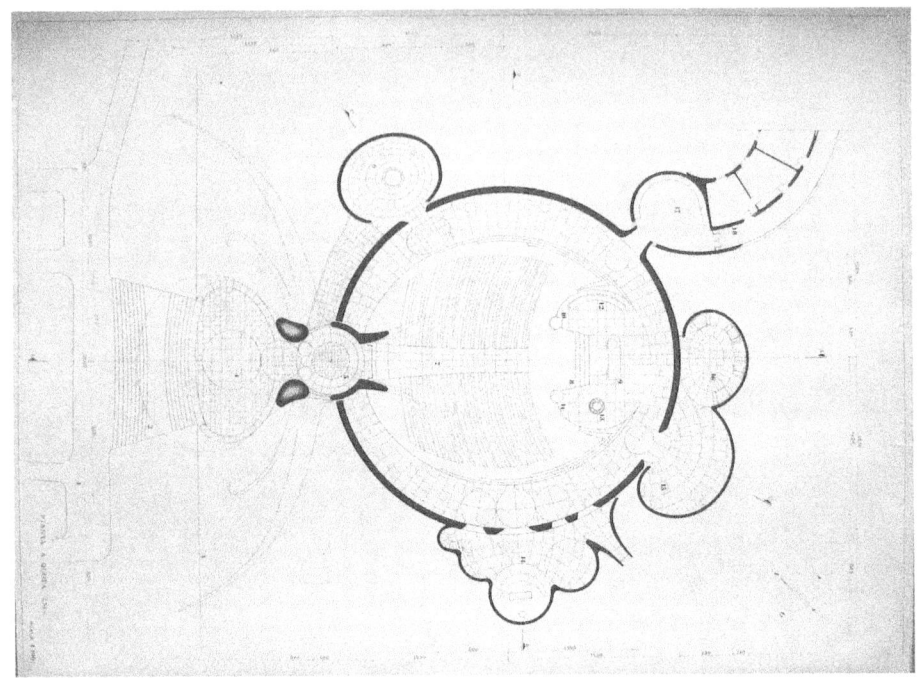

FIGURE 6.4. Luigi Moretti, Sancta Maria Mater Ecclesiae, 1965–1970. Plan. Central State Archive, Rome, Luigi W. Moretti Archive, Box 91, "Relazione."

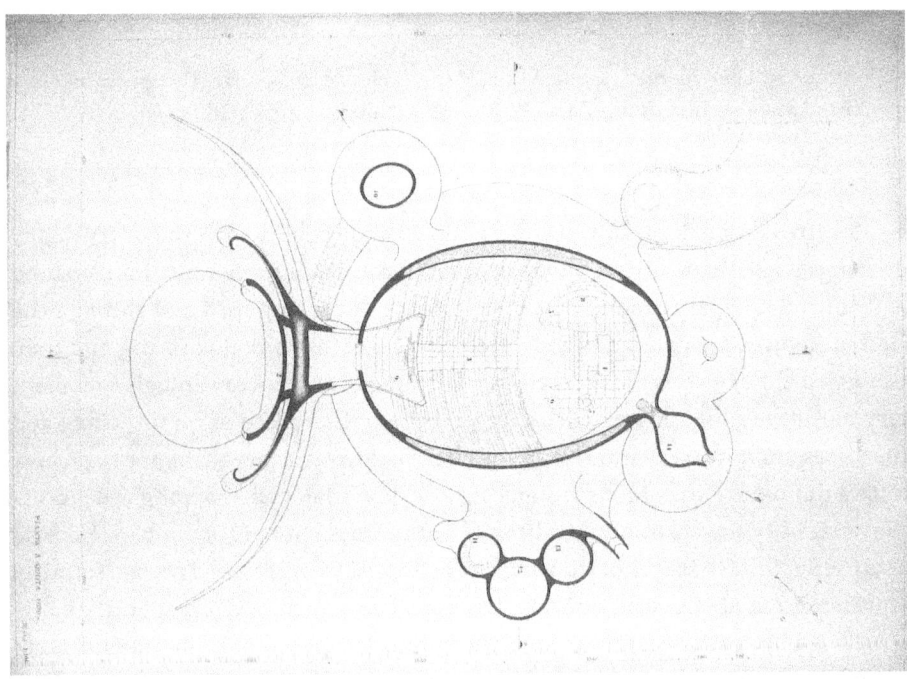

FIGURE 6.5. Luigi Moretti, Sancta Maria Mater Ecclesiae, 1965–1970. Plan. Central State Archive, Rome, Luigi W. Moretti Archive, Box 91, "Relazione."

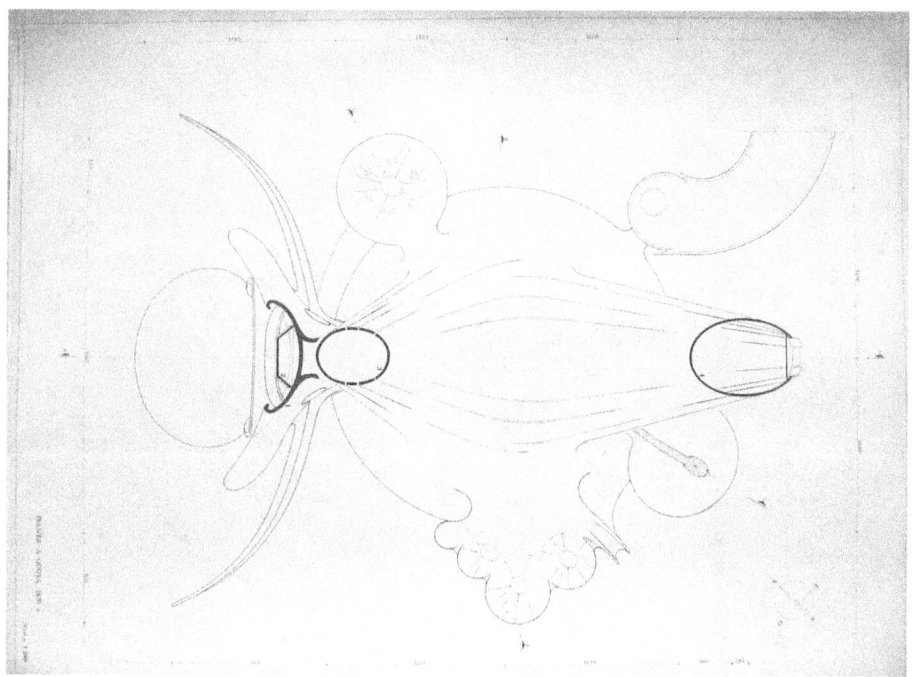

FIGURE 6.6. Luigi Moretti, Sancta Maria Mater Ecclesiae, 1965–1970. Plan. Central State Archive, Rome, Luigi W. Moretti Archive, Box 91, "Relazione."

that seeks to leave behind the external world and prepare for the "magical sacred space" of the assembly.[90] Whereas "sacred space" alone would normally imply some governing ideal other than the gathered assembly, something more akin to *domus dei* than to *domus ecclesiae*, Moretti is intent upon holding them together.

Attending to the plan geometry, a distinct progression develops that also embodies a tension of normally conflicting orders (figures 6.4, 6.5, and 6.6). The plan is a perfect circle at its base, but then as the walls ascend (and following the floor plans cut at successively higher levels; Moretti presents six such plans) the form is entirely transformed: first to a single ellipse, then to an elongated ellipse, and finally to dual ellipses. The idea is to use the shifting form of the walls to effect the change rather than any meeting of disparate forms, so that the aggregate experience transcends any specific form. Moretti also notes the size of the planned church to house a thousand people and to be about 30 meters in diameter, comparing this favorably to the Pantheon (40 meters), S. Maria Maggiore (30 meters) and S. Andrea (26 meters).[91]

A longitudinal section conveys a sense of Moretti's requirement that there be no divisions, joints, or marks of construction (figure 6.7). Indeed, the image is more like a biological entity, more grown than anything constructed. This drawing also shows the two opposing "fountains of light." One faces north and so provides a diffuse, homogeneous "reading" light (Moretti refers to Brunelleschi's

FIGURE 6.7. Luigi Moretti, Sancta Maria Mater Ecclesiae, 1965–1970. Longitudinal section. Central State Archive, Rome, Luigi W. Moretti Archive, Box 91, "Relazione."

S. Spirito in Florence), while the other faces south and features both multicolor and transparent glass (Moretti refers to Gothic cathedrals and to the mystical theology of S. Teresa d'Avila). The hoped-for result is not so easy to render either verbally or visually: "the interior space will be elusive, formed by vaporous, continuous luminosity" (figures 6.8 and 6.9).[92]

Turning then to the place of the clergy, Moretti describes the ensemble of altar, ambos, seats, and tabernacle as deserving special status and so necessarily elevated (figure 6.8). The tabernacle receives emphatic treatment, here being tall and so holding the reserved sacrament aloft, yet also utterly eschewing any further enclosing gesture but rather offering it "isolated like a precious tower" and marking it by a "blade" of light from the "gash/rip" in an otherwise immutable wall (figures 6.5, 6.8, and 6.9).[93]

Moretti sums up the whole as "a 'continuum' for coordinating, molding/forming universality, transcendent and earthly."[94] One relatively minor but telling detail helps express the tension-filled mediation between the mundane and the transcendent that he seems to have in mind: when discussing voice amplification, he proposes a series of microphones be installed unobtrusively in various places all around (altars, ambos, etc.) so that as one moves around the naturally human voice is amplified as if by the very environment.[95] A similarly minor but provocative remnant of his thinking in the process of design can be found in two separate

FIGURE 6.8. Luigi Moretti, Sancta Maria Mater Ecclesiae, 1965–1970. Interior perspective. Central State Archive, Rome, Luigi W. Moretti Archive, Box 91, "Relazione."

FIGURE 6.9. Luigi Moretti, Sancta Maria Mater Ecclesiae, 1965–1970. Model. Central State Archive, Rome, Luigi W. Moretti Archive, 70/275/42279.

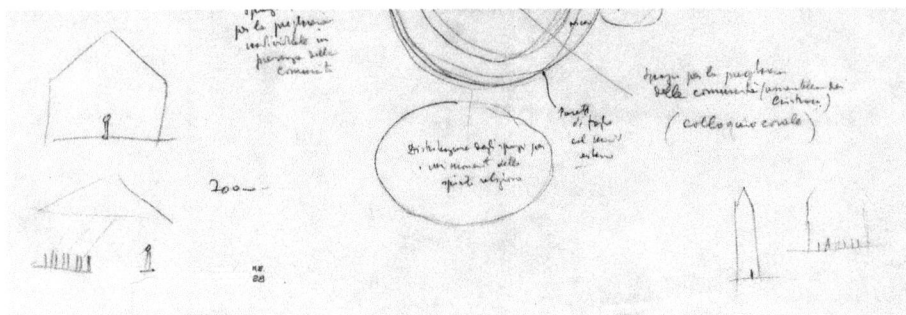

FIGURE 6.10. Luigi Moretti, Sancta Maria Mater Ecclesiae, 1965–1970. Design drawings, detail. Central State Archive, Luigi W. Moretti Archive, 70/275/25OR.

parts of one drawing, where he appears to have sketched out in a diagrammatic way the two commonly opposed models for a church (figure 6.10): if the one is taken to distill to an image the *domus ecclesiae* model with a gathered community and a presider, all enclosed within a domestic shape, the other may be a similar distillation of the *domus dei* model, with more monumental shapes either held high above a community of persons or standing directly behind a single being. That both occupy separate corners of a single sheet seems appropriate to the architect seeking above all to create "a magical gathering space between the visible and the invisible."[96]

CONCLUSION

Luigi Moretti's design of the church that was to celebrate and express the modernizing achievement of the Second Vatican Council is defined by a tension between otherwise opposed ideas, forms, and gestures. That is, it is explicitly not defined by a clear choice of one obvious model over another, be that choice for *domus ecclesiae* over *domus dei*, communal over hierarchical space, or modernism over history. Rather, it is a distinctive tension that seeks to express what Moretti took to be the essence of the challenge of modern religious architecture in the midst of its crisis: to express the relation between the human and the divine, or what he simply calls the "religious spirit" and aligns closely to light. In the midst of the crisis of communicative forms, the church must be utterly modern and new, yet also deeply rooted in the most ancient of traditions.[97]

Recalling Oleg Grabar's suggestion to see ornament as mediation and thereby reconceive the formal aspect of ornament entirely, Luigi Moretti's Sancta Maria Mater Ecclesiae appears to carry modernism to its conclusion by drawing upon the most basic elements of spatial experience in the creation of something entirely new. Indeed, to the degree that one wants to see recognizable, material forms in the design, notions of biomorphism and evocations of Mary's womb emerge. But Moretti nowhere speaks of this. Rather, he seeks to achieve "a transcendent unity" that both focuses upon the gathered community yet in turn orients that community toward the transcendent other.[98]

Moretti draws upon his invention of a phenomenological form, "space-light," in order to evoke an altogether new and unfamiliar environment that nonetheless is rooted experientially in the long tradition of Western church architecture. Moretti uses "space-light" in his descriptions and drawings to convey movement into and through the church. He also uses it to govern this movement according to historical models that are not, however, echoed formally. Central to his entire narrative, both describing the church as well as glossing the contributions of the Council, is the tension between the human and the divine, and this is mapped onto light in theological as well as architectural terms. That is, beyond the formal, spatial, and phenomenological levels of analysis, Moretti is after beauty as a distinctly theological end, as the glory that is invoked by human stances toward the divine but yet remains utterly transcendent. In an almost parenthetical comment at the end of his reflection stemming from the promise of divine presence in the midst of human community ("Dove sono due o tre riuniti nel mio nome . . . [Matteo 18.20]"), Moretti reminds the reader that beauty is "the mirror of divinity." He warns that iconoclasm is to be avoided; one must be courageous and the architect must "sharpen his animus," all the while remembering the distinction between "living beauty" and "worn-out beauty."[99]

Thus, Moretti insists upon locating "living beauty" ultimately in the divine but as made visible through reflection in the works of artists and architects. This puts his aesthetic squarely in line with Maritain, for whom art is an intellectual virtue and the divine beauty is best reflected to the modern world by the most abstract "forms." Yet Moretti takes Maritain's equation of the abstract with the spiritual to its logical conclusion, to the point of positing the immaterial, amorphous form that is "space-light" as the governing motif of his design. It serves as the primary ornament that mediates the experience of the work of architecture, understood here especially in terms of the human-divine encounter that is located within the gathered humanity. Indeed, Moretti distills the Council's call for "full active conscious participation" and its insistence that liturgy be "communal, not individual" into the exaltation of the gathered community in the "magical sacred space" of the church. This is the culmination of the modern project insofar as it pertains to Catholic architecture, for the sacred is hereby fully brought to reside within the people. And where older, historic forms of ornament could be seen as references to a transcendent reality, the ornament of "space-light" connotes rather a triumph of immanentism.

It is therefore ironically appropriate that the Chiesa del Concilio was never built. Moretti's postwar reception was complicated; he was typically dismissed as only a "formalist" or reviled as politically toxic as he combined continuity with the Fascist past with the material successes of postwar modernism and modernization.[100] Indeed, the first treatment of Moretti in these years that appears genuinely unprejudiced is foreign: Robert Venturi's brief discussion of the Casa del Girasole in Rome in *Complexity and Contradiction in Architecture* (1966). Venturi's discussion was followed shortly thereafter by translations of essays from *Spazio* in the American journal *Oppositions*.[101] That Venturi's book would come to be seen as a harbinger of postmodernism is especially relevant, for Moretti's critique of modernity has much in common with various streams of postmodern thought. However underdetermined the "postmodern" surely remains, it often includes a return to transcendence that is rooted in modernity having run its course or otherwise having proven insufficient to the task of providing meaning.[102] Moretti's Chiesa del Concilio is a focused expression of his interpretation of the Second Vatican Council, but it may also serve as a memorable figure for a self-critical modernity marked most of all by its awareness of its own mortality.

NOTES

1. The literature on Moretti is immense, though his religious architecture has been addressed far less often and only quite recently. His religious buildings comprised just seven projects—two Fascist-era memorials, three parish churches, and two sanctuaries—only one of which was built, and it was subsequently demolished. As a noteworthy exception to the historiographical silence, more documentary than interpretive but providing a solid groundwork for future research, see Gemma Belli, *Luigi Moretti: il progetto dello spazio sacro* (Florence: Alinea Editrice, 2003) and "Progetti di chiese nella ricerca di Luigi Moretti," *Palladio* 16, no. 31 (January 2003): 69–86. For general introductions, see Bruno Reichlin and Letizia Tedeschi, eds., *Luigi Moretti: Razionalismo e trasgressività tra barocco e informale* (Milan: Electa, 2010); Federico Bucci and Marco Mulazzani, eds., *Luigi Moretti: Works and Writings*, trans. Marina deConciliis (Princeton, NJ: Princeton University Press, 2002); and Cecilia Rostagni, *Luigi Moretti: 1907–1973* (Milan: Electa, 2008).

2. "Dove sono due o tre riuniti nel mio nome . . . (Matteo 18.20)," *Fede e arte* 15, nos. 4–6 (1967): 8–15, reprinted in Belli, *Luigi Moretti*, 140–143. English translation by Marina deConciliis in Bucci and Mulazzani, eds., *Luigi Moretti*, 201–204.

3. Moretti, "Dove sono due o tre," 8–9: "scarne e nude."

4. For basics on the project, see Belli, *Luigi Moretti*, 75–79, and Rostagni, *Luigi Moretti: 1907–1973*, 216–220.

5. Rostagni, *Luigi Moretti: 1907–1973*, 65.

6. Ibid., 40–41.

7. Moretti, "Dove sono due o tre," 8–10.

8. Accompanying the design drawings, models, and photographs of the project in the Luigi Moretti Archive at the Archivio Centrale dello Stato in Rome are presentation materials of the final design, including a red, cloth-bound book containing Moretti's theoretical and programmatic explanation for the design; see "Relazione," Luigi Moretti Archive, ACS, Box 91. Not referring explicitly to the Sancta Maria Mater Ecclesiae but clearly articulating his views and goals for new churches in light of the Council are also Moretti, "Dove sono due o tre," and "Spazi-luce nell'architettura religiosa," *Fede e arte* 10, no. 1 (1962): 168–198.

9. I thank Dennis Doordan for first making this observation.

10. See Tim Culvahouse, "On Ideas: Hello . . . Is Anybody Out There?" *Harvard Design Magazine* 9 (Fall 1999): 84–88.

11. Oleg Grabar, *The Mediation of Ornament* (Princeton, NJ: Princeton University Press, 1992).

12. *Fede e arte* 10, no. 1 (1962): 168–198.

13. The etymological note under "religion" in the Oxford English Dictionary includes the following: "*re- re- prefix* + a second element of uncertain origin; by Cicero connected with relegere to read over again . . . so that the supposed original sense of 'religion' would have been 'painstaking observance of rites,' but by later authors (especially by early Christian writers) with *religāre* religate v., 'religion' being taken as 'that which ties believers to God.' Each view finds supporters among modern scholars." The two senses of the term loosely align with "ritual studies" and sociologically informed approaches to the study of religion in the first instance and to the tradition of phenomenologically oriented historians of religion, most prominently Mircea Eliade, in the second. For criticism that such methods harbor implicit (and illicit) presumptions concerning "the sacred" to which humans seek to be rebound, see Jonathan Z. Smith, *To Take Place: Toward Theory in Ritual* (Chicago, University of Chicago Press, 1987). See also Eliade, *The Sacred and the Profane: The Nature of Religion* (New York: Harcourt Brace, 1959). For more recent debate about the cogency of the term for the field of religious studies, see Timothy Fitzgerald, *The Ideology of Religious Studies* (New York: Oxford University Press, 2000), and Jonathan Z. Smith, "Religion, Religions, Religious," in *Critical Terms for Religious Studies*, ed. Mark C. Taylor (Chicago: University of Chicago Press, 1998): 269–284.

14. These terms are of course related in complex ways that continue to be debated, as does the interpretation of modernism (in architecture as well as in other fields) with respect to its attitude toward history. For the purposes of this discussion, "modernity" is the broad cultural term indicating a period or place having been marked by the results of "modernization," which in turn includes the dominance of post-Cartesian and especially post-Kantian rationality, industrialization, urbanization, liberal democratic political structures and ideals, and an overarching presumption of progress. Thus various origins are postulated, yet all are dependent upon the distinctly "modern" penchant for historical periodization, within which the present and future are privileged as in some significant sense having surpassed traditional, "premodern" societies. "Modernity" is thus as much an ideological construct as it is a set of phenomena. "Modernism" describes more or less organized movements in particular fields, which seek explicitly to engage modernity rather than merely to oppose it. Objectives of such engagement vary: some mainly champion modernity while others primarily critique it, often in order to mitigate certain negative consequences of modernization. The common orientation amidst these differences is the focus upon the present and the future, typically rejecting or at least distancing oneself from the past in some manner. For just one indication of the ongoing discourse surrounding "modernity" and its cognates, see the interdisciplinary journal *Modernism/Modernity* and its sponsor, the Modernist Studies Association.

15. The "secularization thesis," according to which the waning of religious belief is constitutive of modernity, has surely been challenged in recent years; see, from among many, Talal Asad, *Formations of the Secular: Christianity, Islam, Modernity* (Stanford, CA: Stanford University Press, 2003), and Charles Taylor, *A Secular Age* (Cambridge, MA: Belknap Press of Harvard University Press, 2007).

16. Karsten Harries, *The Bavarian Rococo Church: Between Faith and Aestheticism* (New Haven, CT: Yale University Press, 1983).

17. Ibid., 251.

18. See Adolf Loos, *Ornament and Crime: Selected Essays* (Riverside, CA: Ariadne Press, 1997); Christopher Long, "The Origins and Context of Adolf Loos's 'Ornament and Crime,'" *Journal of the Society of Architectural Historians* 68, no. 2 (June 2009): 200–223.

19. Harries, *The Bavarian Rococo Church*, 248–249.

20. Ibid., 255–258.

21. Ibid., 253–255.

22. Ibid., 9.

23. Jacques Maritain, *Art and Scholasticism with Other Essays* (n.p.: FQ Classics, 2007), 60.

24. See Stephen Schloesser, *Jazz Age Catholicism: Mystic Modernism in Postwar Paris, 1919–1933* (Toronto: University of Toronto Press, 2005), 160–162.

25. See John W. O'Malley, *What Happened at Vatican II* (Cambridge, MA: Harvard University Press, 2008), 301. O'Malley notes that much of the discussion over reform in the liturgy also appealed to *aggiornamento*, commonly translated as "updating," or to the similar approach of "development," yet he argues that *ressourcement* was more widespread and at times the real driving force for change despite a rhetorical gloss that was less threatening.

26. See Geoffrey Herf, *Reactionary Modernism: Technology, Culture, and Politics in Weimar and the Third Reich* (Cambridge: Cambridge University Press, 1984) for the concept, combining explicit celebration and embrace of modern technology with nostalgic appeals to idealized forms of history and tradition, as evident in the case of the rise of National Socialism.

27. See Michael Phayer, *The Catholic Church and the Holocaust, 1930–1965* (Bloomington: Indiana University Press, 2000) for an analysis of the Vatican's failure under Pope Pius XII (1939–1958) to condemn and oppose Nazi atrocities during the war even as it made partial attempts to counter their effects and aid Jews. Phayer attributes this failure to the pope's view of the Soviet Communist threat and his choice to maintain the Church's potential role as mediator in order to minimize further warfare globally. See also Carlo Falconi, *The Silence of Pius XII*, trans. Bernard Wall (Boston: Little, Brown, 1970). Individual Catholics, priests and laypersons, certainly were involved enough in the resistance that Roberto Rossellini's *Roma città aperta* (1946), the first major postwar film and the first globally known Neorealist film (due to winning the Grand Prize at Cannes), portrayed the sacrificial assistance given by the parish priest, Don Pietro.

28. See Nicholas Atkin and Frank Tallett, *Priests, Prelates and People: A History of European Catholicism since 1750* (Oxford: Oxford University Press, 2003).

29. Despite the announcement being short on specifics, it was remarkable both for being couched in positive rather than disciplinary, negative terms (the dominant tradition with councils) and for including an ecumenical invitation to non-Catholics to participate. See O'Malley, *What Happened*, 15–18.

30. For contemporary historiographic evidence of an identity crisis, found in the overwhelming focus on national history at the expense of all other subjects, see S. J. Woolf, "Research into Contemporary History in Italy," in *Contemporary History in Europe: Problems and Perspectives*, ed. Donald C. Watt (New York: Praeger, 1969): 134–150. A similar historiographic limitation prevailed in the interwar years as Italians were surrounded by ideological battles not conducive to historical research; see Furio Diaz, "Federico Chabod e la 'nuova storiografia' Italiana dal primo al secondo dopoguerra (1919–50)," *Storia della Storiografia* 4 (1983): 138–144.

31. See Christopher Duggan and Christopher Wagstaff, eds., *Italy in the Cold War: Politics, Culture, and Society, 1948–58* (Oxford: Berg, 1995).

32. See Emilio Gentile, *The Struggle for Modernity: Nationalism, Futurism, and Fascism* (Westport, CT: Praeger, 2003), 184–185.

33. See Aurelio Lepre, *L'anticomunismo e l'antifascismo in Italia* (Bologna: il Mulino, 1997); David Ward, *Antifascisms: Cultural Politics in Italy, 1943–46: Benedetto Croce and the Liberals, Carlo Levi and the "Actionists"* (Madison, NJ: Fairleigh Dickinson University; London: Associated University Press, 1997); Sandra Pescarolo, "From Gramsci to 'Workerism': Notes on Italian Working-Class History," in *People's History and Socialist Theory*, ed. Raphael Samuel (London: Routledge and Kegan Paul, 1981): 273–278.

34. Argan would later be the mayor of Rome, its first from the Communist Party (PCI), 1976–1979.

35. "Architettura e ideologia," *Zodiac* 1 (1957): 47–52.

36. See Eric Mumford, *The CIAM Discourse on Urbanism, 1928–1960* (Cambridge, MA: MIT Press, 2000), especially chapter 4. See also Alison and Peter Smithson, "The New Brutalism," *Architectural Design* (April 1957): 113.

37. Robert Venturi, *Complexity and Contradiction in Architecture* (New York: Museum of Modern Art, 1966); Aldo Rossi, *L'architettura della città* (Padova: Marsilio, 1966).

38. There was of course a difference in the way in which the respective identity crises were perceived, for while within the architectural community in Italy (and elsewhere) the question of continuity was widely and publicly debated, the postwar institutional Church presented itself as very much in control. There was in fact some consideration of convening a council under Pius XII in the early 1950s, but such possibilities were kept quite secret at the time. O'Malley, *What Happened*, 17.

39. Quoted in David Tracy, "The Uneasy Alliance Reconceived: Catholic Theological Method, Modernity, and Postmodernity," *Theological Studies* 50 (1989): 556. Schillebeeckx was a Dominican theologian associated with the *nouvelle théologie* movement among modern Catholic theologians that was influential in shaping the reforms of the Council.

40. "Per una geografia della situazione italiana (1945–1995)," in Sandro Benedetti, *L'architettura delle chiese contemporanee: il caso italiano* (Milan: Jaca Book, 2000), 15–102; original edition, "L'esperienza religiosa nell'architettura italiana dell'ultimo cinquantennio," in *Profezia di Bellezza. Arte sacra tra memoria e progett*, ed. Mariano Apa (Roma: CISCRA Edizioni, 1996): 205–216.

41. Benedetti, *L'architettura delle chiese contemporanee*, 16–18.

42. Ibid., 19.

43. Ibid., 21–23.

44. Ibid., 49–68.

45. See Glauco Gresleri, *Chiesa e quartiere: storia di una rivista e di movimento per l'architettura a Bologna* (Bologna: Compositori, 2004).

46. Benedetti, *L'architettura delle chiese contemporanee*, 49–56.

47. Ibid., 57–58.

48. Ibid., 61–62.

49. Ibid., 66–68. See also Amedeo Belluzzi, Giovanni Michelucci, and Claudia Conforti, *Lo spazio sacro nell'architettura di Giovanni Michelucci, Archivi di architettura* (Torino; Milano: U. Allemandi; Messaggerie libri, 1987).

50. Belli, *Luigi Moretti*, 15.

51. Rostagni, *Luigi Moretti: 1907–1973*, 38.

52. See Antonella Greco and Salvatore Santuccio, *Foro Italico* (Rome: Clear, 1991).

53. See See Cherubino Gambarella, "Luigi Moretti e il disegno della Palestra del Duce, Scrittura, spazio e prospettiva," *ArQ* 12 (1994): 170–178.

54. There is an account that he met Mussolini personally at the Imperial Fora and discussed great issues concerning urban migration, the relationship between the city and the country, and such themes, but the only testimony to this is from Yvon De Begnac, a sympathetic biographer of Mussolini. See De Begnac's *Luigi Moretti Architetto Romano* (Rome: Agenzia Giornalistica Romana, 1974).

55. Quoted in Bucci and Mulazzani, *Moretti*, 213. See L. Diemoz, "Luigi Moretti architetto. Propositi di artisti," *Quadrivio* 3 (December 12, 1936).

56. Rostagni, *Luigi Moretti: 1907–1973*, 56–60.

57. See Bucci and Mulazzani, *Moretti*, 214; Agnoldomenico Pica, "Luigi Moretti," Luigi Moretti Archive, ACS, Box 98; De Begnac, *Luigi Moretti Architetto Romano*; Belli, *Luigi Moretti*, 15.

58. These included *L'architecture d'Aujourd'hui*, *The Architectural Review*, and the Swedish *Svenska Dagbladet*. See Belli, *Luigi Moretti*, 15.

59. Ibid., 15–16.

60. In *Spazio* 7 (December–April 1952–1953): 9–20.

61. See, for example, Luigi Moretti, "Valori della modanatura," *Spazio* 3, no. 6 (December–April 1951–1952): 5–12.

62. Bucci and Mulazzani, *Moretti*, 29, n. 23.

63. See, for example, the inclusion of his spatial studies in the first National Congress of Sacred Architecture, 1955, in Bologna; for documentation, see Luciano Gherardi, ed., *Dieci anni di architettura sacra in Italia, 1945–1955* (Bologna: Edizione dell'Ufficio tecnico organizzativo arcivescovile, 1956); see also Glauco Gresleri, "La questione del sacro," in *Luigi Moretti: Razionalismo e trasgressività tra barocco e informale*, eds. Bruno Reichlin and Letizia Tedeschi (Milan: Electa, 2010), 295–311.

64. Rostagni, *Luigi Moretti: 1907–1973*, 147, 157, nos. 131–135.

65. Bucci and Mulazzani, *Moretti*, 25–28.

66. The development was administered by the Istituto Nazionale per le Case degli Impiegati dello Stato (INCIS). Salvatore Fruscione, "Quartiere INCIS a Decima," in *La capitale a Roma: città e arredo urbano, 1945–1990*, ed. Daniela Fuina et al. (Rome: Carte Segrete, 1991), 81.

67. Stefano Mavilio, *Guida all'architettura sacra: Roma 1945–2005* (Milan: Electa, 2006), 194. In the interim, however, the commission had gone to Luigi Figini and Gino Pollini in 1978; see Gresleri, "La questione del sacro," 307.

68. O'Malley, *What Happened*, 283–289.

69. Moretti, "Dove due o tre," 8.

70. Achille Maria Ippolito, "La progettazione dello spazio pubblico tra utopia e realtà," in Fuina et al., *La capitale*, 76. See also Rostagni, *Luigi Moretti: 1907–1973*, 260–263.

71. See John W. O'Malley, S.J., "Vatican II: Did Anything Happen?" *Theological Studies* 67 (2006): 3–33. His summary description of the changes embodied in the event of the Council, as seen in its vocabulary, is worth quoting in full: ". . . from commands to invitations, from laws to ideals, from threats to persuasion, from coercion to conscience, from monologue to conversation, from ruling to serving, from withdrawn to integrated, from vertical and top-down to horizontal, form exclusion to inclusion, from hostility to friendship, from static to changing, from passive acceptance to active engagement, from prescriptive to principled, from defined to open-ended, from behavior-modification to conversion of heart, from the dictates of law to the dictates of conscience, from external conformity to the joyful pursuit of holiness." Ibid., 29.

72. To be more precise, the "house church" has been distinguished by L. Michael White from a *domus ecclesiae*, or the "house of the church," with the former indicating an unrenovated house used by the community for worship and the latter meaning a remodeled house given over for dedicated use by the community. In both cases, however, the architectural environment is domestic and nonmonumental in character. See *The Social Origins of Christian Architecture. Volume 1: Building God's House in the Roman World: Architectural Adaptation among Pagans, Jews and Christians* (Valley Forge, PA: Trinity Press, 1996), 102–139.

73. See Josef A. Jungmann, "Constitution on the Sacred Liturgy," in *Commentary on the Documents of Vatican II*, ed. Herbert Vorgrimler (New York: Herder and Herder, 1966): 1–88, 84n5.

74. For Conciliar and post-Conciliar documents, see Austin Flannery, O.P., ed., *Vatican Council II: The Conciliar and Post Conciliar Documents* (Collegeville, MN: Liturgical Press, 1977).

75. The theme of "noble simplicity" seems to have originated with the debate in the 1760s

and 1770s over the relative authority of the Greeks vs. the Romans, an eighteenth-century variation of the slightly earlier (and more French) *querelle des Anciens et des Modernes*. The new debate was spurred by the growing awareness of Greek antiquities amidst excavations of Paestum, near Naples, and featured the German scholar Johann Joachim Winckelmann's promotion of Neoclassicism (pro-Greek) and Giovanni Battista Piranesi's printmaking and architectural design (pro-Roman). Winckelmann positively characterized classical Greek art as one of "noble simplicity and calm grandeur," and the liturgical appropriation of this notion seems to have begun with Edmund Bishop and as a matter of combatting Northern European liturgical inculturation as part of Pius X's attack on modernism. See Edmund Bishop, *The Genius of the Roman Rite* (London: Beaufort House, 1899). See also C. Johnson and A. Ward, "Edmund Bishop's 'The Genius of the Roman Rite': Its Context, Import and Promotion," *Ephemerides Liturgicae* 110, no. 6 (1996): 401–444. The original phrase appears in Winckelmann's essay "Gedanken über die Nachahmung der griechischen Werke in der Malerei und Bildhauerkunst" (1755), in *Winckelmann's Werke*, ed. C. L. Fernow (Dresden: 1808–1835), vol. 1, 31–32.

76. See "Relazione," Luigi Moreti Archive, ACS, Box 91.
77. Ibid., 2.
78. Ibid., 3.
79. Ibid., 4.
80. Ibid., 5–6.
81. Ibid., 7–9.
82. Ibid., 7.
83. Ibid., 7–8.
84. Ibid., 9.
85. Ibid., 10.
86. Ibid., 11.
87. Ibid., 12.
88. Ibid.
89. Ibid.
90. Ibid., 15.
91. Ibid., 16.
92. Ibid., 17.
93. Ibid.
94. Ibid., 20.
95. Ibid., 20–21.
96. Moretti, "Spazi-luce," 189.
97. Ibid., 170.
98. Moretti, "Dove due o tre," 14.
99. Ibid., 15.

100. Manfredo Tafuri and Francesco Dal Co wrote of his later buildings that "he locked himself into a formalism that was its own end." *Modern Architecture*, trans. Robert Erich Wolf (New York: Harry N. Abrams, 1979), 382. For the political toxicity, see Belli, *Luigi Moretti*, 16.

101. Belli, *Luigi Moretti*, 16–17. Venturi, *Complexity and Contradiciton*, 22. The translations appear in *Oppositions* 4 (October 1974).

102. For example, see the theologians of Radical Orthodoxy. As foundational texts, see John Milbank, *Theology and Social Theory: Beyond Secular Reason* (Cambridge: Cambridge University Press, 1993) and Catherine Pickstock, *After Writing: On the Liturgical Consummation of Philosophy* (Oxford: Blackwell, 1998).

7 MODERNISM AND THE CONCEPT OF REFORM
LITURGY AND LITURGICAL ARCHITECTURE

RICHARD KIECKHEFER

On the face of it, the rise of modern church architecture appears closely linked to the development of liturgical reform. Both were anticipated in Western Europe shortly before World War I, became discernible movements after that war, gained mainstream adherence after World War II, and became canonical if not virtually universal after the Second Vatican Council, not only in Roman Catholicism but in mainline Protestant denominations as well. At every stage there were proponents of modern church design who took inspiration and authorization from the work of liturgical reformers. Writers on church architecture of the mid-twentieth century sometimes report with evident astonishment that a church of the 1940s or 1950s anticipated the reforms of Vatican II by several years, but in fact the liturgical documents of the Council represent one moment in a movement of liturgical reform that had been in progress since the early twentieth century, and churches of earlier decades were in some measure indebted to the earlier stages of that reform. Still, the alliance was not simple or inevitable. The link between modern church design and liturgical reform turns out, on closer inspection, to be more complicated and problematic than it first appears. The purpose of this chapter is to explore certain respects in which the two movements worked separately and even at cross-purposes, and then to isolate other respects in which the alliance was nonetheless real.

First of all, the liturgical reform of the early to mid-twentieth century was fundamentally historicist, while modern church design sought to move beyond the historicism of the revival styles. While modernist architects might find inspiration in historical precedent, the past did not have the normative force for them that it had for the liturgical reformers.

When liturgical reforms were carried out, they were inspired or at least justified as a return to early liturgical usage. Already under Pope Pius XII, modest reforms such as the restoration of the Paschal Vigil to the evening of Holy Saturday were represented in that light.[1] Odo Casel's classic book *Das christliche*

Kultmysterium (1932) articulated a conception of worship grounded in an affinity with the mystery cults—an affinity that was recognized by Christian writers as early as the third century, fully manifested in Cyril of Jerusalem's *Mystagogical Catechesis*, and enshrined in Leo the Great's dictum, "What was visible in the Lord has passed over into the mysteries" (meaning the liturgy), or Ambrose's more succinct "I find you in your mysteries."[2] If other liturgical reformers sought to restore particulars of early Christian worship, Casel wished to restore an early conception of its spirit. Not coincidentally, some of the leading voices in mid-twentieth-century liturgical reform were those of liturgical historians. Josef A. Jungmann's massive survey of *The Mass of the Roman Rite* made all those concerned with liturgy more keenly aware of the ways in which the mass had been changed.[3] In and beyond the Anglican Church, Dom Gregory Dix's book *The Shape of the Liturgy* (first published in 1945) had profound influence.[4] One key theme of Dix's work was the transformation of the liturgy in the fourth and fifth centuries after the conversion of Constantine and the influx of multitudes into the Church and into the churches. The Eucharist had originally been a corporate action of the entire congregation: celebrants, deacons, and congregations all played an active role. In the post-Constantinian era, it became increasingly clericalized as "something which the clergy were supposed to do *for* the laity."[5] The celebrant had previously been given the role of speaking the Eucharistic prayer, but new prayers assigned to the clergy were now multiplied. The people's offertory was abandoned. Lay communion declined in frequency. The synaxis (with its scriptural readings) became fused with the Eucharist, and the passivity of the laity in the synaxis became transferred to the Eucharist itself. The laity became hearers—and when Latin became a specialized language understood only by the clergy, hearing became less important and seeing became more so. In tracing this progressive relegation of the laity to a passive role, Dix reinforced a sense that had been important to liturgical reform from the outset: that historical change must be undone and earlier, more authentic norms reinstated. Liturgical reform was radically, rather than eclectically, historicist: on matters ranging from the use of the vernacular to the position of the altar, the position of the priest at the altar, and the posture of communicants (whether kneeling or standing), it appealed constantly to the authority of historical practice.[6]

The most influential theorists of church architecture in the mid-twentieth century, unlike liturgists and liturgical historians, made no claim to be advocating a return to a golden age. For them, the use of historical models of any sort was anachronistic and thus misguided. Peter Hammond, writing in the early 1960s, saw revival-style churches as having "no message for the contemporary world" and as confirming the unbeliever's sense that Christianity itself is "a curious anachronism," the "by-product of a vanished culture."[7] In characteristically aphoristic mode, Hammond declared that "it is better to come before God naked than in period costume."[8] Hammond's collaborator Charles Davis repudiated even the suggestion of past styles, viewing the desire for churches that "look like churches" as a nostalgic attachment to religious sentiment; "to fulfill its purpose properly, a church must be built in a living language."[9] One might have supposed such theorists would be receptive to modes of architecture derived from the same liturgical golden age that liturgists so often saw as the source of their most basic norms. That pre-Constantinian age, however, did not provide useful models, because it was largely an era of house churches and of houses refashioned into places of worship rather than of purpose-built liturgical architecture.

Architectural aversion to historical allusion was, of course, not universal or uniform. One of the most influential of the early German modernists, Dominikus Böhm, subject of a recent volume edited by Wolfgang Voigt and Ingeborg Flagge (2005), consciously adapted Gothic forms in much of his work, not only in his parabolic and pointed arches but also at times in the sequencing of these arches to establish a clear sense of longitudinal direction. While the influence is less obvious, even his round churches claimed indebtedness to fourth-century precedents such as Santa Costanza in Rome.[10] At his Church of Saint John the Baptist in Neu-Ulm, Böhm retained a monumentality on the exterior that has elicited comparison with German Romanesque, while on the interior he combined overtly Gothic forms with equally manifest modern construction and Expressionist use of partly concealed and dramatically mysterious lighting.[11] Still, for all their allusions, one would never mistake Böhm's churches for works of revival style; the difference lies not simply in the degree of freedom with which historical elements are handled, but in the confidence with which Böhm appropriated them to his own governing purposes. In Czechoslovakia, Jože Plečnik attempted to re-create the liturgical space of early Roman basilicas while using modern construction techniques, but his effort was hampered by limited resources and constraints placed on him by clients.[12] Numerous further examples of the blending of historical allusion into modernism can be found, for example, in Bartlett Hayes's *Tradition Becomes Innovation* (1983).[13] The examples Hayes provides rarely give so clear and striking a blend of modernist aesthetic and historical allusion as one sees in Böhm's most successful projects, but still they show the capacity of modernism to absorb historical reference. This capacity, however, was not what Peter Hammond and other mid-twentieth-century theorists of church design sought in modernism. Neither architects nor architectural theorists shared liturgists' commitment to reviving an ideal past.

For a second reason as well, we cannot see the alliance of architectural modernism and liturgical reform as simple and straightforward: the major official documents on liturgical reform were not strongly or clearly supportive of modern architectural design.

If we turn to the liturgical documents of the Second Vatican Council anticipating a clear endorsement of modern church design, we will be disappointed. Indeed, the Council had stunningly little to say about church architecture. The Constitution on the Sacred Liturgy, issued in 1963, addressed the matter with succinctness and vagueness in equal measure: "When churches are to be built, let great care be taken that they be suitable for the celebration of liturgical services and for the active participation of the faithful [*ad fidelium actuosam participationem obtinendam*]."[14] Strictly speaking, this is all the Council had to say about church design. It is more than nothing, and the wording is (as we shall see) in some ways important, but clearly the Council fathers had other concerns far more on their minds. On this as on other themes, their intent can be contextualized by the preparatory documents that came before the Constitution and the instructions for implementation that came afterward. But here we find a mixture of parsimony, reserve, and sometimes even overt traditionalism. The preparatory commission had said that a church building should be a "faithful echo of the sacred assembly . . . hierarchically composed," and the emphasis on hierarchy of clergy and laity was nowhere contradicted in the conciliar documents. The commissions were more concerned with furnishings than with structures: the main altar should be positioned "midway between the presbytery and the people," minor altars should be few in number, and the tabernacle should be appropriately located (usually to the side of the altar). Among liturgical reformers, the position of the celebrant vis-à-vis the congregation was much contested, and eventually celebration *versus populum* or facing the congregation became normative. On this point the instructions for implementation were simple and undogmatic, saying merely, "It is lawful to celebrate Mass facing the people."[15]

The lack of sustained attention to church design is surprising, because already in the late 1940s the German hierarchy had issued an influential document that did address principles of church architecture in somewhat more specific terms. Theodor Klauser, a liturgical historian, wrote these directives on behalf of the Liturgical Commission of the German hierarchy. At the outset, Klauser gave a general statement of principles that deserves our careful attention:

> The church edifice today is intended for the people of our times. Hence it must be fashioned in such way that the people of our times may recognize and feel that it is addressed to them. The most significant and the most worthy needs of modern mankind must here find their fulfillment: the urge toward community life, the desire for what is true and genuine, the wish to advance from what is peripheral to what is central and essential, the demand for clarity, lucidity, intelligibility, the longing for quiet and peace, for a sense of warmth and security.[16]

If there was ever an official statement of what modernity in church architecture should be, this was it—and we shall return to the particulars of this statement more than once. Beyond this opening statement of principles, Klauser's text reads in no small part as a kind of syllabus of errors. He repeated no phrase more often, it seems, than his leitmotif "It would be a mistake to . . ." Thus, we learn that it would be a mistake to separate the church from the parish complex, to build a church directly on a busy street, to build a church in the style of profane architecture, to place the altar in the precise center of the church, to design a church in such a way that the congregation will not feel a sense of oneness, to overlook the need for a quiet space of private prayer, to locate the choir in a rear gallery, to arrange and decorate in the manner of a comfortable bourgeois residence, to imitate the poverty found in a proletarian dwelling, to allow haphazard and arbitrary arrangement and decoration, or to construct a church of excessive size.[17] Central to his vision of both structure and furnishing was fidelity to principles found specifically in the liturgy of Rome. The authority of Roman precedent here must not be missed, because it lends an element of centralizing traditionalism even to what might seem liberal reforms. Thus Klauser endorsed celebration facing the people precisely because he found that tradition in Roman usage. He was sensitive to the need for "orderly procession" for much the same reason: this too was the custom of the Roman church, with its longitudinal basilicas.[18] Klauser would not have been comfortable with the varieties of auditorium seating that had already been developed in some churches between the wars. He was a reformer in the classic sense of that term: a restorer of what to him seemed the most authoritative precedent, and for him (as for liturgical reformers as early as the ninth century) Roman usage was the touchstone of authenticity.

The third caveat in linking liturgical reform to architectural modernism is that the introduction of modern design in church architecture was highly uneven and dependent on local and institutional concerns, while liturgical reform was instituted more uniformly by central authorities. Architects prominently identified as modernists could expect commissions from patrons who shared their convictions, but many were more flexible, more accommodating to the preferences of their clients. Designers could move from historicist to modern idiom, or the reverse. The postwar churches of Chicago provide examples of accommodation in either direction. Architects of long standing in the archdiocese could still be called upon to design a Gothic revival church even in the mid-1950s: the firm of Meyer and Cook, which had done its first Chicago church in the late 1920s, built the monumental Queen of All Saints, one of Chicago's few officially designated basilicas, between 1956 and 1960.[19] In the 1920s Karl Vitzthum had done a Gothic revival design for Saint Thomas Aquinas Church; in the early 1950s he collaborated with John Burns on the highly visible modernist Saint Peter's in the Loop, which alluded to the Gothic only in its monumental portal.[20] But the transition could also work in the opposite direction. In the mid-fifties, Radoslav Kovacevic collaborated with William Pavlecic and Jack Ota on Saint Gall. The pastor there requested a building where the altar would be in the center, so Kovacevic designed a quarter circle with the altar at the corner and the pews arcing around it, with no sharp distinction between nave and sanctuary. At its completion in 1958, Saint Gall was probably the most faithful reflection in Chicago of Continental innovations in church design. A few years later Pavlecic and Kovacevic again collaborated on a modern design for Saint Jane de Chantal. But by the late 1960s, when they worked with R. Markovitch on the Serbian Orthodox church of Saint Simeon Mirotocivi, they accommodated themselves to the policies then common among Serbian immigrants, designing a replica of a fifteenth-century Serbian monastic church (that of Kalenich).[21] In short, even architects who did work in close alliance with a proponent of liturgical reform might just as well serve the purposes of another congregation by reverting to the most straightforward historicism.

For all that, however, there were real points of connection between liturgical reform and modern church design. Five points of contact seem to me salient; one might perhaps easily extend the list, but these five will suffice to illustrate how the movements could connect.

First: Enhanced congregational participation was central both to liturgical reformers and to modernist church designers. From the outset, liturgical reform was meant to stimulate fuller congregational participation, and while the Second Vatican Council said very little about church design, the few words it did devote to that subject were chosen with a very specific purpose: church buildings should be designed for the active participation of the faithful.[22] Articulating this goal is far easier than achieving it; Catholics' reluctance to sing at mass has been noted, and congregations often remain solidly passive even in churches renovated at considerable expense in the name of participation.[23] Cautious reformers warned in the 1960s that celebration *versus populum* would position the priest in the role of a performer and accentuate rather than overcome the passivity of the congregation.[24] The capacity of architecture to mold behavior was perhaps exaggerated on all sides. Still, the goal of increased participation had from the outset been widely shared by liturgists and architects.

Peter Hammond noted a clear parallel here with the principles of theater design stated by Walter Gropius in 1934. To achieve unity between actors and spectators, Gropius advocated abolishing all separation between auditorium and stage. The theater architect, Gropius proposed, should use "all possible spatial means capable of shaking the spectator out of his lethargy, of surprising and assaulting him and obliging him to take a real, living interest in the play." Hammond's case for a parallel follows easily from his basic observation: "Substitute 'sanctuary and nave' for 'stage and auditorium,' and 'liturgy' for 'play,' and you have a very precise description of the aim which has been realized with varying degrees of success in a rapidly growing number of modern churches based on circular or elliptical plans."[25]

Second: Clarity of focus was equally fundamental to liturgical reformers and to modern church architects. On this point Klauser was emphatic in the principles he articulated for the German hierarchy in the late 1940s: the church interior should be designed for the Eucharistic sacrifice and not for private devotions; the eye should be drawn to the altar and not distracted by decorations.[26] This principle too was ratified by the Second Vatican Council in its statements on the artistic environment for worship.[27] Others were suggesting that side altars might be moved to separate chapels or even to a crypt. And this striving for clarity of focus was compatible in execution—even if distinct in origin and motive—with the minimalist thrust of architectural modernism. Frédéric Debuyst surveyed modern churches built through midcentury and suggested that "The main purpose, the 'idea' coming to life in these churches, can be summed up in one phrase: 'the serving of the assembled community *in the simplest possible form*.'"[28] Rudolf Schwarz, who was personally and aesthetically close to Mies van der Rohe, urged that artistic language in the twentieth century, in order to be "absolutely truthful," must say nothing more than could be understood by contemporaries. If that meant saying less than was once said by church designers—making less elaborate theological statements in architecture—then the ensuing reserve would be preferable to architectural statements that would not be understood.[29] Deeper resignation emerges from Paul Tillich's call for a "holy emptiness" in churches, meant as both apophatic and existential, expressing both the presence of an elusive God and the absence of a God for whom the people must wait.[30] These are by no means identical points of view, and in some ways they may not even be compatible, yet in the end the artistic minimalism of a Schwarz or a Mies has reinforced the liturgists' demand to pare away the inessential—whether that is defined as the decorative or as the devotional—and accentuate the essential—whether that is the altar or the emptiness.

Third: Experiments in conscious, explicit symbolism were frequently important both to liturgical reformers and to modern church architects. On this point one must now consult the work of Kerstin Wittmann-Englert, *Zelt, Schiff und Wohnung: Kirchenbauten der Nachkriegsmoderne* (2006).[31] Wittmann-Englert examines the churches designed after World War II in the forms of tents or ships, or as community centers resembling apartment complexes. The first two forms are related to the notion of the church as a pilgrim community, one called out of any fixed location into mission in the world; the third Wittmann-Englert traces to Dietrich Bonhoeffer's call for a "church for others," a church that manifested itself not in attachment to sacred forms (since demythologization required desacralization) but in communal action. All three forms flourished in the postwar decades, and the project of rebuilding in Germany provided numerous examples.

Wittmann-Englert argues that churches built in these forms differ from medieval churches by being, in Günter Bandmann's sense, not bearers of meaning but rather bearers of association: instead of arising from a fixed system of signs, as in medieval culture, they have a function that is more subjective and thus more fluid.[32] This may be so, but the opposite seems at least as likely. A medieval church looked equally unlike a ship, a city, and a garden, and could be interpreted as all three precisely because the symbolism was more implicit than explicit. A mid-twentieth-century church designed to look like a tent was more likely to have a clear resemblance that would make the tent symbolism strikingly more plausible than that of a ship or anything else. And it is this *explicit* consciousness of symbolic meaning that connects such churches most clearly with one strand of liturgical reform. Theodor Klauser was only being conventional when he identified the altar as the sacrificial table, the banquet table, Christ's throne on earth, and a symbol of Christ himself.³³ But Romano Guardini carried such reflections further in his book *Sacred Signs*, which gives sustained meditation on the symbolism of church buildings, of liturgical objects within these buildings, and even of all four compass directions.³⁴ This penchant for making symbolism explicit is surely more a tendency of modern and reform-minded literature than of more traditional culture.

The application of such explicit symbolism to church design has often been questioned. Peter Hammond notes wryly that midcentury churches were built to resemble hands folded in prayer, anchors, fishes, flames, passionflowers, and much else, and concludes by pondering "what all this whimsical symbolism has to do with the planning of churches, or indeed with serious architecture of any kind."³⁵ But this is forceful as an argument not against symbolic meaning in general, but specifically against overly explicit, arbitrary, univocal symbolism. What do parishioners do when they have tired of worshiping inside a fish and decide they would rather worship inside a bird, or a star, or a flower? Significance of this sort, fixed rather than fluid, simple rather than polysemous, quickly seems trite.

Fourth: Both liturgical reformers and modern church designers were in many cases drawn to the ideal of a transposed domesticity. On this point two influential theorists of the 1960s discovered each other as allies: Fréderic Debuyst and Edward Sövik. Debuyst, a Belgian monk, accepted the notion of a church as a kind of living room—an open space in the house of God's family, and a place of hospitality—in which celebration might take place.³⁶ Sövik carried the point further, relying more fully on biblical images of the church as a family and urging that worship be conceived as a kind of family reunion. The worship space should serve as a kind of living-dining room. The entryway or concourse should provide a space for worshipers to gather and mingle before they enter into the worship space proper.³⁷ These conceptions had limited application to the actual design of churches: none of Sövik's buildings has a close resemblance to the house church at Dura Europos, and the similarity with contemporary residential architecture is more suggestive than fully realized. The point is that worshipers should feel a sense of hospitality, comfort, and fellowship, and that the architecture should facilitate this sense by a preference for modesty over monumentality, and for informality and asymmetry over formal symmetry. Both space and furnishings should be arranged in a way that produces a sense of bonding within the congregation. Among liturgical reformers, Theodor Klauser is one of many whose language echoes these themes, but his key point is that if the church is a home it should be "neither bourgeois nor proletarian," and should communicate both the grandeur of God and "'the goodness and kindness of our Saviour' (Titus 3:4)."³⁸

Fifth: Modernity in church design was part of a broader effort at engagement with the modern world that was congenial to many liturgical reformers. A document published by the World Council of Churches in 1968, *The Church for Others and The Church for the World*, characterized as "heretical" those churches that encourage the security of isolation or flight from the world.³⁹ (The title itself already suggests indebtedness to the tradition of Dietrich Bonhoeffer.) But how does a building suggest either closure from or openness to the world outside? Most obviously, by the use of broad windows. Several churches of midcentury are made of minimal frames supporting glass on all sides, usually open not to an urban environment but rather to the natural world. Perhaps more effective is the coordination of worship space with meeting rooms and other spaces that serve social and ministerial functions. Bonhoeffer's notion of a "church for others" inspired the Evangelical Church in Germany to build community centers of this sort.[40] More recently, Archbishop Rembert Weakland in Milwaukee linked his cathedral with rooms for social services that could also provide gathering points for processions.[41]

The postwar directives of the German Catholic hierarchy had specifically warned against too much openness to the world: a church should not be built directly on a busy street, but should provide a buffer zone or atrium so that worshipers might be "inwardly disposed and attuned to the divine atmosphere of the sacred interior."[42] On this point there is, perhaps, a divide among the liturgical reforms. Romano Guardini was emphatic in rejecting a primarily ethical conception of worship: it is meant chiefly as an expression not of *nomos* but of *logos*, not of ethical values but of spiritual meanings.[43] The early liturgical reforms were largely contemplative in spirit, and an alternative form of liturgical renewal emerged only after World War II.

Meanwhile, certain high-profile church commissions manifested a different aspect of engagement with the world: particularly the churches of monastic and other religious orders, which had the resources to engage prominent secular architects, could by doing so signal that they had entered into the forefront of modern culture and were open to rapprochement with the values of that culture. Some of the best-known churches of the 1950s and 1960s were designed by architects who did not belong to the religious communities for which they worked and were often distanced from any religious culture: Le Corbusier's chapel at Ronchamp, Frank Lloyd Wright's Greek Orthodox church in Wauwatosa, and others. When the monks of Saint Procopius in Lisle engaged Edward Dart, they were inspired by the religious convictions of this Episcopalian architect. When the monks of Saint Johns' in Collegeville commissioned Marcel Breuer they were, like many religious communities, reacting dramatically against parochial insularity. Some, like the Dominicans of Plateau d'Assy, reinforced the message by commissioning stained glass, tapestries, mosaics, and other art by the most prominent of midcentury artists, regardless of whether they were believers or unbelievers.[44]

In short, the twentieth century brought no single driving force shared by liturgical reform and modernist church design, but on each side there was a repertoire of themes and concerns that could be and often were shared by the other side of a real if unstable alliance. The relationship between these movements is thus best seen as one of convergence at particular points, which varied from one context to another.

BIBLIOGRAPHICAL SURVEY OF THE LITURGICAL MOVEMENT

One of the best overviews of the liturgical movement is John R. K. Fenwick and Bryan D. Spinks, *Worship in Transition: The Liturgical Movement in the Twentieth Century* (New York: Continuum, 1995), which complements Paul Bradshaw and Bryan Spinks, eds., *Liturgy in Dialogue* (London: SPCK, 1993). The movement was largely the product of theological, liturgical, and historical work among Belgian and German Benedictines, including those of Maria Laach Abbey in Germany. See Ernest Benjamin Koenker's *The Liturgical Renaissance in the Roman Catholic Church* (Chicago: University of Chicago Press, 1954), which was originally the author's dissertation at the University of Chicago.

For evidence of very early Anglican involvement in the renewal, see Walter Howard Frere, *Some Principles of Liturgical Reform: A Contribution Towards the Revision of the Book of Common Prayer* (London: Murray, 1911). A. G. Hebert, *Liturgy and Society* (London: Faber and Faber, 1935), and A. G. Hebert, ed., *The Parish Communion* (London: SPCK, 1937), were highly influential in promoting the notion that the parish as a community should be gathered in a Eucharistic celebration (not simply morning prayer) that would serve as the religious center of its common life. For the sequel to that effort, see David MacDonald Paton, ed., *The Parish Communion To-day* (London: SPCK, 1962), Peter John Jagger, *A History of the Parish and People Movement* (London: Faith Press, 1978), and Donald Gray, *Earth and Altar: The Evolution of the Parish Communion in the Church of England to 1945* (Norwich, UK: Canterbury Press, 1986).

The liturgical movement had ecumenical dimensions from its early years, partly because immersion in the history of the liturgy and recovery of liturgical resources brought the reformers into contact with liturgical traditions other than their own. One of the early leaders of the liturgical movement, Lambert Beauduin, was a Belgian Benedictine who founded Chevetogne Abbey in 1925 as a place where Western and Eastern churches could interact and gain mutual understanding; his view of liturgy is expressed in Lambert Beauduin, *Liturgy the Life of the Church*, trans. Virgil Michel, 2nd ed. (Collegeville, MN: Liturgical Press, 1929). Reciprocal influence between Roman Catholic and Protestant reformers makes it difficult to treat the movement along denominational lines; see Jean Daniel Benoit, *Liturgical Renewal: Studies in Catholic and Protestant Developments on the Continent*, trans. Edwin Hudson (London: SCM Press, 1958). By midcentury, interdenominational conferences on liturgical reform had become prominent means for promoting the cause; see the proceedings of the first National Liturgical Conference, Madison, Wisconsin, 1958: Massey Hamilton Shepherd, ed., *The Liturgical Renewal of the Church* (New York: Oxford University Press, 1960).

Practicing architects took an interest in the movement and wrote about church architecture and its connections with liturgical reform even in the early twentieth century. Among Roman Catholics, the most noteworthy example is Rudolf Schwarz, who was closely linked with the early liturgical reformer

Romano Guardini. Schwarz's own most important writing is *Vom Bau der Kirche*, which originally appeared in 1938 and came out in a new edition in 1998 (Salzburg: Pustet, 1998); the English version is *The Church Incarnate: The Sacred Function of Christian Architecture*, trans. Cynthia Harris (Chicago: Regnery, 1958). For commentary on his own architectural work see *Kirchenbau: Welt vor der Schwelle* (Heidelberg: Kerle, 1960). His historical background is clear from his dissertation, *Frühtypen der rheinischen Kleinkirche* (PhD diss., Technischen Hochschule zu Berlin, 1922). Walter Zahner, in *Rudolf Schwarz: Baumeister der neuen Gemeinde: Ein Beitrag zum Gespräch zwischen Liturgietheologie und Architektur in der liturgischen Bewegung* (Altenberge: Oros, 1992), gives a highly detailed account of how an important church architect was personally involved with and inspired by the early decades of liturgical reform in the Roman Catholic Church. On the Protestant side, the architect Otto Bartning stands out as important both for his designs and for his theoretical writings; see his books *Vom neuen Kirchbau* (Berlin: Cassirer, 1919) and *Vom Raum der Kirche* (Bramsche bei Osnabrück: Rasch, 1958).

Among the liturgical reformers, Louis Bouyer was one with particular interest in church architecture, and with special interest in recovering the Syrian practice of having clergy and congregation clustered together in distinct spaces for the Liturgy of the Word and the Liturgy of the Eucharist; see his *Life and Liturgy* (London: Sheed and Ward, 1956), and *Liturgy and Architecture* (Notre Dame, IN: University of Notre Dame Press, 1967).

Already by the mid-twentieth century the movement had been in existence long enough and had enough consciousness of its own origins and development that some of the leaders, themselves often historians of liturgy, could turn to the movement of which they were a part and trace its history; examples are Olivier Rousseau, *Histoire du Mouvement Liturgique: esquisse historique depuis la début du XIXe siècle jusqu'au pontificat de Pie X* (Paris: Cerf, 1945), and J. H. Srawley, *The Liturgical Movement: Its Origins and Growth* (London: Mowbray, 1954).

NOTES

1. Cheslyn Jones, Geoffrey Wainwright, Edward Yarnold, and Paul Bradshaw, eds., *The Study of Liturgy* (New York: Oxford University Press, 1992), 292.

2. Odo Casel, *The Mystery of Christian Worship*, new ed., ed. Burkhard Neunheuser (New York: Crossroad, 1999).

3. Josef A. Jungmann, *The Mass of the Roman Rite: Its Origins and Development*, trans. Francis A. Brunner (Missarum Sollemnia) (New York: Benziger, 1951–1955).

4. Gregory Dix, *The Shape of the Liturgy* (London: Black, 1945; new ed., New York: Seabury, 1983).

5. Ibid., 7.

6. Ibid., esp. 7–8, 12–15, 45–46, 318–319, 442–443.

7. Peter Hammond, *Liturgy and Architecture* (London: Barrie and Rockliff; New York: Columbia University Press, 1960), 3.

8. Ibid., 157.

9. Charles Davis, "Church Architecture and the Liturgy," in *Towards a Church Architecture*, ed. Peter Hammond (London: Architectural Press, 1962), 157.

10. August Hoff, Herbert Muck, and Raimund Thoma, *Dominikus Böhm* (Munich: Schnell and Steiner, 1962); Rudolf Schwarz, "Dominikus Böhm und sein Werk," *Moderne Bauformen* 26 (1927): 226–240; Gesine Stalling, *Studien zu Dominikus Böhm, mit besonderer Berücksichtigung seiner Gotik-Auffassung* (Bern and Frankfurt/M.: Herbert Lang, Peter Lang, 1974); Wolfgang Voigt and Ingeborg Flagge, eds., *Dominikus Bo/hm, 1880–1955* (Tübingen: Wasmuth, 2005).

11. This is the church featured on the cover of Richard Kieckhefer, *Theology in Stone: Church Architecture from Byzantium to Berkeley* (New York: Oxford University Press, 2004).

12. Wolfgang Jean Stock, *European Church Architecture, 1900–1950* (Munich and London: Prestel, 2006), 130–135.

13. Bartlett H. Hayes, *Tradition Becomes Innovation: Modern Religious Architecture in America* (New York: Pilgrim Press, 1983).

14. *Church Architecture: The Shape of Reform* (Washington, DC: The Liturgical Conference, 1965).

15. Josef Andreas Jungmann, "The New Altar," trans. John J. Galvani, *Liturgical Arts* 37, no. 2 (February 1969): 36–40.

16. *Directives for the Building of a Church, by the Liturgical Commission of the German Hierarchy*, English trans. (Collegeville, MN: Liturgical Press, 1949), reprinted from *Orate Fratres* 24, no. 1 (December 1949). Klauser is not named on the title page, but elsewhere he is acknowledged as the author.

17. Ibid., 4–11. On p. 12 Klauser says it would also be a mistake to introduce too many pews.

18. Ibid., 6–7.

19. George A. Lane, *Chicago Churches and Synagogues: An Architectural Pilgrimage*, with photographs by Algimantas Kezys and George Lane (Chicago: Loyola University Press, 1981), 200–201 (a list of the architects' Chicago churches is on p. 233); Harry C. Koenig, ed., *A History of the Parishes of the Archdiocese of Chicago* (Chicago: Archdiocese of Chicago, 1980), 823–828.

20. Lane, *Chicago Churches and Synagogues*, 168–169, 197; Koenig, *A History of the Parishes of the Archdiocese of Chicago*, 768–774 (Saint Peter), 935–939 (Saint Thomas Aquinas).

21. Lane, *Chicago Churches and Synagogues*, 199, 213 (list on pp. 232 and 234); Koenig, *A History of the Parishes of the Archdiocese of Chicago*, 306–309 (Saint Gall), 461–464 (Saint Jane de Chantal).

22. From the outset, one of the key charges of the reformers was to bring the laity into more active engagement in the liturgy. Gregory Dix's *Shape of the Liturgy* was a study of how the laity had become relegated to passivity; already in the early twentieth century the reversal of this process had been a goal of the movement. For a later statement on the theme, see Bernard Botte, *From Silence to Participation: An Insider's View of Liturgical Renewal*, trans. John Sullivan (Washington, DC: Pastoral Press, 1988).

23. The most widely noted statement of opinion on this question is Thomas Day, *Why Catholics Can't Sing: The Culture of Catholicism and the Triumph of Bad Taste* (New York: Crossroad, 1990).

24. Louis Bouyer, *Liturgy and Architecture* (Notre Dame, IN: University of Notre Dame Press, 1967), 105–112; Jungmann, "The New Altar."

25. Hammond, *Liturgy and Architecture*, 42–43.

26. *Directives for the Building of a Church*, esp. pp. 6–7.

27. *Sacrosanctum Concilium*, sec. 41; but see esp. Appendix to Liturgy Constitution art, 128 (Declarations of Preparatory Commission for a clearer explanation of certain articles), in *Church Architecture: The Shape of Reform*, 98–102, and Instruction for the Proper Implementation of the Constitution on the Sacred Liturgy, September 26, 1964, ibid., 102–104.

28. Frédéric Debuyst, *Modern Architecture and Christian Celebration* (London: Lutterworth; Richmond, VA: John Knox Press, 1968), 55.

29. Hammond, *Liturgy and Architecture*, 55–56.

30. Paul Tillich, *On Art and Architecture*, ed. John Dillenberger and Jane Dillenberger, trans. Robert P. Scharlemann (New York: Crossroad, 1989), 193, 217–218.

31. Kerstin Wittmann-Englert, *Zelt, Schiff und Wohnung: Kirchenbauten der Nachkriegsmoderne* (Lindenberg im Allgäu: Kunstverlag Josef Fink, 2006).

32. Günter Bandmann, *Mittelalterliche Architektur als Bedeutungsträger*, 11th ed. (Berlin: Gebr. Mann, 1998).

33. *Directives for the Building of a Church*, 6–7.

34. Romano Guardini, *Sacred Signs*, trans. Grace Branham, rev. ed. (Wilmington, DE: Michael Glazer; Dublin: Veritas, 1979).

35. Hammond, "A Radical Approach to Church Architecture," in *Toward a Church Architecture*, 24–25.

36. Debuyst, *Modern Architecture and Christian Celebration*, 9–10.

37. E. A. Sövik, *Architecture for Worship* (Minneapolis: Augsburg, 1973), esp. 76–77.

38. *Directives for the Building of a Church*, 10–11.

39. *The Church for Others and The Church for the World: A Quest for Structures for Missionary Congregations. Final Report of the Western European Working Group and North American Working Group of the Department on Studies in Evangelism* (Geneva: World Council of Churches, 1968); the German original is *Die Kirche für andere und Die Kirche für die Welt: Im Ringen um Strukturen missionarischen Gemeinden: Schlussberichte der Westeuropäischen Arbeitsgruppe und der Nordamerikanischen Arbeitsgruppe* (Geneva: Ökumenischer Rat der Kirchen, 1967).

40. Wittmann-Englert, *Zelt, Schiff und Wohnung*, esp. 164–165.

41. See Rembert G. Weakland, "Renovation, Renewal, Restoration," *Catholic Herald* (Milwaukee), January 4, 2001.

42. *Directives for the Building of a Church*, 5.

43. Romano Guardini, *The Spirit of the Liturgy*, trans. Ada Lane (London: Sheed and Ward, 1930; repr., New York: Herder and Herder, 1998), 61–70 ("The playfulness of the liturgy").

44. Kieckhefer, *Theology in Stone*, 229–230 (also 248–253).

PART III

MODERNISM AND DOMESTICITY

INTRODUCTION

MONICA PENICK

During World War II and in the two decades that followed, scores of architects were engaged in the design of the postwar house, a building type that offered extraordinary opportunities and unprecedented challenges. In the United States in particular, the postwar house—single-family, detached, and increasingly built for a middle-class clientele—became, on the one hand, an arena in which a once-stagnant housing industry could expand and thrive; on the other hand, the postwar house offered a venue in which architects could explore progressive ideas. Perhaps more significantly, as the three essays in this section demonstrate, the house became a repository of complex meanings, essential to the formation of postwar character, selfhood, and nationhood. Designers, builders, developers, tastemakers, and consumers understood the expressive possibilities of the postwar house (both the custom-built and mass-developed versions) and transferred onto this singular architectural form the deferred hopes, dreams, and anxieties of a war-torn world.

In this context, the postwar house opened opportunities that were initially linked to absolute need. The wartime mandate to house defense workers, particularly in the United States, was historically unparalleled; this demand was matched and surpassed in the postwar years, fueled by unresolved housing shortages and the increased purchasing power of American consumers (made possible in part by federally sponsored mortgage programs and the GI Bill). The opportunity to design and build during these years produced very real challenges, including a demand for swift construction, innovative building techniques, durable materials, and affordable pricing. Architects were particularly compelled—by both individual clients and the larger housing market—to articulate the ill-defined concept of modernization with open floor plans, flexible interior spaces, "engineered" storage, and up-to-date domestic equipment (especially in the kitchen). These challenges compounded and led again to opportunity, now within the untried laboratories of standardization and prefabrication. SOM's "Experimental Houses" (discussed in this section), Walter Gropius's and Konrad Wachsmann's Packaged House, Levitt and Sons' mass housing developments, the Lustron Houses, and the pioneering efforts within *Arts and Architecture*'s Case Study House Program all broke new ground.[1] These designers probed questions of materials, processes, form, function, and content. Alongside scholars, critics, the professional press, popular media, and cultural institutions, they opened perhaps the most controversial of all postwar debates: what is modern?[2]

The contemporary meaning of modern (and modernism), as it was constructed between about 1940 and 1965, was complex, varied, and contested. To some, modern was reduced to Corbusian *pilotis* and flat roofs; to others, it meant a California ranch house; to others still, a Cape Cod cottage outfitted with an oversized picture window and the latest kitchen gadgetry. Modern was often used as an aesthetic concept, or sometimes spatial, sometimes functional, and sometimes technological. Each essay within this section presents a view of these contested definitions of modern, from the technological modernism of SOM and their prefabricated houses for the Manhattan Project in Oak Ridge, Tennessee, to the modern lifestyle and quasi-organic architecture promoted by *House Beautiful*'s American Style ("modern, but not *too* modern"), to the anxious, "psychologically charged" modern of the fully transparent, exposed (yet isolated), and vulnerable postwar house within its haunted landscape.

Within these three final essays, a secondary and unifying theme emerges. Each author argues not only that modernists engaged in a set of processes, or a way of living, or stylistic conventions, but also that modernism was appropriated for the larger purpose of establishing character or identity. If this identity was permanently linked to the rational, systematized corporate structure at SOM that would eventually perpetuate the legacy of high modernism, it was simultaneously linked to *House Beautiful*'s individualistic, democratic, and nationalistic American Style (a very particular variant of modernism that was positioned as the antithesis of SOM's version of the International Style). The notion of selfhood is bound up in all of these versions of modern character, and, in the final chapter of this volume, modernism (now placed beyond the transparent fabric of architecture and out into the landscape) transforms the notion of character so that it is measured not in terms of mechanization, or individualization, or nationalization, but by its very dematerialization.

Taken together, these three seemingly disparate essays form a cohesive argument: modern was infinitely varied in the postwar decades; definitions, forms, and aesthetic conventions evolved and changed, and (as the final essay suggests) eventually disintegrated. The more compelling and revealing question, then, becomes not "what was modern?" but how was modernism—in all of its competing forms—sanctioned, appropriated, adopted, or adapted in the domestic realm to complete the larger postwar narrative?

NOTES

1. For an excellent summary of the long effort to develop the prefabricated house, see Barry Bergdoll and Peter Christensen, eds., *Home Delivery: Fabricating the Modern Dwelling* (New York: Museum of Modern Art, 2008).

2. This question was addressed in many venues, including the oft-quoted 1948 MoMA symposium on modern architecture. See "What is Happening to Modern Architecture?" A Symposium at the Museum of Modern Art, February 11, 1948, *Museum of Modern Art Bulletin* 15, no. 3 (Spring 1948).

8 "TECHNOLOGICALLY" MODERN
THE PREFABRICATED HOUSE AND THE WARTIME EXPERIENCE OF SKIDMORE, OWINGS AND MERRILL

HYUN-TAE JUNG

INTRODUCTION

Mid-twentieth-century American architecture has been considered a degenerate outgrowth of modern European architecture. It is believed that the overwhelming influences of the era's corporate and consumer culture impeded the proper transplant of modern architecture on American soil. One of the most influential architectural theoreticians in the twentieth century, Colin Rowe, argued that "purged of its ideological and societal content," modern architecture in the United States was reduced to being either a "*décor de la vie* for Greenwich, Connecticut," or the "suitable veneer for the corporate activities of enlightened capitalism."[1] Rowe contended that utopian visions of modern architecture in Europe became empty ornaments for corporate America.

Rowe's theory that good architecture turned bad due to the influence of corporate culture and consumerism is problematic for two reasons. The first is that European modern architecture was never unified and homogeneous. Rather, the perceived uniformity was due to an accidental combination of different factors. The second reason is that postwar American architecture was more influenced by wartime technological experimentation than by European modern architecture of the interwar period. While many architectural historians have reexamined the first misconception, the second has never been appropriately investigated. To grasp how American architecture developed during the war, more focus should be given to the mechanization and systemization of building than to form.

Rowe's comments can easily be applied to the firm Skidmore, Owings and Merrill (hereafter SOM), which has been the main representative of so-called corporate modernism. The firm has been criticized for having commercialized modern architectural language after the war to please its clientele (the government and corporations such as the H. J. Heinz Company and the Connecticut General Life Insurance Company). This kind of criticism, however, is based solely on formal similarities between European modernism and corporate modernism.

Such formal analysis is a way of understanding modern architecture through a perspective based on forms and formal similarities. By refraining from such formal analysis, we will find that SOM was, with regard to technology, a thoroughly modern firm before and during the war.

William Hartmann, one of the early partners of SOM, argued that the New York World's Fair of 1939 was a catalyst in the early history of the firm, which was established in 1936 in Chicago. But it was the Second World War that enabled the firm to become a large-scale architectural organization. The critical moment came in 1942 when the Manhattan Engineer District, a confidential wartime military organization, selected SOM to design the city of Oak Ridge, Tennessee. This town was a crucial part of the atomic bomb development known as the Manhattan Project. When it started working on the town, SOM was a small design firm with limited experience. Its projects prior to 1942 included only small-scale exhibition designs and prefabricated houses. After 1942, the firm grew along with the town of Oak Ridge. By the time the war was over, SOM had become one of the largest architecture firms in the country, with substantial experience to deal with almost any type and size of project.[2] This remarkably rapid transition between 1939 and 1945 was predicated upon SOM's involvement with the John B. Pierce Foundation in prefabricated housing research and construction.

The collaboration between SOM and the Pierce Foundation, one of the most prominent prefabrication research institutions, began in 1939 with a small "Experimental House" as it was named by the foundation. This Experimental House and subsequent collaborative projects allowed SOM to gain sufficient technical knowledge and on-site experience to carry out large-scale military, government, and corporate commissions as well as to design postwar office buildings. It is precisely during this war period that significant changes in SOM's business areas, organizational systems, and architectural forms occurred. Most importantly, their active participation in prefabrication experiments unexpectedly led SOM into the world of the military-industrial complex, which provided the firm with extremely large commissions abroad in the postwar period. In the 1940s and 1950s, SOM's architecture was centered on the vision of a prefabricated, standardized house: the house of mass production.

THE VISION OF THE HOUSE: ABSTRACTION AND FLEXIBILITY

When the United States officially entered World War II in December 1941, the battle was waged not only overseas but also at home. On the home front, the war effort involved complex changes in societal and governmental structures to transform the country into a highly effective supply base. As war production injected sudden energy into an industrial economy still stagnant from the Depression years, the tempo of everyday life accelerated. The new speed of production and distribution created by the booming wartime economy permanently transformed architecture and its production. To meet the wartime requirements for

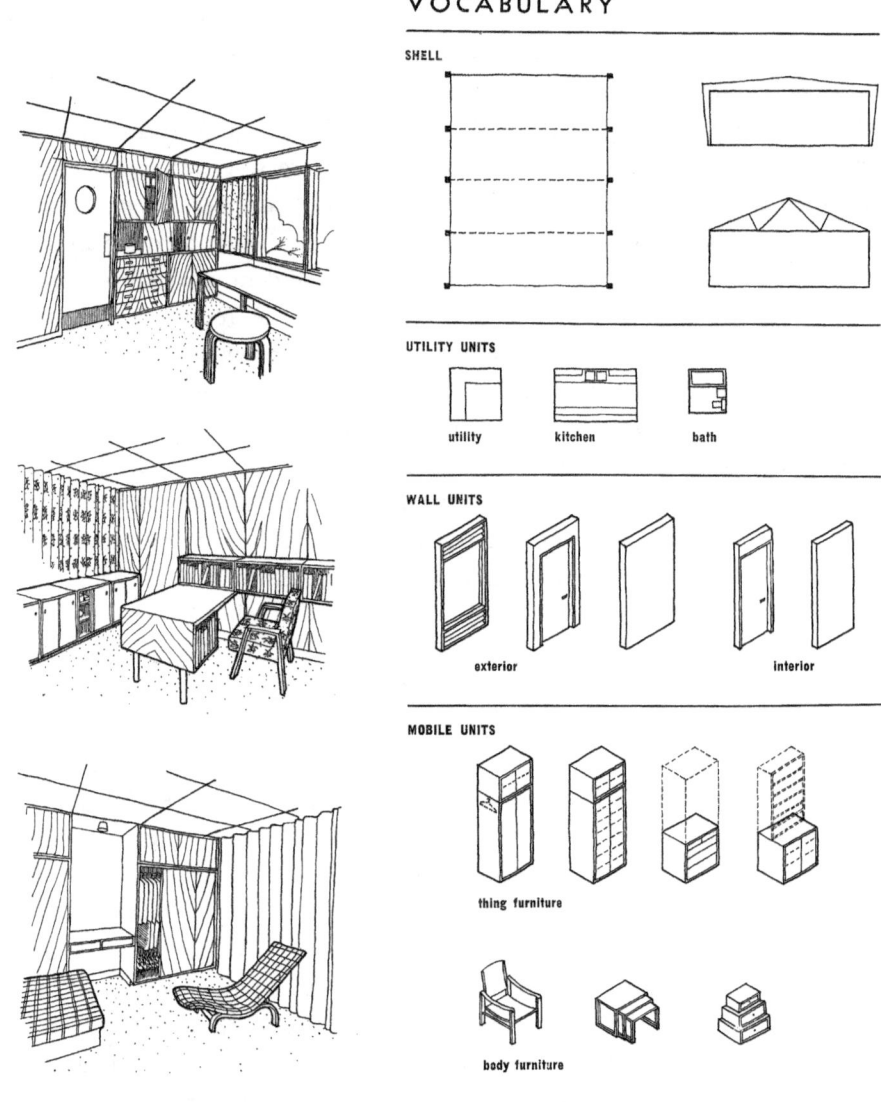

FIGURE 8.1a. SOM, "Flexible Space." *Architectural Forum*, September 1942.

factory buildings and housing for workers, building production and architecture became systemized and standardized. The two processes crystallized sufficiently to replace conventional production, ultimately guaranteeing the predominance of American architecture in the postwar world. The systemization and standardization of wartime housing production, for example, became the basis of postwar building construction. Some members of the John B. Pierce Foundation and SOM applied prefabrication techniques to the research on glass and metal curtain wall in the 1940s and 1950s.

Architectural journals anticipated an increase in postwar production, especially in terms of a response to the increasing shortage of civilian housing. Mass production was considered key to wartime and postwar construction, and standardization of building components seemed the best way to meet the housing demands of the period. Prefabrication technology appeared to be capable of filling this role. An article in the September 1942 issue of *Architectural Forum*, "The New House of 194X," exemplified this thinking. The journal article asked, "How can the House of 194X be made the most-wanted commodity in the competitive postwar market place?" Along with many other journals, *Architectural Forum* engaged the imminent market situation, in which mass production through systemization and mechanization was supposed to replace traditional architectural production. The journal invited thirty-three architecture firms to present their ideas on the standardization and systemization of housing production. One of these firms was SOM, whose article was entitled "Flexible Space" (figure 8.1).

"Flexible Space" was a formula based on standardizing the basic elements of a building and industrializing their production. The composition would meet the diverse requirements of individual occupants by creating numerous variations through slight modifications of a prototype. SOM argued that their formula could meet the various demands of families, even though "every family is different" and "every family changes."[3] The activities of each individual in a family were

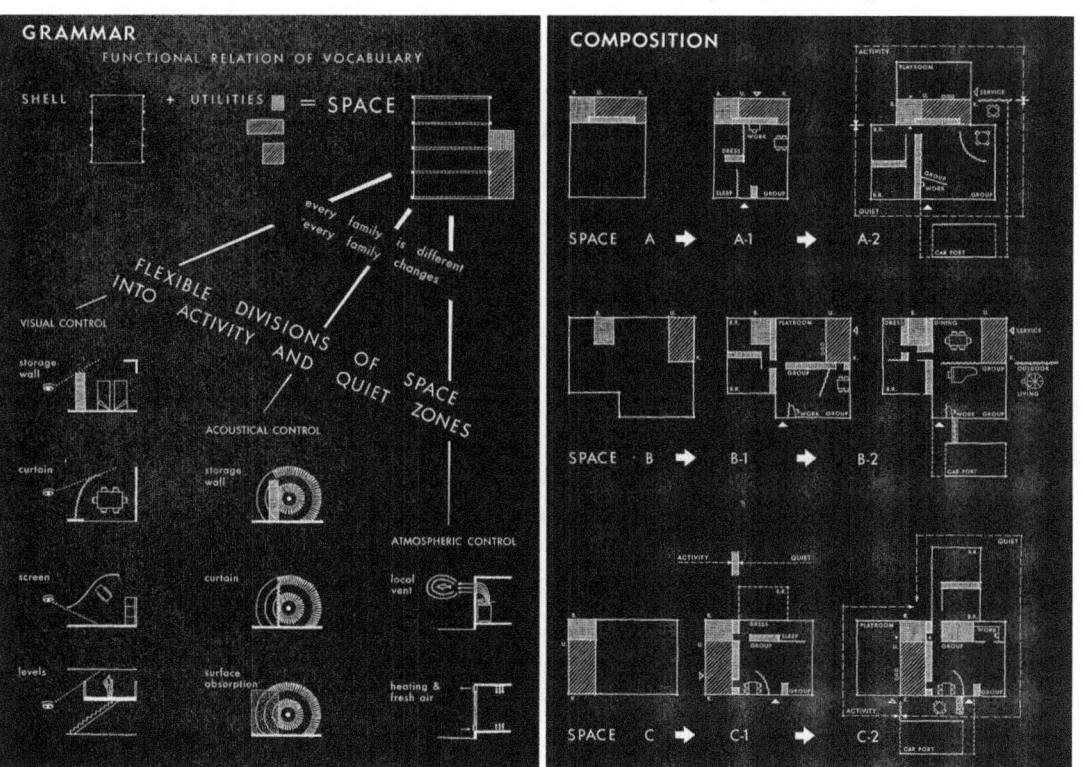

FIGURE 8.1b. SOM, "Flexible Space." *Architectural Forum*, September 1942.

scientifically measured to guarantee the house and its parts could sufficiently accommodate diverse events.

While most of the other proposals were more concrete, SOM concentrated on a fairly abstract idea of space. The firm theorized the flexibility of a spatial system. The goal was to construct a formula of spatial organization in which a building was conceived as being a collection of disassembled parts and dividable functions. Using a crude linguistic model, SOM subdivided architectural production into three stages: "Vocabulary," "Grammar," and "Composition." "Vocabulary" referred to the shell or enclosure of a space, practical units, wall units, and mobile units. "Grammar," or the "functional relation of vocabulary," was a process of combining shell and utilities in order to create spaces that successfully met visual, acoustic, and atmospheric requirements. "Grammar" was to satisfy the diverse demands of each occupant. The final stage was "Composition," which created variations of the spatial system based on certain prototypes.[4]

"Flexible Space" had little to do with materiality, technology, context, or even space; the key to its conceptual paradigm was instead the abstraction with which all mechanical production and reproduction would achieve its projected economic and technological goals. It was devised to justify and facilitate the mass reproduction of a building. In addition, "Flexible Space" prefigured the idea of mass customization.

THE JOHN B. PIERCE FOUNDATION AND EXPERIMENTAL HOUSE NO. 2

The idea of "Flexible Space" came from SOM's previous experience with prefabricated housing research. Starting in 1939, the firm devoted itself to researching the prefabrication of houses and worked on this and other related technological issues in collaboration with the John B. Pierce Foundation. The firm's first opportunity for collaboration came unexpectedly at the New York World's Fair of 1939, where SOM worked with many corporations, including Westinghouse, to design its exhibition pavilion. Joseph F. O'Brien of Westinghouse took charge of preparing the 1939 exhibition and had close relations with the firm. By the end of 1938, O'Brien decided to leave Westinghouse and join the Pierce Foundation as director of Electrical Research; he soon became general manager of the foundation.[5] O'Brien was instrumental in hiring SOM as a consulting architect for the foundation, prompting a short yet intensive period during which the firm accumulated expertise related to prefabricated housing technology and subsequently systematized its architectural language.

The devastation caused by the Great Depression spurred the foundation's research on prefabricated houses. This research intensified during the Second World War. Prefabrication attracted much attention from businessmen and architects in the 1930s who wanted to revive the building industry. It was viewed as an area with the potential to revitalize the Depression-era economy.[6] After a series of reports from February to June 1932 on a housing problem in America, *Fortune* concluded in its July 1932 issue that prefabrication was "the greatest single commercial opportunity of the age."[7] Emphasizing economic reasoning, the magazine presented a concept of design that was far from traditional. The article stated that design was not an aesthetic issue but an industrial one. Accordingly, *Fortune* argued that "design will dictate the form of thousands of units instead of the form of one," as in the case of the automobile industry.[8] The traditional concept of a house as a unique cultural entity thus gave way to economic priorities.

The Pierce Foundation had been established in 1924 by John B. Pierce, then vice president of the American Radiator and Standard Sanitary Corporation, to pursue "educational, technical and scientific work in the general fields of heating, ventilating, and sanitation."[9] From its inception, the foundation declared that it would focus on the physical and physiological human environment. Its Housing Research Division was established in New York in 1931, with the Harvard-educated architect Robert L. Davison as the first director. Davison had long been interested in prefabrication and was well known as a specialist in the field. In 1933 the foundation established another division, a Laboratory of Hygiene, in New Haven, Connecticut. This division specialized in physiological problems in the domestic environment and was supervised by C. E. A. Winslow, who was then head of the Department of Public Health at Yale University and who has often been regarded as the father of public health programs in the United States. The Pierce Foundation's varied interests, including research into prefabricated housing, the use of space in the domestic environment, and physiological and psychological research, were intended to complement each other. For the foundation, prefabrication was the outcome of a scientific understanding of the individual, family life, and the industrialization of a building (figure 8.2). Yet prefabrication did not necessarily mean standardization to the Pierce Foundation. On the contrary, it was understood as a precondition of flexibility.

In 1932 the Pierce Foundation erected the first prefabricated house, later named Experimental House No. 1, on top of the Starrett-Lehigh Building in New York City and tested numerous materials for structural and enclosure purposes.[10] Although the house was the first, the foundation did not publicize it much nor did they develop detailed research projects. Seven years later, with the construction of its second prefabricated house, the foundation established itself as a leader in prefabrication research and production. The second house, called Experimental House No. 2, was completed in 1939. SOM began to work as a consulting architect with the foundation in 1938, and SOM architect J. Walter Severinghaus was appointed as supervisor for construction and design improvement of Experimental House No. 2. The house was built in Lebanon, New Jersey, where Joseph O'Brien's farm was located. The house was a single story with a pitched roof and a porch. The plan of the house was a box divided into two bedrooms, a living room, a bathroom, and a combined kitchen-dining space. The main building material was prefabricated plywood without insulation. After completion of

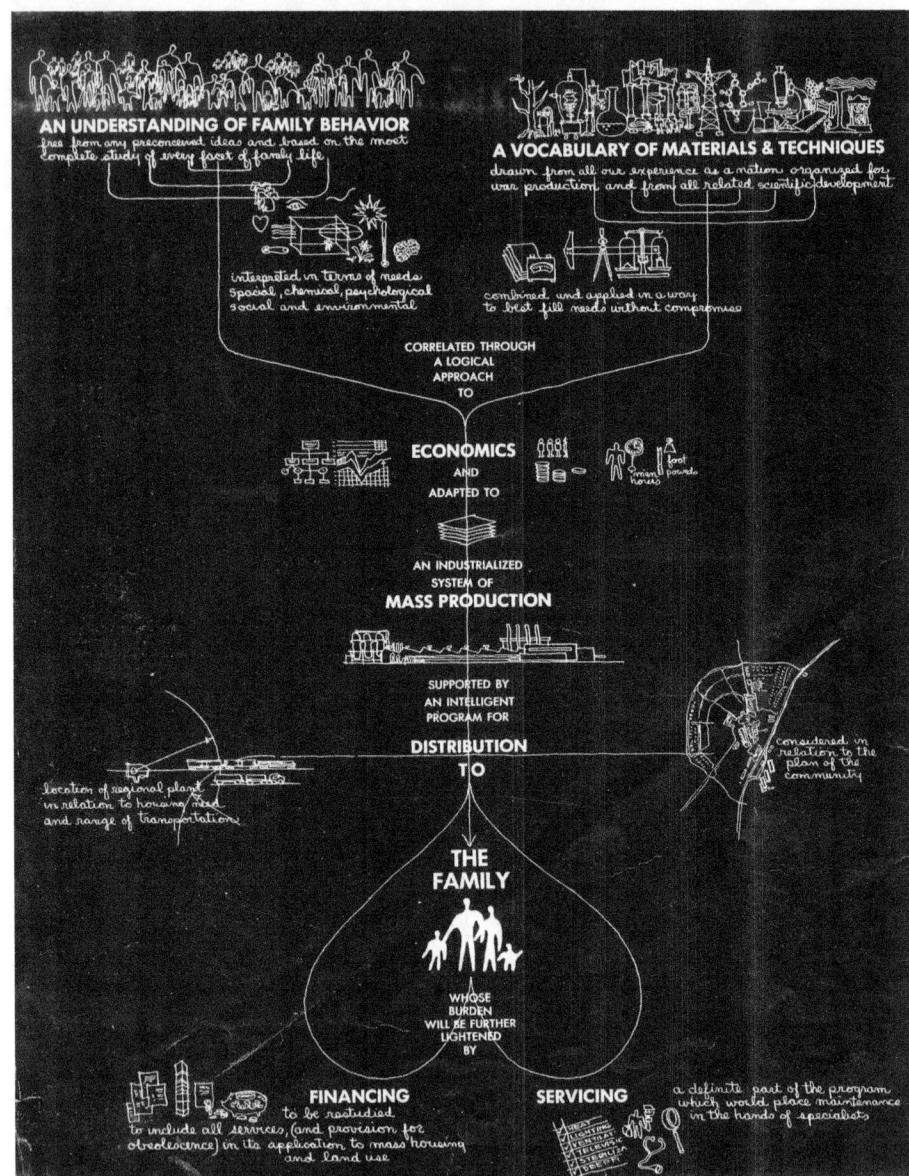

FIGURE 8.2. Charles Eames, "Chart" on Prefabrication. *Arts and Architecture*, July 1944. Courtesy of David Travers.

Experimental House No. 2, SOM immediately developed different versions of the prototype with varying options for orientations and porches, as well as two types of garages. The Pierce Foundation reported that it would build ten more houses with exterior variations prepared by SOM.

This experience with the Pierce Foundation helped SOM to more closely engage in the design and construction of prefabricated houses. In October 1940, *Architectural Forum* commissioned SOM to study all materials related to prefabricated

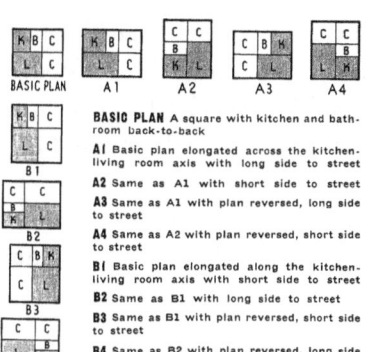

FIGURE 8.3. SOM, Plan Section and Orientation Diagram. *Architectural Forum*, November 1940.

housing that the journal had collected from builders. The journal then asked the firm to present "a basic house design" that only increased the merits of individual house plans. The journal published SOM's drawings the following month with annotations. The basic intentions of the project were not only to present an economical house but also to examine the other prefabricated houses available in the market and provide manufacturers with a standard model for a low-cost dwelling unit.[11] The house by SOM seemingly met all the general conditions for a low-cost house and was flexible and replicable as a prototype. The house was expected to become a housing standard, applicable to any context.

SOM's "Plan Selection and Orientation" diagram (figure 8.3) reveals characteristics of the firm's typical approach to a housing project. The diagram was easy to use, applicable anywhere, and detailed. It included an analysis of existing four-room prefabricated houses, from which the authors found there were only two different types of floor plans: one with the bathroom between the kitchen and a bedroom, and the other with the bathroom between two bedrooms. The first plan was readily chosen by SOM for its housing research; the firm economized on the plumbing by putting the kitchen and bathroom back to back and permitted greater flexibility in the shape of the house and its orientation. As the diagram shows, eight variations were created from the first plan. Each plan could be used in certain orientations that were readily installed in various possible locations according to the diagram. The firm developed the diagram based on such factors as "winter sun and summer breeze on the living room, and kitchen exposures."[12] This simplified, systematic diagram was believed by SOM to be employable in "most parts of the U.S.," although "it should be adjusted to local prevailing wind conditions" and "to sun conditions" of the extreme South.[13] With the eight variations and the diagram, SOM made low-cost housing development easily calculable. The detailed drawings for individual houses aimed at diversity and flexibility confirm SOM's systematic approach to architecture.

One of the key members of the Pierce Foundation's house research, John H. Callender, who later wrote *Time-Saver Standards* (1966), argued that "housing design should be based on family needs. The problem was how to obtain the data on which to base a design for housing not one, but several thousand families."[14] Callender's argument confirmed that the research came from an interest in mass production and that SOM's "Flexible Space" was a continuation of the foundation's research. The Pierce Foundation's research program on family life was highly influenced by sociologist Svend Riemer, who had worked with the Swedish Cooperative Building Society. Riemer's research method, called the "Stockholm Study" (1937), was a continuous record of the activities of each member of a Swedish family. More than two hundred families were studied through interviews and on-site sketches of the interiors in order to closely analyze how people interact with each other and with their domestic built environment. After thorough research on family behavior and use of space, Riemer proposed a new concept of design. Presenting a paper at the Milbank Fund annual conference in New York City in 1939, he contended:

> All too often the designer views the home in its static aspect only. He considers it as comprising so much space with so much furniture, neglecting the fact that it is the setting for many diversified activities of the family and its individuals, occurring in continuous flow and often conflicting . . . in space and time. . . . Design is a problem of conflicts in space and time.[15]

Like Riemer, the Pierce Foundation and Callender and SOM understood the issue of design as "a problem of conflicts in space and time." Obviously, design was not simply an issue of style or aesthetics.

To focus on the conflicts of family living, Callender suggested analyzing housing design in terms of three categories: space, equipment, and environment.[16] Space was measured by the physical occupation of a person and equipment around specific items in the domestic space such as a chair, a table, or even a mirror. The environment was subdivided into physiological and psychological measurements. While the physiological environment included control of moisture, heat, ventilation, light, sound, and sanitation, the psychological environment incorporated control of privacy and consideration of the general appearance and impression of the space and equipment. Aesthetic preferences and social

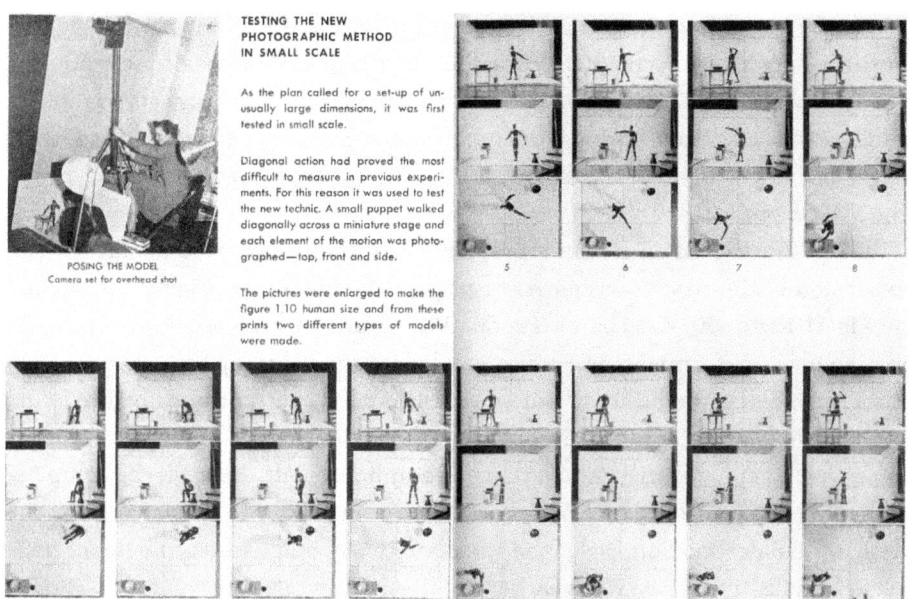

FIGURE 8.4. Experimenting with photography to measure space and motion. Courtesy of the John B. Pierce Laboratory.

standards were considered as psychological factors. Design in this process did not begin with physical walls and their shapes, but with "a human and wrapping around him with the required space, equipment, and environment."[17] The objective spatial measurements of human activities and developments of various furnishings became important parts of design (figure 8.4). The style of a house could be "fairly conventional—possibly even Cape Cod Colonial," when taking into account aesthetic preferences and social standards.[18] This concept of design was internalized by SOM in its work with the foundation and was further advanced during and after the Second World War.

THE HOUSING PROJECT FOR THE GLENN L. MARTIN BOMBER PLANT

On October 7, 1941, a group of businessmen, government officials, and reporters gathered in Baltimore to celebrate the completion of a housing project for the employees of the Glenn L. Martin Aircraft Company. The event was followed by a tour to Middle River, Maryland, where Stansbury Estates, a three-hundred-unit housing project, had just been completed and a second three-hundred-unit housing project, Aero Acres, was under construction. The occasion included speeches by Bror Dahlberg, president of the Celotex Corporation, and Joseph F. O'Brien, then serving as the general manager of the Pierce Foundation, that focused primarily on their respective roles in the construction of the projects.

While the Pierce Foundation and the Celotex Corporation were central figures in these housing projects, SOM contributed significantly to their realization.[19] The firm acted as the primary architect for the projects, creating general plans and specific technical drawings for construction. The Experimental House No. 2 developed by the Pierce Foundation and SOM in 1939 was used as a prototype for the Martin project.

The Glenn L. Martin housing project was initially conceived as part of the expansion of the 1929 Martin aircraft plant in Middle River originally designed by Albert Kahn and Associates. Production of aircraft bombers made it necessary to boost personnel from 17,000 employees to 45,000 by the end of 1941.[20] Anticipating that the influx of war workers would worsen the already dire housing situation of the city of Baltimore, the company decided to build its own housing development, constructed and financed in-house. For this task the company organized the Stansbury Manor Corporation, a subsidiary to be managed by the designer-builder Jan Porel, who had completed a 185-unit garden apartment project at Middle River three years earlier.[21]

In an effort to find the best in low-cost construction techniques, Porel compared thirty-two types of construction methods, from which the Pierce Foundation's method used in Celotex's Cemesto House was finally selected.[22] The Cemesto House was identical to Experimental House No. 2 in shape. The only difference was that it was not made of plywood, but of a new building material called Cemesto, a product of the Celotex Corporation. To prove the efficiency of the construction method and the durability of the Cemesto House, the Pierce Foundation and Celotex built a one-family and a six-family house based on their previous experiments, particularly one involving a project in Lebanon, New Jersey. The six-family house proved to have some technical problems, but the one-family house appeared so convincing that the Martin company decided to build six hundred identical houses on the two sites within walking distance of the bomber plant in Middle River.[23]

SOM and the Pierce Foundation designed the Martin House (figure 8.5) to be compact and rectangular with four and a half rooms—the A3 plan as seen in the "Plan Selection and Orientation" Diagram. The plan followed what the firm specified in its previous research, with two bedrooms directly connected to each other and the bathroom and kitchen adjoined to facilitate plumbing installation. The house was composed of a living room with a dining alcove, two bedrooms, a kitchen, and a bathroom. It had three curtained closets and two storage spaces, and demonstrated careful consideration in minimizing both traffic congestion and sound transmission. Other significant design elements included two large windows in the living-dining area (covered with metal venetian blinds), a covered porch, a linen closet, a coat closet, a shower fixture over a tile-trimmed bathtub, built-in shelves, and cabinets in the kitchen.[24] The house was equipped with electric appliances such as a refrigerator, a water heater, a stove, and an oven. These features were contrived to attract working families and to encourage them to

FIGURE 8.5. Martin House, 1941. Courtesy of the John B. Pierce Laboratory.

remain at the plant in the middle of the war when workers were in short supply and most needed.

The structural system of the Martin House was identical to that of the early Experimental House No. 2 in that it employed a wood skeleton frame and curtain walls. The only major difference between the two houses was that the cladding material changed from plywood to Cemesto board. SOM selected Cemesto as the main building material, including exterior and interior wall finish. Cemesto board consisted of a cane fiber insulation board core sealed with a special compound between two layers of weather-, fire-, and wear-resistant asbestos-reinforced cement.[25] Exterior walls employed one-and-a-half-inch-thick Cemesto board and one-inch-thick interior partitions. All of the boards and structural members were cut to specified sizes by the manufacturer prior to delivery. Assembly work was executed mainly in a field shop on the construction site; a second field shop was set up for the assembly of plumbing, which was under a separate contract. The Martin House was "pre-engineered for mass production with the wall and roof materials factory-made and delivered to the building site."[26]

This new prefabricated construction procedure replaced traditional craftsmanship as well as the traditional concept of housing design. For SOM and the Pierce Foundation, a house became a product. Erecting six hundred identical houses with identical drawings was something the foundation and SOM aspired to achieve when they began their research. Every house in Stansbury Estates

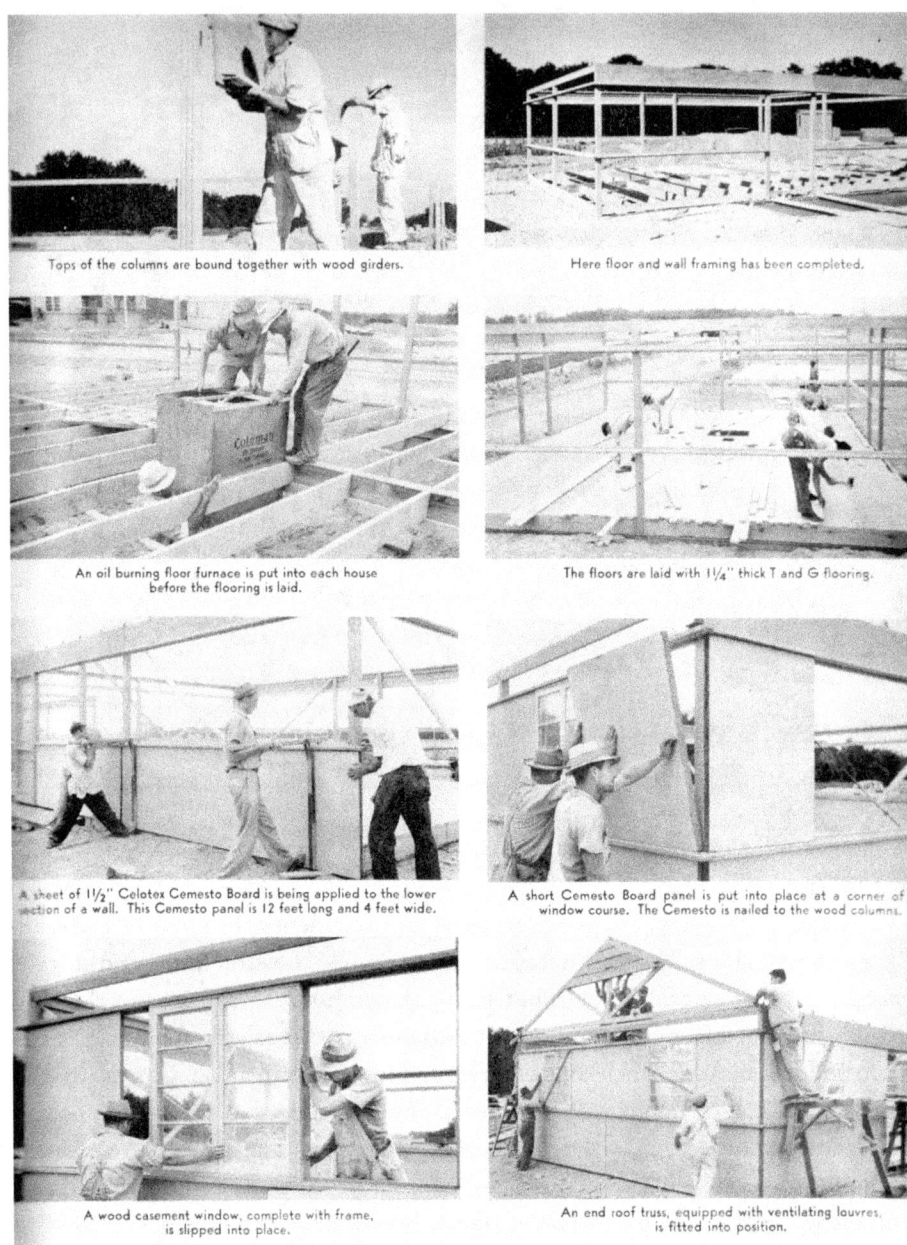

FIGURE 8.6. Construction photos, 1941. Courtesy of the John B. Pierce Laboratory.

and Aero Acres was identical except for the colors of the roofs, window frames, curtains, and other such features. The houses were fundamentally identical, but their cosmetics could be easily modified to produce more variation. Additionally, in order to save time, construction was organized so that the individual trades could concentrate solely on their designated task without needing any idea of how the house as a whole was to be completed (Figure 8.6). Construction workers from each trade performed their own work like assembly-line factory workers, entirely alienated and isolated from the final product.²⁷

THE MANHATTAN PROJECT AND OAK RIDGE

The development of the atomic bomb in the United States began around 1939, when Albert Einstein of the Institute for Advanced Study in Princeton, New Jersey (along with others) urged President Franklin D. Roosevelt to initiate a nuclear research program. This effort enabled the U.S. Army Corps of Engineers to create the Manhattan Engineer District (MED) under the directorship of Brigadier General (later Major General) Leslie R. Groves. There were three major locations for the project: Oak Ridge, Tennessee; Hanford, Washington; and Los Alamos, New Mexico. The community in Los Alamos was directly operated by the military and was the smallest and least complex of the three; the Oak Ridge and Hanford communities were created as unprecedented military-civilian communes, more complex in their organization and operation than Los Alamos. Oak Ridge, designed and built by SOM, was constructed first and became a model for Hanford (Figure 8.7).

Until the end of 1942, the site of the future Oak Ridge community showed few traces of human settlement. In the fall of that year MED purchased through

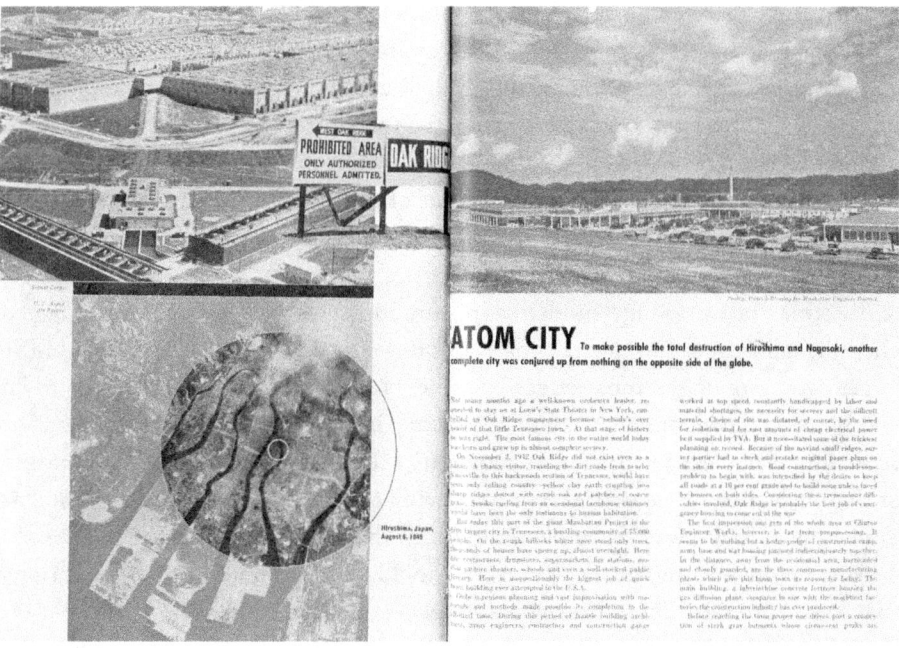

FIGURE 8.7. "Atom City." Nuclear facilities (top left) and a shopping mall (right) in Oak Ridge with an aerial photo of Hiroshima on August 6, 1945 (bottom left). *Architectural Forum*, October 1945.

eminent domain a rectangular plot of fifty-nine thousand acres at a cost of $2.6 million. This fenced site was located a few miles away from Norris Dam and eighteen miles west of Knoxville, Tennessee. MED carefully selected the vast reservation area. It was safe from air attack, had dependable electric power in large quantities supplied by the Tennessee Valley Authority, and had flat areas suitable for building that were separated by natural barriers to make a sufficient town site. There was an abundant water supply from the Clinch River, and the land was cheap (priced at about forty dollars per acre). When the site was selected after short yet intensive considerations, MED ominously called it the "Kingston Demolition Range"; they later ambiguously renamed it Clinton Engineer Works (CEW), which became the official reference to the whole site during the project.[28] The town site was located at the eastern end of the reservation on the slopes of Black Oak Ridge. To avoid unnecessary confusion and to lessen outsiders' curiosity, the name of Oak Ridge began to be employed for the post office address of CEW starting in the summer of 1943.[29]

By the spring of 1942, several methods of extracting the rare isotope Uranium-235 from the more common Uranium-238 had undergone testing by MED scientists at CEW and were nearly ready for pilot plant construction. These methods were the centrifuge, gaseous diffusion, thermal diffusion, and electromagnetic methods of separating Uranium-235.[30] The Tennessee Eastman plant, known as Y-12, comprised a 270-building compound and was the location of the electromagnetic process. Carbide and Carbon Corporation, or K-25, occupying seventy-one buildings, used gaseous diffusion. S-50, operated by the Fercleve Corporation, employed the thermal diffusion method. These nuclear facilities were located in valleys eight to ten miles away from the town site, near the fenced western perimeter of the reservation. X-10, operated by DuPont, was located in a parallel valley. This plant produced a small amount of plutonium. This was only a plutonium research facility, however; the main production plant was at the Hanford Engineer Works in Hanford, Washington.[31]

The town of Oak Ridge suddenly appeared in the sparsely populated, rugged and hilly landscape. The town's construction was an "incidental by-product of the largest and one of the most effective projects for war."[32] In principle, the town and housing development were of secondary importance compared to the construction of nuclear facilities, but providing scientists, engineers, and operators of the nuclear facilities with the proper living environment was still regarded as important.[33] There was an agreement within the army that civilians such as scientists, engineers, and other operators should be given better living conditions than those provided for military personnel.

No one could have anticipated the final size of the town. The city grew larger and larger until it had become "the biggest job of quick town building ever attempted in the U.S.A."[34] In 1942 the land was empty and undeveloped; by 1945 and the end of the war, the area had a population of 75,000 people, with 10,000 family dwelling units, 13,000 dormitory spaces, 5,000 trailers, more than 16,000 hutment and barrack accommodations, and other supplementary facilities for ordinary town life.

SOM was in charge of the majority of the building projects at the town of Oak Ridge. The main considerations in planning and building the town were "speed, saving of critical materials and minimum interference with the local labor supply."[35] It is not surprising that speed was the foremost consideration in many of MED's missions. To MED leaders, the key to winning the war was getting the facilities up and operating quickly and efficiently. Before participating in the operation, however, SOM was only a small design firm and had little experience apart from exhibition halls and prefabricated houses. In 1942 the firm had only about twelve employees in its Chicago offices and twelve more in New York. How, then, could such a small firm have undertaken one of the largest and most confidential wartime projects and completed its mission so successfully? And how did this success affect the firm's development after the war? SOM's activities at Oak Ridge reveal how and why the firm succeeded in its wartime missions that paved the way for its triumph in the postwar period.

In late June of 1942 the Stone and Webster Corporation (S&W) of Boston, one of the prime contractors for the Manhattan Project, agreed to develop the reservation site, including its utility facilities and housing construction. For the next several months, however, District Engineer Colonel James C. Marshall and his staff gradually became aware of S&W's inability to prepare town and housing development plans. There were also occasional delays in plan delivery, which made MED apprehensive.

When S&W submitted its overall plan for CEW to the MED New York headquarters, General Groves, Colonel Marshall, Lieutenant Colonel Kenneth D. Nichols, and others convened on October 26, 1942, to review the proposals. The plans that S&W had prepared revealed many elementary mistakes, including miscalculations in the number of urinals and showers.[36] In addition, Colonel Marshall found another problem in S&W's designs. During a December 17, 1942, telephone communication with August C. Klein, then vice president of the corporation, the colonel expressed dissatisfaction with the design of the houses, describing them as "overdesigned" and "too fancy." Colonel Marshall firmly believed that S&W's designs for the houses should not be accepted.[37]

In the meantime, MED initiated an internal evaluation of S&W's plans. This task was carried out by MED's principal engineer, Wilbur Kelly, and resulted in a brief report on January 3, 1943. Kelly stated that the drawings by S&W did not show any "originality or modern innovations." There was also a much more serious problem. According to Kelly, S&W's work contained major errors in estimating costs. Of the six original house types, only one was matched with the original cost estimate; the rest showed wide gaps between the original estimates and the new estimates. Some of the new estimates were beyond the limit established by law.[38] Kelly argued that the housing development "was not a sideline and should not be treated as such," and contemptuously reported that "plans equal to, or better than, the ones produced up to now could have been obtained from any lumber yard at the cost of printing."[39] He suggested two options to solve the situation: the first was to force a reorganization of the S&W housing team so that the job could be reassigned to competent personnel; the second was to establish a contract "for house design to an architectural firm experienced in low cost work." Kelly clearly preferred the second option, as he and his colleagues had encountered enough troubles with S&W. He finally insisted that a new architecture firm be hired and the corporation be removed from the town and housing design portion of the contract.[40]

MED immediately began searching for an architecture firm on which they could rely. The army was already aware of the Pierce Foundation, which was well known for low-cost prefabricated housing research. MED contacted Joseph O'Brien and arranged a meeting with him.[41] Considering that MED was searching for an architectural firm that had experience in developing low-cost housing, the team of the Pierce Foundation and SOM—a competent housing research foundation and its consulting architecture firm—drew the attention of MED. Having successfully constructed the housing project for the Glenn L. Martin Company (with mass-produced, easily transported, and inexpensive Cemesto-clad units), the team of the Pierce Foundation and SOM appeared an almost ideal leader for the proposed project.

On January 28, 1943, about three weeks after the submission of the evaluation on S&W, a small meeting was held in New York City; in attendance were Captain Ed Block and a Lieutenant Moore of MED, Joseph F. O'Brien of the Pierce Foundation, and Louis Skidmore of SOM. The MED officers organized the meeting to learn more about the team and, in particular, its experience in town planning and housing development. At the meeting, O'Brien and Skidmore promised that in two weeks they could present "complete plans and specifications, a site layout including stores, dormitories, recreational facilities, a hospital, etc., and cost estimates based on any size town."[42] O'Brien persuaded the officers to consider their plans as an alternative to S&W's. The MED officers thought that it would be worth doing more research on the Pierce Foundation and visiting projects it and SOM had completed. They accepted O'Brien and Skidmore's offer, noting that for the preliminary work the foundation and SOM would not claim any expense.[43] Several army officials accompanied by Skidmore and Merrill departed for Baltimore to tour the Glenn L. Martin housing project.

MED was convinced that the Pierce Foundation was one of the leading research institutions in the field of low-cost prefabricated houses and that SOM had sufficient working experience. It was clear to those involved, however, that the military considered the team primarily because of the foundation's reputation.[44] For the first year or so, SOM was not recognized separately from the Pierce Foundation. Partially due to this reason, the firm desperately tried to strengthen its ties to MED to secure the commission. The design of an entirely new city with a network of houses, schools, hospitals, shopping centers, and streets presented a challenge from the very beginning, made more difficult by the extreme secrecy surrounding the project. When the architects asked the officers about the location of the town, for example, they were told that it was confidential. The only information that the designers could obtain amounted to a few aerial photographs and topographical maps without titles or names.⁴⁵ After spending several days collecting this basic information, the SOM planners took four to five days to finish the town planning. The design was then ready to be submitted to MED.

On February 16, 1943, in the MED office, S&W's housing and site plans were put on the table with another set of drawings by SOM. MED leaders called in Leon H. Zach, a Harvard-trained landscape architect and former associate of Olmsted Brothers and chief of the Engineering Branch, Construction Division of the U.S. Army Corps of Engineers, to compare the two plans. Zach harshly criticized S&W for the poor quality of its general scheme, specifically its lack of traffic circulation, narrowness of city blocks, and insufficient consideration of topography, parking, and drainage; on the other hand, he applauded SOM. According to Zach, SOM's plans showed "far more thought and ability."⁴⁶ He preferred to proceed according to the new SOM plans. The meeting resulted in five instructions to the Pierce Foundation (and SOM), which would redirect all of the housing and town developments in Oak Ridge.⁴⁷ After this meeting, the Pierce Foundation and SOM immediately and officially became part of the Manhattan Project. Their first assignment was to design one thousand houses, subsequently increasing to three thousand, five thousand, and finally ten thousand houses within a year. It was the beginning of the most ideal commission any architectural firm could imagine: designing an entire town from scratch.

To streamline the transfer of work from S&W to SOM, a meeting was held on February 24, 1943, among MED, SOM, and S&W. SOM was asked by the military to "provide detailed layout of sections of the town site as rapidly as final locations have been checked and established on the ground," although the design of the drainage system was officially S&W's.⁴⁸ In addition, SOM was required to submit recommended road sections for approval "within the next day or two" and to recommend locations for a temporary trailer camp to house one thousand trailers.⁴⁹ This transfer of work happened immediately. A letter from Lieutenant Colonel Nichols sent to S&W made it clear that they were relieved from the responsibility of overall town planning, preparation of plans, and specifications for dwellings, shopping centers, schools, theater, church, recreational facilities, and the town hall. All of those responsibilities were now in the hands of SOM. Nichols nevertheless made it clear that certain work being done by S&W would remain with the corporation, writing that "the elimination of the work by this letter does not alter your responsibilities for design and construction of the now authorized dormitories, cafeteria, laundry and guesthouse."⁵⁰ The letter also revealed that plans for the hospital were under review. Until this moment, S&W believed that it had the design job for the hospital as well as the other supplementary facilities.

After March 15, when Lieutenant Colonel Robert C. Blair sent a letter to S&W,

an entirely different story unfolded. Referring to the previous letter by Nichols, Blair pointed out that the letter "did not contain any definite statement as to whether you [S&W] would retain responsibility for design of the hospital." The design of the hospital (with all other jobs mentioned above) would also "be assigned to the Pierce Foundation."[51] The transfer of the hospital project was one of many examples in which SOM took over projects from S&W. SOM and O'Brien tried, officially and unofficially, to supplant S&W. O'Brien, for example, sent an informal letter to Captain Block on March 3, 1943, about the apartment and the guesthouse at the town site after studying the S&W plans with the SOM architects. O'Brien found technical mistakes in the S&W drawings and returned those plans with corrections made using a colored pencil. He argued that the corrections were "not intended to be a criticism of the plans drawn up," but intended to call Captain Block's attention to "certain things that seem to be somewhat out of proportion."[52] Soon after, design and construction of the dormitories and the guesthouse were turned over to SOM.

Later on in the process, SOM took advantage of personal relationships with MED officers as a means to attract projects unrelated to Oak Ridge. The design and construction of some facilities in the Chicago area clearly demonstrated this tactic. Captain Joseph T. Ware had close personal and professional ties with the SOM partners, having worked as one of the liaison officers between the firm and MED in 1943. On September 5, 1944, Captain Ware sent a letter to the MED headquarters about modification of a commercial building in the Chicago area. He insisted that the job be given to SOM rather than S&W. Ware was in favor of hiring SOM and argued that "investigation by the contractor revealed that the firm of Skidmore, Owings and Merrill, with offices in Chicago and New York, was in a position to begin design work immediately."[53] After working for about a year and a half, the small design firm had become competitive and trustworthy. MED personnel who worked closely with the firm thought highly of SOM and recommended it over larger organizations.

"TECHNOLOGICALLY" MODERN

When MED finally approved the town and housing plan, SOM was asked when it could send a team out to the site to begin work. The answer was "immediately." It was right after February 24, 1943, just a week after the final meeting between S&W, SOM, and MED, that John O. Merrill along with five other SOM architects and planners, including Albert Goers, Louis Scesa, and Walter Metschke, left for the site. The travel arrangements were rather unusual: they were instructed by a MED officer to be at Pennsylvania Station in New York City at a precise time, without a clue as to their destination. They received their tickets in sealed envelopes. After boarding the specified train, the crew opened the envelopes and discovered that their destination was Knoxville, Tennessee. The day after arriving in the city, they met Colonel Nichols for the necessary instructions and moved to

CEW. On the site, Merrill set up a temporary field office in the rear of a garage and started surveying the area on foot.[54] The SOM crew inspected all of the road locations on foot in order to avoid topographical obstacles and checked all potential locations for houses.

The site plan initially selected and approved by MED was only based on a contour map and some aerial photographs. The architects believed that the schematic site plan would only be used for preliminary planning purposes and not for construction. MED, however, thought otherwise. There was no time to develop a new site plan derived from the context. SOM thus had to adopt a strategy for supplementing the submitted plan with thorough exploration of the whole site, rather than preparing another site plan based on the actual context. This procedure was put in place because replanning would take too long. Walter Metschke, who took on a critical role in developing the original plan, remembers the process as follows:

> The first move was to randomly stake an alignment which the survey party would accurately locate in the field as a basis for preparing a computed vertical and horizontal alignment. This stationed alignment was then staked in the field. It was again walked for required adjustments. The roads were located on top of the ridges and in many situations had to be precisely on the center line of the ridge to accommodate housing on both sides . . . Each time the road was restaked in the field it was again walked for possible revisions, a new alignment prepared, computed and restaked. This procedure was repeated as many times as necessary to achieve as nearly perfect an alignment as possible to avoid construction errors and delays.[55]

This repetitive operation in the field to avoid any delay was constantly required, since there was no time to correct errors or change anything. Once the position of the roads was indicated, the rest of the procedures were almost automatic. Right after construction orders were issued from MED, a full construction crew as well as equipment followed the survey team. As the SOM team scrambled along the rugged landscape, staking out roads, sewers, and water lines, the construction crew followed close behind them.[56]

The housing was essential to properly accommodate the personnel operating the plant, so the road and housing construction set the pace for the whole project at CEW.[57] MED required SOM to prepare complete site plans of fifty houses for the day's housing construction. Each lot was staked in the field, applying existing plans for the four corners of the house, and the centerline of the road was established so that the finished floor plans could be applied by field inspection. Trees were cut only when they were located within the boundaries of the walls of a house. To save time, new construction methods were systematically and enthusiastically devised. As in the Glenn L. Martin project, the construction process was divided into separate operations, each of which was processed one by one.

But compared to this previous project, the operation at Oak Ridge was better organized and much faster. Each element, such as pouring a foundation or erecting walls, was in process for a group of houses at a time; when the first crew was ready to move on, another crew took over along the construction sequence clarified by the firm. In this way thirty to forty houses a day were completed and ready for occupancy.[58] This speedy construction of prefabricated houses was later continued and popularized by private industry mass developers such as Levitt and Sons.

The physical shape of Oak Ridge was a narrow strip approximately one mile wide and over six miles in length, stretching along a major ridge (east-west axis) and crisscrossed by minor ones. This linear layout proved to be "adaptable to rapid expansion on the difficult, hilly site. Houses were placed to take advantage of the lovely view and existing trees, but to necessitate a minimum of roadway construction."[59] The network of streets in general was demarcated by the topography of the landscape, which was the best way to save time and construction costs and to allow easy expansion. All the streets looked conventional and familiar. The city appeared almost picturesque on the map, avoiding the grid pattern typical of modern planning despite being designed from scratch. This conventional-looking layout was also a result of the army's requirement—that the percentage of grade on the roads should not exceed 8 percent (later, at SOM's request, the requirement was raised to 12 percent because of the topography of the site).[60]

To avoid the confusion of disorderly names in a street system, SOM created a systemized nomenclature: major north-south thoroughfares and three principal east-west streets were designated as "Avenues"; the connecting roadways were called "Roads"; loops were called "Circles"; dead-end streets were identified as "Lanes" or "Places." The avenues were named for states such as Pennsylvania and Nebraska, and all streets served by one avenue employed the same first letter as that avenue. For example, all streets served by Kentucky Avenue had names beginning with the letter "K," like Kelvin Lane, Kenwyn Road, Kimball Lane, and Kingsley Road. The alphabetical system was employed everywhere except for the three east-west arterials: Oak Ridge Turnpike, Bear Creek Road, and Bethel Valley Road.[61] The street naming proved to be simple and efficient.

The original Experimental House of 1939 and its numerous variations developed by the Pierce Foundation and SOM up until 1943 played an important role in determining the future character of Oak Ridge (figure 8.8). The houses were diverse in size. The A and B types were small two-bedroom houses, the C house had an extra bedroom, and the D had a dining room. The A, B, and C types were linear and ranch style in plan and form, while the D was L-shaped. Some other types of houses and apartments were also constructed. All of the houses had picture windows in the living rooms, hardwood floors, and a blower air circulation system. Like the Martin houses, all Oak Ridge houses were equipped with stoves, refrigerators, garbage cans, and venetian blinds or shades at all windows. They were heated by coal furnaces.[62]

FIGURE 8.8. Aerial view of Cemesto houses. Photo by James E. Westcott, ca. 1945. U.S. Department of Energy Photograph Collection.

In designing the city, houses, and facilities, there was "no requirement of stylistic design" from MED.[63] However, there existed a certain homogeneity in the designs of houses and other facilities such as the guesthouse, dormitories, and supermarkets. All of them looked conventional at a glance, but to the more trained eye they appeared to be more of a hybrid of an old image and modern technology. There were three reasons for this. First, SOM employed the Experimental House developed by the firm and the Pierce Foundation as a generic template. Second, there was no time to develop new designs and MED was comfortable with the original designs. Lastly, pseudo-conventional designs were preferred. This third point deserves further explanation. The initial three thousand Cemesto houses were intended to accommodate well-educated engineers, scientists, and their families. MED asked SOM "to provide an environment which would offer no unavoidable conflict with their temperament, their routines and their habitual standards." It was assumed that many of the new settlers were not from larger urban areas such as Los Angeles and New York City but from all over the country, including places where generally modern architecture was still not popular. The amenities that MED believed new settlers desired, however, such as fireplaces, electric kitchens, a built-in heating system, and porches, were encouraged and authorized by the army.[64] This effort to lessen the readjustment difficulties of the personnel no doubt contributed to the conventional image of the town.

FIGURE 8.9. Guest House, ca. 1945. Photo by James E. Westcott. U.S. Department of Energy Photograph Collection.

It should be noted that Experimental House No. 2 and its variations were not developed for a specific context or climate. Rather, they could be built anywhere with minor modifications. The Pierce houses were technically determined and built for the site. As Colonel Nichols recalled, "Oak Ridge was a city without past, and it was not designed to have much of a future. We tried to design only for the duration of the war, in order to conserve money, materials, and labor."[65] The ephemeral nature of the town was a perfect condition for the Pierce houses, technologically modern but formally indefinable. For the time being, the houses could be called prefabricated houses, with vague allusions to the country house. However, the style of the houses meant little; they could adopt another style whenever needed. All parts of the houses and other buildings were manufactured in factories, delivered by train, and assembled on site. Building parts were elaborately standardized with careful consideration paid to systematized construction so that assembly was easy and quick.

According to the contemporary architectural historian Peter B. Hales, the excellence of SOM's entire Oak Ridge development was due to "its combination of conservation and innovation, its melding of the mythic qualities of past American utopias with the modern vision of centralization and government management."[66] The houses united conventional images and advanced mass production technology. The town and houses irresistibly evoked images of traditional villages, and the organic shapes of the streets and traditional shapes of houses were good testimony to the imagery of past America. The technology employed in construction symbolized the other side, a mechanical and futuristic America (figure 8.9). In this sense, Hales's comment seemingly epitomizes the essence of

Oak Ridge. At the same time, it should not be forgotten that many of the organic images were forced by the army's time and cost restrictions.

Critical to the design, however, was that SOM designed buildings with anonymous nostalgic images in order to produce conventional yet mystical sentiments, which contributed to the centralization and governmental management of CEW. There was no tension between the centralized, governmental ownership and management of the town and the design aesthetics. They were already part of the well-controlled whole. If there was nostalgia for the American past at Oak Ridge, it was an outcome of the speedy construction and the tight military control of the town. The nostalgic images actually belonged to the flexibility of modular technology. The design was thus neither modern nor traditional. It was a hybrid, transformative and technological.

The final image of the town was based on systematic mass reproduction. In some sense, asking whether the style of houses was modern or conventional is the wrong question. All of them were extremely modern, technologically. In each, the issue of style was nothing but an issue of precarious taste.

BECOMING A LARGE FIRM AT OAK RIDGE

During the operation at Oak Ridge, SOM was forced to reinvent its own practice as the size of the project grew and the firm's involvement became more complex. The project transcended the typical commission of architectural practice. To complete the work, SOM needed to become a new architecture-engineering firm that could perform road and housing construction, hospital and school design, town planning, equipment preparation, and interior design. The town of Oak Ridge was a laboratory for the firm to build a new kind of professional structure, which anticipated the future corporate architectural practice.

SOM's first contract with MED officially spanned from February 1943 to July 1943. The main focus was "the design of all structures required for a community to house approximately 12,000 inhabitants," which included "the design of dwelling units, store groups, theatres, churches, grade schools, high school, hospital, recreation buildings and other buildings as required for the community."[67] In the first phase SOM designed site planning for roads and house locations, three thousand dwelling units based on six architectural types, two shopping centers, a town administration building, a hospital, a nurses' home, an elementary school, two apartment buildings, a gas station, a recreation hall, and neighborhood store areas. SOM would receive the lump sum of $130,000, with supplemental compensation for overtime and additional services.[68] The amount in total would later prove to be millions of dollars as the firm attracted more jobs in other MED-related areas during and right after the Second World War.

None of the designers at SOM had any idea how many schools, supermarkets, hardware stores, and barbershops would be needed for the initial population of twelve thousand inhabitants. Having little experience in urban planning or large-scale projects, the designers made reasonable estimates, relying upon data in almanacs and the wisdom of experts.[69] They studied a similar-sized city, Lawrenceburg, Indiana, which was the birthplace of Louis Skidmore, and then developed a technique based on coefficients per person to approximate needs. For example, there was a certain number of barber chairs in the city. That number was divided by the number of men. Each man of the city theoretically needed 0.0012 percent of a barber chair. In the same way, each woman required 0.00658 percent of a beauty shop. By multiplying the expected community population by these numbers, SOM designers produced scientific estimates applicable to MED's changing population estimates.[70]

The second major contract spanned from September 6, 1943, to August 1, 1944. During this phase, the scale of SOM's task grew much larger and more complex. The estimated population of this phase became 44,000 residents, which soon grew to 66,000. The scope of work included overall site plans; 9,250 new family dwelling units excluding the 3,000 units already under construction; new men's dormitories to accommodate 1,600; women's dormitories to house 6,000; cafeterias; laundries; schools; and other structures to complete the development of the city. SOM's project list also included distribution facilities in the town, which previously belonged to S&W. SOM, now serving as an engineering firm as well, was asked to design the various sewer, water, and power facilities.[71] Likewise, SOM played an increasingly important role as the expansion of the plants created a need for more housing and other buildings necessary for ordinary town living.

At the end of 1944, about twenty months after the first team of six SOM employees was sent to the future site of Oak Ridge, the firm hired about 650 employees for Oak Ridge alone. The New York and Chicago offices also grew significantly. SOM transformed into an entirely different firm in its organization, operation, and capability. In March 1943, while John O. Merrill and others were working in Oak Ridge from dawn to dusk, seven days a week, the small New York office on East Fifty-Seventh Street was full of architects, engineers, and draftsmen producing plans for Oak Ridge houses. William Brown, who was then only thirty-four years old, was put in charge of the housing project at Oak Ridge. He later took charge of the special buildings as well as the housing. Robert Cutler designed the hospital and Arne Engberg the Town Center. By this time, Merrill had set up an office in the administration building at the site and worked primarily on site planning and building location.[72]

The SOM New York office was the headquarters for its Oak Ridge project until late 1943. Drawings were produced in the office and sent to the MED headquarters located in Manhattan. Because of security reasons, the communication between the firm's New York office and the Oak Ridge office was modulated by the military team. Several MED officers, Colonel Blair, Captain Ed Block, and Captain Ware, were assigned to the mission and stayed in the office almost continuously. Their job was to guide and check all drawings and act as liaisons between the firm, MED, and CEW.

In August 1943, Colonel Marshall, the top-ranked military engineer at Oak Ridge, was promoted to brigadier general and assigned another job entirely separate from the Manhattan Project. The deputy engineer, Kenneth Nichols, became the leader of MED under General Groves. Realizing the strategic importance of CEW, he decided to transfer the district's headquarters from Manhattan to the administration building at Oak Ridge, which was called "the Castle." Accordingly, the majority of the SOM design team moved from New York to Oak Ridge in the same month. The design team encountered a number of difficulties at the new location, including the need to acquire office space, telephones, and furniture.[73] Nevertheless, the whole situation for SOM improved significantly. First of all, the complicated communication problem between MED and the SOM New York and Oak Ridge teams was resolved, so the firm could instantly respond to certain unexpected situations or difficulties occurring at the site. Secondly, MED firmly recognized SOM staff as architect-engineers and gradually relied on the firm for any issue related to town and housing design and construction. At the early stage, until the end of 1943, SOM was regarded as part of the Pierce Foundation. When the main design team of the firm, along with other related crews in the New York office, finally moved to the site, its presence was instantly felt by MED. For the military, this meant that SOM was immediately and continuously available for the diverse demands of the project. The firm was constantly pressed by MED to take on many different roles. This created great pressure, but great opportunity as well. Working at the site of one of the most confidential projects in the Second World War, SOM now had to restructure all loosely related areas of architecture-engineering under its own aegis; this was the true beginning of the modern, bureaucratic architectural firm.[74]

In the fenced town of Oak Ridge, SOM took on a quite exclusive yet inclusive role. As the only architecture-engineering firm in the town, SOM's scope of responsibility turned out to be "challenging," and MED gave them "many interesting roles to play." It was "alarmingly all-inclusive."[75] Anything remotely connected with planning, building, furnishing, or equipping of the town was referred directly to the firm. This was quite beyond the conventional boundary of architectural services. The situation forced the firm's leaders, Skidmore and Owings, to get help in unfamiliar fields. Traditional architectural work had to be supplemented by a wide variety of professionals when tackling large, complex projects at the site. To meet various demands, the firm restructured its organization by bringing in competent professionals from entirely different disciplines. For instance, the L. S. Ayers department store in Indianapolis dispatched, at Owings's personal request, its key merchandizing manager. In addition, Skidmore asked Robert Moses of New York to send the chief engineer of the Tri-borough New York–New Jersey Bridge Authority to head the traffic and highway department. SOM hired a complete construction company from Grand Rapids, Michigan, to become the construction division of the firm. Construction manager Jan Porel, with whom SOM had worked on the Glenn L. Martin project, also joined the team.[76]

Importing personnel from other fields was to some degree compelled by the second contract SOM made with MED. "The Architect-Engineer was required to maintain his complete staff, and conduct all his operations at Oak Ridge," wrote Samuel Baxter, then the contracting officer's representative at MED. After working with the firm during all stages of the contract, he reported that "an adequate and competent organization was maintained throughout the period of the contract."[77] Those in charge of the various departments were "experienced and capable men in their respective fields." This evaluation of the firm was in part the result of importing personnel from other practices. Baxter similarly indicated that the business administration of SOM was "well organized and functioned efficiently and that accounts, files and property records kept up to date and in good order with the result that final accounting and auditing of the contract should be completed in a minimum time after the completion of technical services."[78] Ironically, the strength of the architecture-engineering firm had little to do with quality of design, but rather more to do with its level of organization.

During the operation, MED sometimes thought that the schedule for completing housing, special buildings, roads, and utilities was almost impossible. SOM, however, surprised the military by producing a significant amount of drawings and specifications within the allotted time frame. MED perceived SOM as quite an efficient and competent organization.[79] In addition, SOM sufficiently impressed MED with its operation at the site. Meanwhile, the firm completed the previous contract "in the shortest time," while restructuring its organization. A small architecture firm had transformed itself into a well-modulated architecture-engineering firm, capable of undertaking a complicated engineering project that would have otherwise been assigned to a traditional engineering firm such as S&W. Working under a difficult schedule, SOM overcame all obstacles and became a large, complex, yet flexible organization. The various roles that SOM architects were forced to fill at Oak Ridge helped them carry out far-reaching projects, which most architecture firms of that period could not have been expected to undertake.

William Brown, one of the early partners of the firm, recalled that the Oak Ridge project significantly increased the scale of the firm's operations and the number of its staff, and that the personnel of the firm "successfully handled the problems involved in coordinating many different types of technicians toward a single result."[80] As he described it, the Oak Ridge project would later enable the firm to qualify for large-scale military and government projects as well as projects for corporate headquarters such as the U.S. Military Compound in Okinawa, the Creole Petroleum Corporation in Venezuela, the U.S. Air Force Academy in Colorado Springs, and the Connecticut General Insurance Company. The physical infrastructure to support the American military force after the Second World War and during the Cold War years in foreign countries such as the Philippines, Japan, and Morocco was designed by SOM. Without considering the Oak Ridge project, it is not possible to explain the evolution of SOM. In fact, it is reasonable to argue that the small firm finally became SOM only after the experience in Oak Ridge. The size, scale of business, and organizational structure of the firm fundamentally changed during the war. Simplified architectural design, advanced technology, and efficient organization of a large-scale labor force were unified. The modern aesthetics for which the firm was known was in fact inseparable from the consideration of systemization and mechanization of architecture and the emergence of a bureaucratic firm.

CONCLUSION

With the detonation of atomic bombs at Nagasaki and Hiroshima in 1945, SOM abruptly completed its brief yet transformative evolution, one that had begun with a single, small experimental house in New Jersey. The first Experimental House No. 2 in 1939 turned out to be a seed for several thousand houses within about five years. The house led to many different types of buildings such as dormitories, hospitals, schools, shopping centers, and offices in the city of Oak Ridge. In the end, the journey culminated in the formation of a formidable architectural powerhouse that combined standardization and systemization of a building with the idea of flexible space. The massive architecture-engineering firm was the structural incarnation of the small prefabricated house.

With an introduction of the 'bureaucratically' organized firm to the field of architecture, the architects began to take different roles from those of the traditional artist-architect. Within the firm, building design now became quite a minor part of its overall operation and was reorganized to be a combination of all building-related considerations. Architects were encouraged to incorporate technological, political, economic, and cultural issues in their design process. The architects of SOM as a group developed an efficient, flexible organizational machine that could produce its systematic results in any circumstance. All of these changes were initiated at Oak Ridge, when the architects worked under the immense pressure of speed, with little pressure on design.

SOM's presence at Oak Ridge was not limited to the wartime period, but continued well into the postwar period. From the late 1940s on, the firm undertook a new mission of transforming the temporary military-civilian complex into a permanent city. From then on, SOM designed new buildings to replace the temporary, poor-quality buildings previously erected or brought from other areas during the war. What was intriguing about these buildings was their design. Their forms were undoubtedly modern from almost any perspective. Schools, for example, boasted modern appearances such as flat roofs and sleek glass-steel surfaces (figure 8.10). However, it should be remembered that the modern forms were produced by the same architects who had worked on the conventional-looking pitched roof buildings during the war. There was no gradual transition in style from conventional to modern designs, as though they were in essence identical. It seemed as if the modern form was already embedded in its production system as a ready-made.

LEFT: *Attractive, multistoried apartments provide modern homes overlooking wooded hills.* **ABOVE:** *Exceptionally fine two-family garden apartments have convenient carports.*

OAK RIDGE, U.S.A., WORLD'S 8th WONDER
IN TENNESSEE'S HILLS THE PATTERN OF DESTINY IS BEING SHAPED

LEFT: *Ultramodern educational facilities are available to Oak Ridge youth in this fine high school and,* **RIGHT:** *Elementary schools are designed in contemporary manner.*

Photos, HEDRICH-BLESSING, Chicago

Only a few years ago the quiet of the Tennessee hills was shattered by construction activities unprecedented in all history. The world's No. 1 atomic energy community was being created. With few exceptions living facilities were temporary, pending community development according to a Master Plan. Since war's end architectural and engineering progress has been transforming the pioneer Oak Ridge into a model which may well influence planning for other defense communities throughout the nation. SLOAN is especially proud that its Flush Valves were selected for Oak Ridge—another example that explains why . . .

SLOAN VALVE COMPANY · CHICAGO · ILLINOIS

more **SLOAN** *Flush* **VALVES**
are sold than all other makes combined

SLOAN FLUSH VALVES are specified for closets, urinals, service sinks, hospital sterilizers, etc., and once regulated to the requirements of the fixture, will deliver a uniform flush at all pressures between 10 and 100 pounds.

FIGURE 8.10. Sloan Flush Valve advertisement. Images include apartments (top) and schools (bottom) after the end of World War II. *Progressive Architecture*, June 1951. Courtesy of Sloan Valve Company.

The small prefabricated house developed by SOM and the Pierce Foundation was technologically designed. In addition, it was built to be a prototype, exemplifying the standardization of building parts and the systemization of design and construction. The basic elements of the house were repeated over and over again, evolving into different houses and facilities. This evolution later culminated in the glass-steel modern corporate headquarters of postwar American architecture. Those anonymous corporate buildings in the postwar American urban and suburban areas were the offspring of wartime building technology. At least in the case of SOM, the modern European forms found in the firm's postwar buildings were coincidental. Thus, rather than trying to find formal similarities with European modernism, it is more appropriate to attempt to discover how postwar American architecture grew from its autochthonous historical and technological developments.

NOTES

1. Colin Rowe, "Introduction," in *Five Architects: Eisenman, Graves, Gwathmey, Hejduk, Meier* (New York: Wittenborn and Company, 1972), 4.

2. William Hartmann, *Oral History of William Hartmann*, interview by Betty Blum (Art Institute of Chicago, 2003), 71–72.

3. "The New House of 194X," *Architectural Forum*, September 1942, 100–103.

4. Ibid.

5. *New York Times*, November 12, 1938, 26.

6. Alfred Bruce and Harold Sandbank, *A History of Prefabrication* (New York: Arno, 1972), 7. This book was originally published in July 1943 by the John B. Pierce Foundation.

7. Ibid., 11–12.

8. "Five Questions . . . and a Striking Answer," *Fortune*, July 1932, 61.

9. Bruce and Sandbank, *A History of Prefabrication*, 11–12.

10. Ibid.

11. "The *Architectural Forum* Defense House by Skidmore, Owings and Merrill, Architects," *Architectural Forum*, November 1940, 444.

12. Ibid.

13. Ibid.

14. John H. Callender, *Introduction to Studies of Family Living*, John B. Pierce Foundation, December 1943, 5.

15. Svend Riemer, quote in Callender, ibid., 8. Riemer's paper was later published. Svend H. Riemer, "Family Life as the Basis for Home Planning," in *Housing for Health*, American Public Health Association, Committee on the Hygiene of Housing, Lancaster, PA, 1941.

16. Callender, *Introduction to Studies of Family Living*, 12–13.

17. Ibid.

18. Ibid., 15.

19. Speeches on "The Cemesto House" by Bror Dahlberg and J. F. O'Brien, *A Vital Contribution* (Chicago: Celotex Corporation, 1941).

20. "Building for Defense," *Architectural Forum*, November 1941, 335–337.

21. "Houses for Defense," *Architectural Forum*, November 1941, 321–322.

22. *A Vital Contribution*, 7.
23. "Houses for Defense," 322.
24. Ibid.
25. *A Vital Contribution*, 10.
26. Ibid., 7.
27. "Six Houses a Day," *Business Week*, September 13, 1941, 65. The magazine reports, "This Lebanon house is the spiritual father of homes for airplane workers which are going up at the rate of six a day at the Glenn L. Martin Co. Plant, Middle River, Md."
28. Charles O. Jackson and Charles W. Johnson, "The Urbane Frontier: The Army and the Community of Oak Ridge, Tennessee, 1942-1947," *Military Affairs*, February 1977, 9.
29. Leslie R. Groves, *Now It Can Be Told: The Story of the Manhattan Project* (New York: Harper, 1962), 25–26.
30. "Construction for Atomic Bomb Production," *Engineering News-Record*, December 13, 1945, 113.
31. Louis Falstein, "Oak Ridge: Secret City," *New Republic*, November 12, 1945, 636.
32. Ernest A. Wende, "Building a City from Scratch," *Engineering News-Record*, December 13, 1945, 149.
33. Daniel Lang, "The Atomic City," *New Yorker*, September 29, 1945, 52.
34. "Atom City," *Architectural Forum*, October 1945, 103.
35. Wende, "Building a City from Scratch," 149.
36. General Leslie Groves mentioned, "Too many urinals and showers; not enough toilets. Ratio of 1:12 about right; change. Cut one row showers, add 4 toilets, eliminate 4 urinals. 24 wash bowls too many, to be reduced." "Notes on conference in District Office, 9:45 a.m., October 26, 1942," File MD-337, "Meetings and Conferences, District Office," Box 28, RG 4nn-326-85005, National Archives and Records Administration, Southeast Region Depository, East Point, GA (hereafter, NARA).
37. Transcript of Conversation between Klein and Marshall, 5:40 p.m., December 17, 1942, File MD-600.1, "Construction and Installations," Box 41, RG 4nn-326-85005, NARA.
38. Wilbur E. Kelly, "Report on Housing Plans—Summary of Status and Recommendations," January 3, 1943, File MD-624, "Housing," Box 52, RG 4nn-326-85005, NARA. "It is not desirable to build houses of the types designed by Stone and Webster at the costs indicated, and of course, the law prohibits construction of any single dwellings costing over $7500.00."
39. Ibid.
40. Ibid.
41. William S. Brown, manuscript sent to Owings, October 1970, Box 49, The Papers of Nathaniel A. Owings, Library of Congress.
42. "Conference with J. B. Pierce Foundation with Reference to Town Planning and Housing Development," January 29, 1943, File MD-337, J. B. Pierce Foundation, Box 29, RG 4nn-326-85005, NARA.
43. Ibid.
44. Nathaniel A. Owings, *The Spaces in Between: An Architect's Journey* (Boston: Houghton Mifflin Co., 1973), 86.
45. Stephane Groueff, *Manhattan Project: The Untold Story of the Making of the Atomic Bomb* (Boston: Little, Brown and Company, 1967), 163.
46. "Conference—Housing," February 17, 1943, File MD-337, "Meetings and Conferences, District Office," Box 28, RG 4nn-326-85005, NARA. "A. Pierce Foundation to go ahead as quickly as possible on 1000 house layout, including shopping and recreation facilities for same, using survey parties and draftsmen in field with a view to starting road construction Monday, February 22. B. Pierce Foundation to proceed with plans and specifications of

houses in order to have them ready for bidding in approximately two weeks' time. C. Pierce Foundation to furnish detailed street layout as soon as possible in order to arrange conference with Stone and Webster relative to utilities, as Stone and Webster will do this work. D. Pierce Foundation to work up and submit a schedule for construction of 1000 houses by July 1 with recommendations on number of contractors necessary, etc. E. Pierce Foundation to furnish plans for a women's apartment dormitory."

47. Ibid.

48. "Memorandum to the Files," February 25, 1943, File MD-337, "Meetings and Conferences, District Office," Box 28, RG 4nn-326-85005, NARA.

49. Ibid.

50. A letter by Lt. Colonel K. D. Nichols to R. T. Branch of S&W, February 17, 1943, File MD-600.1, "Construction and Installations," Box 41, RG 4nn-326-85005, NARA.

51. A letter by Colonel Robert C. Blair to R. T. Branch of S&W, March 15, 1943, File MD-600.1, "Construction and Installations," Box 41, RG 4nn-326-85005, NARA.

52. A letter by J. F. O'Brien of the J. B. Pierce Foundation to Captain Block, March 3, 1943, File MD-624, "Housing," Box 52, RG 4nn-326-85005, NARA.

53. "Chicago Area—Construction Contracts," September 5, 1944, File MD-600.1, "Construction and Installations," Box 41, RG 4nn-326-85005, NARA. This letter was written by Joseph T. Ware, who was stationed in the SOM New York office in early 1943 before transferring to the MED Chicago Office.

54. Groueff, *Manhattan Project*, 164–165.

55. Walter G. Metschke, *Memoir of Walter G. Metschke* (Art Institute of Chicago, 1998), 38–39.

56. Owings, *Spaces in Between*, 96–97.

57. Groueff, *Manhattan Project*, 165.

58. "Atom City," 105.

59. Ibid.

60. Metschke, *Memoir*, 38.

61. "How Oak Ridge Street Program Grew," *The American City*, April 1948, 102–103.

62. Martha Cardwell Sparrow, *The Oak Ridgers* (Department of History, Mississippi State University, 1980), 41–43.

63. Joseph T. Ware, letter to Owings, October 7, 1970, Box 49, The Papers of Nathaniel A. Owings, Library of Congress.

64. Owings, *Spaces in Between*, 90.

65. K. D. Nichols, "My Work in Oak Ridge," in *These Are Our Voices: The Story of Oak Ridge, 1942–1970*, ed. James Overhold (Oak Ridge, TN: Children's Museum of Oak Ridge, 1987), 116.

66. Peter Bacon Hales, *Atomic Spaces: Living on the Manhattan Project* (Urbana and Chicago: University of Illinois Press, 1997), 85.

67. "Design Progress Report: Skidmore, Owings and Merrill," June 15, 1943, File MD-600.914, "(Skidmore, Owings & Merrill) Design Progress Report," Box 4, RG 4nn-326-85005, NARA.

68. Ibid.

69. Groueff, *Manhattan Project*, 164.

70. Owings, *Spaces in Between*, 87–91.

71. A letter by Captain Samuel S. Baxter to T. C. Williams, Project Manager of S&W at CEW, October 4, 1943, File MD-600.914, "(Skidmore, Owings & Merrill) Design Progress Report," Box 4, RG 4nn-326-85005, NARA.

72. William S. Brown, manuscript sent to Owings. Many young architects of SOM developed into key members of the firm at Oak Ridge during the Second World War. In 1949,

when the founders decided to expand the firm's leadership, William Brown and Robert Cutler with two others became full partners.

73. Ibid.

74. Henry-Russell Hitchcock described SOM as an example of "Architecture of Bureaucracy" in "The Architecture of Bureaucracy and the Architecture of Genius," *Architectural Review*, January 1947, 3–6.

75. Nathaniel A. Owings, "From Oak Ridge to Manhattan and Way Stations." Lecture given to the Chicago Wayfarers Club, October 15, 1946, Speeches and Writings File, Box 53, The Papers of Nathaniel A. Owings, Library of Congress.

76. Owings, *Spaces in Between*, 87–88.

77. Captain Samuel S. Baxter, "Completion Report of Skidmore, Owings and Merrill, Contract No. W-7401-eng.69," October 9, 1944, File MD-600.914, "Skidmore, Owings & Merrill, Completion Report," Box 51, RG 4nn-326-85005, NARA.

78. Ibid.

79. Ibid. Baxter concludes, "It is the opinion of the undersigned officer [Captain Samuel S. Baxter] that Skidmore, Owings and Merrill discharged work under this contract in a highly satisfactory and efficient manner, that competent men were placed in charge of the various parts of the work, that schedules were met in most instances, and that the work produced fulfilled the requirements of the District Engineer in an economical manner. The partners, the project manager, and the department heads of Skidmore, Owings and Merrill cooperated with the undersigned officer in every way possible, and left nothing undone in their efforts to complete the job in the best manner in the shortest time."

80. William S. Brown, manuscript sent to Owings.

9 "MODERN BUT NOT *TOO* MODERN"

HOUSE BEAUTIFUL AND THE AMERICAN STYLE

MONICA PENICK

In May 1950, *House Beautiful*'s editor-in-chief Elizabeth Gordon announced a new brand of postwar architecture: the "American Style."[1] In a full-color feature, complete with a nine-point manifesto, Gordon presented the American Style as a cohesive set of design principles with identifiable aesthetics and an adherent set of architects. Gordon presented the American Style as a "mature" national architecture—indigenous, ingenious, and fully modern. In the pages of *House Beautiful*, the style represented both a new spirit and a new look. With its emphasis on site- and purpose-specific plans, climatic responsiveness, emerging technologies, and "common-sense" design, Gordon argued that the American Style addressed crucial architectural issues of the day, all in a form that seamlessly integrated comfort, beauty, and utility. The American Style was, for the magazine, "characteristically American"; as such, it offered a domestic paradigm for postwar modernism that could aggressively compete with other lines of "imported" modernism—particularly the resurgent International Style.[2] With an emphasis on the style's inherent American-ness, the implication of the American Style reached far beyond its viability as an architectural solution to postwar building: Gordon and *House Beautiful* positioned the American Style as the new symbol of democracy and capitalism, and a powerful material expression of American national identity. At this pivotal moment in the postwar architectural discourse, Gordon and *House Beautiful* introduced the American Style as a symbol of the nation's social maturity and cultural independence and simultaneously opened a public forum for architectural criticism, debate, and reform.

"MODERN BUT NOT *TOO* MODERN"

As editor-in-chief of *House Beautiful*, a shelter magazine concerned with the "business of better living," Elizabeth Gordon was in constant search of the perfect postwar house.[3] For Gordon, the American home offered more than mere shelter; it extended both materially and metaphorically beyond its own walls to become the source of "the good life" and the very heart of the American family. The home was, then, the simultaneous container for both social and architectural values. From the beginning of her tenure at *House Beautiful* in 1941, and earlier still with her 1937 book *More House for Your Money* (coauthored with Dorothy Ducas), Gordon began to address what she understood as the most pressing concerns of the home-buying public: form, function, content, and cost.[4] In sum, she sought good design. *House Beautiful*, with its broad middle-class audience and focus on domesticity, provided a forum in which Gordon could further explore these crucial social and architectural issues tied to the development of postwar housing—specifically the single-family home.

At the close of World War II, as the demand to house millions of Americans escalated to near-crisis levels, Gordon asked *House Beautiful* readers, architects, and the building industry to consider "how much change will people want in postwar homes?"[5] Their answer was not a lot, or, certainly not all at once. Armed with readers' mail responses, consumer questionnaires, and government survey statistics, Gordon and *House Beautiful* proclaimed that the American public wanted "modern but not *too* modern."[6]

The public perception—accurate or not—of modern architecture as European, avant-garde, minimalist, and functionalist had been established as early as 1932, in part by the Museum of Modern Art's *Modern Architecture: International Exhibition*.[7] Curated by Henry-Russell Hitchcock and Philip Johnson, *Modern Architecture* introduced the European avant-garde of the 1920s to the American public, under the newly coined label of the "International Style."[8] With black-and-white photographs and decontextualized architectural models, the exhibition presented a uniform and austere image of modernism, represented by the work of, among others, Le Corbusier, Walter Gropius, and Mies van der Rohe.[9] Hitchcock and Johnson's accompanying book, *The International Style*, offered a historical context for the exhibited projects—a perspective that cemented, for many, the view of modernism as a homogeneous, placeless aesthetic. Into the 1940s, prominent historians, curators, critics, and the architectural press continued to rely on Hitchcock and Johnson's definitions, and continued to celebrate the International Style's sober and severe aesthetic.

In the postwar years, as the dream of home ownership became a reality for a wider segment of the American population, Hitchcock and Johnson's definition of modernism remained for the most part uncontested. The image of the modern house as a Corbusian block or Miesian pavilion—a monochromatic, cubic mass on stilts—dominated the American public's architectural imagination. However, many consumers—and the federal infrastructure that would ultimately fund their purchases—resisted the International Style's emphasis on industrial materials (steel and concrete), stark character, and inherent *existence minimum*.[10] Though some architects offered softened translations of the International Style (for example, designers who participated in *Arts and Architecture*'s

Case Study House Program after 1945), consumer-desires survey data suggested the average American remained apprehensive.[11] For those professionals who sought to modernize postwar design, this consumer hesitancy presented a significant challenge.

Gordon, at *House Beautiful*, was among the many editor-critics to recognize that modernist strategies of simplification and rationalization were desirable (and even necessary in the postwar economy), but the physical and aesthetic manifestations of these ideas were perhaps too radical or too revolutionary. She recognized that architectural taste was slow to form and even slower to transform. Though she was convinced that postwar architecture would continue to modernize, she believed that even in transition, it would "always [keep] its design roots in the near past."[12] Gordon argued that extremes would not sell architecture, at least not to the audience who constituted the greatest portion of the postwar market, the very same audience who subscribed to *House Beautiful*. If a radical architectural revolution was destined to fail, Gordon believed that an evolutionary approach that built upon America's architectural heritage could succeed.[13] The first step, in her view, toward achieving a fusion of past and present was to address issues of performance, technology, and livability. Simply put, the task at hand was to prioritize desired lifestyle over architectural style. In Gordon's studied analysis, the postwar consumer wanted "the function of modern architecture, without the look of modern."[14]

Gordon was not the only magazine editor to promote architecture that was "modern but not *too* modern."[15] Other figures within the shelter press and women's magazines recognized the very same conservatism in American residential taste. Many editors (and some who were trained as architects), such as John Normile at *Better Homes and Gardens* and Mary Davis Gillies at *McCall's*, made similar claims, substantiated through their respective publications' consumer desires surveys. Change and progress were not undesirable, as *Woman's Home Companion* observed, but the American public seemed to want a "modern inside" and a "warm traditional exterior."[16] Despite a clearly documented desire for modernization, the majority of postwar consumers were likely to choose something between the extremes presented by the architectural profession. Consumers did not want "push button palaces of metal and glass and plastic," nor would they settle for the outmoded Cape Cod cottage.[17]

Informed by years of observation and volumes of housing research, Gordon asserted that the postwar consumer wanted modern functionality without the modernist steel-and-glass aesthetic.[18] Given this documented preference, she believed that American modernism should instead merge the best of the past (pitched roofs, stone hearths, and wood cladding), with the best of the present (adroit planning, large expanses of carefully placed glass, and uncomplicated forms).[19] The formal solution to the problem of the postwar house, argued Gordon, was to be found in neither revivalism nor radical revolution, but within "the forgotten saga of our own [America's] indigenous design history."[20]

Gordon believed that a "home-grown" American architecture that prioritized comfort, convenience, and practicality would appeal to the postwar housing market, specifically young middle-class families in search of their first homes.[21] Yet she felt this emerging consumer group was not yet equipped to make good design decisions; they had yet to develop "good taste" or the capacity to demand improved quality (from either designers or manufacturers). Gordon did not fault the public for this, because, as she argued, they "didn't realize that they could have more . . . so how could they want it?"[22] She instead placed the blame squarely upon those who she believed disseminated limited information and narrow architectural visions. In Gordon's view, most shelter magazines, that segment of the popular press tasked with informal design education, had thus far failed in their mission. While these magazines did spread ideas to a wide audience, they did not provide their readership with any "standards to shop with or by."[23] Professional architectural journals suffered from the same deficiencies, as did taste-making cultural institutions like the Museum of Modern Art. Gordon's aim with *House Beautiful* was to fill this informational void.

With this as her mission, Gordon launched a crusade to establish "good design" criteria, under which she could promote the best in postwar modern architecture.[24] She sought to educate and elevate middle-class taste, and to simultaneously encourage a dialogue between consumers (prospective home buyers) and producers (architects and builders). As a self-appointed critic and tastemaker, she clearly positioned herself to vie with Philip Johnson at MoMA and perhaps even John Entenza at *Arts and Architecture*, who in 1945 had launched the Case Study House Program as his solution to the problem of the postwar house. Men such as Johnson and Entenza offered one vision, but in Gordon's assessment, their resolutions were financially and aesthetically unappealing to the mainstream. As an alternative, Gordon offered a vision of modernism for the Average American, a synthetic and real-world approach that blended the "practical, the everyday, the ingenious, the technical."[25]

THE AMERICAN STYLE

In May 1950, Elizabeth Gordon and *House Beautiful* announced "the emerging American Style" (figure 9.1).[26] Gordon introduced this style as the manifestation of the American way of life and American character, something that emerged gradually from grassroots origins and grew from region to region, to finally mature as a national design style with social implications.[27] Applicable to architecture, interior design, landscape design, and the decorative arts, the American Style represented a "new kind of beauty . . . a new spirit and look."[28] The hallmark of this new style was its ability to respond to a marked change in postwar design values, most notably a new emphasis on performance, comfort, and informality.

Gordon and her *House Beautiful* staff, including architect James Marston Fitch and writer Jean Murray Bangs, recognized that the American Style had deep

FIGURE 9.1. "The Emerging American Style." *House Beautiful* (May 1950): 121.

---

roots in the late nineteenth and early twentieth centuries. Fitch in particular recognized the influence of European modernists such as Le Corbusier, Walter Gropius, and Mies van der Rohe, but argued that the process of "selection, adaptation and modification to the special conditions of American life"[29] had resulted in a version of modern architecture that Bangs described as "freed . . . from the burden of having to use borrowed forms."[30] In this assessment, the American Style had emerged as an autonomous line of architecture and, importantly for the development of American cultural identity (as separate from, for example, European cultural identity), served as a sort of "cultural declaration of independence coming about 175 years after the political one."[31] The American Style was billed as both "native" and "regional"; as such, it offered not only an alternative

FIGURE 9.2. "The Station Wagon Way of Life." *House Beautiful* (June 1950): 103.

to but also a criticism of the foreign and generic International Style. Unlike its European rival, the American version of modernism was neither esoteric nor, as Gordon would later imply, dogmatic. This was, for *House Beautiful* at least, a "common-sense" modern design that evolved from the down-to-earth American way of life.[32]

As a companion to the American Style feature, *House Beautiful* lavishly illustrated a postwar lifestyle that implied both a sociocultural value system and an architectural setting. The magazine's version of the American way of life—literally and symbolically represented by the American station wagon and the California ranch house—was independent, comfortable, and family-oriented (figure 9.2).[33] It embraced informal yet gracious living, implicitly filled with leisure.

It was defined by the luxury of space, freedom from constraint, and freedom from care.

In *House Beautiful*, American domestic life was easy, casual, and social. Inspired by the suburban boom and a romanticized view of California living, "easy" described both the typical American postwar character and a simple life free from pretension. This easy life was filled with maintenance-free goods, durable materials, and cleanable surfaces. The easy life adopted "engineered" storage that increased domestic organization and reduced clutter. Importantly, this new life included labor-saving appliances and state-of-the-art electronics (such as high-fidelity sound equipment and television sets).

"Casual" indicated an analogous easygoing social attitude, one that translated architecturally into the informal, flexible floor plans with multipurpose spaces found in the California ranch house and illustrated in *House Beautiful* with the work of Los Angeles–based designer Cliff May. In this model of casual living, the formal, separate dining room disappeared and the family rumpus room took its place. A growing intimacy between houses and landscape encouraged indoor-outdoor living, but privacy was retained at all costs. In design terms, the private backyard patio—again a key component of the California ranch house, and again illustrated by examples of Cliff May's work—became the new heart of the

FIGURE 9.3. Cliff May, Ranch House Classic (Cliff May Residence #3), Los Angeles, 1939. Cliff May pictured enjoying an "ideal" family life (ca. 1945), in the privacy of his backyard patio. Photo by Maynard L. Parker. Image courtesy of the Huntington Library, San Marino, CA.

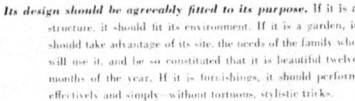
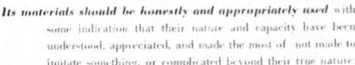
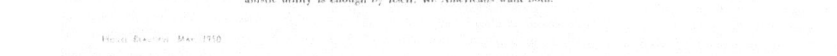

FIGURE 9.4. "How to Recognize The American Style." *House Beautiful* (May 1950): 158.

American Style house (figure 9.3). Social life and domestic life intertwined, and the family merged activities into public zones with the needs of children incorporated into the home's architectural program. All in all, the postwar American lifestyle demanded what *House Beautiful* described as an architecture of democracy, where "better things [were] available to more people," and where "everyman" helped perfect the American Style.[34]

To provide a material counterpart to (and theoretical framework for) these cultural and social values, *House Beautiful* outlined a specific set of design principles for the American Style. In "How to Recognize the American Style," the magazine (Gordon was the likely author) offered a manifesto of sorts, in the grandest of modernist traditions (figure 9.4).[35] The article paraphrased several

FIGURE 9.5. Harwell Hamilton Harris and students from the University of Texas at Austin School of Architecture, *House Beautiful* Pace Setter 1955, Dallas, 1954. Southern Pine advertisement brochure, ca. 1954. Reproduced with permission from the Southern Forest Products Association. Harris Papers, the Alexander Architectural Archive, University of Texas Libraries, University of Texas at Austin.

key tenets drawn from modern architectural theory, and many of these approximated Frank Lloyd Wright's principles of organic design. Among the nine points presented, *House Beautiful* placed a particular emphasis on purpose- and site-specific design, honest use of natural and common materials (reminiscent of both Wright and the Arts and Crafts movement), frank expression of structure, and the use of integrated rather than superfluous architectural ornament (figures 9.5, 9.6, and 9.7).

FIGURE 9.6. Anshen and Allen, Silverstone House, Taxco, Mexico, 1949. Published in *House Beautiful* (January 1951) as a representation of the principles of the American Style and naturalism. Photo by Maynard L. Parker. Image courtesy of the Huntington Library, San Marino, CA.

The magazine's preference for a softer, perhaps more humanistic (or naturalistic) version of modern design was evident through the guide to the American Style, yet technology still ranked third on the list of tenets. *House Beautiful* argued here and elsewhere that advancing technologies made "things perform better, wear longer, require less upkeep."[36] In this context, though, consumer technologies outranked advancing construction techniques and to some degree industrialized materials and processes; this emphasis underscored a key difference between the American Style and its International Style competitors (most

FIGURE 9.7. Edla Muir, Zola Hall House, Los Angeles, ca. 1951. Published in *House Beautiful* (July 1951) and on the cover of Joseph Barry, *The House Beautiful Treasury of Contemporary American Homes* (New York: Hawthorne, 1958). Photo by Maynard L. Parker. Image courtesy of the Huntington Library, San Marino, CA.

---

obviously, Le Corbusier and Mies van der Rohe). For *House Beautiful*, the American Style "harnessed" technology for the domestic interior, in the form of appliances, gadgetry, new maintenance-free materials, heating, ventilation, and solar shading. And significantly, the American Style—meant to be adopted in suburbs across the nation—adeptly accommodated the most influential technology of the twentieth century: the automobile. This was, after all, the architectural analogue to what *House Beautiful* had called "the Station Wagon Way of Life" (see figure 9.2). American Style carports and push-button garages were therefore synchronized with the latest consumer enthusiasms.

Perhaps most importantly—and as a direct link to Gordon's larger editorial agenda—the "how to" guide presented an architectural language that was specifically "an American version of Modern," albeit an adaptation, modification, and simplification of both early twentieth-century American design traditions and the "European version" of modern design.[37] The past work of architects such as H. H. Richardson, Frank Lloyd Wright, and Greene and Greene were of particular importance (and praised elsewhere in the magazine) (figure 9.8).[38] *House Beautiful* believed that this "native" brand of modern would appeal to an American sense of beauty, utility, and common sense over the "intellectual stunts or tricks"

FIGURE 9.8. Harwell Hamilton Harris and students from the University of Texas at Austin School of Architecture, *House Beautiful* Pace Setter 1955, Dallas, 1954. Photo by Maynard L. Parker. Digital print courtesy of Harris Papers, the Alexander Architectural Archive, University of Texas Libraries, University of Texas at Austin. Image rights courtesy of the Huntington Library, San Marino, CA.

---

that Gordon believed were the trade of European modernists (and particularly those associated with the International Style).[39]

Through short features like the American Style guide, Gordon used *House Beautiful* as an instrument of reform; in the pages of the magazine she codified the American Style, provided a forum for its popularization, and attempted to unite members of what has thus far been a fragmented architectural movement. Her approach publicized alternative models of modernism, disseminated these to the broader public, and, perhaps most significantly, empowered the postwar consumer to become a partner in the process of design.

THE AMERICAN STYLE POLITICIZED:
"THE THREAT TO THE NEXT AMERICA"

Though Gordon had long supported the American public's freedom to blend design styles and develop independent (and individualized) aesthetic taste, she had never been overly concerned with the larger implications of architectural choice. This began to change with her introduction of the American Style in 1950;

three years later she launched a new (and highly controversial) editorial agenda that connected domestic design with a larger political, cultural, and social context.

The first years of the 1950s provided the impetus for Gordon's new agenda. At the precise moment that the American housing market experienced a jolt (with 1.95 million housing starts in 1950 alone), world politics became intensely charged.[40] In the space of a few short years, China fell to Mao and became the People's Republic, the Soviet Union raised its "Iron Curtain" around Eastern Europe, and North Korea crossed the thirty-eighth parallel to engage the United States in war. The threat of worldwide Communist domination triggered fear at home, exacerbated by Wisconsin senator Joseph McCarthy's efforts to expose Communists working within the U.S. State Department and by the growth of the Hollywood blacklist.[41] Gordon, who observed from a seemingly disconnected position as a shelter magazine editor, viewed this political peril as prelude to a cultural—and by extension, architectural—threat.

If free markets and free minds were at risk, then in Gordon's assessment the American Style (as the democratic form of modern architecture) was simultaneously under siege. For many, Gordon included, the danger was realized in architectural terms as the postwar incarnation of the International Style, which retained its lingering associations (exaggerated or untrue as they may have been) with socialism, communism, fascism, and anticapitalist ideologies. For Gordon, the United Nations Headquarters (1950) and SOM's Lever House (1952) were prominent symbols of this very type of encroachment, as was Mies van der Rohe's much revered and equally feared Farnsworth House (1951). Though these projects could be readily interpreted as products of a thriving democratic and capitalistic system, or, in the case of Farnsworth House, an assimilated architecture commissioned by an independent, professional, and progressive "New Woman," Gordon found these architectural images disturbing and un-American.

In April 1953, *House Beautiful* published Gordon's "The Threat to the Next America," a scathing critique of the International Style (figure 9.9). In this controversial editorial, she declared an imminent threat to the quality of American design. The battleground was aesthetic, political, and social. Gordon accused the International Style's leading practitioners—the "artistic dictators" Mies, Gropius, and Le Corbusier—of subverting democratic individuality and ignoring basic human requirements. Gordon believed that certain "self-chosen elite" positioned at highly visible museums (for example, MoMA), architecture magazines (for example, *Architectural Forum*), architecture schools (for example, Harvard and IIT), and in professional practice were guilty of thoughtlessly promoting the "mystical idea that less is more," which in her view was "simply less."[42]

Gordon condemned the International Style as "anti-reason" itself, characterized by the "unscientific, irrational and uneconomical—[by] illogical things like whole walls of unshaded glass . . . [and] heavy buildings up on thin, delicate stilts."[43] Using her interview with Edith Farnsworth for specific evidence, Gordon argued that Mies and his followers created an architecture of unlivable

FIGURE 9.9. Elizabeth Gordon, "The Threat to the Next America." *House Beautiful* (April 1953): 126–127.

"stripped-down emptiness."[44] In her view, these European modernists (even those working in the United States) simply ignored the basic human need for individuality, comfort, and convenience (such as storage). The problem, for Gordon, was that this "hair shirt school" valued appearance over performance.[45]

The danger for the American consumer, argued Gordon, was that an aversion to "comfort, convenience, and functional values" was coming from "highly placed individuals and highly respected institutions."[46] Such "totalitarian" influence was detrimental to the formation of free taste. For Gordon, this was the seed of a greater social threat. Her goal was to expose this threat and to simultaneously unmask the shortcomings of what she saw as a "narrow, ignorant" interpretation of modernism. In turn, she proposed an alternate version of modern that was, as she wrote, home-grown and commonsensical. She hoped to redirect public taste toward a modernism of good judgment, specifically, the American Style.

Gordon's "Threat to the Next America" provoked a substantial public response. Her views garnered a great deal of national attention, including printed responses in *Progressive Architecture* and a full-page rejoinder in *Architectural Forum*. In June, July, and October 1953, *House Beautiful* reprinted excerpts from over sixty letters to the editor (a mere fraction of the hundreds received), both in support and in opposition to Gordon's essay. According to *House Beautiful*, 85 percent were in "hearty approval," while the remaining 15 percent were divided between "those who say we are flogging a dead horse and those who say we are attacking the greatest designers and architects alive."[47]

Opposition was particularly fierce. Gordon's professionalism, judgment, and knowledge—not to mention her personal politics—were called into question. For example, W. E. Ross from Jackson, Mississippi, wrote to *House Beautiful*: "Your Elizabeth Gordon is an uninformed masterpiece.... Why don't you have this bigoted female educated before you let her preach further?"[48] Others were shocked that she dared to attack Mies, Gropius, and Le Corbusier in such an "emotional" and "irrational" manner, and for the "obvious purpose of selling 'possessions.'"[49] At least one respondent was so offended that he canceled his subscription.[50] Philip Johnson called her tone Fascist. Peter Blake of *Architectural Forum* branded Gordon as the real threat to the Next America. He announced that she had penned her own epitaph: "Here lies *House Beautiful*, scared to death by a chromium chair."[51]

Given Gordon's previous support of the Bay Region School, William Wurster's protest was perhaps the most unexpected. Accompanied by thirty prominent California designers including Lawrence Halprin, Garrett Eckbo, Theodore Bernardi, and Donn Emmons, Wurster rejected Gordon's implication that modern architects were seditious or harbored the intent to undermine American freedom.[52] Collectively, these designers protested Gordon's evaluation of architecture based on what they perceived as "political criteria" and objected to her "attack on European art and architecture and the implication that all good art has its roots in America and all that is European is subversive, perverted or sick."[53]

Former friends turned foe, particularly offended by Gordon's apparent political extremism. Although she chose to highlight the International Style as foreign and as un-American, her editorial policies were less reflective of her personal politics than of the popular anti-Communist, antitotalitarian rhetoric of the day.[54] Indeed, her rhetorical strategies were just as likely meant to stir emotion and stimulate action.

Despite such heated opposition, Gordon's supporters were many. Allegiance came from Lewis Mumford, Bruce Goff, Karl Kamrath, and others. An unexpected and positive turn of events came when she received a telegram that read, "Surprised and delighted. Did not know you had it in you. From now on at your service. Sending you the latest from my standpoint.—GODFATHER."[55] Gordon had no idea who her "Godfather" was, but would soon learn that Frank Lloyd Wright had come to her defense. This proved a pivotal moment for Gordon, for *House Beautiful*, and for Wright himself.

Wright's encouragement was perhaps the most empowering of all that Gordon would receive. She had long admired his ideas, if not his designs. She had published a favorable account of Taliesin West in 1946 (though she commented, confidentially and outside of print, that she had not been impressed with the aesthetic).[56] At the time, Gordon likely understood that his work suffered from many of the flaws for which she later criticized International Style modernists—including "cantilevering things that don't need to be cantilevered..."[57] Thus few of *House Beautiful*'s published images belonged to Wright, but many of the magazine's positions owed something to his theory. As Gordon introduced the American Style in 1950, she upheld Wright as its "spiritual leader."[58] Upon Wright's death in 1959, she recalled that she had always "tried to edit by Wrightian precepts and principles," though in reality, prior to 1953 she had avoided any overt connection to organic architecture or the term "organic" (as used in the Wrightian sense).[59] Nevertheless, from the moment of Wright's public declaration of support in 1953, *House Beautiful*'s concept of the American Style as the modern architecture for the Next America became synonymous with Wright's brand of organic design.

The relationship between *House Beautiful* and Wright was further cemented when members of his Taliesin Fellowship joined Gordon's editorial staff. When architectural editor James Marston Fitch resigned "in protest" against the editorials of 1953, Gordon replaced him with Wright's apprentice John deKoven Hill.[60] Ahead of all others, Hill became Gordon's close confidant and was highly influential within the publication.[61] Hill, who entered the Taliesin Fellowship in 1938, had spent the previous fifteen years working closely by Wright's side as both architect and interior designer. Gordon hired Hill as the new architectural editor and later promoted him to executive editor. He occupied a large role: he not only guided the editorial content of the magazine but also was reportedly responsible for designing nearly one-quarter of what *House Beautiful* published between 1953 and 1963. While Wright had thought to position Hill as a voice for organic architecture, Hill became a force of his own. The Taliesin connection grew stronger when Gordon and Hill recruited Curtis Besinger, a Taliesin apprentice from 1939 to 1955 and later a professor at the University of Kansas, to contribute architectural essays to *House Beautiful*. Kenn Lockhart, another Taliesin Fellow, also joined the magazine's ranks. Gair Sloan, trained in Aaron Green's San Francisco office, was hired as *House Beautiful*'s in-house draftsman. Wright's 1953 telegram had helped Gordon when she had "felt mighty alone," but his apprentices proved to be of even greater assistance. Wright's support, Hill's design talent, Besinger's critical writing, and Sloan's able hand "allowed *House Beautiful* to . . . design & build & show [their] alternative to the Bauhaus," and as Gordon wrote, "that was better than a lot of verbage [sic]."[62]

AMERICAN STYLE GOES ORGANIC

As the architecture department at *House Beautiful* became increasingly tied to Wright, Gordon was able to suggest an environment in which the American Style, now reformulated as a popularized form of organic architecture, could thrive. Between the world wars, organic architecture had experienced demise. It had not ceased to exist or to be practiced, but it had faded from public view. Competing visions of modernism, including the International Style, had subsumed the organic. Gordon's American Style brought it to the fore, but it was her 1953 article that truly opened a venue for its resurgence. By challenging the notion of what it meant to be modern, by reinterpreting organic architecture as a humanistic and practical alternative, Gordon suggested a new life for an old design philosophy. And importantly, *House Beautiful* lent organic architects—beyond just Wright— a mainstream audience. By championing these men who the historian Esther McCoy has called the "architectural misfits" of the 1950s, and by attacking the competition, Gordon risked professional rejection.[63] Her actions, however, galvanized an otherwise scattered and peripheral organic movement.

Gordon knew that Wright was at the center. By 1953 he had reached the apex of his fame, with the AIA Gold Medal in 1949, *Sixty Years of Living Architecture* in 1951, completed Usonians numbering in the hundreds, and his plans for the Guggenheim Museum often in the press. She also knew that his apprentices—such as Fay Jones, Alden Dow, and Aaron Green—were establishing independently successful practices. And architects who had not studied under the master (such as Alfred Browning Parker) were nonetheless adopting his architectural mannerisms and principles.[64] Still, as Gordon wrote years later, enthusiasm for this kind of modern architecture was limited. Though "Frank Lloyd Wright was creating new, exciting containers . . . for most people, he was too far ahead. His taste was not for the average family. People were afraid. . . . Progress was fine, but it mustn't look different!"[65] This recalled again her long-held support of mitigated modernism, one that was "modern but not *too* modern."[66]

What Gordon could achieve that Wright could not was an essential repackaging of organic design. Gordon's strategy was to link Wright's organic architecture to her own concept of the American Style. The challenge was to reformulate the Wrightian brand so that it could simultaneously capture the spirit of progress and become sellable to a mass market. Even so, Wright would not be the star; he would remain the shadow of inspiration and the source of legitimacy.

With her concept of a revitalized and essentially popular form of organic architecture, Gordon explored the middle ground between facsimile (of Wright) and fetish (of, for example, Bruce Goff). Wright may have pioneered modern organic space, but it was the subsequent generation of architects, Gordon's American Stylists, that made it truly popular and essentially livable. In the pages of *House Beautiful*, and particularly with the magazine-sponsored Pace Setter House Program (1948-1965), Gordon created the opportunity for designers such as Cliff May, Alfred Browning Parker, Harwell Hamilton Harris, Vladimir Ossipoff, Roger Rasbach, and John deKoven Hill to demonstrate their viability (figures 9.2, 9.3, 9.5, and 9.6, above; figure 9.10). For Gordon, these designers proved that the American Style could incorporate Wright's influence, yet move beyond his concept of organic to become wholly contemporary and original.

Upon Gordon's death in September 2000, the *Economist* wrote that with "The Threat to the Next America," she became embroiled in the "politics of architecture."[67] On the one hand, she opened professional polemics to a nonarchitectural

FIGURE 9.10. John deKoven Hill, *House Beautiful* Pace Setter 1960, Cincinnati, Ohio. *House Beautiful* (February 1960): 104.

audience; on the other hand, she invoked seemingly irrational rhetoric that perhaps threatened her own credibility. The battle between competing postwar modernisms—an emerging American Style and a dominating International Style—had been building since at least 1946; even so, Gordon's attack of 1953 could be read as a political act of anger and retribution. While Gordon never committed this to print, her longtime associate editor (and former Taliesin apprentice) Curtis Besinger attested in a 1986 letter to Robert Venturi that the trigger for Gordon's attack was outright and unexpected rejection. Besinger wrote:

> *House Beautiful* was asked by the U.S. Department of State to "do" the furnishings for a "typical builders house" ... to be exhibited in Europe to show how Americans live. The "decorators" of the magazine shopped the market and put together a package of furnishings for this "typical" house. But when the exhibition opened in Europe the "package" had been replaced with one that could have appeared in a [Museum of Modern Art] "Good Design" show.⁶⁸

Whether provoked by anger or other motivations, Gordon certainly impacted postwar domestic architecture. Her "Threat" essay represented a critical moment at which the tides turned.

CONCLUSION

Elizabeth Gordon announced her retirement from *House Beautiful* in January 1965. Amidst growing animosity within the Hearst machine, she refused to surrender her editorials to "the service of advertisers" and subsequently risk the trust of her readers.⁶⁹ Instead, she resigned.⁷⁰

Gordon may have been forced into professional exile, but her role in the postwar architectural discourse nevertheless remains significant. Though her line of argument was highly problematic and at times logically inconsistent or purposefully selective, her effort to reopen and then close a long-standing controversy between organic modernism and functionalist modernism—or, in her terms, the American Style and the International Style—was considerable. She was certainly not the only critic to assert such views, but her voice was loud and her audience large. As Besinger later observed, she publicly questioned the path of modernism "13 years before Robert Venturi's *Complexity and Contradiction* . . . 21 years before Peter Blake [in "Follies of Modern Architecture"] . . . and 24 years before Charles Jencks in his *Language of Post-modern Architecture*."⁷¹ As Besinger suggested, Gordon had long been an advocate of reform and of good, livable modern design. Her effort to reframe modern domestic architecture went beyond her now-infamous essay of 1953. With *House Beautiful*, Gordon created a forum in which competing versions of modern design could grow and flourish. To critics like Gordon, it was clear that several models of modern architecture did and could exist simultaneously; she sought a viable public path for one of these lines.

With the codification of the American Style, organicized and, by 1953, highly politicized, Gordon offered a new model for modernism in postwar America. The identification and consolidation of a simple set of architectural principles were only part of her contribution. Under Gordon's influence, a popular audience was given a mechanism with which to understand design developments around them;

selected architects were likewise provided with a venue in which to offer an alternative to the canonical vision of modernism that so dominated the professional journals of this era. Thanks in part to a large national circulation and, after 1953, to the support of Frank Lloyd Wright, Gordon was able to give voice to a new movement and to "sanction modernism" in a way that most mass-market publications could not.

NOTES

I would like to thank Anthony Alofsin and Christopher Long for their insight and guidance in the development of this research. Jennifer A. Watts, Erin Chase, and the staff at the Maynard L. Parker Collection (Huntington Library) have offered their invaluable assistance with many of the images for this essay. Beth Dodd, Nancy Sparrow, and the staff at the Alexander Archives (School of Architecture, University of Texas at Austin) have also provided archival assistance for which I continue to be grateful. At the University of Wisconsin–Madison, I would like to thank the Design Studies Department and the Graduate School for their support of my work; I am particularly grateful to my research assistant Julia Dane for her diligence, patience, and excellent work. I would like to thank my colleagues Vladimir Kulić and Timothy Parker for their collaborative spirit, enthusiasm, and perseverance throughout this project.

1. Elizabeth Gordon, "The New American Style Grew from America's Way of Life," *House Beautiful* 92 (May 1950): 122–123. *House Beautiful* first used the term "modern but not *too* modern" in 1948 to describe emerging design trends that Gordon would eventually label American Style. For usage of this phrase, see Jedd S. Reisner, "Modern but not *Too* Modern," *House Beautiful* 90 (April 1948): 120–125.

2. Gordon featured the phrase "characteristically American," which referenced philosopher Ralph Barton Perry's attempt to "characterize" American society, culture, and values in a series of lectures published in book form in 1949. Gordon published feature articles by Perry and frequently referenced his ideas as she wrote about the American Style. See Ralph Barton Perry, *Characteristically American* (New York: Knopf, 1949).

3. The phrase "business of better living" appeared in *House Beautiful*'s masthead. Elizabeth Gordon began her tenure as editor-in-chief at *House Beautiful* in October 1941 and retired in December 1964. Her first exploration of the ideal "postwar house" appeared in *House Beautiful* in 1942, though her full-scale investigation of the housing "problem" began four years later, with *House Beautiful*'s Golden Jubilee (fiftieth anniversary) issue in December 1946. Under Gordon's editorship, architecture became a focal point of the magazine, while comparable women's journals or shelter magazines such as *Ladies' Home Journal*, *McCall's*, or *Better Homes and Gardens* focused on gendered topics such as entertaining, cooking, gardening, and interior decorating. Under Gordon, *House Beautiful* transcended the industry stereotype to become what many architects such as Harwell Hamilton Harris considered "a serious architectural influence." For Harris's comments on the role of *House Beautiful* in this context, see the series of speeches made on the occasion of Gordon's American Institute of Architects Awards Presentation (AIA National Convention, Orlando, June 1987, AIA Archives). For more on Gordon and *House Beautiful*, see Monica Penick, "The Pace Setter Houses: Livable Modernism in Postwar America" (PhD diss., University of Texas at Austin, 2007).

4. Elizabeth Gordon coauthored the consumer-oriented "how-to" book *More House for Your Money* with Dorothy Ducas in 1937. In this book, Gordon and Ducas offered practical advice for Americans looking to build a "quality" new home for the least amount of money. Its contents included advice on financing, purchasing, planning, and designing the single-family home. See Gordon and Ducas, *More House for Your Money* (New York: William Morrow and Company, 1937). For more on the book's content and on Ducas, see Penick, "The Pace Setter Houses."

5. Elizabeth Gordon, "People Want Sensible Things . . . ," *Architectural Forum* 82 (April 1945): 119–126.

6. For Gordon's and *House Beautiful*'s description of modern, see, for example, "How Modern Got This Way," *House Beautiful* 88 (December 1946): 175, 255–257 and Reisner, "Modern but not *Too* Modern."

7. *Modern Architecture: International Exhibition* opened at the Museum of Modern Art in New York on February 10, 1932, and ran through March 23, 1932. See Terence Riley, *The International Style: Exhibition 15 and The Museum of Modern Art* (New York: Rizzoli, 1992).

8. For a historical account of Hitchcock and Johnson's involvement and the creation of the exhibition, see Riley, *The International Style*.

9. *Modern Architecture* argued for the international applicability of this emerging style and included projects from Belgium, Austria, the Netherlands, Switzerland, Sweden, Finland, Spain, Japan, England, Czechoslovakia, the USSR, Italy, France, Germany, and the United States. The work of J. J. P. Oud, Le Corbusier, Walter Gropius, and Mies van der Rohe received the greatest emphasis. Among the designers practicing in the United States (some of whom were European by birth), Howe and Lescaze, Raymond Hood, Richard Neutra, and Frank Lloyd Wright were represented. For the range of projects displayed at the exhibition, see Riley, *The International Style*.

10. In the postwar years the U.S. government offered financial assistance to perspective home buyers, particularly military veterans. The Federal Housing Authority (FHA) administered loans and mortgages that enabled millions of Americans to purchase their own homes. With federal assistance, however, came policies and guidelines. These were of great concern for designers and builders: the majority of all homes constructed after the war were to be financed—either from the builder side or the buyer side—through the FHA. Regional offices were often opposed to aesthetic experiments, officially described as architectural "nonconformity." This term was often ascribed to modern design, and—as experimentation did not represent a sound investment—overtly modern architecture was often denied funding. For more on FHA policies, see "Modern Design" in United States Federal Housing Administration, *Technical Bulletin No. 2*, March 15, 1936 (Washington, DC: Federal Housing Administration/U.S. Government Printing Office, 1936): 8–9. For more on the FHA assistance and the troubled housing industry, see Gwendolyn Wright's chapter "New Suburban Expansion and the American Dream" in Wright, *Building the Dream: A Social History of Housing in America* (Cambridge, MA: MIT Press, 1981).

11. Between 1939 and 1952, scores of housing research surveys were conducted under the auspices of government agencies, foundations, and consumer magazines. The Building Research Advisory Board, the National Housing Agency, the FHA, the Survey Research Center, the Institute for Social Research at the University of Michigan, the Small Homes Council at the University of Illinois, the National Research Council, the National Academy of Sciences, and the John B. Pierce Foundation were among the most noted contributors. Likewise, the popular press (*Better Homes and Gardens*, *Collier's*, *McCall's*, *House Beautiful*, etc.) launched a significant effort to create and publish "desires" surveys. Professional magazines such as *Architectural Record*, *Architectural Forum*, and *Merchant House Builder* likewise surveyed numerous families between 1936 and 1950. Builders were not to be

left out of the research frenzy: Fritz Burns and Levitt and Sons both reported their own in-house research and development departments, the purpose of which was to collect data that could inform design and development choices. See *A Survey of Housing Research in the United States* (Washington, DC: Housing and Home Finance Agency, 1952).

12. Gordon, "People Want Sensible Things," 120.

13. Ibid., 119.

14. Ibid.

15. Reisner, "Modern but not *Too* Modern."

16. See "House Omnibus," *Architectural Forum* 81 (April 1945), featuring *Better Homes and Gardens* (91–100), *McCall's* (101–108), *Ladies' Home Journal* (109–118), *House Beautiful* (119–126), *Parents* (127–133), *Woman's Home Companion* (134–139), and *Country Gentleman* (141–159). For the "modern inside" commentary, see "House Omnibus," *Woman's Home Companion* section, 135.

17. "House Omnibus," *Better Homes and Gardens* section, 91.

18. Gordon relied heavily on data produced by social science surveys as well as in-house consumer research that was completed in the early 1940s. In particular, she would have likely referred to forty-one surveys that were published in various form between 1948 and 1955, which appear in aggregate in Edward T. Paxton, *What People Want When They Buy a House*. Prepared by Housing and Home Finance Agency, U.S. Department of Commerce (Washington, DC: U.S. Government Printing Office, 1955).

19. In 1948, 42 percent of survey respondents nationwide preferred "modern"—and the majority of these (65 percent) resided in the western portion of the United States. "Modern" included the "ranch house" and "contemporary," while "traditional" encompassed "Cape Cod" and "colonial." See Paxton, *What People Want*, 17.

20. "How Modern Got This Way," 257.

21. Gordon was conscious that in the early 1950s, her audience was predominantly middle-class and female. She clearly understood—partly through her own path to professional success—that these same women had become a powerful and swayable force in the marketplace. For the rise in buying power and influence of postwar women, see Mary Ellen Zuckerman, *A History of Popular Women's Magazines in the United States, 1792–1995* (Westport, CT: Greenwood Press, 1998), and Ruth Schwartz Cowan, *More Work for Mother: The Ironies of Household Technology from the Open Hearth to the Microwave* (New York: Basic Books, 1983).

22. Elizabeth Gordon, "How Did I Get to Be Me?" Unpublished autobiography in MS 241.A.3.135, Besinger Collection, Dept. of Special Collections, University of Kansas.

23. Ibid.

24. Gordon's "good design" campaign in many ways offered a companion to MoMA's own "good design" concepts, disseminated through the museum's *Good Design* exhibitions launched in 1950 in partnership with the Merchandise Mart in Chicago and under the direction of MoMA's Edgar Kaufmann Jr. While Gordon's views (particularly with regard to Scandinavian design) on the quality of everyday "useful" objects aligned with many views expressed by MoMA, she would eventually rail against the institution's program and style of tastemaking. For the announcement of *Good Design*, see the Museum of Modern Art, "First Showing of Good Design Exhibition in New York," December 1, 1950 (501116-70). Museum of Modern Art Press Release Archives.

25. Gordon, "The New American Style Grew from America's Way of Life," 123.

26. For the announcement of the arrival of the American Style, see ibid. For Gordon's list of principles, see "How to Recognize the American Style," *House Beautiful* 92 (May 1950): 158.

27. Gordon, "The New American Style Grew from America's Way of Life," 123.

28. Ibid.

29. James Marston Fitch, "The New American Architecture Started 70 Years Ago," *House Beautiful* 92 (May 1950): 135.

30. Jean Murray Bangs, "Prophet without Honor," *House Beautiful* 92 (May 1950): 138.

31. Ibid.

32. For Gordon's characterizations of the American Style (and direct comparisons to the International Style or European modernism), see especially "How to Recognize the American Style" and, later, the embedded criticisms within "The Next America," *House Beautiful* 95 (April 1953): 111 and Elizabeth Gordon, "The Threat to the Next America," *House Beautiful* 95 (April 1953): 126–131, 250–251.

33. "The Station Wagon Way of Life," *House Beautiful* 92 (June 1950): 103.

34. Mary Roche, "The American Ideal of Leveling Up," *House Beautiful* 92 (May 1950): 128.

35. "How to Recognize the American Style," 158.

36. Ibid.

37. Ibid.

38. For example, in the lengthy discussion on Greene and Greene in Jean Murray Bangs, "Prophet without Honor." Bangs was not only a staff member at the magazine but also the wife of architect Harwell Hamilton Harris, whose Texas State Fair house was selected as *House Beautiful*'s Pace Setter 1955.

39. "How to Recognize the American Style," 158.

40. For housing starts between 1889 and 1964, see U.S. Department of Commerce, Bureau of the Census, *Housing Construction Statistics 1889 to 1964*, Table A-5, "United States—Number of New Housing Units Started and Constructions Cost: Annually, 1889–1964," 24–25.

41. Such accusations of Communist activity appeared in Senator Joseph McCarthy's "Wheeling Speech," delivered in Wheeling, West Virginia, on February 9, 1950. Paul Boyer's short account of the Cold War's impact on American culture, "Fear, Security and the Apocalyptic World View: The Cold War's Cultural Impact and Legacy," in *Contemporary Issues* Series No. 11 (Carlisle, PA: Clarke Center at Dickinson College, 2001), is useful in this analysis. For the relevance of atomic warfare to developments in American culture, see Boyer's *By the Bomb's Early Light* (New York: Pantheon, 1985).

42. Gordon, "The Threat to the Next America," 126.

43. Ibid., 129.

44. Ibid., 126.

45. Ibid., 251.

46. Ibid., 127.

47. "Public Opinion on 'The Threat to the Next America,'" *House Beautiful* 95 (June 1953): 29.

48. Ibid.

49. For the accusation of irrationality, see W. C. English Jr.'s letter, ibid. Henry Hill of San Francisco specifically accused Gordon of attacking Mies in an effort to boost consumption of possessions.

50. For cancellations of subscriptions, see ibid., 92. For this line, see Edward Farrell's letter in "More Readers' Mail on: The Threat to the Next America," *House Beautiful* 95 (July 1953): 6. Other respondents who questioned her judgment included Cecil D. Elliot (assistant professor of Architecture, North Carolina State College), Donald H. Honn (architect, Tulsa), and James Klutz (lumberman, Concord, NC).

51. "More Readers' Mail on: The Threat to the Next America," 92.

52. For the complete list of signers, see Penick, "The Pace Setter Houses," and complete

letter in Curtis Besinger, MS 132, Wright Collection, Box 3, Dept. of Special Collections, University of Kansas.

53. The objections and signatures were printed in full, and, according to Curtis Besinger, a copy of the letter was sent to all the "leading architectural magazines and schools." Besinger to Gordon, MS 132, Wright Collection.

54. Personal correspondence about Gordon has described her as an "Eisenhower Democrat," associated with such figures as social critic Arthur Schlesinger Jr. Elizabeth Gordon's 65th Birthday Binder, author's collection.

55. Frank Lloyd Wright to Gordon, telegram, Phoenix, [March] 24, 1953. Frank Lloyd Wright Archives, John deKoven Hill Papers. The telegram and subsequent letters are dated March 1953, though the "Threat" article did not run until April. This suggests either that Gordon sent Wright an advance copy, that Wright had access to an early-release subscription copy, or that the date is simply wrong. The advance copy would not be surprising, as Gordon and Wright had corresponded several times in 1949 and 1950 and again in January 1953 for a discussion of "the choice between organic architecture and the International Style."

56. With the exception of the 1946 article, prior to 1953 Gordon had rarely published Wright's work; this was possibly due in part to an agreement between Wright and *Architectural Forum*, which Wright apparently revoked after 1953. This lack of coverage was also due in part to a disagreement between Gordon and Wright over *House Beautiful*'s published features on naturalism and the term "organic" (and Wright's role in the development of both) that occurred in 1949 and 1950. For more on this, see note 58 below and Penick, "The Pace Setter Houses."

57. Gordon, "The Threat to the Next America," 126.

58. Gordon to Wright, December 5, 1950, Hill Papers. Wright wrote to Gordon to express his displeasure with her series of articles on naturalism, which he felt "falsified the nature of organic architecture." Gordon was deeply affected by this, and likely took his criticism into account as she moved forward with her editorials of 1953.

59. Diane Maddex, *Frank Lloyd Wright's House Beautiful* (New York: Hearst Books, 2000), 38–39.

60. Fitch recounted, "I resigned from the editorial board of *House Beautiful* in the spring of 1953. The decisive issue was, of all things, whether the Gropius/Miesian/Bauhaus version of modern architecture was "communistic," hence somehow un-American, while that of the San Francisco Bay region which the magazine editorially supported was safely "American . . ." For complete comments, see "James Marston Fitch," in *Brief Biography of James Marston Fitch*, James Marston Fitch Charitable Foundation.

61. In addition to designing and directing the exhibit at the Los Angeles County Fair in 1954, Hill designed many interiors that were featured in *House Beautiful* (and assisted other architects, including Harwell Hamilton Harris). He was named Pace Setter architect in 1960. For more on Hill, see Penick, "The Pace Setter Houses."

62. Gordon to Besinger, November 26, 1986, MS 241.A.3.133, Correspondence: Elizabeth Gordon, Besinger Collection.

63. Esther McCoy, "Sim Bruce Richards," in *Nature in Architecture*, San Diego Natural History Museum, April–June 1984.

64. For more on Parker, see Penick, "The Pace Setter Houses." See also Randolph C. Henning, *The Architecture of Alfred Browning Parker: Miami's Maverick Modernist* (Gainesville: University Press of Florida, 2011).

65. Gordon, "How Did I Get to Be Me?," 6.

66. Reisner, "Modern but Not *Too* Modern."

67. Obituary, Elizabeth Gordon, *The Economist* 30 (September 2000): 101. Clippings, Hill Papers.

68. Besinger to Robert Venturi, June 5, 1986. MS 241.A.3.137–39, Correspondence: Elizabeth Gordon, Besinger Collection.

69. Diana J. Sims, "Beyond House Beautiful," *Hagerstown*, September 3, 1987. From MS 241.A.3.133, Correspondence: Elizabeth Gordon, Besinger Collection.

70. John deKoven Hill suggested that Gordon was forced out by the Hearst administration. For this assessment, see John deKoven Hill and Maggie Valentine, *John deKoven Hill* (Los Angeles: Oral History Program, University of California).

71. Curtis Besinger, letter to The Design Committee, A.I.A., n.d., but ca. June 1986. Correspondence: Elizabeth Gordon, Besinger Collection.

10 HOUSE AND HAUNTED GARDEN

SANDY ISENSTADT

In the opening scene of *The Birds*, Alfred Hitchcock's 1963 thriller, Melanie Daniels, played by Tippi Hedren, meets Mitch Brenner, played by Rod Taylor, in a pet shop in San Francisco, where they admire a pair of lovebirds in a cage. In light of what follows—birds ravaging a small town up the California coast—the lovebirds clearly stand in for the ideal relationship between mankind and nature, at least as mankind imagines it: nature in repose, a repository of virtue and easy visual pleasure. The metal cage, a trifle for human industry, is the instrument that makes this relationship possible. But it also relies upon the benevolent, and even adorable, character of nature.

However, soon after Hedren and Taylor leave behind the big city for a bucolic setting, nature rebels. The typically innocuous temperament of ordinary birds deforms into avian rage. Possessed by a malevolent spirit, the birds bring nature back to a nineteenth-century, Darwinian-era vision: nature, red in tooth—beak, in this case—and claw. In the film's most dramatic scene, Hedren finds herself in a phone booth, unable to escape, helplessly buffeted by roiling skies of angry birds. She is caged within a glass box, an archetype if ever there was one of the modern house: a thin metal frame, a distance-dissipating technology (a telephone) at its heart, and entirely open to nature through its walls of glass. Horrified, Hedren can do nothing but watch as birds fling themselves against the glass, smashing it, and as they peck at the life of a man, who also crashes against the booth (figure 10.1). She watches, in short, as the murderous birds turn the terms of mankind's relationship with nature inside out, literally, as the townsfolk rush to lock themselves indoors. There are no words in this scene, no human language; rather, the sound of screeching birds fills Hedren's exposed refuge, which now looks less like the confident proof of human dominion over nature than it does the flimsy and brittle construction it truly is. Walls of glass are suddenly a weakness; they function as intended only when the outside world of nature is at rest.

With Hedren wordless and able only to look, the booth is clearly as much a

FIGURE 10.1. The "crack in the picture window" in *The Birds* is due not to the unfulfilled promises of suburban life but to a presumably benevolent nature turned suddenly homicidal. Alfred Hitchcock (director), film still from *The Birds*, Universal Pictures, 1963. The view is that of Melanie Daniels, played by Tippi Hedren.

metaphor for the camera as it is for the modern house, an analogy that in fact became common in the postwar era. In a 1952 magazine spread on the modern designs of Marcel Breuer, for instance, his houses were said to look like cameras, "rectangular boxes perched on a small stone base as if on a tripod, one large glass wall focused straight at the view." More significantly, such views through glass also established the proportions of modern architecture's relationship with nature: "Breuer's attitude toward nature is that of an observer, of the man behind the camera: he likes to look at it." As such, the houses were "observation posts" from which to admire the natural world.[1] The unspoken presumption, of course, is that nature had agreed to go along with this arrangement. Hedren, too, is looking out from her glass-walled box, but her attitude is not the bemusement of detached observation. As *The Birds* suggests, the unexamined premise of picturesque plenitude gathered through glass can be overturned in a moment.

The postwar period was rife with anxieties: the birth of the nuclear industry, a Cold War portending sudden annihilation, intercontinental missiles and accurate remote guidance devices, the Eisenhower-era emergence of a military-industrial defense economy, and technological skepticism, along with rapid urbanization and demographic change. But one anxiety in particular seems to have attached itself to the modern house: an otherwise bucolic setting infiltrated by a natural world that seems bent on revenge. *The Birds* offers just one example. Where it was once more common to depict a house that was haunted, a range of stories and films appears in the postwar decades to describe a haunted setting for the house.

To understand this development, it is necessary to look back to nineteenth-century discussions that articulated an ideal relationship between a freestanding house and its setting that fused the two into the domestic amalgam of "character." Although modernism recast this relationship, it nevertheless absorbed the terms that comprised it. In the passage from the nineteenth to the twentieth century, character, understood as the expression of otherwise unseen virtues of a house as well as its occupants, shifted in terms of how and where it was localized. At first, character was observed as part of the physical fabric of the house and represented the inner nature of the inhabitants to a larger community. A surrounding landscape, even in its diminutive version of suburban yard, simultaneously framed the house and gave voice to the home's moral tenor.

Modernism, however, rejected such sentimental notions and dismissed ideas of character outright. By emphasizing modern materials and methods of construction, modernism aimed to erase the patina of idiosyncratic occupation that settled upon a house over time. Polished and scrubbed, modernism's representative surfaces gave no traction for character to accumulate, as if it were precipitated from the moral atmosphere generated by the occupants. Nevertheless, relations with the outdoors remained important for modern architects as walls were opened wider and wider with glass. Indeed, many architects suggested that the home's architectural merit might be measured foremost by its relations with the surrounding landscape. At a time when houses might be mass produced, the landscape might even prove to be the source of distinction. Character, in other words, might be found outdoors rather than within the home's physical fabric. The surrounding landscape was taken less as a public expression of personal virtue, however, than as a form of private visual pleasure. In turn, the locus for judging the house shifted from a viewer looking from the street toward the house to a point inside the house looking out onto a private view.[2] In short, the house had long contained within it a shadow. The modern house and its ideal of transparency had seemingly banished shadows, but as it turns out, they had only moved outdoors, into the landscape.

CHARACTER DETERMINED

The creation of character was a mainstay of nineteenth-century American domestic architecture. Never truly defined, which was likely a factor in its power, character was summarized best by Horatio Greenough as the visible record of function. Writing at the same time, Andrew Jackson Downing thought that domestic character in particular was registered most clearly by chimneys and windows. These were, he wrote in 1842, "the two most essential and characteristic features of dwelling-houses."[3] The chimney intimated a warming hearth within, with the dual function of radiating heat outward and drawing toward it the family, while generous windows not only brought light and air indoors but also expressed a secure relationship with the surrounding environment. Somatic and visual needs were thereby served and made visible. Taken together, these elements portrayed domestic character; that is, they externalized contemporary notions of dwelling, with the family as both the central social unit and the crucible for individual development.

More generally, character was an artifact of Picturesque subjective aesthetics, appearing in sustained fashion in the house design literature that emerged first in eighteenth-century England. It drew attention to the effects that forms had upon a spectator, rather than toward the principles that might generate form. Since dwellings were the building type most closely linked to the rounds of daily life, they could as a consequence indicate the dwellers' character as well. An asymmetrical plan, for example, could signal a commonsense concession to convenience and, in turn, an unaffected sensibility belonging to those who lived there. The aim, as James Malton put it in a 1798 essay, was "to perpetuate on Principle that Peculiar mode of building which was originally the effect of chance." Circumstance, rather than transcendent principle, would govern the making of architecture.[4] But as Joshua Reynolds noted at the same time, such an emphasis tended to make architecture more like scenery, akin to the picturesque landscape itself. This was especially the case when effects of chance were conventionalized and used as signs rather than as authentic expressions of character. Although character was coeval with organic notions of form following function, it usually involved such "associated elements," as Colin Rowe called them; that is, character was stated in architectural motifs that conjured an "implied impression of artistic individuality and the expression, either symbolic or functional, of the purpose for which the building was constructed."[5] Rowe, writing in the early 1950s, was attempting to fill out the history of ideas that the modern architects he championed had thought they had discarded.

Regardless, as the architectural notion of domestic character developed in the nineteenth century, dwellings were more and more frequently said not simply to shelter a family but also to represent it. In the United States, modest houses, and almost always rural ones like log cabins, could stand in for avowedly American traits of humility, honest labor, and an incorruptible nature. As a result, these houses could become political icons. In contrast, urban types were anathema. Thomas Gunn's 1857 *Physiology of the New York Boarding Houses*, for instance, links an assortment of bad foreign characters to boardinghouses, concluding that a good home is a check against a mean disposition.[6] At the same moment, Emerson linked the connection between family and house to an idea of national character. Following the widely quoted phrase from his essay on character—". . . it is the privilege of truth to make itself believed. Character is this moral order seen through the medium of an individual nature"—the house might resonate with and represent human variation sufficiently to build up, unit by unit, a stable and just society.[7]

In a presumed homology, attaining the status of subjecthood was premised upon possession of real property in Enlightenment philosophy; real property was the entity that related, or rather, that performed the relation between self and society.[8] Indeed, prior to standards for assessing creditworthiness, and with few institutions engaged solely in lending money, good character was the crucial factor needed to earn credit in order to purchase a home or, for that matter, start a business. To this end, character could be assessed by canvassing the opinions of merchants and neighbors. Overt displays of wealth, for instance, might diminish a borrower's ability to repay a loan, as well as indicate a streak of vanity. Marriage signaled an acceptance of responsibility, as well as assuring the free labor of a wife and, usually, children, all of whom might be counted among a man's assets. Personal character, in short, was a financial asset, although thriftiness was usually understood more as a willing deferral of gratification rather than an embrace of abstinence. Property, both personal and real, underpinned all forms of character, as house design discussions often appeared alongside not only advice on financing a house but also attitudes toward money more generally. Private property advertised personal economy and thus externalized moral character. As the Reverend Edward Everett Hale wrote in 1874, land and personal character were the two legs of social standing: "real estate . . . the only estate, except character, which is *real*."[9]

The connection between character and credit also makes evident that character was assumed to be not simply a distinguishing trait but also an enduring one. Implications of stability aligned neatly with architectural principles regarding durability, evident with such prominent writers as John Ruskin. In this context, the idea of repose was advocated to describe an ideal for both house and family; it stood unmoving and opposed to the perceived acceleration of everyday life sparked by a technologically advanced civilization.[10] With middle-class single-family houses unable to rely upon the usual coordinates of aesthetic merit such as noble materials or rich ornamentation, character and its implications of integrity helped to legitimize the type and thus to warrant professional attention. Character was understood as the visible portion of a representational circuit; that is, it posited a quality whose existence underpinned the validity of its appearance. In this way, a modest house could intimate the otherwise unseen presence of humility, say, rather than simply being an index of a family's limited means. Put another way, the symbolic projection of humility, for instance, presumed a basis upon which such projection rested. "It needs the combined personality of the family to make the character of the house," as interior designer and tastemaker Candace Wheeler wrote in 1903.[11] Character, then, was not an accessory; it was an essential trait of private houses.

CHARACTER UNDONE

With moral, financial, and aesthetic factors bearing on the architectural character of the single-family house, home ownership became both a vehicle for and an emblem of self-determination, which is why the most revealing insights into character appear in that literature where selfhood comes undone, namely,

FIGURE 10.2. With a shared character and a soul common to all—evident in the image of brother, sister, and hearth—family and house decay simultaneously. "The Fall of the House of Usher" by Albert Edward Sterner for Edgar Allan Poe, *The Works of Edgar Allan Poe, Vol. 1, Tales of the Grotesque and Arabesque*, eds. Edmund Clarence Stedman and George Edward Woodberry (Chicago: Stone and Kimball, 1894), facing p. 131.

psychologically charged tales of the haunted house. Emerging in tandem in the eighteenth century, the literatures of single-family house design and haunted houses presume reciprocity between house and self. House design manuals tell how to put houses together; haunted house stories describe how they fall apart. Right from the start, in Horace Walpole's 1764 *Castle of Otranto*, the formula is in place: a twisted house not only establishes an atmosphere but also defines the "characters" in the story. For example, as circulation through the Castle is inscrutable, so is the troubled past of Manfred, Prince of Otranto.[12] An especially condensed emblem of a foul spiritual realm that bears upon otherwise unself-conscious domestic life is the "Dweller of the Threshold," a ghostly presence devised by Lord Edward Bulwer-Lytton in *Zanoni*, from 1842. The dweller is a spirit "surpassing in malignity" that is discovered only when a prohibition against entering an inner chamber is violated.[13] And the innermost or at least final chamber, as suggested by numerous hauntings, such as those suffered by the quasi-supernatural Heathcliff in Emily Brontë's *Wuthering Heights* (1847), is the grave itself.

In the American setting, Edgar Allan Poe is the best example of this sort of literature, as the entwining of house and occupant is a recurrent—no, obsessive—theme with him (figure 10.2). H. P. Lovecraft observed that in Poe's 1839 "Fall of the House of Usher," Roderick, Madeline, and their house were as one: "a brother, his twin sister, and their incredibly ancient house all sharing a single soul and meeting one common dissolution at the same moment."[14] The narrator begins his story with an inventory of house elements, as if finding in each decaying lintel some support for his own despair. His amorphous and dark state of mind is discerned and thereby manifested in the distinct features of the house. Horror in Poe is usually unnoticed, just underfoot, a pulse of life dimming—desperate but unheard—behind the very wall the protagonist casually leans upon. Horror is built into the structure of everyday life, with the reader learning that what passes for reality is but a fine membrane between unthinking routine and absolute terror. Undoing the structure of the house or tearing down a wall, an action frequent with Poe, will reveal the otherwise unseen horror. It is precisely this reversal of construction that Poe thematizes in his invention of the very genre of detective stories. To "de-tect" means, literally, to remove the roof, to dismantle a tectonic assembly. To take apart a house is to uncover the undying character of the person who lives, or, as in much of Poe, recently expired there. Secrets are brought to light in such stories; hidden guilt is uncovered.[15] In contrast, in Poe's lesser-known landscape essays "The Landscape-Garden" (1842), "The Domain of Arnheim" (1847), and "Landor's Cottage" (1849), the figure of the garden appears as a site for restitution and exaltation.

As Walter Benjamin put it, Poe was the "first physiognomist of the interior," referring to the newly formed private sphere of the bourgeoisie that was an expression of and stage for a new sense of interiority and personal depth.[16] In the process of disassembly, what was once as familiar as the face of a loved one becomes something strange, or uncanny, as Freud described just this sensation. The sense of unease, Freud thought, arose from two related feelings: first, an uncertainty regarding whether an object long presumed to be inanimate might truly harbor a melancholy or malign spirit, and second, the doppelgänger, a spiritual double that is free to cause havoc in one's own name. The haunted house is both these things: a pile of materials that comes to life in a form commensurate with the self and at times acts in the name of the self. Just as the literature regarding sound economic practices and potential for personal bankruptcy made clear what might happen if economic discipline were lost, so did the haunted house stories make clear the consequences of a loss of self-control. It is no coincidence that in many such stories, family wealth has been squandered and all that remains is a house that has also been hollowed. Just as a family with a house congruent to its virtues was a modal type for self-control, so was the combination of decayed house and corrupt individual an exact inverse, an image of the dissolution of self.

Henry James's "The Jolly Corner," published in 1908, several years after his first prolonged return to the United States after almost thirty years living abroad, exemplifies these themes. The protagonist, Spencer Brydon, returns from Europe after thirty-three years to have a final look at his boyhood home, the eponymous "jolly corner," which he has agreed to have demolished to make way for an apartment building. Walking about the house at night, Brydon senses a presence, an "unexpected occupant," discerned in "the blank face of the door" and other bits of the house. He then meets "his other self," the self that might have been had he not moved away—"a compartment of his mind never yet penetrated"—who gradually emerges from the gloom of the doomed house. James was particularly sensitive to contemporary changes in house style and planning, and so specifies that it is a Victorian warren of discrete rooms rather than the flowing space of open plans that kindled Brydon's impressions:

The house, as the case stood, admirably lent itself; he might wonder at the taste, the native architecture of the particular time, which could rejoice so in the multiplication of doors—the opposite extreme to the modern, the actual almost complete proscription of them; but it had fairly contributed to provoke this obsession of the presence encountered telescopically, as he might say, focused and studied in diminishing perspective . . .[17]

Although he disapproved of recent developments in architecture such as the open plan, implying that character and memory find no footing there, James nonetheless has Brydon imagine the unlived life he encounters in his doppelgänger to be that of a modern and avaricious architect: "If he had but stayed at home he would have anticipated the inventor of the sky-scraper. If he had but stayed at home he would have discovered his genius in time really to start some new variety of awful architectural hare and run it till it burrowed in a gold mine." When, finally, Brydon meets his doppelgänger face to face, he disintegrates: "Then harder pressed still, sick with the force of his shock, and falling back as under the hot breath and the roused passion of a life larger than his own, a rage of personality before which his own collapsed." Even as volition is kidnapped, this "rage of personality" is anticipated, even prepared for, in thoroughly architectural terms; the most prominent metaphors of psychic affect belong to the house. Brydon seeks evidence of the ghost in doors inexplicably ajar; he opens a window to jump through in case he does come upon the ghost; and he realizes that throughout the city "hard-faced houses" and "[g]reat building voids" under cover of night don "a sort of sinister mask" and so form a "large collective negation." At night an invisible city appears composed of the unlived lives of all its citizens, with individual homes an index from which potential agency issues. In "The Jolly Corner," selfhood is projected onto that object most like itself, which becomes in turn a canvas for misgivings and misbegotten traces of the soul.[18]

CHARACTER REJECTED

Modernism precluded the notion of character. As a set of conventionalized forms, character often relied on historical motifs rather than, say, structural principles, which was how it might be asserted when it was not truly present, a possibility anathema to nascent notions of architectural honesty. A broad and sheltering roof, for example, might conjure a competent and generous character, but it could just as easily mask an uncomfortable and inefficient plan. In contrast, many modernists argued that authentic architectural character was epiphenomenal to the accommodation of function or the articulation of structure; it could not be evoked simply by pasteboard motifs that had come to be generally associated with such matters. Commonplace analogies between faces and house facades, with window mullions likened to lines of age and, thus, a kind of wisdom, became more and more suspect.[19] Whereas "facade" formerly referred to a complex interface between private and public realms worthy of detailed design attention, the term began to be one of scorn. Charges of "facadism" suggested a perverse subordination of individual needs to social appearances. Having a facade meant to surrender personal integrity, that is, the integration of one's various bits, to the scrutiny of others. A facade was what "other-directed personalities," in David Riesman's famous formulation, put on to appear in public.[20] "Facade" was the front that belonged to others and was believed to diminish the self that, as a result, belonged to no one. In a postwar book on house design, Robert Woods Kennedy cited Otto Fenichal, a Freudian psychoanalyst, to explain that modern clients were objective and secure and cared little for the composition of a facade, suggesting in turn that traditionalists needed to shore up their fragile egos with a face everyone would agree on. Modern clients had no need to articulate social status with a symbolic language of form that reflected "archaic pictorial thinking." Rather, they were concerned with using technical means to demonstrably improve the quality of their everyday life.[21] Modernism, in other words, simply had no use for character.

In fact, even before modernists dismissed it, character had already been in retreat from consumer culture. Critics complained that clients, mesmerized by a market mentality, were in danger of snuffing out character on their own. For example, as glass became cheaper in cost and better in quality, clients wanted more of it. As a result, houses came to have more and larger windows. But too many windows evacuated character, one early twentieth-century English traveler said, and resulted in a featureless "glazed void."[22] Several years later, in 1914, Ruby Goodnow explained: "Large windows shattered the sense of enclosure necessary for the creation of domestic character . . . People demand windows everywhere! Each room must have two and often three." She felt the need to explain to clients besotted by cheaper building products that "in architecture the important thing is to express the *character* of a building. . . . Somehow we associate our ideas of home with a certain snugness, a certain security. It is this quality which makes the difference in character between a public building and a home. . . . This feeling vanishes for most of us, if we try to imagine such a scene in a house which is all windows" (figure 10.3). Windows, Goodnow saw, focused the inhabitants' attention not on the unique figure of the home but rather on the mundane ground outside.[23]

CHARACTER IN THE LANDSCAPE

But having so permeated the American popular consciousness—and unconsciousness—it would be surprising for character to have disappeared altogether, as modernists would have it. Indeed, Rowe himself makes clear the argument that the notion of character is itself fundamentally modern. Rather, as Warren Susman and scholars inspired by him have suggested, character migrated in the early twentieth century into ideas of personality, a collection of meanings that

What the house below might have looked like if its designer had known more about architecture.

Modern American Domestic architecture,—alas!

FIGURE 10.3. Muntins resolve the architectural scale more finely than massing or the balance of solid and void. By doing so they suggest intimate practices of inhabitation and, thus, character attributes shared by the house and its occupants. Similarly, the delicate dormers and entry of traditional design contrast with the coarse, square, and staccato patterns of the modern design, suggesting a feminine and less assertive design sensibility, which was deemed more appropriate for and reflective of the domestic realm. Ruby Ross Goodnow, *The Honest House* (New York: Century, 1914), 109.

has thrived since then.²⁴ But character blossomed elsewhere as well. The architectural character of a home, formerly understood as a property of the physical fabric of the house, was, especially with modernism, projected onto the landscape surrounding the house. In other words, the character of a modern dwelling would by the mid-twentieth century come to be measured in terms of an intimacy with nature. Character, then, did not disappear so much as it was displaced to the outdoors. Correspondingly, the sense of the home as a refuge and place of safety was transposed onto that nature.

To be sure, landscape had been adjunct to private homes well before the twentieth century. Uvedale Price, for instance, related houses to the surrounding scenery, arguing that they could borrow landscape effects by, for instance, taking on the colors of local materials or by becoming generally shaggier. Later, commenting on the same matter, Downing wrote, "The scenery, amid which it [the villa] is to stand, if it is of a strongly marked character, will often help to suggest or modify the character of the architecture."²⁵ And, no doubt, nature has been a mainstay more generally of American notions of national character.²⁶

In the twentieth century, however, having the house take on visual effects of landscape was felt to be regressive, but relations with landscape nonetheless came to be preserved in a particular form: views through large windows, precisely the ones feared by Ruby Goodnow. Indeed, no less a figure than Henry-Russell Hitchcock, at the conclusion of his 1929 book, *Modern Architecture: Romanticism and Reintegration*, one of the first histories of modernism, suggested as much. Hitchcock argued throughout the book that architecture had disintegrated under the influence of the Picturesque, which located aesthetic comprehension within individual observers and, as a result, precipitated the separation of architectural design from engineering. The effect on architecture was corrosive as buildings were considered merely an accent to a larger landscape. In contrast, the "New Pioneers" of his own time were on the verge of reintegrating these long-separated modes so that the continuing concern for modern architecture would soon prove to be the aestheticization of structure.²⁷

Yet, with a very pregnant "Yet" that begins the book's final statement, Hitchcock raised the surprising point that there is something among the splendidly rational New Pioneers that recalled the peak of Romanticism: "cutting the cards another way," he mused, the Romantic disintegration and the modernist reintegration of architecture may have much in common. Specifically, "All the New Pioneers . . . are very careful to relate their architecture as fully as possible to the natural surroundings, although without in any sense merging it therewith." Modern architecture, in other words, was not so much *like* nature, as with Picturesque design. Rather, it was *next* to nature. Despite its insistence on technologically inspired form, modern architecture had a character that a citizen of the eighteenth century might embrace: "Uvedale Price, the great authority on the picturesque," continued Hitchcock, "would have approved both terraces and ribbon windows. In a sense indeed he recommended them more than a century ago when he suggested that houses might be 'picturesquely' designed solely with the idea of making the most of the circumambient view." Subsequently, the contrast of nature and dwelling became an imperative for modern architecture.[28]

Popular venues similarly registered the adjacency of house and landscape as a crucial factor in modern house design. For the general public, the benefit of the modernist dematerialization of enclosure was greater visual presence of the outdoors rather than, say, dramatic structural expression. Correspondingly, architectural merit no longer inhered in a secure and mostly opaque enclosure or in the enchanted attraction of the hearth. With modernism, merit could be measured by generous visual relations with landscape. To open up the home to the larger world implied that in some sense the world itself had become domesticated and thus swiftly summoned the mythic figure of the pioneer, the hearty man who mastered nature that he might love it and make it docile for the generations to follow (figure 10.4). Unsurprisingly, then, any number of midcentury sociological and literary works strove to explain national character in terms of frontier history, with the postwar suburb frequently appearing with a cast of pioneers, settlers, and single-family homes. As a representative piece in the *New York Times* put it, "The ranch-style house in our ever-expanding suburbs and exurbs is not too different from the log cabin of the man in the doeskin breeches. Nor are those who inhabit them." Husband and wife and even the kids were likened to "the hardy pioneers."[29] As David Lowenthal put it some years later, "Our forefathers mastered a continent; today we celebrate the virtues of the vanquished foe: To love nature is regarded as uniquely American."[30] A home open to the outdoors could therefore appear to continue and to culminate a national narrative of spatial conquest. Domestic character, as a corollary, was no longer to be represented in the body of the house from the viewpoint of someone on the street so much as it was registered in a view outward, from the point of view of someone inside looking out.

By the mid-twentieth century, a private landscape view, seen through glass from inside the house, expressed the modern form of domestic character. It visibly registered a physical distance from work upon which the growing suburbs were premised, providing therapeutic relief from urban anxieties; it was a visual metaphor for freedom and lack of restraint and so rehearsed another motif of suburbanization, recalling even a leading narrative of nationhood; and its various benefits could be bought and sold. Moreover, because it did not directly depend on the amount of land owned, or, with easier credit, on the client's ability to pay, a landscape view was not restricted to the wealthy. Domestic satisfaction therefore might be measured by degrees of openness to a landscape. Wall could dissolve to window because the landscape itself had been domesticated, that is, drawn into the *domus*, the circle of human inhabitation. At the same time, a private landscape view from the living room was a visual correlate of the urban-scale social atomism that underpinned postwar suburbanization. Unpopulated views are only possible in suburbs when neighbors agree to look at their yards, rather

FIGURE 10.4. Walls of glass emphasize the outdoors and are nearly always imagined as providing a view of domesticated nature, visually replicating a narrative of national character. Libbey-Owens-Ford advertisement, *Town and Country*, January 1933. Courtesy of Canaday Center for Rare Books and Special Collections/University of Toledo.

than at each other. What was looked over was property, which is defined in legal terms by the right to exclude others. Replaying the flight from the city, the landscape picture idealized in picture windows was a literalization of social distance.

Regarding the economic side of matters, while an assessment of personal character was no longer necessary to borrow money to buy a house, landscape had in fact become an important and explicit factor in the cost of a home. Only in the postwar era did real-estate appraisers begin to routinely note that landscape views were not only pretty but had market value as well. In particular, views alone, appraisers suggested, might be sufficient to generate individuality just as houses were becoming more and more standardized—characterless—in large developments such as Lakeview, California, or the various Levitt suburbs. Even more, when adequate landscape was lacking, real-estate appraisers began advising clients to invent their view. As one real-estate appraiser wrote in 1951, "Artificial view is becoming more and more a necessity in those areas where duplicate houses, similar in shape, size, color, and construction limit the possibilities of natural pictures."[31] Architectural distinctiveness, or, to use a familiar word, "character," might be gauged more by the scope and quality of view than by any aspect of the home's formal traits.

THE HAUNTED LANDSCAPE

Corresponding to the migration of domestic character from the house to the landscape, the horror of postwar haunted house literature began to move outdoors, too, with a volitional and oftentimes malevolent landscape displacing a domesticated and acquiescent one. This often took the form of other people appearing in what had been a private view, a trope that signals a collapse of social distance comparable with the appearance of inner demons that were prelude to psychic collapse in nineteenth-century haunted house stories. Fears that the home might harbor wickedness certainly continued, but new anxieties appeared regarding the overbearing presence of others. One of the first postwar writers to take on such issues was Shirley Jackson. Her first published story, "The Lottery," from 1948 and now much anthologized, followed a neighborly gathering as it turned into a public execution. The rustic, small-town setting became an impassable contradiction to the unwanted intimacy of a dispassionate death. The neighbors, like-minded to the point of murder, were all too easily likened to the conformity of the postwar suburb. Jackson's short novel, *The Sundial*, appeared ten years later. Halloran House, where the story takes place, was witness to murder and ghosts, prophetic visions, a foreboding atmosphere, unexplained events, and the threat of annihilation. Throughout it all, a sundial, always visible outside yet oddly off-center in the manicured gardens, stands as a symbol of the Halloran family's isolation and its ultimately unverifiable but suggestively supernatural fate. Jackson herself made the link to nineteenth-century haunted house literature explicit with a reference to the Castle of Otranto.[32]

Jackson's full-length novel of horror was *The Haunting of Hill House*, from 1959. The protagonist is Eleanor Vance, a meek woman uncomfortable at best with her own family, and now at an isolated country house with a small team of investigators trying to lay bare the house's reputation for weird incidents. Various things happen, from sudden shifts in temperature to disembodied voices, ghosts,

FIGURE 10.5. A brooding tree absorbs a ghostly human figure and, seconds later, the car and the life of its driver. This view through her windshield is the last thing seen by Eleanor Vance, played by Julie Harris. Robert Wise (director), film still from *The Haunting*, Argyle Enterprises and Metro-Goldwyn-Mayer, 1963.

inexplicable bloodstains, and so on. Most of the action takes place within the house, which is animated by an ill will and seems to desire Eleanor. Whether she in turn becomes enamored of the house or else simply goes mad is left for the reader to decide. She meets her demise, however, in the yard, as her car hits a tree that had been brooding there throughout the story (figure 10.5). Although landscape is not thematized as the source of malevolence—just sudden death—what is most suggestive about Shirley Jackson's writing career is her lesser-known work in family-oriented fiction for shelter magazines such as *Good Housekeeping*, *Woman's Day*, and *McCall's*. For these journals, Jackson wrote about happy houses, togetherness, and lovable mishaps, precisely the everyday surface of life through which her horror fiction slashes.[33]

Landscape is imaginatively refigured in Richard Matheson's 1956 novel, *The Shrinking Man*, the story of Scott Carey who, through an unlikely combination of insecticide and radiation, begins to shrink. He is attacked outside his own door by a bird, a common sparrow, and chased into the cellar of his home, where he becomes imprisoned while his wife and daughter presume him dead. As he continues to shrink, the cellar becomes a vast terrain, with caverns and cliff faces, a thunderous furnace, and a monstrous spider that dwells at the far end of a desert and that torments Carey and inhabits his fears. With each incremental diminishment of his stature, Carey adjusts to a new landscape, making his own clothes, questing for food and water, and turning household castoffs into primitive tools for his continued survival. At full size, a physical correlate of power, Carey could dominate his home that so seamlessly served his needs as to slip beneath conscious observation; as he shrinks, the home itself becomes

FIGURE 10.6. The lawn that once cradled Scott Carey's suburban home is reimagined as a treacherous landscape, with domesticated pets turned murderous. Jack Arnold (director), film still from *The Incredible Shrinking Man*, Universal International Pictures, 1957. Grant Williams, pictured, as Scott Carey, and Orangey as his cat.

a perpetually unfamiliar and endless place, the frontier landscape of suburban mythology in its primitive, untamed state (figure 10.6). Lawn chairs, for instance, the paraphernalia of outdoor suburban leisure, rise up into looming and treacherous mountains. The spider in particular becomes a symbol of an impenetrable otherness, as Carey thinks, "the spider had come to symbolize something to him; something he hated, something he couldn't coexist with," a new nature hostile to man's rule. Carey has become the mythic pioneer inside his own home. He reenacts the national narrative of triumph over nature, which suburban growth was recapitulating, not only by subduing the spider but also simply by surviving each ordeal bodily and, as he enters the microscopic realm, spiritually. In the final scene he makes his way outside to his own lawn, which he finds "a wonderland." He anticipates that despite having left the human world far behind, "He might not have to be alone."[34] His yard, at various points a social buffer and then a hazard, finally becomes his own manifest destiny, the ground for possible union with others. In the film version, *The Incredible Shrinking Man*, produced the following year, the lawn becomes an even more prominent emblem for Carey's plight. At first, curious newsmen appear on it as he stares out from the window; then when he is confined to stay in a dollhouse, he has to dash across the idealized ersatz lawn of the living room carpet to escape the monster that was once his pet cat; in the final scene he ventures, primitively armed and garbed, out of the house and into the infinite lawn.[35]

Venomous landscapes subsequently became a refrain in horror literature and cinema. Stephen King's 1975 story "The Lawnmower Man" refashions the effort it takes to maintain that suburban lawn into an autonomous force that literally devours Harold Parkette, the home owner.³⁶ Steven Spielberg's film *Poltergeist*, from 1982, tells the story of Steve Freeling, a real-estate broker, no less, whose family is terrorized by ghosts released from the earth when a cemetery is razed to build houses. In *Poltergeist*, ghosts replace neighbors as the people who have been removed from the land in order that it might be enjoyed as a picture of privacy. The ghosts appear in the television, the picture in the living room that replaced— explicitly in contemporary house design literature—the picture window. Their return in *Poltergeist* is thereby multiply coded in terms of the histories of colonial settlement, postwar suburbanization, and looking at landscape.³⁷

The most evocative haunted house book that explicitly thematizes landscape is *The House Next Door*, published by Anne Rivers Siddons in 1978. In this novel, a husband and wife, Walter and Colquitt Kennedy, watch as a once empty and supposedly unbuildable lot next door becomes the site for a new house. A series of misfortunes follow, from miscarriage to murder and from dementia to diarrhea, while the Kennedys watch from their windows and back porch. The source of the evil is Kim Dougherty, the young genius architect whose dark forebears imprint his otherwise thoroughly modern character. He has an uncanny propensity for organic architecture so powerful that the house he designed was less constructed upon the earth than grown from it, "like an elemental spirit that had lain, locked and yearning for the light, through endless deeps of time, waiting to be released."³⁸ Or, as Frank Lloyd Wright, another, perhaps better known organic architect put it years before, "Out of the ground, into the light."³⁹ The house next door was an emanation from the land rather than from the people who lived and, tragically, died there. In addition to seeming to grow from the land and, presumably, featuring complexly interrelated parts and a correspondence of form to function, the house next door was available for the Kennedys to identify with, that is, it served as an organic artifactual embodiment of selfhood.

Once completed, the house is simultaneously a breathtaking masterwork and a murderous terror, but as the story continues, the real horror is the suburban setting itself. Only in retrospect, then, does it become clear how Siddons set up the reader from the very first pages. The formerly empty lot had been the basis for a fantasy of isolation, "giving one the feeling of being cloistered away in a mountain retreat even though our street is only a block off one of the city's main thoroughfares. Our bedroom windows overlooked it," as did a planned home office, the breakfast room, and the patio. The neighbors on the other side of the lot, the Guthries, shared the fantasy. They "loved the lot, I knew, for the same reasons we did. They are, as are most of us on this street, people who treasure space and greenness and privacy." A house built on the lot "would stare directly into the core of our living." This was a particular problem for Colquitt because she had "a rather shameful penchant" to walk naked in her yard.⁴⁰

When Colquitt learns the lot next door will be built on, she is aghast, and realizes that through her visual occupation of the landscape she had acquired a sense of ownership. It had become a part of her sense of self, part of, to use a neglected term, her character. When Walter reminds her that the lot does not in fact belong to her, she protests, based on the evidence of her own eyes: "But it does, I said back. . . . I looked out the kitchen window at the piece of ground that did not belong to me." As the story moves on, the Kennedys witness the immanent malice of the house grown from the land and finally tell the authorities. But for giving voice to secrets of the suburbs, the neighbors turn against them, not only shunning the Kennedys but also, emblematically, vandalizing their lawn, thereby ruining the view from their big front windows.[41] The Kennedys had violated the suburban premise of a community composed of atomized individuals, each looking out upon an otherwise unpopulated view. With Colquitt musing on her and Walter's self-sufficiency as well as the communal premise of seclusion, the real horror turns out to be social intimacy, the avoidance of which is made manifest in the presence of landscape. The apron of lawn surrounding the suburban house is shown to be not only a symbolic register of independence but also a mechanism for maintaining social distance. Colquitt was intimate with the nature of the lot next door, even getting naked with it, but when she learns another neighbor's secret, she thinks, "This sort of shattering disclosure makes most of us almost unbearably uncomfortable. It is harder to live with than almost anything I know. Our set shrinks from it. In distance there is decency."[42] Whereas with frontier imagery an unpopulated landscape signified a social realm that had yet to arrive, in the modern suburb the imagined absence of others was a distinct refusal of the social realm.

With the private and unpopulated view a visual correlate of social distance, the suburban landscape becomes haunted when it can exercise volition and show itself to be every bit as intolerant as the citizens who dwell there. Whereas in the Victorian house horror had to do with the exposure of an otherwise dark side of oneself, in the postwar period horror involved simply having one's banal self be seen. To put it another way, Victorian horror rested on the corruption of one's character, whereas modern horror was to be exposed as lacking in character. For the reader, horror shifted from sharing the point of view of the one who is detecting or, rather, de-tectonicizing, dark secrets to become aligned with those who have been turned into objects for detection. Terror shifts from the discovery of hidden parts of oneself to the unwanted exposure of oneself to others. Whereas in the nineteenth century darkness had incubated anxiety, in the postwar era distance kept the demons at bay. In either case, when darkness can no longer contain it or when distance is transgressed, the self has lost control and the domestic sphere collapses.

Perhaps one more story can help make the point: Stephen King's *The Shining*, from 1977. The plot is likely familiar, at least from the 1980 Stanley Kubrick film, so I focus on the setting, an old hotel named "the Outlook" for having the best views in the country, situated on a high and isolated point in the Rocky Mountains. Although a hotel, it is home to a single family one winter, or rather, like in Siddons's book, a series of families. King himself likens the hotel to a grand house, like a family castle, even beginning with an epigraph from Poe's "Masque of the Red Death" and mentioning Walpole too along the way. The large and self-sufficient hotel in turn seems almost a caricature of suburban life, with the desire for privacy soon becoming the curse of isolation. Indeed, as the hotel closes for the season and Jack Torrance, the protagonist, is left alone, the landscape rises up: "It gave Jack a curious shrinking feeling, as if his life force had dwindled to a mere spark while the hotel and the grounds had suddenly doubled in size and become sinister, dwarfing them with sullen, inanimate power."[43]

Torrance had previously worked in landscaping "people's lawns and bushes and hedges," even trimming topiary, landscape in sentient form. He thought that by wintering in the hotel, the distance from the distractions of urban life would allow his creative side to blossom, which it does at first. But distance also presages the loss of society's civilizing influence. Isolation diminishes Jack, and without social limits he goes out of control, with the loss of control arrogated to the hotel itself. Outside, in the garden, topiary animals come alive, clutching and scratching and, in the final scene, allying with Jack's son, Danny, to subdue and finally to kill Jack. An animated landscape de-animates a living man. Danny's particular gift, a kind of supernatural empathy—an uncommon and uncommonly intimate connection with others—that provides the book's title, is directly at odds with Jack's neurotic self-involvement. Although Danny and his daddy are closely identified in the story, they stand at opposite ends of a spectrum of distance: Danny is abnormally connected to others, including those he has never met, even including nature, while Jack is unconnected with his own family and, as he psychically merges with former winter caretakers, even with himself. As with other postwar haunted house stories, social isolation takes the form of what at first is a fabulous view over an unpopulated landscape. But soon enough that isolation, initially desired as a condition of individual expression, becomes as much of a blight as that which the suburban exodus supposedly left behind. As Jack Torrance says, shortly after he first calls the hotel "home" and sees it as riven with natural beauty and human tragedy, "I think this place forms an index of the whole post–World War II American character."[44] (figure 10.7).

CONCLUSION

Under the influence of modernism, between the mid-nineteenth and the mid-twentieth century, the visible character of domestic architecture migrated in location from the fabric of the house to the landscape surrounding the house. It shifted in purpose as well, moving from being a correlate of the home owner's moral complexion to become a source of distinctiveness and a protective perimeter necessary to assure individual gratification. The house itself, as a corollary,

FIGURE 10.7. Characters, house, and garden collapse one upon the other in this transitional shot from outdoors to indoors, which is soon followed by another overlaid transition in reverse. Stanley Kubrick (director), film still from *The Shining*, Warner Bros. Pictures, Hawk Films, Peregrine, and Producers Circle, 1980. The backs of Jack Nicholson, Shelley Duval, and Danny Lloyd, pictured, as Jack, Wendy, and Danny Torrance, respectively.

---

shifted from being a crucible for socialization to become a bastion of privacy. Modernism participated in this shift by licensing changes in the spatial organization of the house, which in turn conditioned the developmental possibilities for personhood within the house.

In the nineteenth-century house, varied room sizes and specific functions provided the spatial resources for an individual to develop his or her own intimate and social sides. Psychic stability involved a conscious balancing of a rich repertoire of psychological textures, just as daily life involved moving through the home's differentiated spaces. Selfhood was not compromised by complexity of character. In turn, anxieties regarding character, as seen through the literature of haunted houses, centered on the unseen presence of irrational parts of a complex psyche and a deep memory, which could be revealed through the disassembly of either the house or the self, usually both.

In the postwar house, though, anxieties came to be centered on the collapse of social distance. As authenticity became a popular personal virtue in the postwar period, the individual was seen as being more or less homogeneous, self-similar from one setting to another. Psychic stability was in this version more a matter of casting inner and outer from the same material, being honest with oneself or honest in all situations. House plans conceived in terms of discrete rooms with determinate character and within a definite enclosure gradually gave way to an interior conceived more in terms of circulation and fluid relations between inside and out, the emblem of which was a private view of landscape. The spatial continuum of the modern house, premised upon openness both within the home and to the outdoors, allowed the self to appear constant regardless of changes in social setting or whether inside or outside the home. The conception of the self as authentic is remarkably akin to transparency in this architectural sense.

The suburbs, of course, are the larger context for the transfer in the nature and location of domestic architectural character. At one level, a demographic shift from cities to suburbs, typified by single-family houses centered in a surrounding apron of lawn, made the management of landscape a concern for families with modest economic status, even if the leading icons of modern design were surrounded by acres of private land. The apprehensive imaginings in postwar horror literature demonstrate just how important private, if diminutive, landscapes had become to the psychic mechanisms of self-control. Distance in particular became the means to protect this visually open realm from optical trespass, which helps to explain the simultaneous fascination and threat of narrowed distances in general and of shrinking in particular. Anxieties regarding a controllable domain are evident in the frequent appearance in this literature of dollhouses and models—*The Shining*, for instance, features a number of models, including an outdoor playhouse that is the "exact replica" of the hotel, as well as an indoor model of the garden labyrinth outside—paralleling the characterization of suburbs as being themselves a sort of "miniature" by Robert Wood in his 1958 book, *Suburbia*.[45] A miniature landscape surrenders itself to an omniscient gaze, whereas a miniaturized viewer is at the mercy of giants. The postwar house proposed the former but feared the latter.

At another level, the suburban ideal of an "enclave," a retreat to a manageable society of shared values, evident in protracted postwar battles over exclusionary zoning, becomes almost a parody in haunted house literature. When character emanated from the self, its unraveling likewise arose from within; in the postwar era, with character appearing only in the absence of others, its demise involves unhappy neighbors. What made the 1956 film *Invasion of the Body Snatchers* the most unsettling of the many postwar alien invasion films was precisely that the threat came from neighbors, who finally turn into an army of soulless automata in what must be the apotheosis of the horror of suburban conformity. With a private landscape a proxy for the absence of others and their challenge to selfhood, neighbors who have lost their humanity are a symbolic inversion of anxieties regarding the viability of the self. In this context, it seems more than coincidence that the source of the trouble comes in the form of a batch of bad seeds otherwise destined to enhance suburban lawns.[46]

The difference between nineteenth- and twentieth-century horror about houses is neatly captured in the contrast between Poe's de-tecting and the "shattering disclosure" of Siddons, that is, from an apparently reasoned deconstruction of the irrational interior to the unsettling effect of someone else's uninvited revelation. The horror comes not from within oneself, based on a nineteenth-century notion of individual merit arising from the qualities of one's complete and complex character, but from outside—the gaze returned from the landscape—in keeping with descriptions of selfhood, such as those of Riesman, where the individual is composed in response to the opinions and expectations of others. Such people open themselves to others for approval with the understanding that no one will look too closely as long as the emblems of conformance are in place. They are beholden to others for their consensual disengagement with community.

Correspondingly, the means of shielding oneself from the psychological threat of either disassembly or disclosure shifts by the postwar era from darkness to distance. In Poe, spaces are dank: the closeness of a wall cavity, the pitch of a cellar or tomb, the murk of a pit, the gloom of an invalid's bedroom; in Siddons, spaces are open and flow one into another, alike in physical attributes but with distance to distinguish them—recall that Colquitt Kennedy's neighbors share the same extended view but are hidden one from the other. The underside of Victorian virtue dwelled in dark places, whereas in the postwar period horror emerges with exposure and, in between, the anxiety is anticipated with oversized windows that diminish the ability to regulate the interior's emotional temperature.[47] Nineteenth-century horror literature required inhabitation, the uncanny that dwells within the familiar; postwar horror concerns visibility itself.

Common to both the Victorian and the modern localization of character is the rehearsal of psychic self-control by architectural proxy. House and home grounds are each in their turn objective correlates, material manifestations of psychic structures, which are conditioned by social forms. Subconscious forces threatening autonomic functioning are kept in darkness in the nineteenth century, whereas external threats to self-stability are diminished with distance in the twentieth. As private property, home and home grounds are legally protected from social trespass; they mediate self and society and produce a protective layer in which selfhood may ripen. In turn, the self becomes prey to anxieties harbored in that which would protect it.

NOTES

1. "Marcel Breuer, Teacher and Architect," *House and Home* 1 (May 1952): 104–115.
2. This argument is presented in a different context in Sandy Isenstadt, "Four Views, Three of Them Through Glass," in *Sites Unseen: Landscape and Vision*, ed. Dianne Harris and J. Fairchild Ruggles (Pittsburgh: University of Pittsburgh Press, 2007), 213–240.
3. Andrew Jackson Downing, *Cottage Residences* (New York: Wiley and Son, 1842), 56.
4. Discussed in John Woodforde, *The Truth about Cottages* (London: Routledge and K. Paul, 1969), 29–31.
5. Colin Rowe, "Character and Composition; or Some Vicissitudes of Architectural Vocabulary in the Nineteenth Century," *Oppositions* 2 (January 1974): 41–60, and reprinted in Colin Rowe, *The Mathematics of the Ideal Villa and Other Essays* (Cambridge, MA: MIT Press, 1976), 59–88.

6. Thomas Butler Gunn, *The Physiology of New York Boarding-Houses* (New York: Mason Brothers, 1857), 255, 299. For more on boardinghouses, see Elizabeth Cromley, *Alone Together: A History of New York's Early Apartments* (Ithaca, NY, and London: Cornell University Press, 1990), 20–27.

7. Emerson's larger point is to be true to one's own nature, regardless of circumstance. Ralph Waldo Emerson, "Character" [1855], in *Essays and English Traits* (New York: Harvard Classics, P. F. Collier and Son, 1909), 195.

8. The argument is elaborated in Grant Kester's dissertation, "The Faculty of Possession: Property and the Aesthetic in English Culture, 1730–1850" (PhD diss., University of Rochester, 1996), 82.

9. Edward Everett Hale, *Workingmen's Homes: Essays and Stories* (Boston: Osgood and Co., 1874), 9. The history of credit in the United States is discussed in Lendol Calder, *Financing the American Dream: A Cultural History of Consumer Credit* (Princeton, NJ: Princeton University Press, 1999). See also Margot Finn, *The Character of Credit: Personal Debt in English Culture, 1740–1914* (New York: Cambridge University Press, 2003).

10. For a further discussion of repose as a decorating ideal, see "The Psychic Value of Repose," in Sandy Isenstadt, *The Modern American House: Spaciousness and Middle-Class Identity* (New York and London: Cambridge University Press, 2006), 85–88.

11. Candace Wheeler, "Character in Houses," in *Principles of Home Decoration* (New York: Doubleday, Page and Co., 1903), 17.

12. As is well known, Walpole's story evolved from the purchase and renovation of his own Gothic-inspired home, Strawberry Hill. Walpole suggested in his preface that "some real castle" is behind the story's supernatural occurrences, in Horace Walpole, *The Castle of Otranto* [1764] (New York: Pearson Longman, 2007), 3, and discussed in Martin Kallich, *Horace Walpole* (New York: Twayne Publishers, 1971), 79–80.

13. Edward Bulwer-Lytton, *Zanoni* (New York: Harper and Co., 1842), especially books 4 and 5.

14. H. P. Lovecraft, "Supernatural Horror in Literature," in *At the Mountains of Madness* (New York: Modern Library, 2005), 137. Lovecraft also suggests that the tension in Poe is drawn between his recognition of the psychological complexity of horror and an almost scientifically precise writing. For a history of American haunted house literature more generally, see Dale Bailey, *American Nightmares: The Haunted House Formula in American Popular Fiction* (Bowling Green, OH: Bowling Green State University Press, 1999).

15. The dual meaning is already present in the Latin root *detegere*, literally to take off the roof and figuratively to unveil or lay bare. Plautus, for example, described a wind that unroofed a villa, while Quintilian suggested a man's manner of speaking can reveal (*detegit*) his inner secrets. My thanks to Ruth Bielfeldt for these and many other examples. Although the literature on Poe is vast, two essays seem especially apt. Richard Wilbur describes Poe's motif of enclosure in his "The House of Poe," in *Poe: A Collection of Critical Essays*, ed. Robert Regan (Englewood Cliffs, NJ: Prentice-Hall, 1967), 98–120, while David Leatherbarrow reads Poe for insights into architecture in "A Study of the Writings of Edgar Allan Poe," *Via* 8 (1986): 6–15. Regarding psychic identification with particularly small spaces, see Emily Apter, "Cabinet Secrets: Fetishism, Prostitution, and the Fin de Siècle Interior," *Assemblage* 9 (June 1989): 6–19.

16. Walter Benjamin, "Louis-Philippe, or the Interior," in *Reflections*, trans. Edmund Jephcott (New York: Schocken, 1986), 154–156.

17. Henry James, "The Jolly Corner," *The English Review* 1, no. 1 (1908): 24.

18. Ibid., throughout.

19. Mullions, as a technical device and a factor in the construal of character, are discussed in Isenstadt, *The Modern American House*, 180–191.

20. David Riesman, *The Lonely Crowd: A Study of the Changing American Character* (New Haven, CT: Yale University Press, 1950).

21. See, for example, John Gloag, "Advertising in Three Dimensions," *Architectural Review* 74 (September 1933): 111; Russell Walcott, "Facadism," *Architectural Record* 80 (November 1936): 385–389. Robert Woods Kennedy, *The House and the Art of Its Design* (New York: Reinhold, 1953), 382–385.

22. From James John Hissey, *The Charm of the Road* (London: Macmillan, 1910), 102.

23. Ruby Ross Goodnow, *The Honest House* (New York: Century, 1914), 84–92.

24. Warren Susman, "Personality and the Making of Twentieth Century Culture," in *Culture as History* (New York: Pantheon Books, 1984), 271–285. See also Karen Halttunen, "From Parlor to Living Room: Domestic Space, Interior Decoration, and the Culture of Personality," in *Consuming Visions: Accumulation and Display of Goods in America, 1880–1920*, ed. Simon Bronner (Winterthur, DE: Winterthur Museum, 1989), 166–170, and Richard Sennett, "Personality and the Private Family," in *The Fall of Public Man* (New York: Knopf, 1977).

25. Downing, *Cottage Residences*, 271.

26. For an overview, see Alfred Kazin, *A Writer's America: Landscape in Literature* (New York: Knopf, 1988).

27. Henry-Russell Hitchcock, *Modern Architecture: Romanticism and Reintegration* [1929] (New York: Da Capo, 1993), 8.

28. Ibid., 220. The relation of house and nature in Frank Lloyd Wright and Le Corbusier, for example, was an enduring model for others, according to Sigfried Giedion, *Space, Time and Architecture: The Growth of a New Tradition* [1941] (Cambridge, MA: Harvard University Press, 1967), 414–417, 525–529.

29. "Topics of the Times," *New York Times*, October 7, 1957, 26.

30. David Lowenthal, "Not Every Prospect Pleases," *Landscape* 12, no. 2 (Winter 1962): 19.

31. Leonard Cowley, "The Value of a View," *Appraisal Journal* (April 1951): 239–242.

32. Shirley Jackson, *The Sundial* (New York: Farrar, Straus and Cudahy, 1958), 188–189, discussed in Richard Pascal, "New World Miniatures: Shirley Jackson's *The Sundial* and Postwar American Society," *Journal of American and Comparative Cultures* 23, no. 3 (Fall 2000): 100.

33. Shirley Jackson, *The Haunting of Hill House* (New York: Viking, 1959). The film, *The Haunting*, is from 1963, directed by Robert Wise (Argyle Enterprises, Metro-Goldwyn-Mayer). A sample of Shirley Jackson articles would include "Nice Day for a Baby," *Woman's Home Companion* 79 (July 1952): 34–35; "How to Enjoy a Family Quarrel," *McCall's* 84 (September 1957): 37ff.; "Pleasures and Perils of Dining Out with Children," *McCall's* 84 (March 1957): 54–5ff.

34. Richard Matheson, *The Shrinking Man* [1956] (New York: Tom Doherty Associates, 1994), 172, 204.

35. Directed by Jack Arnold. Universal Pictures, 1957.

36. Stephen King, "The Lawnmower Man" [1975], in *Night Shift* (New York: Doubleday, 1978).

37. Story by Steven Spielberg. Directed by Tobe Hooper. Produced by Frank Marshall and Steven Spielberg. MGM, 1982. See also Mark Wigley, "The Electric Lawn," in *The American Lawn*, ed. Georges Teyssot (New York: Princeton Architectural Press, 1999), 155–195.

38. Anne Rivers Siddons, *The House Next Door* (New York: Simon and Schuster, 1978), 32.

39. In Edgar Kaufman, ed., *An American Architecture* (New York: Horizon Press, 1955).

Wright expressed his views on the relation of architecture to landscape in "The Character of the Site Is the Beginning of Architecture," *House Beautiful* 97 (November 1955): 248–249ff.

40. Siddons, *The House Next Door*, 21.

41. Ibid., 262–263.

42. Ibid., 111.

43. Stephen King, *The Shining* (Garden City, NY: Doubleday, 1977), 99–100.

44. Ibid., 186.

45. Miniatures appear in nearly all the titles discussed. See Richard Pascal, "New World Miniatures: Shirley Jackson's *The Sundial* and Postwar American Society," *Journal of American and Comparative Cultures* 23, no. 3 (Fall 2000): 99–111. Similarly, the front lawn itself was likened to a miniature of a picturesque estate. See, for example, J. B. Jackson, "Ghosts at the Door," *Landscape* 1, no. 2 (Winter 1951–1952).

46. Directed by Don Siegel, Walter Wanger Productions. A similar claim could be made for Alfred Hitchcock's *The Birds*, from 1963.

47. Postwar anxieties regarding overexposure continued to coalesce around windows: "Is there a picture in your picture window," ran the title of one article from 1950, or, ten years later, "Does your front lawn belong to you, or the whole neighborhood?" In "Is There a Picture in Your Picture Window?" *House Beautiful* 92 (January 1950): 34–35; Elizabeth Gordon, "Does Your Front Lawn Belong to You?" *House Beautiful* 102 (May 1960): 152–163. The May 1960 issue is dedicated to achieving privacy on modestly sized lots.

FURTHER READING

PART I. MODERNISM AND THE STATE

Aggregate. *Governing by Design: Architecture, Economy, and Politics in the Twentieth Century*. Pittsburgh: University of Pittsburgh Press, 2012.

Akcan, Esra. *Architecture in Translation: Germany, Turkey, and the Modern House*. Durham, NC, and London: Duke University Press, 2012.

Åman, Anders. *Architecture and Ideology in Eastern Europe During the Stalin Era: An Aspect of Cold War History*. New York: Architectural History Foundation, Inc.; Cambridge, MA, and London: MIT Press, 1992.

Belluzzi, Amedeo, and Claudia Conforti. *Architettura italiana 1944–1994*. Rome and Bari: Laterza, 1994.

Blagojević, Ljiljana. *Modernism in Serbia: The Elusive Margins of Belgrade Architecture, 1919–1941*. Cambridge, MA: MIT Press, 2003.

Bozdoğan, Sibel. *Modernism and Nation Building: Turkish Architectural Culture in the Early Republic*. Seattle: University of Washington Press, 2001.

Castillo, Greg. *Cold War on the Home Front: The Soft Power of Midcentury Design*. Minneapolis: University of Minnesota Press, 2010.

Devos, Rita, and Mil de Kooning, eds. *L'architecture moderne à l'Expo 58*. Brussels: Fonds Mercator et Dexia Banque, 2006.

Dobrenko, Evgeny, and Eric Naiman, eds. *The Landscape of Stalinism: The Art and Ideology of Soviet Space*. Seattle and London: University of Washington Press, 2003.

Isenstadt, Sandy, and Kishwar Rizvi, eds. *Modernism and the Middle East: Architecture and Politics in the Twentieth Century*. Seattle: University of Washington Press, 2008.

Harris, Steven E. *Communism on Tomorrow Street: Mass Housing and Everyday Life after Stalin*. Woodrow Wilson Center Press/Johns Hopkins University Press, 2013.

Kulić, Vladimir. "National, Supranational, International: New Belgrade and the Symbolic Construction of a Socialist Capital." *Nationalities Papers: The Journal of Nationalism and Ethnicity* 41, no. 1 (January 2013): 35–63.

Kulić, Vladimir, Maroje Mrduljaš, and Wolfgang Thaler. *Modernism In-Between: The Mediatory Architectures of Socialist Yugoslavia*. Berlin: Jovis, 2012.

Loeffler, Jane C. *The Architecture of Diplomacy: Building America's Embassies*. 2nd ed. New York: Princeton Architectural Press, 2010.

Lu, Duanfang, ed. *Third World Modernism: Architecture, Development and Identity*. London and New York: Routledge, 2011.

Mëhilli, Elidor. "The Socialist Design: Urban Dilemmas in Postwar Europe and the Soviet Union." *Kritika: Explorations in Russian and Eurasian History* 13, no. 3 (Summer 2012): 635–665.

Molnár, Virág. *Building the State: Architecture, Politics, and State Formation in Postwar Central Europe.* London and New York: Routledge, 2013.

Mrduljaš, Maroje, and Vladimir Kulić, eds. *Unfinished Modernisations—Between Utopia and Pragmatism: Architecture and Urban Planning in Former Yugoslavia and its Successor States.* Zagreb: CCA, 2012.

Paperny, Vladimir. *Architecture in the Age of Stalin: Culture Two.* Cambridge and New York: Cambridge University Press, 2002.

Péteri, György, ed. Nylon Curtain. *Transnational and Transsystemic Tendencies in the Cultural Life of State-Socialist Russia and East-Central Europe.* Trondheim, Norway: TSEECS, 2006.

Quek, Raymond, Darren Deane, and Sarah Butler, eds. *Nationalism and Architecture.* London and Burlington, VT: Ashgate, 2012.

Reid, Susan E., and David Crowley, eds. *Socialist Spaces: Sites of Everyday Life in the Eastern Bloc.* Oxford and New York: Berg, 2002.

Sabatino, Michelangelo. *Pride in Modesty: Modernist Architecture and the Vernacular Tradition in Italy.* Toronto and Buffalo: University of Toronto Press, 2010.

Scott, James C. Seeing Like a State: *How Certain Schemes to Improve the Human Condition Have Failed.* New Haven, CT, and London: Yale University Press, 1999.

Scrivano, Paolo. "Signs of Americanization in Italian Domestic Life: Italy's Postwar Conversion to Consumerism." *Journal of Contemporary History* 40, no. 2 (April 2005).

Smith, Mark B. *Property of Communists: The Urban Housing Program from Stalin to Khrushchev.* DeKalb: Northern Illinois University Press, 2010.

Švácha, Rostislav. *The Architecture of New Prague, 1895–1945.* Cambridge, MA: MIT Press, 1995.

Tafuri, Manfredo. *History of Italian Architecture, 1944–1985.* Translated by Jessica Levine. Cambridge, MA: MIT Press, 1989.

Vale, Lawrence J. *Architecture, Power, and National Identity.* 2nd ed. London: Routledge, 2008.

Wharton, Annabel Jane. *Building the Cold War: Hilton International Hotels and Modern Architecture.* Chicago: University of Chicago Press, 2001.

Zarecor, Kimberly Elman. *Manufacturing a Socialist Modernity: Housing in Czechoslovakia, 1945–1960.* Pittsburgh: University of Pittsburgh Press, 2011.

PART II. MAKING RELIGION MODERN

Adams, William Seth. *Moving the Furniture: Liturgical Theory, Practice, and Environment.* New York: Church Publishing, 1999.

Asad, Talal. *Formations of the Secular: Christianity, Islam, Modernity.* Stanford, CA: Stanford University Press, 2003.

Bakker, Hans, and Rijksuniversiteit te Groningen. *The Sacred Centre as the Focus of Political Interest: Proceedings of the Symposium Held on the Occasion of the 375th Anniversary of the University of Groningen, 5–8 March 1989.* Groningen: E. Forsten, 1992.

Berger, Peter L., ed. *The Desecularization of the World: Resurgent Religion and World Politics.* Grand Rapids, MI: W. B. Eerdmans, 1999.

Brown, David, and Ann Loades. *The Sense of the Sacramental: Movement and Measure in Art and Music, Place and Time.* London: SPCK, 1995.

Brown, Frank Burch. *Religious Aesthetics: A Theological Study of Making and Meaning.* Princeton, NJ: Princeton University Press, 1989.

———. *Good Taste, Bad Taste, and Christian Taste: Aesthetics in Religious Life*. Oxford and New York: Oxford University Press, 2000.

Bühren, Ralf van. *Kunst und Kirche im 20. Jahrhundert: die Rezeption des Zweiten Vatikanischen Konzils*. Paderborn: Ferdinand Schöningh, 2008.

Dupré, Louis K. *Passage to Modernity: An Essay in the Hermeneutics of Nature and Culture*. New Haven, CT: Yale University Press, 1993.

Fitzgerald, Timothy. *The Ideology of Religious Studies*. New York: Oxford University Press, 2000.

Flannery, Austin. *The Liturgy: Renewal and Adaptation; Liturgical Reform in the Roman Catholic Church: All Major Documents on Liturgy, with Commentary*. Dublin: Scepter Books, 1968.

———, ed. *Vatican Council II: The Conciliar and Post Conciliar Documents*. Collegeville, MN: Liturgical Press, 1977.

Harwood, Elain. "Liturgy and Architecture: Liturgical Reform and the Development of the Centralised Eucharistic Space." *Twentieth Century Architecture* 3 (1998): 49–74.

Hayes, Bartlett. *Tradition Becomes Innovation: Modern Religious Architecture in America*. New York: Pilgrim Press, 1983.

Heathcote, Edwin, and Iona Spens. *Church Builders*. Chichester: Academy Editions, 1997.

Jodock, Darrell, ed. *Catholicism Contending with Modernity: Roman Catholic Modernism and Anti-modernism in Historical Context*. Cambridge and New York: Cambridge University Press, 2000.

Jones, Lindsay. *The Hermeneutics of Sacred Architecture: Experience, Interpretation, Comparison*. 2 vols. Cambridge, MA: Harvard University Press; Harvard University Center for the Study of World Religions, 2000.

Jungmann, Josef A. "Constitution on the Sacred Liturgy." In *Commentary on the Documents of Vatican II*, edited by Herbert Vorgrimler, 1–88. New York: Herder and Herder, 1966.

Kieckhefer, Richard. *Theology in Stone: Church Architecture from Byzantium to Berkeley*. Oxford and New York: Oxford University Press, 2004.

Kilde, Jeanne Halgren. *When Church Became Theatre: The Transformation of Evangelical Architecture and Worship in Nineteenth-Century America*. New York: Oxford University Press, 2002.

O'Connell, Marvin Richard. *Critics on Trial: An Introduction to the Catholic Modernist Crisis*. Washington, DC: Catholic University of America Press, 1994.

O'Malley, John W. "Vatican II: Did Anything Happen?" *Theological Studies* 67 (2006): 3–33.

———. *What Happened at Vatican II*. Cambridge, MA: Harvard University Press, 2008.

Pickstock, Catherine. *After Writing: On the Liturgical Consummation of Philosophy*. Oxford: Blackwell, 1998.

———. "Liturgy, Art, Politics." *Modern Theology* 16, no. 2 (April 2000): 159–180.

Runkle, John Ander, ed. *Searching for Sacred Space: Essays on Architecture and Liturgical Design in the Episcopal Church*. New York: Church Publishing, 2002.

Schloeder, Steven J. *Architecture in Communion: Implementing the Second Vatican Council through Liturgy and Architecture*. San Francisco: Ignatius Press, 1998.

Schloesser, Stephen. "Against Forgetting: Memory, History, Vatican II." *Theological Studies* 67 (2006): 275–319. Reprinted in *Vatican II: Did Anything Happen?* Edited by David G. Schultenover, 92–152. New York: Continuum, 2007.

———. *Jazz Age Catholicism: Mystic Modernism in Postwar Paris, 1919–1933*. Toronto: University of Toronto Press, 2005.

Schultenover, David G., ed. *Vatican II: Did Anything Happen?* New York: Continuum, 2007.

Sedgwick, Mark. *Against the Modern World: Traditionalism and the Secret Intellectual History of the Twentieth Century*. Oxford: Oxford University Press, 2004.

Stock, Wolfgang Jean, ed. *European Church Architecture 1950–2000*. Munich: Prestel, 2002.

Taylor, Charles. *A Secular Age*. Cambridge, MA: Belknap Press of Harvard University Press, 2007.

Weber, Joanna M. "The Sacred in Art: Introducing Father Marie-Alain Couturier's Aesthetic." *Worship* 69 (1995): 243–262.

White, Susan J. *Art, Architecture, and Liturgical Reform: The Liturgical Arts Society (1928–1972)*. New York: Pueblo Publishing, 1990.

Yates, Nigel. *Liturgical Space: Christian Worship and Church Buildings in Western Europe 1500–2000*. Aldershot, UK: Ashgate, 2008.

Young, Victoria Marie. "St. John's Abbey Church, Collegeville, Minnesota (1953–1961): The Benedictines and Marcel Breuer Search for the Sacred." PhD diss., University of Virginia, 2003.

PART III. MODERNISM AND DOMESTICITY

Castillo, Greg. *Cold War on the Home Front: the Soft Power of Midcentury Design*. Minneapolis: University of Minnesota Press, 2010.

Colomina, Beatriz. *Domesticity at War*. Cambridge, MA, and London: MIT Press, 2007.

———. *Privacy and Publicity: Modern Architecture as Mass Media*. Cambridge, MA: MIT Press, 1994.

Constant, Caroline. *The Modern Architectural Landscape*. Minneapolis and London: University of Minnesota Press, 2012.

Decker, Julie, and Chris Chiel. *Quonset Hut: Metal Living for a Modern Age*. New York: Princeton Architectural Press, 2005.

Filler, Martin. *Makers of Modern Architecture*. New York: New York Review Books, 2007.

Friedman, Alice T. *American Glamour and the Evolution of Modern Architecture*. New Haven, CT: Yale University Press, 2010.

———. *Women and the Making of the Modern House: A Social and Architectural History*. New York: Abrams, 1998.

Gibbs, Jocelyn, and Nicholas Olsberg. *Cliff May and the Romance of the Ranch House*. New York: Rizzoli, 2012.

Goldhagen, Sarah, and Réjean Legault, eds. *Anxious Modernisms: Experimentation in Postwar Architectural Culture*. Cambridge, MA: MIT Press, 2000.

Gottfried, Herbert, and Jan Jennings. *American Vernacular Buildings and Interiors, 1870–1960*. New York: W. W. Norton and Co., 2009.

Gregory, Daniel. *Cliff May and the Modern Ranch House*. New York: Rizzoli, 2008.

Harris, Dianne Suzette. *Little White Houses: How the Postwar Home Constructed Race in America*. Minneapolis: University of Minnesota Press, 2013.

Hess, Alan, and Alan Weintraub. *Organic Architecture: The Other Modernism*. Layton, UT: Gibbs Smith, 2006.

Hines, Thomas S. *Architecture of the Sun: Los Angeles Modernism, 1900–1970*. New York: Rizzoli, 2010.

Isenstadt, Sandy. *The Modern American House: Spaciousness and Middle Class Identity*. Cambridge: Cambridge University Press, 2006.

Kaplan, Wendy, ed. *California Design, 1930–1965: Living in a Modern Way*. Cambridge, MA: MIT Press, 2011.

Keil, Rob. *Little Boxes: The Architecture of a Classic Midcentury Suburb*. Daly City, CA: Advection Media, 2006.

Leighton, Sophie. *The 1950s Home*. Oxford: Shire Publications, 2009.

Marling, Karal Ann. *As Seen on TV: The Visual Culture of Everyday Life in the 1950s*. Cambridge, MA: Harvard University Press, 1994.

Rapaport, Brooke Kamin, and Kevin L. Stayton. *Vital Forms: American Art and Design in the Atomic Age, 1940–1960*. New York: Brooklyn Museum of Art, 2001.

Rice, Charles. *The Emergence of the Interior: Architecture, Modernity, Domesticity*. London and New York: Routledge, 2007.

Schuldenfrei, Robin. *Atomic Dwelling: Anxiety, Domesticity, and Postwar Architecture*. Abingdon, Oxon; New York: Routledge, 2012.

Shanken, Andrew Michael. *194X: Architecture, Planning, and Consumer Culture on the American Home Front*. Minneapolis: University of Minnesota Press, 2009.

Smith, Elizabeth A. T., Julius Shulman, Peter Goessel, et al. *Case Study Houses*. New York: Taschen, 2002.

Watts, Jennifer A., ed. *Maynard L. Parker: Modern Photography and the American Dream*. New Haven, CT: Yale University Press, 2012.

Wright, Gwendolyn. *USA: Modern Architectures in History*. London: Reaktion Press, 2008.

CONTRIBUTORS

DENNIS DOORDAN, author of *Twentieth Century Architecture* and coeditor of *Design Issues*, a journal devoted to the history, theory, and criticism of design, is an architectural and design historian and museum consultant and the Associate Dean of Research, Scholarship and Creative Work at the University of Notre Dame School of Architecture. He has a PhD from Columbia University and a BA from Stanford University. He holds a joint appointment in the University of Notre Dame School of Architecture and the Department of Art, Art History, and Design.

SANDY ISENSTADT teaches the history of modern architecture at the University of Delaware. His writings range from essays on postwar reformulations of modern architecture in a global context to American material culture. He is currently working on a book examining novel luminous spaces introduced by electric lighting in the twentieth century.

HYUN-TAE JUNG is an Assistant Professor of Architecture at Lehigh University. He has a doctorate in history and theory of architecture from Columbia University and has earned his master's and bachelor's degrees in architecture from the University of Seoul in South Korea. Before coming to Lehigh, he served as an Assistant Professor in the College of Architecture at the University of Nebraska–Lincoln. He has published numerous articles in both American and South Korean journals, including *In.Form: The Journal of Architecture, Design, and Material Culture*, *Review of Architecture*, and *Building Science and Space*.

RICHARD KIECKHEFER is the John Evans Professor of Religious Studies at Northwestern University. His research interests focus mainly on the late Middle Ages, with special interest in church architecture and in the history of witchcraft and magic. Dr. Kieckhefer's books include *European Witch Trials* (Routledge and Kegan Paul, 1976), *Repression of Heresy in Medieval Germany* (University of

Pennsylvania Press, 1979), *Unquiet Souls* (University of Chicago Press, 1984), *Magic in the Middle Ages* (Cambridge University Press, 1989), *Forbidden Rites* (Sutton and Penn State University Press, 1997), and *Theology in Stone* (Oxford University Press, 2004). A theme underlying much of his research is the way in which communities create and sustain a sense of shared culture in the face of difference, dissension, and dispute.

VLADIMIR KULIĆ holds a PhD in architectural history from the University of Texas at Austin and teaches architectural history and design at Florida Atlantic University. He is the author of *Modernism In-Between: The Mediatory Architectures of Socialist Yugoslavia* (with Wolfgang Thaler and Maroje Mrduljaš, 2012). In collaboration with Maroje Mrduljaš he authored and directed the international research project *Unfinished Modernisations—Between Utopia and Pragmatism* (2010–12), which brought together over thirty researchers from the region of the former Yugoslavia. Vladimir is the winner of the Bruno Zevi Award for a Critical/Historical Essay in Architecture, the Trustees Merit Citation from the Graham Foundation, and the ACLS/SSRC/NEH International and Area Studies Fellowship.

JULIANA MAXIM is an Associate Professor at the University of San Diego, where she teaches the history and theory of art and architecture. Her work centers on twentieth-century art, architecture, and urbanism in Eastern Europe and on the relation between state power and representation in architecture, painting, and film. She earned her PhD in the history, theory, and criticism of art and architecture from MIT. She is at work on a book titled *The Socialist Life of Modern Architecture: Bucharest, 1948–1965*, which examines the various expressive and dramatic contexts through which modern architecture developed in postwar Romania. She is the recipient of the National Council for Eastern European and Eurasian Studies Research Award, and of the American Council of Learned Societies Early Career Grant.

TIMOTHY PARKER is an architect and an architectural historian and theorist. He earned his PhD in architectural history and theory at the University of Texas at Austin, focusing upon the interpretation of modern religious architecture and the historiography of modernism. He has received several substantial fellowships and awards, including the Carter Manny Award from the Graham Foundation for Advanced Studies in the Fine Arts, and has presented his research broadly, from community settings to international professional conferences. He is an Assistant Professor in the School of Architecture + Art at Norwich University, Vermont.

MONICA PENICK studied at Stanford University and received her doctorate in architectural history from the University of Texas at Austin, with expertise in American architecture, interior design, and decorative arts. Her research and publications have ranged from an investigation of the image and meaning of postwar modern design as created by the American popular press to an examination of the relationship between nationalism, regionalism, cultural identity, and architecture. Penick's work has been supported by fellowships from the Andrew W. Mellon Foundation/ACLS, the American Association of University Women, and the Beverly Willis Architecture Foundation. She is an Assistant Professor in Design Studies at the University of Wisconsin–Madison.

ROBERT PROCTOR is a Lecturer in the History of Architecture in the Mackintosh School of Architecture at the Glasgow School of Art. He studied architectural history at Edinburgh and Cambridge Universities. His research interests include midcentury modern architecture in Britain, particularly churches, and fin-de-siècle architecture and design in France, on both of which he has published in academic journals and edited books. He is currently completing a book on Roman Catholic church architecture in Britain between 1955 and 1975, due to be published by Ashgate in 2014.

MICHELANGELO SABATINO was trained as an architect and architectural historian in Italy, Canada, and the United States. After completing a postdoctoral fellowship at Harvard University's Department of the History of Art and Architecture and teaching at Yale University's School of Architecture, he was appointed at the Gerald D. Hines College of Architecture of the University of Houston. His book *Pride in Modesty: Modernist Architecture and the Vernacular Tradition in Italy* (2010) has won four national awards including the 2012 Alice Davis Hitchcock Book Award from the Society of Architectural Historians. Sabatino has lectured in universities in the Americas, Europe, and Asia. He has received fellowships and grants from the Canadian Centre for Architecture, Canada Council, Graham Foundation for Advanced Studies in Fine Arts, Georgia O'Keeffe Research Museum, Houston Architecture Foundation, Japan Foundation, MacDowell Colony, Rice Design Alliance, Wolfsonian-FIU, and the Social Sciences and Humanities Research Council of Canada.

KIMBERLY ELMAN ZARECOR is Associate Professor of Architecture and Director of the Bachelor of Design Program in the College of Design at Iowa State University where she teaches courses in architectural history and design. She holds a M.Arch (1999) and PhD (2008) from the Graduate School of Architecture, Planning, and Preservation at Columbia University. Her research examines the cultural and technological history of architecture and urbanism in the former Czechoslovakia. She is the author of *Manufacturing a Socialist Modernity: Housing in Czechoslovakia, 1945-1960* (University of Pittsburgh Press, 2011). Her work has also appeared in *Architektúra & urbanizmus, East European Politics and Society, Home Cultures*, and *Umění*, as well as a number of edited volumes and conference proceedings.

INDEX

Page numbers in *italics* indicate illustrations.

Aalto, Alvar, 147
Abrams, Bradley, 69, 86
Abruzzese, Felicia, 147
abstract art, 143
Abstraction, 37, 46, 50, 53, 55, 63, 95, 142, 190
Academy of Applied Arts (Zagreb, Croatia), 46
Accademia di San Luca, 149
Aero Acres (Middle River, Maryland), 195, 198
aesthetics, 42, 52, 67–68, 81, 120–121, 146, 194, 209, 213, 219, 247, 270
Agati, Michele, 102, *102*
AIA Gold Medal: Frank Lloyd Wright and the, 235
Albani, Maria Teresa, 149
Albergo Rifugio Pirovano (Cervinia, Italy), 98
Albert Kahn and Associates: designs for Martin Aircraft Plant (Middle River, Maryland), 196
Albini, Franco, 98, 99
Ambrose, 169
America, 179, 186, 191, 208
American consumer, 183, 232
American Institute of Architects (AIA), 149, 238
American modernism, 221
American Radiator & Standard Sanitary Corporation, 191

"American Style": *House Beautiful* and the, 184, 219, 222–224, *223*, 226, 228–232, *228*, 234–238, 240–241
American way of life, 222, 224
Anderson, Benedict, 61, 65
Anshen and Allen, Silverstone House (Taxco, Mexico), *228*
Antonioni, Michelangelo, *Gente del Po*, 98
Aprilia (Italy), 94
Aragon, Louis, 63
Architectural Forum, 188, *188*, 189, 192, *193*, 199, 215–216, 231–233, 239–240, 242; publications on SOM and prefabricated housing, 188–189, *188*, *189*, 192–193, 199, 215–216
Architectural Record, 1, 6, 239, 267
Architectural Review, 48, 64, 106, 138, 166, 218, 267
architecture-engineering firm: SOM and development of, 209, 211–213
architecture of democracy, 226
Architektura ČSR, 67, 72, 74, 76, 81, 85, 87–89
Archizoom, 146
Argan, Giulio Carlo, 145, 165; "Architettura e ideologia," 145, 165
Arhitectura, 12, 16, 21, 27, 32–36
Arp, Hans, 45
Arts & Architecture. See Case Study Program
Association for Organic Architecture, 101
Association of the Communist Youth of Yugoslavia, 43, 44
Austria, 63, 64, 239
avant-garde, 8, 23, 44–47, 52, 62–64, 67–68, 70, 73, 80, 84–85, 87, 92, 113, 220

277

Aymonino, Carlo, 103

Bailey, Arthur, 123
Bailey, C. H. R., 119, 122, 136
Balta Albă (Bucharest, Romania), 26
Baltimore (Maryland), 195, 196, 202
Bandmann, Günter, 174, 180
Bangs, Jean Murray, 222, 223, 241
Banham, Reyner, 93, 105–106, 136
Barcelona (Spain), 49–50, 64
Barr, Alfred, Jr., 48
Bartning, Otto, 178
Basilicata (Italy), 98, 102
Bauhaus, 22, 35, 45, 145, 234, 242
Baxter, Samuel, 212, 217–218
Bay Region School, 233
BBPR. *See* Studio Architetti BBPR
Beauduin, Lambert, 177
Beck, George A., 126, 138
Behne, Adolf, 36
Belgium, 64, 239. *See also* Brussels
Belgrade (Serbia), 37, 42–45, 53–54, *54*, 56, 62–65, 269; New Belgrade, 8, 52, 269; Sephardic cemetery, 53; Surrealist group, 37, 43; University of Belgrade, 44, 53
Benedetti, Sandro, 146–147, 165
Benjamin, Walter, 250, 266
Bernardi, Bernardo, 50, 64
Bernardi, Theodore, 233
Besinger, Curtis, 234, 237, 242–243
Better Homes & Gardens, 221, 238–240
Birmingham University, 117
Bishop, Edmund, 167
Black Oak Ridge (Tennessee), 200
Blagojević, Ljiljana, 65, 269
Blair, Robert C., 203–204, 210, 217
Blake, Peter, 233, 237
Block, Ed, 202, 204, 210, 217. *See also* Manhattan Engineer District (MED)
Block of Progressive Architectural Associations, 71
Bogdanović, Bogdan, 37–38, 42–44, 53–61, 63, 65; *The Futile Trowel* (*Zaludna mistrija*), 56–57; Jasenovac Memorial Complex (Jasenovac, Croatia), 60; Monument to the Jewish Victims of Fascism (Belgrade, Serbia), 53–54, *54*; Slobodište (Kruševac, Serbia), 57, 58, 59, *59*; *Small Urbanism* (*Mali urbanizam*), 54–55, 57; "Sun Gate" (*see* Serbia: Slobodište); "winged souls" (*see* Serbia: Slobodište)
Bohemia, 69
Böhm, Dominikus, Church of Saint John the Baptist, 170
Bonhoeffer, Dietrich, 174, 176
Borba, 54
Borromini, Francesco, 56
Bosnia and Herzegovina, 40–41, 63
Bouyer, Louis, 178–179
Bramante, Donato, 56
Brazil, 64; Brasilia, 8
Breton, André, 63
Breuer, Marcel, 165, 176, 245, 272
Brno University of Technology, 81
Brontë, Emily, *Wuthering Heights*, 249
Brown, William, 210, 212, 216–218
Brunelleschi, Filippo, S. Spirito (Florence, Italy), 157, 158
Brussels (Belgium), 46–50, *47*, *48*, *49*, 52, 64, 90–92, *91*, 105. *See also* Universal and International Exposition
Brutalism, 113, 114
Bucharest, 12, 13–15, 17–19, 21–22, 24–26, 28–31, *29*, 34–35; Floreasca, 2, *12*, 16, *16*, *17*, 19–25, *21*, 27–34, *27*, 36; Floreasca Towers, *12*, 24, 25, *27*, *29*, 28–30, *31*; IPB (Institut Proiect București), 20; 1935 Master Plan, 19, 23; Rachmaninoff Street, 11, 14
Building Research Advisory Board, 239
Buler-Lytton, Edward, *Zanoni*, 249, 266
Burles, Newton & Partners, 113, 114
Burns, Fritz, 240

Cafiero, Vittorio, 150
California, 224–225, 233, 244, 257
California ranch house, 183, 224–225. *See also* ranch house
Călinescu, G., *Black Chest*, 15, 34
Callender, John H., 194, 215; *Time-Saver Standards*, 194
Calvino, Italo, 99, 106
Cambellotti, Duilio, 99, 106
Canada, 64, 276
Carbide and Carbon Corporation. *See* K-25
Casabella-Continuità, 101, 104
casa colonica, 96, 102–103
casa in linea, 103
casa torre, 103

case a schiera con ballatoio, 103
Casel, Odo, *Das christliche Kultmysterium*, 168
Case Study Program, 183, 220–222, 273
Cassou, Jean, 48
Castelli romani, 96, 103
Castex, Jean, 27
Castiglioni, Enrico, 146
Castle (Oak Ridge, Tennessee). *See* Oak Ridge (Tennessee): Adminstration Building
Catholic Church, 6
Cattaneo, Cesare, 146
Celotex Corporation, 195–196; Cemesto House, 196, 207, *207*
Cemesto board, use of at Martin House, 197, *197*, *198*
Centre for Worship and Religious Architecture (Birmingham, UK), 117–118
Centro di Studio e Informazione per l'Architettura Sacra, 147
Chandigarh (India), 8
Chevetogne Abbey (Belgium), 177
Chicago (Illinois), 45, 63, 172, 179, 187, 201, 204, 210, 217, 240
Chiesa del Concilio. *See* Moretti, Luigi: Sancta Maria Mater Ecclesiae
Chiesa e quartiere, 147, 165
China, 231
Churchill, Henry Stern, 6
CIAM (Congrès Internationaux d'Architecture Moderne), ix, 22–23, 25, 35, 55, 63, 65, 72, 116, 145, 165; Charter of Athens, 25
City Hall (Zagreb, Croatia), *40*
Classicism, 54, 56–57, 90–92, 94–96, 105–106
Clinch River (Tennessee), 200
Clinton Engineer Works (CEW), 200–201, 205, 209–211, 217
Cofimprese, 149
Cold War, ix, 5, 9, 10, 39, 62, 164, 212, 241, 245, 269–270, 272
Collegio San Giuseppe, 147
Colorado Springs (Colorado), 212
Communism, 19, 23, 33, 46, 86, 145, 231; and Catholicism, 145; opposition to, 145
Communist Party of Czechoslovakia, 66–70, 81, 85
Communist Party of Yugoslavia, 44–45, 63

Condee, Nancy, 38, 62
Connecticut General Life Insurance Company Building (Bloomfield, Connecticut), 186, 212
Constitution on the Sacred Liturgy, 125–126, 137, 140, 151, 152, 166, 170, 180, 271. *See also* Second Vatican Council
Constructivism, 45, 46, 47
consumerism, 106, 186, 270
consumer taste, 48, 64, 179, 221, 222, 230, 232, 240
contextualism, 101
corporate culture, 186
Croatia, 41, 43, 60; Jasenovac, 58, 60, *60*; Rab, 41, *41*, 63; Zagreb, 37, 40, 42–46, 52, 63, 64
Croce, Benedetto, 146, 164
cultural identity, 223, 276
Cutler, Robert, 210, 218
cvartal, 19–26, *21*, 28, 35
Cyril of Jerusalem, *Mystagogical Catechesis*, 169
Czechoslovak Building Works, 79
Czechoslovakia, 5, 8, 10, 62, 66–71, 73, 76, 80, 81, 85–86, 89, 170, 176, 239, 270; Block of Progressive Architectural Associations, 71; Brno University of Technology, 81; Kladno, 66, 73, 74, 76–77, 79, 83, *83*, 87–89; Ministry of Labor and Social Affairs, 66, 73; Ministry of Technology (MT), 72, 87, 88; Model Housing Development Program, 66–67, 71–72, 74, 76, 77, *77*, 78, 80, 82, 83, 84; Most, 66, 73–74, *74*, 83, 88–89; National Front, 68–69; Ostrava, 66, 70, 73–74, *74*, 76–82, *77*, 78, 80, 82, 87–89; Two-Year Plan, 66–67, 72–73, 76–77, 79–80, 84, 87; Two-Year Plan Apartments, 72–73, 77, 80; Zlín, 70
Czech Republic, 5, 66, 68, 73, 81, 83, 85, 89

Dahlberg, Bror, 195, 215
Dal Co, Francesco, 167
Daniel, Werner, 100–101, *100*
Dart, Edward, 176
Davis, Charles, 118, 127, 136–137, 169, 179
Davison, Robert L., 191
De Begnac, Yvon, 165
Debuyst, Frédéric, 174–175, 180
De Carlo, Adolfo, 91
De Carlo, Giancarlo, 99, *100*, 102, 107

decoration. *See* ornament
Del Debbio, Enrico, 148
De Martino, Ernesto, 103, 107
Denmark, Copenhagen, 72
Dessau (Germany), 22
Diocese of Bologna, 146, 147
Diocese of Clifton, 114, 129, *131*, *132*, *133*
Dix, Dom Gregory, *The Shape of the Liturgy*, 169, 178
Dobrović, Nikola, 63
domestic character, 246–247, 252, 255, 257; and Andrew Jackson Downing, 246
domesticity, vi, 181, 220, 272, 273; interior, and technology, 221, 228, 229, 240; and liturgical reform, 175
Dow, Alden, 235
Downing, Andrew Jackson, 246, 254, 265–267
Dresden (Germany), 45
Ducas, Dorothy, 220, 239
DuPont. *See* X-10
Dura Europos (Syria), 175
Durell Stone, Edward, Pavilion of the USA, Universal and International Exposition (Brussels, Belgium), 91

E42 (1942 World's Exposition), 91, 150
Eames, Charles, *192*
Eastern Europe, 3, 5, 37–38, 61, 67, 231, 269, 275
East Kilbride (UK), St Bride's Roman Catholic Church, 116, *117*
Eckbo, Garrett, 233
Eco, Umberto, 56
economic growth: role of war production in, 187
Economist, 235, 243
economy: wartime, 187
Eiermann, Egon, Pavilion of Germany, Universal and International Exposition (Brussels, Belgium), 91
Einstein, Albert, 199
Eliade, Mircea, 111, 163
Emerson, Ralph Waldo, 247, 266
Emmons, Donn, 233
Engberg, Arne, 216
England, 135, 138, 177, 239; Devon, Buckfast Abbey, 127; Harlow, 116, 127; Liverpool, 113–116, 118–120, 122, 126–131, 133–137
Enlightenment aesthetics, 142, 143

Entenza, John, 222
Entwistle, Clive, 119, 122
Esposizione Universale Roma (EUR) (Rome, Italy), 150
Europe, 5, 9, 34, 113, 164, 237, 250, 270
EXAT 51, 46, 52, 64; "Manifesto," 46, 64
Existenzminimum, 103
EXPO '58. *See* Brussels; Universal and International Exposition

Fallani, Giovanni, 150
Fanfani, Amintore, 93
Farnsworth, Edith, 231
Fascism, 71, 92–93, 98, 102–103, 105, 145, 148, 164, 231; and Catholicism, 144–145; New Towns, 94, 102–103; opposition to, 145
Fede e Arte, 139, 162, 163
Federal Housing Authority (USA), 239
Fencl, Ferdinand, 88
Fenichal, Otto, 252
Fercleve Corporation, 200
Finland, 64, 239; Helsinki, 72
Fiorentino, Mario, 101, 103; Monument to the Fosse Ardeatine, 101
Fitch, James Marston, 222–234, 241
Flagge, Ingeborg, 170, 179
"Flexible Space": SOM and, *188*, 189–190, *189*, 194, 213
Forbat, Fred, 23
Forrest, John B., 124–125
Fortune, 191, 215; on prefabrication, 191
Fossataro, Count Adolfo, 149
Fourier, Charles, Phalanstère, 83
Fragner, Jaroslav, 87
France, 64, 68, 145–146, 239, 276; Paris, 43, 48, 63, 164; Plateau d'Assy, 176
Frankfurt (Germany), 22–23, 27
Freud, Sigmund, 111, 250
Freudian psychology, 53, 252
Friedlová, Anna, 74, 76, 76–77, 77, 88
Fuchs, Bohuslav, 87
functionalism, 43, 67, 85, 116, 122, 145, 147; scientific, 71, 74
Futurism, 92, 164

Galić, Drago, 43
Gardella, Ignazio, 91
Garnier, Tony, Industrial City, 73
Gaudí, Antoni, 56, 58

General Assembly Building (New York, New York), 1
Germany, 49, 63–64, 68, 91, 101, 146, 174, 176–177, 239, 269; Dresden, 45; Hannover, 63; Maria Laach Abbey, 177
Gesamtkunstwerk, 49
Gibberd, Frederick, *115*, *119*, *120*, 124–129, *128*, 131, 134, 136–138; Harlow New Town, 116; Metropolitan Cathedral of Christ the King (Liverpool Metropolitan Cathedral), 114–116, *115*, 118–120, *119*, *120*, 122, *128*, 134–137
Giedion, Sigfried, *A Decade of New Architecture*, 93
Gillespie, Kidd & Coia, 115–117, *117*, 136
Gillies, Mary Davis, 221
Giovannoni, Gustavo, 101, 147
Glenn L. Martin Aircraft Company, 195, 202
Glenn L. Martin housing project, 196, 202, 205, 211, 216
Goalen, Gerard, 119, 127; Church of Our Lady of Fatima, 127
Goers, Albert, 204
Goff, Bruce, 233, 235
"good design," 220, 222, 237, 240
Goodhart-Rendel, H. S., 114, 136
Good Housekeeping, 258
Goodnow, Ruby, 252–254, *253*, 267
Gordon, Elizabeth, 4, 219–222, 224, 226, 229–243, 268; and postwar architectural discourse, 219, 237; and "The Threat to the Next America," 230–233, *232*, 235, 241–242
Gorio, Frederico, 102, *102*, 103
Gottwald, Klement, 81, 85
Grabar, Oleg, 141–142, 160; *The Mediation of Ornament*, 141, 163
Grabrijan, Dušan, 40, 62, 63
Gramsci, Antonio, 98, 103, 105; *Letteratura e vita nazionale*, 98
Grassi, Giorgio, 93
grattacielo straiato, 104
Graves, Michael, 55
Great Britain, 64, 68, 111, 113–114, 118, 124–125, 130, 135, 137, 276
Great Depression, 190
Greece, 148; Paestum, 167
Green, Aaron, 234, 235
Greenberg, Clement, 39
Greene and Greene, 229, 241

Greenough, Horatio, 246
Gropius, Walter, 2, 6, 173, 183, 220, 223, 231, 233, 239, 242; and Konrad Wachmann, Packaged House, 183
Groves, Leslie R., 199, 201, 211, 216
Guardini, Romano, 175–176, 178, 180; *Sacred Signs*, 175
Guarini, Guarino, 56
Guggenheim Museum: Frank Lloyd Wright and the, 235
Guidi, Ignazio, 150
Gunn, Thomas, *Physiology of the New York Boarding Houses*, 247, 266

Haig, Henry, 129
Hale, Edward Everett, 248, 266
Hales, Peter B., comments on Oak Ridge development, 208, 217
Halprin, Lawrence, 233
Hammond, Peter, 117–118, 122, 124, 130, 136–138, 169–170, 173, 175, 179–180; *Liturgy and Architecture*, 124, 137, 178–180
Hanford Engineer Works, 200
Harries, Karsten, *The Bavarian Rococo Church: Between Faith and Aestheticism*, 142, *143*, 163–164
Harris, Harwell Hamilton, 227, 230, 235, 238, 241–242
Harrison, Norman, 122, 136
Hartmann, William, 187, 215
Harvard, 231, 276
haunted house, 249, 250, 257, 260, 262, 263, 264, 266
Havlíček, Josef, 67, 73, 74, 76–77, 83, 87–89
Hayes, Bartlett, *Tradition Becomes Innovation*, 170, 179, 271
Hebebrand, Werner, 22
Hedren, Tippi, 244, *245*
Heenan, Archbishop John C., 120–121, 123, 125–127, 134, 136–137
Hellmuth, Yamasaki & Leinweber, Pruitt Homes and Igoe Apartments (St. Louis, Missouri), 96
Highway, exhibition, 45
Hill, Henry, 241
Hill, John deKoven, 234–236, *236*, 242–243
Hilský, Václav, 67, 73, 74, 77, 87
historicism, 170; and liturgical reform, 168–170

Hitchcock, Alfred, *The Birds*, 244–245, 245, 268
Hitchcock, Henry-Russell, 218, 220, 239, 254, 267; *Modern Architecture: Romanticism and Reintegration*, 254, 267; and Philip Johnson, *The International Style*, 220, 239
Hitler, Adolf, 106, 149
H. J. Heinz Company, 186
Holland, 64
Holocaust, 144
Hood, Raymond, 239
House Beautiful, 4, 184, Ch. 9, 223, 224, 226, 228, 229, 230, 232, 236
housing: low-cost, 193, 194; mass production, 189; prefabrication, 187, 190–193, 197, 202; prototypes, 193; standardized, 189, 193; systemization, 189; wartime, 187–188
Howard, Ebenezer, Garden City, 73
Howe and Lescaze, 239

Ibler, Drago, 43, 63
Illinois Institute of Technology (IIT, Chicago, Illinois), 45, 231
India, 8
Indianapolis (Indiana), 211
Institute for Advanced Study (Princeton, New Jersey), 199
Institute of Design at IIT (Chicago, Illinois), 45
International Center for Aesthetic Research, 150
International Style, 3, 9, 39, 95, 101, 184, 219, 220, 224, 228, 230, 231, 233, 234, 236, 237, 239, 241, 242
Invasion of the Body Snatchers, 264
Iron Curtain, 5, 9, 12, 49, 231
Istituto de Merode, 147
Istituto Nazionale per la Ricerca Matematica e Operativa per l'Urbanismo (IRMOU), 150
Istituto Nazionale per le Case degli Impiegati dello Stato (INCIS), 166
Italianness, 93
Italy, 5, 50, 52, 64, 90–99, 101–103, 105, 106, 140, 141, 145, 146, 148, 150, 164, 239, 270, 276; Aprilia, 94; Bologna, 146, 165–166; *Castelli romani*, 96, 103; Fascist regime, 91, 93–99, 105, 139, 144; Genoa, 93, 96; INA-Casa, 93, 94, 94, 96, 104, 106; Lazio, 150; Littoria, 94; Milan, 5, 50–51, 51, 93, 96, 99, 101, 145–146, 149; New Town, 94, 102, 103; Pomezia, 94; Pontinia, 94; Rome, 5, 91, 93–94, 96, 101–102, 104, 139, 140, 146–150, 154–159, 162, 165, 170, 172; Sabaudia, 94; Salò, 149; Tiber river, 151; Turin, 50, 93, 96, 98, 146, 150; UNRRA-Casas, 94, 96, 106

Jackson, Shirley: "The Haunting of Hill House," 257, 267; "The Lottery," 257; *The Sundial*, 257, 267–268
James, Henry, "The Jolly Corner," 250, 251, 266
Janů, Karel, 87, 88
Japan, 239; Hiroshima, 199, 213; Nagasaki, 213
Jeftić, Miloš, 63
John B. Pierce Foundation, 187–188, 190–192, 194–197, 202–204, 206–207, 211, 215–217, 239; Experimental House No. 1, 187, 191, 206; Experimental House No. 2, 190–191, 196–197, 208, 213; and Henry-Russell Hitchcock, *The International Style*, 220, 239; Housing Research Division, 191; Laboratory of Hygiene, 191; Martin House, 196–197, 206
Johnson, Philip, 220, 222, 233, 239
Jones, Fay, 235
Jung, Carl Gustav, 65
Jungmann, Josef A., 166, 169, 178–179, 271
Jurkovič, Dušan, 86

K-25 (Oak Ridge, Tennessee), 200
Kamrath, Karl, 233
Kant, Immanuel, 143
Karađorđević dynasty, 43
Kaufmann, Edgar, 240
Kelly, Wilbur, 201–202, 216
Kennedy, Robert Woods, 252, 267
Khrushchev, Nikita, 22, 25, 62
Kiesler, Frederick, 45
King, Stephen: "The Lawnmower Man," 260; *The Shining*, 261, 263
King Alexander I of Yugoslavia, 42
Kingston Demolition Range. *See* Clinton Engineer Works
Klauser, Theodor, 171–175, 179
Klein, August C., 201, 216

Koněrza, Miroslav, 74, 87
Košice Program, 1945, 68
Kovacevic, Radoslav, and William Pavlecic, Saint Jane de Chantal, 172, 179
Kovacevic, Radoslav, with William Pavlecic and Jack Ota, Saint Gall, 172, 179
Kovařík, Emil, 74, 87
Krejcàr, Jaromir, 22
Krleža, Miroslav, 43–44, 63
Kroha, Jiří, 81–83, *82*, 87, 89
Kubrick, Stanley, *The Shining*, 261, 263
Kuthan, Karel, 88

Ladies' Home Journal, 238, 240
Lakeview (California), 257
La Martella (Matera, Italy), 94–95, 96, 102–103, *102*, 107
La Sarraz (Switzerland), 23, 35
Lasdun, Denys, 119, 122, *122*, 136
Lawrenceburg (Indiana), 210
League of Communists of Yugoslavia, 46, 52
Leatherbarrow, David, 266
Lecaro, Cardinal Giacomo, 147
Le Corbusier, ix, 2, 8, 40, 73, 127, 145, 147, 176, 220, 223, 229, 231, 233, 239, 267; City for Three Million Inhabitants, 73; Notre Dame du Haut, Ronchamp (France), 127, 145, 176; Palace of the League of Nations, Geneva (project), ix; retrospective, 40; United Nations Headquarters, New York (New York), ix, 6
Ledoux, Claude-Nicolas, 56
Leonidov, Ivan, 47
Leo the Great, 169
Levi, Carlo, *Christ Stopped at Eboli—The Story of a Year*, 98–99, *99*, 106
Levitt and Sons, 183, 206, 240
Lévy-Bruhl, Lucien, 57, 65
Lewin, Kurt, vii
Libby-Owens-Ford, 256
Libera, Adalberto, 92–93, *92*, 95, 104–105, *104*; Casa Malaparte (Isle of Capri, Italy), 92, *92*, 105; Tuscolano III (Rome, Italy), 93, 95, 104–105
Littoria, 94, *104*
Liturgical Movement, 113, 118, 122, 123, 124, 125, 130, 134
livable modern design, 237, 238
Lockhart, Kenn, 234

London (UK): Architectural Association, 132; Tate Gallery, 52
Loos, Adolf, 142–143, 163
Los Angeles (California), 207, 225, *225*, 229, 239, 242; Los Angeles County Fair, 1954, 242
Lovecraft, H. P., 249, 266
Lowenthal, David, 255, 267
Lucania (Basilicata, Italy), 98
Lugli, Piero Maria, 95, 102, *102*
Lukić, Sveta, 62
Lurçat, André, 22
Lustron Houses, 183
Lutyens, Sir Edwin, 121, 129
Luzarra, 99

Magnitogorsk (Russia), 23, 35
mahala, 29, 35
Malton, James, 247
Manhattan Engineer District (MED), 187, 199
Manhattan Project, 184, 187, 199, 201, 203, 211, 216–217
Mao Zedong, 231
Marinetti, Filippo Tommaso, 92
Maritain, Jacques, 143–144, 151, 161, 164; *Art and Scholasticism*, 143, 164
Markovitch, R., 172
Marshall, James C., 201, 211, 216
Marshall Plan, 93
Marx, Karl, 46, 111
Marxism, 146, 39, 45, 81, 153, 69
Maryland, 195, 196, 202, 216
Matheson, Richard, *The Incredible Shrinking Man*, 259, *259*
Maxwell, Robert, 116, 136
May, Cliff, 225, *225*, 235, 272
May, Ernst, 22, 27, 35
McCall's, 221, 238–240, 258
McCarthy, Joseph, 231, 241
McCoy, Esther, 235, 242
McKenna, Thomas, 126, 137
Meduna, Vladimír, 74, 88
Merchandise Mart, the, 240
Merchant House Builder, 239
Merrill, John O., 204, 210
Metron, 101, 107
Metschke, Walter, 204–205, 217
Mexico, 64, 228
Meyer, Hannes, 22, 47

Meyer, Hannes, Petersschule, 47
Meyer and Cook, Queen of All Saints, 172
Michelucci, Giovanni, 147, 165
Michigan, Grand Rapids, 211
microraion, 24–28, *26*
Middle River (Maryland), 195, 196, 216; Aero Acres, 195, 198
Middle River, Stansbury Estates, 195, 197
Mies Van der Rohe, Ludwig, 49, 64, 174, 220, 223, 229, 231, 233, 239, 241, 242; Farnsworth House, 231; Pavilion of Germany, 49
Milan Triennale, 1936, *100*, 101; 1951, 99, *100*; 1960, 150; 1963–1964, 50–52, *51*
"minor architecture," 96, 101
Mississippi, Jackson, 233
Mitchell, William, 129
Modern Architecture Research Group (MARS), 114
"modern but not too modern," 219–221, 235, 238–240, 242
modernism, ix–xi, 1–6, 8–10, 13, 16, 30–32, 35–36, 38–41, 48–49, 54–56, 61–62, 64–65, 67, 80, 90–93, 95–98, 101, 103–107, 111, 114, 116–117, 132, 135, 139, 141–142, 144–146, 151, 160–164, 167, 170, 172, 174, 179, 180, 183–187, 207, 215, 219–224, 230–232, 234–239, 241–242, 245–246, 251–252, 254–255, 262–263, 269, 270–273; American, 186, 220, 223, 231, 234, 242, 272; and character, 248, 251, 254, 264; corporate, 5, 184, 186–187, 215; and design, 2, 45, 172, 213, 224, 228–229, 237, 239, 245, 253, 264; domestic, vii, 175, 183, 219, 237, 246, 253, 255, 273; European, 5, 41, 62, 93, 105–106, 186, 215, 220, 241; and heresy, 144; historiography of, x, 5, 142; and history, x–xi, 3, 4, 32–33, 55, 142, 160, 163, 247; and the modern house, 220, 244–246, 255, 264, 269, 272; and modernity, modernization, x, 2, 8, 9, 35, 38–40, 54–55, 61–62, 65, 67, 85, 109–110, 135, 142, 144, 151, 161–165, 171, 175, 183, 221, 270–271, 273; and the Modern Movement, vii, x, 14, 20, 33–34, 36, 107; and MoMA's *Modern Architecture: International Exhibition*, 220, 239; and morality, 145; and nature, 245, 254–255, 256; and politics, 92, 145, 164; reactionary, 144; regionalist, Bosnia, 40; regionalist, Italy, 90, 93, 95–96, 98; residential (*see* modernism: domestic); and secularization, 142; and technology, 3, 144, 187, 189–190, 204, 207–209, 213, 215, 221; theological, 144; and utopian visions, 52; varieties of, 113–114, 134–135, 172–173

Moholy-Nagy, László, 45, 50
Mollino, Carlo, Casa del Sole hotel (Cervinia, Italy), 98
Mollino, Carlo, ski lodge at Lago Nero (Sauze d'Oulx, Italy), 98
MoMA. *See* Museum of Modern Art
Montenegro, 54
Moore, Lieutenant, 202. *See also* Manhattan Engineer District
Moravia, 66, 69, 86
More House for Your Money, 220, 239. *See also* Gordon, Elizabeth; Ducas, Dorothy
Moretti, Luigi, 111, 139–142, 146–162, 165–167; Commemorative Chapel at the Foro Mussolini (Sacrario dei Martiri) (Rome, Italy), 139, 148; Fascist-era work, 139–141, 147–148; Foro Mussolini (Rome, Italy), 139, 148; INCIS Decima housing development (Rome, Italy), 151; Sacrario dei Martiri (Rome, Italy), 139, 148; Sancta Maria Mater Ecclesiae (Chiesa del Concilio), 139–141, *140*, 146, 150–152, 154–160, *154*, *155*, *156*, *157*, *158*, *159*, *160*, 161–162; "Space-Light in Religious Architecture," 150; *Spazio*, 149, 162, 166; "Strutture e sequenze di spazi," 149; "Where two or three are gathered in my name . . ." (Matthew 18:20), 139
Morocco, 212
Moscow (Soviet Union), 5, 14, 20, 22–24, 47, 68; Lenin Library, 47
Moses, Robert, 211
Movimento Studi Architettura, 101
Moya, Hidalgo, 123, 137
Mrduljaš, Maroje, 51, 62, 64
Muir, Edla, Zola Hall House (Los Angeles, California), 229
Mulazzani, Marco, 150, 162, 165, 166
Mumford, Lewis, 57, 233
Mungiu, Christian, *4 Months, 3 Weeks, and 2 Days*, 13
Munich Pact (1938), 68
Muratori, Saverio, 146

Muratori, Saverio, S. Maria dell'Assunzione, 146
Murray, Gregory, 130
Museum of Modern Art (New York), 52, 185, 220, 222, 231, 237, 239, 240; *Modern Architecture: International Exhibition*, 220, 239
Mussolini, Benito, 94, 148, 149, 165, 206

Napoleon III, 147
National Academy of Sciences (United States), 239
National Congress of Sacred Architecture (Bologna, 1955), 166
National Front (Czechoslovakia), 68–69
National Housing Agency (United States), 239
Neidhardt, Juraj, 40, 41, 42, 62, 63; *Architecture of Bosnia and the Way to Modernity*, 40, 62
neo-classicism, 106, 167
Neo-Liberty, 93, 106, 145
Neo-Rationalism, 93, 101
Neorealism, 98, 101, 103, 106
Nervi, Pier-Luigi, Palace of Labor (Turin, Italy), 50
Netherlands, 239
Neutra, Richard, 239
New Brutalism, 116
New Churches Research Group (NCRG), 117–118
New Empiricism, 113–114
New Haven (Connecticut), 191
New Jersey, Lebanon, 191, 196, 216
New Jersey, Princeton, Institute for Advanced Study, 199
New Mexico, Los Alamos, 199
New York, Albany, 8
New York, New York, 1, 83, 191, 194, 202, 204, 207; Manhattan, ix, 210–211, 218; Museum of Modern Art, 52, 185, 220, 222, 237, 239–240; Starrett-Lehigh Building, 191
New York Times, 215, 255, 267
New York World's Fair, 1939, 187, 190
Nichols, Kenneth. D., 201, 203, 204, 208, 211, 217
Nietzsche, Friedrich, 110–111
Normile, John, 221
Norris Dam (Tennessee), 200
North Korea, 231

nostalgic images, 209
nouvelle théologie, 144, 165
Novotný, Jiří, 88
Nový, Otakar, 78, 88
nuclear facilities, 199, 200. *See also* Manhattan Project; Oak Ridge
Nunan, R. G. P., 123, 137

Oak Ridge (Tennessee), 199; Administration Building, 209–211; house size (types A, B, C, and D), 206; as military-civilian complex, 199, 216; site plan, 203, 205, 209, 210; street nomenclature, 206, 217; and "stylistic design," 206; and town planning, 202, 203, 209, 216; transformation to a permanent city, 213
O'Brien, Joseph F., 190–191, 195, 202, 204, 215, 217
Okinawa (Japan), U.S. Military Compound, 212
Olmsted Brothers, 203
Opera Nazionale del Balilla, 148
Oppositions, 162
organic architecture, 101, 234–235, 242, 260, 272; and design, 227, 234–235; and modernism, 237
ornament, 141, 143, 172–174
Ossipoff, Vladimir, 235
Ostrava-Bělský Les (Czechoslovakia), 81
Ostrava Chemical Enterprise (Czechoslovakia), 73
Ostrava-Karvina Regional Coal Mines (Czechoslovakia), 73
Ostrava-Stalingrad (Czechoslovakia), 81
Ostrogović, Kazimir, City Hall (Zagreb, Croatia), 40
Oud, J. J. P., 239

Pace Setter House Program, 227, 230, 235, 236, 238–239, 241–242
Pacini, Giorgio, 150
Pacioli, Luca, 56
Pagano, Giuseppe, 100, 101, 107
Pagano, Giuseppe, and Werner Daniel, *Architettura rurale italiana: Funzionalità della casa rurale*, 100, 101
Palladio, Andrea, 56, 162
Pane, Roberto, "Literature and Architecture," 101
Panerai, Philippe, 27, 35

Pantheon (Rome), 157
Parker, Alfred Browning, 235, 242
Parker, Maynard, 225, 228–230, 238, 273
Pasolini, Pier Paolo, 98
Pavlecic, William, 172
Paxton, Edward T., *What People Want When They Buy a House*, 240
Pečat, 43
people's democracy, 68
Percy Thomas Partnership, 114, *115*, *131*, *132*, *133*
Perry, Ralph Barton, 238
Perugini, Giuseppe, 91, 101
Phayer, Michael, 164
Philippines, 212
Piacentini, Marcello, 101
Piano Fanfani, 93, 206
Picelj, Ivan, 44–45
picturesque landscape, 245, 247, 254–255, 268
Pierce Foundation Experimental House No. 2 (New York), 191
Pilát, Karel, 71, 73, 85, 87–88
Piper, John, 116, 119, 127, 129
Piranesi, Giovanni Battista, 56, 167
Plečnik, Jože, 41, 54–55, 170
Poe, Edgar Allen, "Fall of the House of Usher," 249, *249*
Poelzig, Hans, 45
Poland, 35, 68
Pomezia (Italy), 94
Pontifical Commission for Sacred Art in Italy, 150
Pontifical Office for the Preservation of the Faith and the Provision of New Churches in Rome, 150
Pontinia (Italy), 94
Pope John XXIII, 144, 151
Pope Paul VI, 150
Pope Pius X, 144–146, 151, 167
Pope Pius X, *Pascendi Dominici Gregis*, 144
Pope Pius XII, 144–146, 151, 164–165, 168; *Mediator dei*, 146
Popović, Konstantin-Koča, 63
Porel, Jan, 196, 211
Porumboiu, Corneliu, *12:08 East of Bucharest*, 13
postmodernism, 6, 55–56, 61–62, 65, 146, 162
Prague (Czech Republic), 5, 66, 68, 73, 81, 83, 85, 89

prefabrication, 32, 71, 187–192, *192*, 215
Price, Uvedale, 254
Progressive Architecture, 214, 232
Protić, Miodrag B., 62
Puiu, Christi, "The Death of Mr. Lazarescu," 13
Pythagoreanism, 57

Quaroni, Ludovico, 91, 93, 95, *95*, 96, 102, *102*, 103; La Martella (Matera, Italy), 94, 95, *95*, 96, 102–103, 107
questione meridionale, 103

Rab, Island of (Croatia), 41, *41*
Radić, Zvonimir, 45
Radice, Mario, 146
Rădulescu, Corneliu, 21
Radvanovský, Zdeněk, 70, 85–87
ranch house, 183, 224–225, 240, 272. *See also* California ranch house
Rasbach, Roger, 235
rationalism, 10, 25, 30, 55, 106
Ravnikar, Edvard, 40–42, *41*, 63; Memorial Complex in Kampor (Rab, Croatia), 41, *41*, 63
Regio Scuola de Architettura, 147
Repubblica Sociale Italiana, 148
ressourcement, 144
Reynolds, Joshua, 247
Reyntiens, Patrick, 116, 119, *128*, 129
Ricci, Corrado, 147
Ricci, Renato, 147
Richards, Ceri, *128*, 129
Richardson, H. H., 229
Richter, Vjenceslav, 37–38, 42–53, 60–64; Museum of the Revolution of the Nations and National Minorities of Yugoslavia (Belgrade, Serbia), 52; Pavilion of Yugoslavia, International Labor Exhibition (Turin, Italy), 50, *50*; Pavilion of Yugoslavia, Universal and International Exposition, 1958 (Brussels, Belgium), 47–49, *47*, *48*, *49*, 64; Pavilion of Yugoslavia, XIII Triennale (Milan, Italy), 51, *51*; *Sinturbanizam*, 52, 63–64
Ricoeur, Paul, 111
Ridolfi, Mario and Ludovic Quaroni, Tiburtino (Rome, Italy), 93–97, *94*, *97*, 103–104
Riemer, Svend, 194

Riesman, David, 252, 265–267
Ristić, Marko, 43–44
Robert Matthew, Johnson Marshall and Partners (RMJM), University of York (UK), 133
Rogers, Ernesto, *91*, 91, 93, 101, 105; Italian Pavilion, Universal and International Exposition, 1958 (Brussels, Belgium), *91*
Roman Catholic Church, 5, 111, 113–114, 177–178, 271; and modernity, 113, 114
Romania, 3, 5, 10, 12, 13, 15, 17, 19–26, *21*, *26*, 31–32, *31*, 34, 35, 275
Romania, Bacău, 22, 35
Romania, Socialist Republic of, 12, 17, 23, 25, 34; State Committee for Architecture and Construction (CSAC), 18
Rome (Italy), 5, 91, 93–94, 96, 101, 104, *104*, 106, 139, 146–150, 162, 165, 170, 172; Esposizione Universale Roma (EUR), 150; Foro Mussolini, 139, 148; INCIS Decima housing development, 151; Pantheon, 157; Sacrario dei Martiri, 139, 148; S. Andrea, 157; Santa Costanza, 170; S. Maria Maggiore, 157; Tiburtino, 93, 94, *94*, 95, 96, 97, 103, 104; Tuscolano III, 93, 94, 95, 96, 103, 104, *104*
Roosevelt, Franklin D., 199
Rosa, Alberto Asor, *Scrittori e popolo: Saggio sulla letteratura populista in Italia*, 98
Ross, W. E., 233
Rossellini, Roberto, *Roma città aperta*, 164
Rossi, Aldo, 93, 146, 165; *L'architettura della Città*, 146, 165
Rostagni, Cecilia, 148, 162, 165, 166
Roth, Alfred, *The New Architecture Presented in 20 Examples*, 93
Rowe, Colin, 186, 215, 247, 252, 265
Rudderham, Joseph E., 129, 138
rural architecture, 100, 101, 102, 107
Ruskin, John, 248

S-50 (Oak Ridge, Tennessee), 200
Sabaudia (Italy), 94
Sacrario dei Martiri (Rome, Italy). *See* Moretti, Luigi: Commemorative Chapel at the Foro Mussolini
Sacrosanctum Concilium. *See* Second Vatican Council: Constitution on the Sacred Liturgy
Samonà, Giuseppe, 99
S. Andrea (Rome, Italy), 157
San Francisco (California), 234, 241–242, 244
Santa Costanza (Rome, Italy), 170
Sant'Elia, Antonio, 92, 93
sassi, 102, 103, 107
Scandinavia, 67, 76, 240
Scesa, Louis, 204
Schillebeeckx, Edward, 146, 165
Schlesinger, Arthur, 242
Schmidt, Hans, 23, 35
Scholasticism, 143, 164
Schütte-Lihotzky, Margarete, 22
Schwagenscheidt, Walter, 22
Schwarz, Rudolf, 174, 177, 178, 179
Scotland, Glasgow, 113
Scott, Adrian Gilbert, 129
Scott, Felicity, 61, 65
Scott, Giles Gilbert, 121, 129, 136; Anglican Cathedral (Liverpool, England), 121, 129
Scott, James C., 8, 10
Second Vatican Council, 110, 113, 114, 125, 134, 136, 139, 141, 144, 147, 150, 151, 160, 162, 168, 170, 173, 271; Constitution on the Sacred Liturgy (*Sacrosanctum Concilium*), 125, 137, 140, 141, 151–153, 166, 170, 180, 271
Second World War. *See* World War II
Secretariat Building (New York), 1
secularization, 109, 113, 142, 163
Sedlák, Jan, 67, 85
Serbia, 55, 57, 59, 63, 172, 173, 269; Kruševac, 57, 58, 59; New Belgrade, 8, 52, 269; Slobodište, 59; Smederevo, 55
Sert, Jose Luis, 23, 35
Severinghaus, J. Walter, 191
Siddons, Anne Rivers, *The House Next Door*, 260, 267, 268
Silesia, 69
Sixty Years of Living Architecture, 235
Skidmore, Louis, 186, 202, 204, 210, 211, 215, 217, 218. *See also* Skidmore, Owings & Merrill
Skidmore, Owings & Merrill (SOM), 183–184, 186–197, *188*, *189*, *193*, 199, 201–213, 215, 217, 218, 231; and corporate architectural practice, 202, 203, 209, 211; evolution of, 209–213; Lever House, 231; and U.S. Military Compound (Okinawa), 212; and "vocabulary," "grammar," and "composition," 189–190

Slabý, Otto, 74, 88
Slavic Agricultural Exhibition, 1948, 81
Sloan, Gair, 234
Sloan Flush Valve Company, 214
Slovenia, 41
S. Maria Maggiore (Rome, Italy), 157
Smederevo (Serbia), 55
Smithson, Alison and Peter, Hunstanton Secondary School (Norfolk, England), 116
Socialist Aestheticism, 39, 62
socialist modernism, chapter 2, 37, 38, 65, 80
Socialist Party of Romania, Central Committee, 18, 34; Resolution 2448, 17, 34
Socialist Realism, 3, 20, 25, 35, 37, 39, 42–45, 53, 61–63, 67, 68, 80, 81, 83, 85
Società Generale Immobiliare, 149
Sövic, Edward, 175, 180
Soviet Union, 3, 22, 24, 35, 45, 66, 68, 69, 81, 231, 270; Five Year Plan, 22; St. Petersburg, 81
space, 183, 188–191, *188*, *189*, 194, 195, *195*, 213, 216–218; and spatial experience, 149; spatial organization and spatial system, 190. *See also* "Stockholm Study"
"space-light," 150, 153, 155, 161
Spain, 239
Spence, Sir Basil, Coventry Cathedral (England), 120, 127, 129, 136
Spielberg, Steven, *Poltergeist*, 260
spontaneous architecture, 99, 100
Srnec, Aleksandar, 44, 45
Stalin, 62, 85, 269, 270
Stalinism, 22, 23, 38, 45, 50, 61, 89
Stam, Mart, 23, 35
standardization, 10, 20, 22, 30, 32, 34, 68, 79, 183, 188, 189, 191, 213, 215; T-series, 79–81, 83
Stansbury Estates (Middle River, Maryland), 195, 197
Stansbury Manor Corporation, 196
Starrett-Lehigh Building (New York), 191
Starý, Oldřich, 87
"Station Wagon Way of Life, The" 224, 229, 241
Stavoprojekt, 67, 68, 70, 78–80, 83–85, 88, 89
S. Teresa d'Avila, 158
"Stockholm Study," 194
Stone & Webster Corporation (S&W), 201–204, 210, 212, 216, 217
Storch, Karel, 72, 76, 87, 89
Strand, Paul, 99
Strand, Paul, and Cesare Zavattini, *Un Paese: Portrait of an Italian Village*, 99, 106
Strižić, Zdenko, 45; Kharkiv Opera House (Ukraine), 45
Studio Architetti BBPR, 91, 93, 101, 145; Monument to the Dead in the Concentration Camps in Germany, 101; sun-therapy colony in Legnano, 93; Torre Velasca (Milan, Italy), 145
Štursa, Jiří, 67, 71–74, *74*, 76, 77, 87, 88
Subcarpathian Ruthenia, 66, 69
Sudetenland, 66
Superstudio, 146
Surrealism, 44, 45, 53, 56
Survey Research Center, 239
Susman, Warren, 252, 267
Sweden, 239; Stockholm, 63, 72
Swedish Cooperative Building Society, 194
Switzerland, 64, 146, 239
symbolism, 53, 55, 117, 118, 119, 122, 127, 130, 131, 174, 175
synthesis of the arts, 46, 47, 53
Syrkus, Helena, 35
Syrkus, Simon, 35

Tablets of Stone, 53
Tafuri, Manfredo, 92, 106, 107, 167, 270
Taliesin Fellowship, 234
Tapié, Michel, 150
taste. *See* consumer taste
Taylor, Rod, 244
Team 10 (Team X), 55, 145
techno-utopia, 61, 65
Teige, Karel, 67, 71, 85, 87
Templ, Stephan, 67, 85
Tennessee: Knoxville, 200; Oak Ridge, 184, 187, 199–201, 204, 206, 208–213, 216–218
Tennessee Eastman Plant (Oak Ridge), 200
Tennessee Valley Authority, 200
Terragni, Giuseppe, Casa del Fascio (Como, Italy), 92
Texas State Fair, 241
Tillich, Paul, 174, 180
Time-Saver Standards, 194. *See also* Callender, John H.
Tito, Josip Broz, 39

town planning. *See* Oak Ridge, Tennessee: and town planning
Trifunović, Lazar, 62
Trincanato, Egle, *Venezia minore*, 101
Turek, Jaroslav, 74, 77, 78, 88
Turin (Italy), 50, 50, 93, 96, 98, 146, 150
Turkey, 8, 10, 269
typification, 10, 22, 68, 79, 89

United Nations, ix, 1, 6, 67, 76, 88, 231; Headquarters, ix, 6, 231; United Nations Relief and Rehabilitation Administration (UNRRA), 66, 94, 96
United States of America, 3, 45, 64, 182, 186, 187, 191, 199, 231, 232, 239–241, 247, 250, 266
Universal and International Exposition (Brussels, Belgium), 1958, 46, 90; Atomium, 90; Pavilion of Germany, 91; Pavilion of Italy, 90–91, 91, 105; Pavilion of the USA, 90; Pavilion of Yugoslavia, 46–50, 47, 48, 49
University of Illinois, Small Homes Council, 239
University of Michigan, Institute for Social Research, 239
University of Texas at Austin, 227, 230
U.S. Air Force Academy (Colorado Springs, Colorado), 212
U.S. Army Corps of Engineers, 199, 203
Usonian (Usonia), 235
USSR, 43, 239

Valori, Michele, 95, 102, *102*
van Loghem, J.B., 22
Velarde, F. X., 114
Venezuela, Creole Petroleum Corporation, 212
Venturi, Robert, 56, 146, 161, 162, 165, 167, 237, 243; *Complexity and Contradiction in Architecture*, 146, 162, 165, 237
Verga, Giovanni, *I Malavoglia*, 98
vernacular, 10, 40, 67, 70, 80, 81, 83, 86, 90, 92–99, 101–105, 152, 169, 270, 272
Vienna (Austria), 44, 63
Visconti, Luchino, *La Terra Trema*, 98
Vítkovice Ironworks, 73
Vitzthum, Karl, with John Burns, Saint Peter's in the Loop (Chicago, Illinois), 172

Vitzthum, Karl, Saint Thomas Aquinas Church (Chicago, Illinois), 172, 179
Voigt, Wolfgang, 170, 179
Voženílek, Jiří, 78, 87, 88

Wachsmann, Konrad, 183
Wagnerschule, 40
Walpole, Horace, 249, 262, 266; *Castle of Otranto*, 249, 257, 266
Ware, Joseph T., 204, 210, 217
Washington, Hanford, 199, 200
Waterkeyn, André, Atomium (Brussels, Belgium), 90
Weakland, Rembert, 176, 180
Weeks, Ronald, 114, 130–132, *131*, *132*, 134, 135, 138; Cathedral of Saints Peter and Paul (Clifton Cathedral, England), 114, *115*, *131*
Weightman & Bullen, 113
Western Europe, 3, 17, 168, 180, 272
West Germany, 64
Westinghouse, 190
Wheeler, Candace, 248, 266
White, L. Michael, 166
Wilbur, Richard, 266
Winckelmann, Johann Joachim, 167
Wingfield, Nancy, 69, 86
Winslow, C. E. A., 191
Wisconsin, Madison, 177
Wise, Robert, *The Haunting*, 258
Wittmann-Englert, Kerstin, *Zelt, Schiff und Wohnung: Kirchenbauten der Nachkriegsmoderne*, 174, 180
Woman's Day, 258
Woman's Home Companion, 221, 240, 267
Wood, Robert, *Suburbia*, 264
Workers' Party of Romania, 34; Central Committee, 18, 34
World Council of Churches, 175, 180
World's Fair Exposition, 1942 (E42), 150
World War I, 168
World War II, ix–xi, 1, 3, 8, 9, 10, 13, 14, 22, 37, 46, 66–68, 86, 90, 91, 93, 110, 113, 144, 168, 174, 176, 182, 187, 190, 209, 211–212, 214, 217, 220
Wright, Frank Lloyd, 176, 227, 229, 233–235, 238, 239, 242, 260, 267, 268; Greek Orthodox church in Wauwatosa, 176; Taliesin West, 233
Wright, Lance, 130, 138

"Wrightian," 234, 235
Wurster, William, 233

X-10 (Oak Ridge, Tennessee), 200

Y-12 (Oak Ridge, Tennessee), 200
Yale University, 191
Yugoslavia, 5, 9, 10, 37–65, 269, 270; Belgrade (Serbia), 37, 42–45, 53–54, 54, 56, 62–65, 269; Jasenovac (Croatia), 58, 60, 60; Kruševac (Serbia), 57, 58, 59; New Belgrade (Serbia), 8, 52, 269; Pavilion of, International Labor Exhibition (Turin, Italy), 50, 50; Pavilion of, Universal and International Exposition, 1958 (Brussels, Belgium), 47–49, 47, 48, 49, 64; Pavilion of, XIII Triennale (Milan, Italy), 51, 51; Rab (Croatia), 41, 41, 63; self-management, 39, 45, 50, 51; Socialist Aestheticism, 39, 62; Surrealism, 44, 45, 53, 56; Zagreb (Croatia), 37, 40, 42–46, 52, 63, 64

Zach, Leon H. *See* Olmsted Brothers
Zagreb (Croatia), 37, 40, 42–46, 52, 63, 64; Academy of Applied Arts, 46; University of Zagreb, 44
Zavattini, Cesare, 99, 106
Zemlja, 43
Zevi, Bruno, 101, 104, 107

www.ingramcontent.com/pod-product-compliance
Lightning Source LLC
Chambersburg PA
CBHW081541300426
44116CB00015B/2710